Confraternity of Penitents

HANDBOOK
of the
CONFRATERNITY OF PENITENTS

EIGHTH EDITION

*Living the Original Third Order Rule of Saint
Francis as a Lay Person in the Modern World*

The Confraternity of Penitents was refounded from the Brothers and Sisters of Penance on August 22, 2003, the Feast of the Queenship of Mary. Thus Mary, Queen of Heaven, along with Saint Francis of Assisi, is patron of the Confraternity of Penitents.

"May the Blessed Virgin Mary help me to live a holy life and die a holy death. Then at the last instance of my life, may she come to my assistance and lead me to heaven." *St. Francis Xavier*

Prayer of St. Aloysius to the Blessed Virgin Mary

O Holy Mary, my Mistress, into Thy blessed trust and special keeping, into the bosom of Thy tender mercy, this day, every day of my life and at the hour of my death, I commend my soul and body; to Thee I entrust all my hopes and consolations, all my trials and miseries, my life and the end of my life, that through Thy most holy intercession and Thy merits, all my actions may be ordered and disposed according to Thy will and that of Thy Divine Son. Amen.

Published by: The Confraternity of Penitents Copyright: 2014 http://www.penitents.org
Eighth Edition (First Edition Published in 2000 as Handbook for the Brothers and Sisters of Penance)

Nihil Obstat:
Very Reverend Mark A. Gurtner, J.C.L.,
Censor Deputatus

Imprimatur:
Most Reverend Kevin C. Rhoades,
Bishop of Fort Wayne-South Bend,
August 12, 2014

ISBN: 1452877386
ISBN-13: 9781452877389

TABLE OF CONTENTS

ACKNOWLEDGEMENTS

Materials in this Handbook were conceived, written, revised, or suggested by many individuals, many of whom are members of the Confraternity of Penitents. We thank especially the following clergy and religious for their input: First, Cardinal Hugolino de Conti de Segni (later Pope Gregory IX) for writing our Rule in 1221. Then Father Julian Stead OSB, Sister Dominica Brennan OSB, Father Francis Kelly, Father David Engo FFM, Father Valerius Messerich OFM, Rev. Msgr. William I. Varsanyi, Rev. Msgr. John J. Darcy, Sister Jacqueline Dickey SSCh, Father John of the Trinity Erem TO Carm, Father Jay Finelli, Father Martin Mary Fonte FI, Sister Veronica of Jesus CN, Father Michael Sisco, Father Mark Gurtner, and Father Jacob Meyer, for their input and prayers. We are grateful to the Most Reverend Robert E. Mulvee, Bishop Emeritus of the Diocese of Providence, Rhode Island, to the Most Reverend Thomas J. Tobin, Bishop of the Diocese of Providence, Rhode Island, and to Bishop Kevin Rhoades, Bishop of Fort Wayne - South Bend, Indiana, for their support.

Finally, our profoundest gratitude goes to the Holy Spirit through Whose inspiration the Confraternity of Penitents began and through Whose guidance this Handbook was written. May He bless with increased grace all who use this Handbook and who proceed into embracing, for the love of the Lord, a life of penance lived with joy.

DEDICATION

This Handbook is lovingly dedicated to Stephanie Natalie Carlson Sullivan, the first penitent to formally pledge for life to live our Rule and Constitutions and the first to enter eternal life. May God reward her for her faith, prayers, and good works.

ORDER INFORMATION

Order from: Confraternity of Penitents, 1702 Lumbard Street, Fort Wayne IN USA 46803, 260/739-6882, bspenance@hotmail.com Suggested donation $30 includes postage, shipping, and handling to all USA locations. For overseas delivery, please contact us. All donations, over and above cost of materials received, are tax deductible. Please make checks payable to the Confraternity of Penitents.

Thank you for your generosity and may God bless you.

DOING PENANCE AS MEANS OF SURRENDER TO GOD

Are you a Roman Catholic lay person who is looking for more in life? What is your goal? Might it be something like one of these?

- Being at peace.
- Growing closer to God.
- Surrendering to God.
- Becoming holier.
- Becoming the person God created you to be.
- Getting to heaven.
- Doing God's Will.
- Helping others to know about God's love.
- Helping others get to heaven.
- Loving God better.
- Doing penance for sin.
- Assisting the Catholic Church in her mission.

If one of these, or something similar, is your goal, and you wish you had some guidance as well as the support of others in reaching that goal, then read on!

Did you know that living a Rule of Life that has been accepted by the Church is a marvelous way to begin to accomplish these goals? Why? Because the Church promises that those who follow such Rules faithfully are guaranteed eternal life. Many Religious Orders, Congregations, and Associations of the Faithful, whose Members follow a Rule of Life, exist in the Catholic Church. Each of these has a unique charism that is reflected in the organization's Rules, Statutes, Constitutions, and other governing materials. If you wish to achieve any or all of the above goals, could you do better than living a Rule of Life?

Many people believe that such Rules exist only for consecrated religious like nuns and brothers. That is not true! Thankfully many wonderful Rules of Life, accepted and encouraged by the Catholic Church, exist for lay people to follow. The graces that come from following a Rule of Life are many.

- You give up your own will to follow the Rule.
- You grow in humility.
- You grow more detached from worldly possessions.
- You learn self-discipline.
- You practice love of neighbor by serving others.
- You practice love of God through prayer and worship.

Does it make sense that a Rule of Life that causes you to give up more of your own will, to grow more in humility, to become more detached from possessions, to practice more self-discipline, to engage in greater service to your neighbor, and to pray more to our God, is a Rule that will speed you along the spiritual journey to help you achieve your spiritual goals? With the grace of the Holy Spirit, the Confraternity of Penitents can assist you in all of these ways and more!

The Rule of 1221

The Confraternity of Penitents is a group of Roman Catholic lay people who are living a modern adaptation of a Rule of Life which was given by Saint Francis of Assisi to lay people to live in the year 1221. On February 11, 2009, the Bishop of the Diocese of Providence Rhode Island (USA) confirmed the canonical status of the Confraternity of Penitents (CFP) as a Roman Catholic, private association of the faithful. This status was recognized by Bishop Kevin Rhoades of the Diocese of Fort Wayne - South Bend Indiana (USA) when the Confraternity of Penitents relocated to that Diocese.[1]

Confraternity members worldwide are living the CFP Rule in their own homes in total obedience to all the teachings of the Roman Catholic Church, to the Holy Father, and to the Magisterium. The Constitutions to this Rule indicate how the Members live the Rule in the modern world. The Bishop of the Diocese of Fort Wayne - South Bend, Indiana, USA, has given the Confraternity of Penitents permission to live the Rule and Constitutions found in these pages and to spread the message of penance (conversion) to others.

Members of the Confraternity of Penitents recognize that they are sinners. They acknowledge past sins and are sorry for them. They are striving to avoid sin but recognize their weaknesses. Knowing that they need God's grace to do good, they voluntarily enter into a life of penance (ongoing conversion) to help them to grow in surrender to God's

---

1   See Appendix U of the Directory in this Handbook for a copy of both Bishop's letters.

way of doing things. Joyfully they accept Christ's atoning sacrifice and God's redeeming love. In all of this, they are like the penitents who lived this Rule in the year 1221.

Here is some background on the Rule of 1221.

- Saint Francis of Assisi wrote a Rule in 1221 for his religious brothers. That Rule is not the Rule which is followed by the Confraternity of Penitents.
- The Confraternity of Penitents follows a Rule written for lay people in the year 1221. At the request of Saint Francis, the Rule of 1221 for the laity was composed by Cardinal Hugolino de Conti de Segni, the Cardinal Protector of Saint Francis's Order. Cardinal Hugolino later became Pope Gregory IX.
- The people who followed the Rule of 1221 were called penitents by the general public. The Rule called them "the Brothers and Sisters of Penance."
- The penitents lived the Rule in their own homes and families.
- The Rule prescribed prayer, fasting, abstinence, community, types of clothing, evangelization, caring for others, and personal holiness.
- The Rule forbad oaths, weapons, grudges, scandal, and anything that causes, fosters, or continues division and sin.

The Rule of 1221 had been embraced with joy by the lay followers of Saint Francis. The Rule underwent a minor adjustment in 1289 but remained essentially unchanged until 1883. In that year the Rule of 1221 was abrogated (withdrawn) and a new Rule substituted for it. In 1978, the 1883 Rule was abrogated and a new Rule substituted. Today Secular Franciscans live the Rule of 1978, also called the Pauline Rule.

In 1994, one individual who had learned about the Rule of 1221, felt a persistent, interior call to live it in the modern world and, a few months later, to pray that others would live it also. The small local group that developed from this has evolved into the international Confraternity of Penitents.

What Makes the Confraternity Unique

A few groups make reference to the Rule of 1221 in their Rules of Life and some attempt to follow it in some way. Some of the wording regarding how they follow the Rule is similar or even the same as in the Confraternity of Penitents. However, there are significant differences.

Differences in how a Rule is lived come from how a group views the Rule. This view is reflected in the Vision of the group. The Confraternity of Penitents has a unique Vision which determines how its Members live the Rule of 1221. That Vision is:

To give glory to God and surrender to His Will through the living of a medieval, penitential Rule of Life, the Rule of 1221. This Rule is lived as closely as possible to its original intent, and in one's own home, in peace with all others, and in obedience to the Roman Catholic Church, its Pope, and its Magisterium.

The key phrase that separates the CFP from all other groups is this: *"This Rule is lived as closely as possible to its original intent."*

Why Live the Rule of 1221 As Closely As Possible to Its Original Intent?

All Rules of Life, if lived well, are means to achieving holiness. Those living any Rule of Life can achieve holiness if they are obedient to how their group is living the Rule in the modern world.

The call to the Confraternity of Penitents was to "live the Rule of 1221" and to "pray that more people will live the Rule of 1221 and enter this fraternity." This implies that the Rule was to be lived as written, as much as is possible in today's world and in keeping with current Church practices. While no one knows the mind of God, we might speculate on why the call to "live the Rule" was given. Might God have wanted to make it easier for some people to attain holiness because they "live the Rule of 1221"? At first glance to the modern eye, the Rule seems difficult to live, although those who are living it find it joyful and liberating. They have discovered that living the Rule "as closely as possible to its original intent" brings many graces and spiritual fruits. Many saints and blesseds lived the Rule of 1221. Several of these were religious but over thirty were lay people.

Might God want all those who today "live the Rule of 1221" to have a chance at achieving such levels of sanctity? We in the Confraternity of Penitents hope so!

The Intent of the Rule of 1221

The Rule of 1221 was intended to be a religious Rule of Life for lay people. Those living the Rule were considered to be part of a religious Order for the laity. Even though they were laity, they conducted themselves like religious. This meant that

- The penitents had certain days of fasting and abstinence.
- They prayed certain prayers.
- They lived modest lives in witness to Christ.
- They met in community monthly for instruction, support, and prayer.
- They supported their own needy Members with prayers and alms.
- They participated in works of charity.
- They were to take the first steps toward reconciliation and to be at peace with all.

How Does the Confraternity of Penitents "Live the Rule of 1221 As Closely As Possible to Its Original Intent?"

Here are some ways in which all the Members of the Confraternity of Penitents live the Rule of 1221 as closely as possible to its original intent. These unique ways distinguish the Confraternity from other lay Catholic organizations, associations, and Orders.

- Just like religious do in convents and monasteries, penitents lived their Rule twenty-four hours a day, seven days a week without relaxation or mitigation other than following the Church custom of not fasting or abstaining on Sundays and Solemnities. This is the case in the Confraternity of Penitents.
- Depending on whether the fabric was of animal or plant fibers, clothing for medieval penitents would have been any shade of "earth tones," "neutral colors," white or black (Rule, Chapter 1). The CFP mandates the same colors for continual wear.
- Penitents were to be inconspicuous in doing penance (Rule, Chapter 1). The CFP maintains this intent by allowing penitents to wear solid colored blue articles of clothing as well as neutral tones. Blue reminds the penitent of his or her consecration to the Blessed Mother, the patron of the Confraternity, and also, because it is a color, helps conceal from others the fact that penitents are doing penance in the area of clothing.
- Reading Chapter 1 of the original Rule indicates that penitential garb, while specific in some ways, was varied among the penitents. Hence, no specific habit was mandated. The CFP retains this intent by having its lay Members mix and match their garb so that they do not appear to be wearing habits. Nor may they receive permission to wear a habit. It is the opinion of the Diocese of Fort Wayne - South Bend, whose Bishop has accepted the CFP Rule and Constitutions, that the wearing of a habit is intended for vowed religious.
- "Vain adornments" were to be put aside (Rule, 2, 4). The CFP maintains this intent by having its Members relinquish all jewelry except functional pieces like watches, wedding bands, earring studs, and a cross or crucifix pendant, ring, or lapel pin.
- Fur garments were limited to "lamb's wool only" (Rule, 4). The CFP maintains this intent by stating that fur garments must be lamb's wool or lamb's wool imitation.
- "Except for the feeble, the ailing, and those traveling," the Rule mandated two meals a day (Rule, 6). The CFP maintains this stipulation while allowing a "bite to eat" "if needed" at one other time during the day.
- Penitents who were engaged in fatiguing work were allowed to "take food three times a day" during the time of year when this strenuous, outdoor work was done (Rule, 11). The Rule implies that the abstinence provisions (no meat) were to be followed. The CFP retains the "three times a day" limit for fatiguing work, with abstinence from meat being observed on Mondays, Wednesdays, Fridays, and Saturdays as the Rule states (Rule, 6).
- Penitents were to abstain from meat four days a week (Rule, 6). The CFP retains this intent. If penitents are eating out on abstinence days, they should select meatless dishes. However, if they are served meat as guests in the homes of others,

they should eat what is set before them so as not to embarrass the host. This is in line with Rule, 6 and Rule, 9.

- Penitents were to pray an Our Father both before and after meals. If they skipped a meal as a fast, they were not exempt from praying. In that case, they were to pray three Our Fathers (Rule, 7). The CFP has retained this.
- The Rule of 1221 defined fasting as the way the Church fasted at that time. Penitents were to follow the Church's fasting guidelines, not their own (Rule, 8). The CFP has its Members follow the Church's guidelines, not their own, while fasting.
- All penitents were to attend Matins "in the fast of St. Martin and in the great fast, unless inconvenience for persons or affairs should threaten." (Rule, 14). Today public attendance at Mass has replaced attendance at Matins. Therefore, CFP penitents are to attend Mass unless there is a "serious inconvenience."
- Penitents were to confess three times a year (Rule, 15), which was considered to be frequent during medieval times when most people made confession only once in a lifetime. Today monthly confession is the norm although yearly confession is required. To retain the intent of confession more frequent than the norm, the CFP requires twice monthly confession.
- Ill penitents were to be visited weekly and to be reminded of their obligation to live their Rule ("remind him of penance") (Rule, 22). The CFP recommends weekly visits in which the ill penitent is not only encouraged and prayed for but is also reminded of his or her obligation to do penance even while ill.
- The official Church representative, the Visitor, was a priest as implied by his power to dispense from the Rule (Rule, 37) and to impose Church penalties (Rule, 39). The CFP requires that its Visitor be a priest.
- Only the Church representative, the Visitor, could determine what "satisfaction" would have to be performed by a penitent who acted contrary to the pledge (Rule, 30). The CFP has retained this power to the Visitor only.
- Only the bishop could declare a person cleared of heresy (Rule, 32). The CFP allows only the bishop to have this power.
- Only the Church representative, the Visitor, had the power to dispense penitents from living certain parts of the Rule (Rule, 37). The CFP has retained this power as belonging to the Visitor only.
- Only the Visitor could expel someone "from the brotherhood" (Rule, 35). The CFP maintains the intent of the original Rule by allowing this power only to the Visitor.

A few other groups and several individuals, who do not belong to any group, either follow the Rule of 1221 or take it as an ideal, but their observances differ from those of the CFP. Even though they may be living the Rule a bit differently than we are in the CFP, we wish all these groups and individuals well and pray for them daily, asking God to prosper them in their promotion of and living of the Rule of 1221. The more people who embrace this way of personal conversion, the better!

Those exploring the Confraternity of Penitents should understand that, in addition to the above differences, the following procedures make the Confraternity unique among the other groups and individuals who are also following the Rule of 1221:

- Formation: Every Member and Associate of the CFP must complete four years of written formation. The only exception would be those who cannot read or write. They may have their lessons read to them and may complete their answers orally.
- Pledging: Only Members who have completed four years of formation may pledge to live the Rule. The only exception would be for those whose death is imminent, according to the testimony of two physicians. Then the penitent must receive permission from the CFP Visitor and Minister General to pledge, with the stipulation that formation will continue as usual if the medical prognosis is incorrect.
- Formators: Only Members may become formators.
- Governance: Only Members may vote or hold office.
- Leadership: Only life pledged Members may hold the highest positions of leadership in the CFP.
- Communications: Every Member, Associate, Affiliate, and Inquirer in the CFP has full and free access to every other by phone, email, postal mail, internet, in person, or any other means. The CFP operates like a family of brothers and sisters in Christ.

Are there other ways in which the Confraternity of Penitents is unique in following the Rule of 1221? Definitely! You can find these by comparing the Confraternity Constitutions with the Statutes and Constitutions of other groups. Carefully look for additions, omissions, and changes between the groups. Ask the Holy Spirit to enlighten you. Remember that any Rule of Life is not an end in itself but rather a means to help you to surrender to God in every aspect of your life. Pray that the Lord will enlighten you as to which group and Rule will help you to achieve this. The Lord will guide you.

Penance as a Vocation

Might a vocation to live a life of continual penance (conversion) in the manner of the Confraternity of Penitents be for you? Only the Holy Spirit knows! But you can be sure that He wants you to find out. If you are fourteen years of age or older, you can be part of the Confraternity of Penitents.

- Roman Catholics may become Members by completing the CFP four year formation program in the Catholic faith and in living the Rule gradually over those years. By the end of four years, the penitent is living the entire Rule and may then apply to pledge to live the Rule and Constitutions for life.

- Non-Catholics and Catholics with impediments may complete the four years of formation as Associates, even though they cannot pledge.
- Those who cannot or do not wish to do formation are invited to become Affiliates who live in peace with all and who support the Confraternity.
- Transfers from other Lay Associations or Third Orders will enter formation at a level determined by the similarity of their current Rule and Constitutions to those of the CFP. See the FAQ (Frequently Asked Questions) section of this Handbook for more information.

Explore these pages for more information and pray about what God wants of you. Then follow the words of our Blessed Mother to the waiters at the wedding feast of Cana and "do whatever He tells you."

May you receive all the blessings God has in store for you!

Please pray for all those in the CFP, for those discerning, for our Visitor, Diocesan officials, and spiritual advisors and assistants. And may God bless you and lead you into His perfect Will for your life!

BIBLIOGRAPHY

The following books were used in compiling this Handbook.

Armstrong, Regis. Clare of Assisi: Early Documents. Saint Bonaventure, New York: Franciscan Institute Publications, 1993.

Collins Liturgical Publications, The Code of Canon Law, The Pitman Press, Bath, England, 1983.

Francis of Assisi: Early Documents. Ed. Regis J. Armstrong, O.F.M. Cap., J. A. Wayne Hellman, O.F.M. Conv., William J. Short, O.F.M. New City Press: New York. Volume 1: The Saint: c. 1999. Volume 2: The Founder: c. 2000. Volume 3: The Prophet: c. 2001.

Englebert, Omer. St. Francis of Assisi: A Biography. Ann Arbor, Michigan: Servant Books, 1965.

Flannery, Austin, O.P., Vatican Council II: The Conciliar and Post Conciliar Documents, Volume 1 & 2, The Liturgical Press, 1992.

Habig, Marion A. St. Francis of Assisi: Writings and Early Biographies: English Omnibus of the Sources for the Life of St. Francis. Quincy, Illinois: Franciscan Press, 1991.

Handbook of the Brothers and Sisters of Penance. Brothers and Sisters of Penance: Middletown, Rhode Island: 2000.

Handbook of the Confraternity of Penitents. Confraternity of Penitents: Middletown, Rhode Island: Editions 2003, 2006, 2010.

Libreria Editrice Vaticana, <u>Catechism of the Catholic Church,</u> Catholic Book Publishing Company, 1994.

McGaghan, Florence Rudge. "Confraternities of Penitents." Transcribed by Donald J. Boon. <u>The Catholic Encyclopedia: Volume XI</u>. Robert Appleton Company, 1911. Online edition c. 2003 by Kevin Knight for New Advent.

National Conference of Catholic Bishops. <u>Christian Prayer: The Liturgy of the Hours.</u> Catholic Book Publishing Co., New York, 1976.

Pazzelli, Raffaele. <u>St. Francis and the Third Order</u>. Quincy, Illinois: Franciscan Herald Press, 1989.

Poppi, Fr. Maximus. <u>The Rules of the Third Order of St. Francis: Texts for Comparative Study.</u> Saint Bonaventure, New York: The Franciscan Institute, 1945.

Stewart, Robert M. <u>"De Illis Qui Faciunt Penitentiam" The Rule of the Secualar Franciscan Order: Origins, Development, Interpretation.</u> Rome, Italy: Istituto Storico Dei Cappuccini, 1991.

The Confraternity of Christian Doctrine, <u>The New American Bible,</u> Benziger, Inc., New York, Beverly Hills, 1968.

USA Inflation Calculator: http://www.usinflationcalculator.com/

THE RULE OF LIFE
OF THE
CONFRATERNITY OF PENITENTS

"Mary's sole object in this world was to keep her eyes constantly focused on God so as to discover His will. Then when she had found out what God wanted, she did it." *St. Bernadine of Siena*

Prayer to Our Lady

Immaculate Mother of Jesus,

We honor you as God's chosen one, beautiful, beloved, and free from all sin. Keep watch over us, pray that we may rise above our sins and failings and come to share the fullness of grace. Be a Mother to us in the order of grace by assisting us to live your obedience, your faith, your hope and your love. Amen.

RULE OF LIFE FOR THE CONFRATERNITY OF PENITENTS

This is the Rule of Life[2] for the Confraternity of Penitents. Penitents live this Rule according to the Constitutions of the Confraternity of Penitents.

THE PRIMITIVE RULE OF 1221

Here begins the Rule of the Continent Brothers and Sisters: In the Name of the Father and of the Son and of the Holy Spirit. Amen.

The memorial of what is proposed for the Brothers and Sisters of Penance, living in their own homes, begun in the year of our Lord 1221, is as follows.

CHAPTER I: DAILY LIFE

1. The men belonging to this brotherhood shall dress in humble, undyed cloth, the price of which is not to exceed six Ravenna soldi[3] an ell[4], unless for evident and necessary cause a temporary dispensation be given. And breadth and thinness of the cloth are to be considered in said price.

2. They shall wear their outer garments and furred coats without open throat, sewed shut or uncut but certainly laced up, not open as secular people wear them; and they shall wear their sleeves closed.

3. The sisters in turn shall wear an outer garment and tunic made of cloth of the same price and humble quality; or at least they are to have with the outer gar-

---

2   The Rule has no footnotes. Footnotes were added by the Confraternity to explain terms which are unfamiliar to modern penitents.

3   Six Ravenna soldi was the equivalent of $5.37 United States of America money in January 2014.

4   An ell is one man's arm length, approximately 5/8 to 1 yard.

ment a white or black underwrap or petticoat, or an ample linen gown without gathers[5], the price of an ell of which is not to exceed twelve Pisa denars.[6] As to this price, however, and the fur cloaks they wear a dispensation may be given according to the estate of the woman and the custom of the place. They are not to wear silken or dyed veils and ribbons.

4. And both the brothers and the sisters shall have their fur garments of lamb's wool only. They are permitted to have leather purses and belts sewed in simple fashion without silken thread, and no other kind. Also other vain adornments they shall lay aside at the bidding of the Visitor.

5. They are not to go to unseemly parties or to shows or dances. They shall not donate to actors[7], and shall forbid their household to donate.

CHAPTER II: ABSTINENCE

6. All are to abstain from meat save on Sundays, Tuesdays, and Thursdays, except on account of illness or weakness, for three days at bloodletting, in traveling, or on account of a specially high feast intervening, namely, the Nativity for three days, New Year's, Epiphany, the Pasch of the Resurrection for three days, Assumption of the glorious Virgin Mary, the solemnity of All Saints and of St. Martin[8]. On the other days, when there is no fasting, they may eat cheese and eggs. But when they are with religious in their convent homes, they have leave to eat what is served to them. And except for the feeble, the ailing, and those traveling, let them be content with dinner and supper. Let the healthy be temperate in eating and drinking.

7. Before their dinner and supper let them say the Lord's prayer once, likewise after their meal, and let them give thanks to God. Otherwise let them say three Our Fathers.

CHAPTER III: FASTING

8. From the Pasch of the Resurrection to the feast of All Saints they are to fast on Fridays. From the feast of All Saints until Easter they are to fast on Wednesdays and Fridays, but still observing the other fasts enjoined in general by the Church.

9. They are to fast daily, except on account of infirmity or any other need, throughout the fast of St. Martin from after said day until Christmas, and throughout the greater fast from Carnival Sunday[9] until Easter.

---

5   A lady's undergarment required 2 1/2 ell, and an overlock (cape) 3 to 3 1/2 ell. A woman's dress might require 10 ell.

6   Twelve Pisa denars were somewhat equivalent to six Ravenna soldi. Towns minted their own coinage at the time the Rule of 1221 was written.

7   In 1221, all plays were bawdy and mocked religion.

8   November 11, Saint Martin's Day, was a Solemnity at the time the Rule was written. Today it is a Memorial.

9   The Sunday before Ash Wednesday.

10. Sisters who are pregnant are free to refrain until their purification from the corporal observances except those regarding their dress and prayers.

11. Those engaged in fatiguing work shall be allowed to take food three times a day from the Pasch of the Resurrection until the Dedication feast of St. Michael[10]. And when they work for others it will be allowed them to eat everything served to them, except on Fridays and on the fasts enjoined in general by the Church.

CHAPTER IV: PRAYER

12. All are daily to say the seven canonical Hours, that is: Matins[11], Prime[12], Terce[13], Sext[14], None[15], Vespers[16], and Compline[17]. The clerics are to say them after the manner of the clergy. Those who know the Psalter are to say the Deus in nomine tuo (Psalm 54) and the Beati Immaculati (Psalm 119) up to the Legem pone (Verse 33) for Prime, and the other psalms of the Hours, with the Glory Be to the Father; but when they do not attend church, they are to say for Matins the psalms the Church says or any eighteen psalms; or at least to say the Our Father as do the unlettered at any of the Hours. The others say twelve Our Fathers for Matins and for every one of the other Hours seven Our Fathers with the Glory Be to the Father after each one. And those who know the Creed and the Miserere mei Deus (Ps. 51) should say it at Prime and Compline. If they do not say that at the Hours indicated, they shall say three Our Fathers.

13. The sick are not to say the Hours unless they wish.

14. All are to go to Matins in the fast of St. Martin and in the great fast, unless inconvenience for persons or affairs should threaten.

CHAPTER V: THE SACRAMENTS, OTHER MATTERS

15. They are to make a confession of their sins three times a year and to receive Communion at Christmas, Easter, and Pentecost. They are to be reconciled with their neighbors and to restore what belongs to others. They are to make up for past tithes and pay future tithes.

10	September 29.
11	Office of Readings
12	Early Morning Prayer
13	Midmorning Prayer
14	Midday Prayer
15	Midafternoon Prayer
16	Evening Prayer
17	Night Prayer

16. They are not to take up lethal weapons, or bear them about, against anybody.

17. All are to refrain from formal oaths unless where necessity compels, in the cases excepted by the Sovereign Pontiff in his indult, that is, for peace, for the Faith, under calumny, and in bearing witness.

18. Also in their ordinary conversations they will do their best to avoid oaths. And should anyone have sworn thoughtlessly through a slip of the tongue, as happens where there is much talking, he should the evening of the same day, when he is obliged to think over what he has done, say three Our Fathers in amends of such oaths. Let each member fortify his household to serve God.

CHAPTER VI: SPECIAL MASS AND MEETING EACH MONTH

19. All the brothers and sisters of every city and place are to foregather every month at the time the ministers see fit, in a church which the ministers will make known, and there assist at Divine Services.

20. And every member is to give the treasurer one ordinary denar[18]. The treasurer is to collect this money and distribute it on the advice of the ministers among the poor brothers and sisters, especially the sick and those who may have nothing for their funeral services, and thereupon among the poor; and they are to offer something of the money to the aforesaid church.

21. And, if it be convenient at the time, they are to have some religious who is informed in the words of God to exhort them and strengthen them to persevere in their penance and in performing the works of mercy. And except for the officers, they are to remain quiet during the Mass and sermon, intent on the Office, on prayer, and on the sermon.

CHAPTER VII: VISITING THE SICK, BURYING THE DEAD

22. Whenever any brother or sister happens to fall ill, the ministers, if the patient let them know of it, shall in person or through others visit the patient once a week, and remind him of penance; and if they find it expedient, they are to supply him from the common fund with what he may need for the body.

23. And if the ailing person depart from this life, it is to be published to the brothers and sisters who may be present in the city or place, so that they may gather for the funeral; and they are not to leave until the Mass has been celebrated and the body consigned to burial. Thereupon each member within eight days of the demise shall say for the soul of the deceased: a Mass, if he is a priest; fifty psalms,

---

18   The smallest value coin minted at the time the Rule was written.

if he understands the Psalter, or if not, then fifty Our Fathers with the Requiem aeternam[19] at the end of each.

24. In addition, every year, for the welfare of the brothers and sisters living and dead, each priest is to say three Masses, each member knowing the Psalter is to recite it, and the rest shall say one hundred Our Fathers with the Requiem aeternam at the end of each.

25. All who have the right are to make their last will and make disposition of their goods within three months after their profession, lest anyone of them die intestate.

26. As regards making peace among the brothers and sisters or nonmembers at odds, let what the ministers find proper be done; even, if it be expedient, upon consultation with the Lord Bishop.

27. If contrary to their right and privileges trouble is made for the brothers and sisters by the mayors and governors of the places where they live, the ministers of the place shall do what they shall find expedient on the advice of the Lord Bishop.

28. Let each member accept and faithfully exercise the ministry of other offices imposed on him, although anyone may retire from office after a year.

29. When anybody wishes to enter this brotherhood, the ministers shall carefully inquire into his standing and occupation, and they shall explain to him the obligations of the brotherhood, especially that of restoring what belongs to others. And if he is content with it, let him be vested according to the prescribed way, and he must make satisfaction for his debts, paying money according to what pledged provision is given. They are to reconcile themselves with their neighbors and to pay up their tithes.

30. After these particulars are complied with, when the year is up and he seems suitable to them, let him on the advice of some discreet brothers be received on this condition: that he promise he will all the time of his life observe everything here written, or to be written or abated on the advice of the brothers, unless on occasion there be a valid dispensation by the ministers; and that he will, when called upon by the ministers, render satisfaction as the Visitor shall ordain if he have done anything contrary to this condition. And this promise is to be put in writing then and there by a public notary. Even so nobody is to be received otherwise, unless in consideration of the estate and rank of the person it shall seem advisable to the ministers.

31. No one is to depart from this brotherhood and from what is contained herein, except to enter a religious Order.

32. No heretic or person in bad repute for heresy is to be received. If he is under suspicion of it, he may be admitted if otherwise fit, upon being cleared before the bishop.

---

19   Eternal rest grant unto them, O Lord, and may perpetual light shine upon them.

33. Married women are not to be received except with the consent and leave of their husbands.

34. Brothers and sisters ejected from the brotherhood as incorrigible are not to be received in it again except it please the saner portion of the brothers.

CHAPTER VIII: CORRECTION, DISPENSATION, OFFICERS

35. The ministers of any city or place shall report public faults of the brothers and sisters to the Visitor for punishment. And if anyone proves incorrigible, after consultation with some of the discreet brothers he should be denounced to the Visitor, to be expelled by him from the brotherhood, and thereupon it should be published in the meeting. Moreover, if it is a brother, he should be denounced to the mayor or the governor.[20]

36. If anyone learns that a scandal is occurring relative to brothers and sisters, he shall report it to the ministers and shall have opportunity to report it to the Visitor. He need not be held to report it in the case of husband against wife.[21]

37. The Visitor has the power to dispense all the brothers and sisters in any of these points if he finds it advisable.

38. When the year has passed, the ministers with the counsel of the brothers are to elect two other ministers; and a faithful treasurer, who is to provide for the need of the brothers and sisters and other poor; and messengers who at the command of the ministers are to publish what is said and done by the fraternity.

39. In all the above mentioned points no one is to be obligated under guilt, but under penalty; yet so that if after being admonished twice by the ministers he should fail to discharge the penalty imposed or to be imposed on him by the Visitor, he shall be obligated under guilt as contumacious.

HERE ENDS THE RULE OF THE CONTINENT.

Author: Cardinal Hugolino dei Conti dei Segni who wrote this Rule at the request of St. Francis of Assisi, 1221
Source: Franciscan Omnibus of Sources

---

20   Medieval towns and cities were small in comparison to modern metropolitan areas. In addition, religion and government were intricately bound together. Penitents, like everyone else, were to adhere to public laws. Penitents were living public lives of purported conversion and supposedly striving for holiness. Public faults of penitents would be well known. To avoid bringing scandal to the Church community, penitents who committed public crimes and did not repent were to be denounced not only to the Church authority (Visitor) but also to public authorities (mayor and governor).

21   Penitents were not to become involved in domestic disputes.

CONSTITUTIONS

"O sinners, be not discouraged…Call Mary to your assistance, for you will always find her ready to help. It is God's Will that she should help in every need." *St. Basil*

<u>Mary, Immaculate Queen</u>

O Mary, Immaculate Queen,
Look down upon this distressed and suffering world.
You know our misery and our weakness.
O you who are our Mother, saving us in the hour of danger,
Have compassion on us in these days of great and heavy trial.
Jesus has confided to you the treasure of His grace,
And through you He wishes to grant us pardon and mercy.
In these hours of anguish, therefore, your children come to you as their hope.
We recognize your Queenship, and we ardently desire your triumph.
We need a Mother, and a Mother's heart.
You are for us the bright dawn, which scatters the darkness and points out the way to life.

In your mercy, obtain for us the courage and confidence of which we have such need.
Most holy and adorable Trinity,
You have crowned with glory in Heaven the Blessed Virgin Mary, Mother of the Savior.
Grant that all her children on earth may acknowledge her as their sovereign Queen,
That all hearts, homes and nations may recognize her rights as Mother and Queen.
Amen.

CONSTITUTIONS OF THE CONFRATERNITY OF PENITENTS

I. FAMILY IN THE CHURCH

Members of the Confraternity of Penitents (CFP) strive to surrender to God through the living of a Rule of Life given to penitents in the year 1221, at the request of St. Francis of Assisi and written by Cardinal Hugolino de Conti de Segni, later Pope Gregory IX. The Constitutions of the Confraternity of Penitents delineate how Members are to live the Rule today.

II. JURIDICAL SITUATION

The Confraternity of Penitents is an international, private, Catholic, lay association of the faithful, existing with the permission of the Bishop[22] of the Diocese of Fort Wayne - South Bend, Indiana, USA, and headquartered in his Diocese. Because the Bishop has deemed the Rule and Constitutions acceptable to live, he has indicated that the CFP Way of Life is a safe guide to holiness. If penitents live this life in humility and love, they will move deeper into their own personal conversion.

III. SUBJECTION TO THE CHURCH

The Pope, by virtue of being head of the Roman Catholic Church, is also head of the Confraternity of Penitents. The Bishop of the Diocese of Fort Wayne - South Bend, Indiana, USA, is the primary representative of the Church regarding the Confraternity of Penitents and has confirmed the canonical status of the Confraternity of Penitents as a

---

22   The term "Bishop" used in these Constitutions, as well as in any other documents of the Confraternity of Penitents, refers to the Bishop of the Diocese of Fort Wayne - South Bend, Indiana, USA, unless otherwise noted.

private association of the faithful (Bishop Kevin Rhoades in a letter dated 3 January 2014. This follows a previous letter by Bishop Thomas Tobin, dated 11 February 2009[23], issued when the Confraternity was headquartered in Rhode Island, USA.). The Confraternity acknowledges the authority of the Bishop over its affairs and will follow his directives.

All Members of the Confraternity, as well as its spiritual advisors, Spiritual Directors, and Visitor, are in complete conformity to all the directives of the Magisterium of the Roman Catholic Church and of the Holy See to whom belongs the authentic interpretation of the Rule and Constitutions. The practical interpretation of the Rule and Constitutions belongs to the Bishop of the Diocese of Fort Wayne - South Bend, in consultation with the Visitor and Minister General of the Confraternity who may also consult the Confraternity Council.

IV. THE OBJECT OF THE COMMITMENT

The Object of the Commitment is for the individual pledged member to lead a penitential life in union with Christ and with all the faithful. Penance is ongoing, putting on the mind of Jesus Christ to "Turn away from sin and be faithful to the Gospel" (Mark 1:15). Penance is conversion from doing things in worldly, selfish ways to doing them God's way. This cannot be done without some self-denial, for the Lord Himself said that we must "deny ourselves, take up our crosses, and follow Him" if we are to be His disciples. (Luke 9:23)

Members of the Confraternity of Penitents are to live converted to God and in a loving, Christ-like relationship with each other and with all. They are to participate in some form of the Spiritual and Corporal Works of Mercy. They are to maintain chastity according to their state in life and are to follow the dictates of the Church regarding sexual activity and family planning. Unless communities of penitents are formed according to Church law and following the CFP Rule and their own Constitutions, penitents are to live in their own homes as they, by the grace of the Holy Spirit, simplify and sanctify their lives.

Without the permission of their spiritual director, or religious superior, penitents should not undertake physical acts of self denial or mortification beyond those delineated in the Rule and Constitutions.

V. FRUITS OF THE COMMITMENT

Some graces given to those who live a penitential life under their freely chosen promise to God are:

a. To enable penitents to understand the transitory nature of this life and the superficiality of a worldly existence (poverty/moderation).

---

23   Letters reproduced in Appendix U of the Directory in this Handbook.

b. To direct penitents in the surrender of their own will to the Rule and to the spiritual director so that they may accept more joyfully the discipline and direction that God gives (obedience).

c. To draw penitents into a deep union with God Who wishes all people to surrender everything to Him (contemplative prayer).

d. To enable penitents to experience in a small way the self-emptying willingly embraced by Our Lord Jesus Christ (abandonment to the will of God).

e. To foster an increase of love for God the Father, Son, and Holy Spirit, and for human beings, since they are made in God's image. True love is to seek the others' good before one's own (loving, selfless service of God and of others).

VI. PURPOSE (CHARISM)

The Confraternity recognizes that God is Lord, Creator, and Father. It endeavors to assist the penitent in surrendering his or her life totally to God's Divine Will as manifest through the teachings of Christ, the authority of the Church, and the motion of the Holy Spirit in the penitent's life, as confirmed by the counsel of the penitent's spiritual director.

Thus, the Purpose (Charism) of the Confraternity of Penitents is to promote penance (conversion), that is, doing things God's way instead of human ways. The Purpose (Charism) is developed in its Vision, Prayer, Mission, Motto, Action, Song, and Symbol.

VISION

To give glory to God and surrender to His Will through the living of a medieval, penitential Rule of Life, the Rule of 1221. This Rule is lived as closely as possible to its original intent, and in one's own home, in peace with all others, and in obedience to the Roman Catholic Church, its Pope, and its Magisterium.

PRAYER

"Most High, Glorious God, enlighten the darkness of my mind, give me right faith, a firm hope and perfect charity, so that I may always and in all things act according to Your Holy Will. Amen." (Saint Francis's prayer before the San Damiano Crucifix)

MOTTO

"You shall love the Lord your God with your whole heart, with your whole soul, and with all your mind, (and) you shall love your neighbor as yourself." (Jesus's words as recorded in Matthew 22:37-38)

MISSION

"Go and repair My House which, as you can see, is falling into ruin." (The message given to St. Francis in a voice from the San Damiano Crucifix.)

ACTION

To pray for God's specific direction in one's life so that, through humbly living our Rule of Life, each penitent may help to rebuild the house of God by bringing love of God and neighbor to his or her own corner of the world.

SONG

"No Longer I" is the theme song of the Confraternity of Penitents.

SYMBOL

The San Damiano Crucifix is the Symbol of the Confraternity of Penitents.

VII. HISTORICAL OVERVIEW

Briefly, in the Diocese of Providence, Rhode Island USA, the Confraternity of Penitents began in 1994 with an interior call by the Holy Spirit to one individual to "live the Rule of 1221." This Rule was made known to others in 1995 and the "Brothers and Sisters of Penance" begun with six members.

In 1998, Bishop Robert Mulvee of the Diocese of Providence gave his permission to live the Rule and Statutes and the Confraternity began a formation program and went on the world wide web.

In 1999, another group also living the original Rule of 1221 joined with the Brothers and Sisters of Penance, but, due to differences among the leaders, the merger was severed in 2003. The Brothers and Sisters of Penance was dissolved and then refounded as the Confraternity of Penitents.

In 2013, the Confraternity of Penitents relocated to the Diocese of Fort Wayne-South Bend, Indiana USA.

An expanded Historical Overview can be found in Appendix E to these Constitutions.

VIII. ELIGIBILITY FOR MEMBERSHIP

Members are those persons considered to be part of the Confraternity of Penitents. All baptized Catholics who are fourteen years of age[24] or older, who are in complete har-

---

24   Applicants under the age of 18 need parental permission in order to become Members of the Confraternity.

mony with all the teachings of the Roman Catholic Church and the Magisterium, are eligible to enter formation as Members.

Members include those who have pledged to live the CFP Rule and Constitutions as well as those who are pursuing formation in the CFP at the Postulancy level or above and who have no impediments to pledging if their formation were complete.

ASSOCIATES

Those who wish to live the CFP Rule, but who have impediments to full Membership, may become Associates of the Confraternity. Associates are nonmembers who are in formation, or have completed formation, with the CFP.

AFFILIATES

Affiliates are nonmembers who support and pray for the CFP but who do not participate in formation.

IX. GOVERNANCE

The Confraternity of Penitents is a private Catholic lay association of the faithful with a hierarchical structure of governance. It is primarily governed by its Rule, Constitutions, and Directory as well as by the Code of Canon Law. Supplementary governance is provided by its Articles of Incorporation and bylaws, originally filed with the State of Rhode Island on August 19, 2003, and amended thereafter, and by the regulations in the State of Rhode Island Non Profit Corporations Act. On November 12, 2013, the Confraternity of Penitents was granted a Certificate of Authority to operate in Indiana as a Non-Profit Foreign Corporation. Foreign means "out of state." The Confraternity retains its original incorporation under the State of Rhode Island.

X. STRUCTURE

Penitents are first and foremost members of the Church which is the body of Christ. Within the CFP, they are Members of the international Confraternity first, secondly of their Regions, and thirdly of any local Chapter or Circle of the Confraternity.

The simplified governing structure is:

Minister General (*International*)
|
Regional Minister *(Regional)*
|
Chapter or Circle Minister *(Local)*

This simplified structure reflects the Order of Governance and the Order of Appeal, proceeding from the local level up to the International level. If the lower level, in conjunction with the religious advisor(s) on that level, cannot address the question or matter of concern, it is referred to the next level. The answer is, in turn, relayed down through the levels to the petitioner.

The highest levels of appeal rest in the Magisterium, that is in the Bishop of the Diocese of Fort Wayne - South Bend and in the Pope through the Apostolic Nuncio.

WORLD

The Confraternity of Penitents is a worldwide organization. All CFP Members, Associates, and Affiliates are ultimately under the governance of the Minister General in consultation with the CFP Council. All Members, Associates, and Affiliates are also subject to the Visitor and Bishop.

The Confraternity of Penitents is self-governing and self-supportive, receiving its funding through donations from its Members and from others worldwide.

REGION

Regions are geographical subdivisions of the world which simplify governance. Subject to the Minister General and CFP Council, Regional Ministers shall govern their Regions following the guidelines within the Rule, Constitutions, and Directory.

LOCALITY

Local gatherings form when two or more CFP Postulants, Novices, and/or Pledged Members, from at least two different families, meet together in person at least monthly. A CFP Circle consists of at least two Members while a CFP Chapter must consist of at least five.

Chapters and Circles are governed by their own Officers subject to their Spiritual Assistant. They are then subject to their Regional Minister and ultimately to the Minister General and Visitor in consultation with the CFP Council.

XI. RIGHTS, DUTIES, AND OBLIGATIONS

Several individuals exercise leadership in the Confraternity of Penitents. The principal ones of these are:

VISITOR

The Confraternity of Penitents' Visitor is a spiritual guide and immediate representative of the Roman Catholic Church. He shall be a priest appointed by the Bishop of the Diocese of Fort Wayne - South Bend, Indiana. If he is also a Religious, the Visitor must have the permission of his superior to serve. The CFP shall have only one Visitor unless the Bishop, in consultation with the Minister General, deems that more are needed.

MINISTER GENERAL

The office of Minister General is the highest non-clerical office in the Confraternity of Penitents. The Minister General is responsible for the efficient operation of the CFP and oversees it in every regard. The Minister General is the primary contact with all Bishops regarding the Confraternity, protects and promotes the Purpose (Charism), and endeavors, with prayer to the Holy Spirit for guidance, to develop and expand the CFP and the message of penance (conversion) worldwide. With prayer and the advice of the CFP Officers and Lay and Spiritual Advisors, the Minister General shall make the final decisions, subject to approval by the Visitor, on all matters involving the Confraternity of Penitents. The only exceptions to this are decisions in the following five areas in which the elected Minister General must have the unanimous consent of those legally named as Council members, plus the consent of the Visitor, to implement a decision:

- The dissolution of major assets or the spending of 20% or more of CFP funds
- Change to the CFP Name, Legal Status as a 501c3 Organization, and Purpose (Charism) as detailed in the Vision, Action, Prayer, Motto, Mission, Song, and Symbol
- Change to the CFP Rule[25] or Constitutions[26]
- Change to the CFP Governance and Structure
- Change to the CFP Formation Program

CFP OFFICERS[27]

Confraternity Officers ensure that the CFP is running smoothly on an international level. Confraternity Officers are the CFP Ministerial Assistant, CFP Messenger, and CFP Treasurer. They assist and advise the Minister General in the operation of the Confraternity.

---

25   The Rule for the Confraternity of Penitents is the Rule of 1221. As such, it is a historical document and cannot be changed. However, the Rule and Constitutions complement each other. Since the Constitutions detail how the Rule is to be lived today, they are subject to modification.

26   The Historical Overview section of these Constitutions may be updated as necessary without the permission required by this part of the Constitutions.

27   The Minister General is also a CFP Officer.

ADDITIONAL COUNCIL MEMBERS

Additional Council Members serve as advisors to the Minister General.

REGIONAL MINISTERS

Regional Ministers insure that formation is being properly conducted in their Regions, both with isolated Members and Associates and with those in Chapters and Circles.

XII. TERM OF OFFICE

Elections and confirmation of appointments are conducted annually. The term of office for all Officers and leaders, other than the Minister General and Formators, begins on January 1 following their election or appointment and ends on December 31. If a term of office becomes vacant before December 31, a replacement will be appointed to fill the office until January 1. Unless factors of incapacity or inability are present, all Life Pledged Members are eligible to nominate, vote, and hold office.

XIII. FORMATION

Formation assures that those entering the Confraternity of Penitents will be adequately formed in the way of life required by the Rule and Constitutions, will develop and advance in the spiritual life, and will grow in knowledge of the teachings of the Roman Catholic Church. Each person in formation is assigned a Formator to review their lessons and to assist them with formation.

Formation is open to Members and Associates of the Confraternity of Penitents. It consists of 51 lessons, which include 12 Postulant lessons, 12 lessons for each of the three years of Novice formation, and 3 lessons prior to pledging. One lesson is completed monthly, with the exception of those in the August Postulancy who complete two lessons per month. Each year of formation must be completed successfully before applications can be accepted for the next year of formation or for pledging.

Applications are made to the CFP Chapter or Circle Minister (if applicable), the Regional Minister, and the CFP Office, for Inquiry, for each year of formation, for pledging, and for vowing.

The stages of formation are:

PRE-INQUIRY

A pre-inquirer is an individual who contacts the Confraternity, or any Member of it, for information, advice, and/or prayer about discerning a possible vocation to the Confraternity, but who has not completed an Inquirer application.

INQUIRY

Inquiry is the first level of formal contact with the Confraternity. Inquirers are exploring the CFP way of life and discerning a possible vocation to it.

POSTULANCY

The Postulancy is an introduction into the formation process. Postulants reflect on certain teachings of the Roman Catholic Church, on penance, and on the spiritual journey. They study the CFP Rule and Constitutions and begin to follow them in certain ways. The Postulancy is a time of further discernment of a vocation to the CFP.

NOVITIATE

The principal years of formation are the three years of the Novitiate, each consisting of at least twelve full months during which the Novice regularly participates in at least one Spiritual or Corporal Work of Mercy. The Novice also undertakes a study of Scripture and of the Catechism of the Catholic Church. Each year of formation integrates different prescriptions of the Rule and the Constitutions into the Novice's life. Those prescriptions are: for Novice 1, prayer; for Novice 2, fasting and abstinence; for Novice 3, simplicity of life. At the end of three years of Novice formation, the penitent shall be praying certain prayers for a certain amount of time daily, shall fast and abstain weekly, and shall have greatly simplified his or her wardrobe and possessions.

XIV. FORM OF COMMITMENT

PLEDGE

A Pledge is a voluntary commitment, before God, to live the CFP Rule and Constitutions either for a year or for life. Making a Pledge is an important and grace filled step in the life of a penitent because a Pledge is a binding promise to live according to the CFP Rule and Constitutions, although not under pain of sin. Prior to pledging, the Member must be at least eighteen years old, must be confirmed in the Roman Catholic Church, and must have successfully completed all four years of formation plus three additional lessons which discuss the seriousness of the pledge. The pledge is made to a Roman Catholic priest, deacon, religious, or to the penitent's spiritual director.

VOW

A vow is the deepest commitment one can make to live the CFP Rule because it is binding under pain of sin, as long as it can be kept. With the permission of the spiritual director, a CFP Life-Pledged Member may take private vows to observe the Rule and Constitutions for life as well as additional vows approved by the Church, such as Consecration to Our Lady.

XV. PROPERTY

Any equipment, property, or other assets purchased by the CFP, either internationally, regionally, or locally, for use by and in the Confraternity, remain the property of the CFP entity (International Council, Regional Council, Chapter or Circle Council) which purchased them.

XVI. THE GENERAL ASSEMBLY

A yearly conference and retreat, open to all Members of the Confraternity, will be held annually if at all possible. The Visitor or another priest, deacon, male or female religious, will preside at this gathering which shall promote Catholic spirituality particularly through penance (conversion) and which shall unite the total Confraternity. Other groups within the Church may be invited to send delegates to this event.

XVII. MEETINGS

Chapters and Circles shall meet monthly in their local communities. Electronic gatherings shall be held monthly, if possible, for those unable to participate in local meetings.

XVIII. FINANCIAL POLICIES

The Confraternity of Penitents is a nonprofit association. It has no mandatory dues, fees, or assessments. If money is needed, the Treasurer may solicit donations.

XIX. ADDITIONAL PROCEDURES

Additional procedures are delineated in the CFP Rule and Directory.

XX. APPLICATIONS OF THE RULE OF 1221

PREAMBLE

In keeping with the Preamble of the Rule, here begin the Constitutions of the Continent (those who give up things) Confraternity of Penitents. In the Name of the Father and of the Son and of the Holy Spirit. Amen.

CHAPTER I: DAILY LIFE

1. In keeping with section 1 of the Rule:

1a. Those belonging to this Confraternity shall dress in humble and inexpensive cloth. Subdued, solid colors, as opposed to patterns and designs, should be chosen. Colors shall be neutral shades (black, white, cream, ivory, beige, tan, camel, brown, gray, charcoal, etc.) in conformity with the colors worn by the first penitents and blue in honor of the Blessed Mother who is the patron of the Confraternity of Penitents. The penitent should strive to have only the least expensive and minimum amount of clothing needed for comfort, employment, and utility.

1b. The penitent should mix and match styles and colors so as appear indistinguishable from other seculars and to avoid the appearance of a wearing a habit. Thus penitents will do penance privately and inconspicuously.

1c. For evident and necessary cause, a temporary dispensation on clothing colors and quality may be given.

2. In keeping with section 2 of the Rule:

2a. Visible undergarments such as socks or stockings may be of solid neutral colors or blue. Clothing that is not visible may be of any color or pattern.

2b. Men's ties should be simple, conservative, and tasteful and may be patterned and of any color or color combination provided that the ties are subdued in appearance and not "flashy."

2c. Colorful ornamentation and fancy jewelry are not to be worn unless a dispensation is given. Engagement rings, wedding bands, watches, and any other similar adornments, and tasteful and unostentatious religious jewelry such as medals are permitted. Small pierced earring studs, in a simple and inexpensive style, may be allowed if needed to keep earring holes from closing.

2d. For special events, a dispensation is given for the wearing of earrings, other jewelry, and clothing that falls outside the regular garb of the followers of this Rule.

2e. The use of perfumes, after shave lotions, and so on should be avoided unless necessary. Wherever possible, unscented hair sprays, soaps, lotions, and so on should be chosen.

2f. Female penitents may use cosmetics if necessary but should keep their makeup as conservative as possible so as not to draw attention to its use. The use of extensive makeup is discouraged.

2g. At all times in public, a simple cross or crucifix must be visibly worn either around the neck or in the form of a brooch or lapel pin. The style chosen should be in keeping with poverty, humility, and simplicity according to the penitent's state in life. If a penitent is already wearing a religious habit of a First, Second, or Third Order community, the habit of the Order will suffice. A penitent can be excused from the wearing of a cross, crucifix, or habit if to do so may endanger the penitent's life or impede the penitent's manner of earning a living.

3. In keeping with section 3 of the Rule:
   3a. All clothing and accessories must be modest and chaste. They must also be simple and inexpensive unless a dispensation is given according to the estate or employment of the person and custom of the place.
   3b. Penitents should attempt to live as simply and inexpensively as possible according to their state in life. With the consent of their spouses and families, they are to have the minimum number of and least sophisticated appliances, furniture, furnishings, electronic aids, and vehicles as necessary. However, the following of this section of the Rule must not create more work or inconvenience for penitents or other family members.

4. In keeping with section 4 of the Rule:
   4a. Outer winter garments shall be either of lamb's wool, or a comparable imitation, only, or of any non-fur material. They shall be of either a solid neutral or blue color, simple and modest, and shall conform to the Constitutions under section 1.
   4b. Purses should be of either a solid neutral or blue color. Suitcases and carry bags such as back packs should be of these colors if possible.

5. In keeping with section 5 of the Rule:
   5a. Attendance at immodest functions or events at which immodest or immoral behavior is exhibited or fostered, except to condemn such behavior, is forbidden. This would include movies, parties, plays, and so on.
   5b. The penitent should avoid the near occasions of sin in all circumstances and should strive always to give good example to others.

CHAPTER II: ABSTINENCE

6. In keeping with section 6 of the Rule:
   6a. For penitents, all Mondays, Wednesdays, Fridays, and Saturdays are days of abstinence (that is, meatless days) unless directed otherwise by a physician. Meat is allowed on Tuesdays, Thursdays, and Sundays.
   6b. Abstinence will follow current Church regulations which are listed in Appendix A of these Constitutions.
   6c. Except for Sundays and Solemnities, penitents are to eat but two meals daily throughout the year unless advised otherwise by a physician. However, a third, small "bite to eat" of beverage and solid food may be taken if needed at one other time during the day. Beverages such as fruit juice, milk, coffee, and so on may be taken at any time between meals.
   6d. Except for Sundays and Solemnities, between meal snacks of solid food should be avoided.
   6e. At all times, penitents should be temperate in eating and drinking.

6f. In their own homes, penitents should attempt to prepare foods that other household members enjoy even if this means that penitents must sometimes prepare an individual dish for themselves in order to follow this Rule.

6g. In order to be hospitable, penitents may eat small, between meal snacks if they are entertaining guests or if they are guests in the homes of others.

6h. When eating with others in a group setting, the penitent should endeavor to allow others to choose their foods first as long as this penitential practice can be kept hidden and not call attention to the penitent.

6i. Travelers while in transit to their destinations and those who are ill, weak, pregnant, or breastfeeding are exempt from following the fasting and abstinence provisions of this Rule.

7. In keeping with section 7 of the Rule:

7a. Before and after meals, let the penitents reverently say either their regular meal prayer, or the Lord's prayer once, and let all give thanks to God. If they forget or if they are fasting completely from food, they are to say three Our Father's. These prayers may be prayed out loud or silently with head bowed unless to do so would either be dangerous to the penitent or highly offensive to the company kept.

CHAPTER III: FASTING

8. In keeping with section 8 of the Rule:

8a. All Fridays are days of fast for penitents. From the Feast of All Saints until Easter, penitents are to fast on Wednesdays as well. Wednesdays and Fridays are also days of abstinence, following section 6 of the Rule.

8b. Fasting guidelines shall follow current Church law and are listed in Appendix A of these Constitutions.

8c. The amount of food eaten on fast days will be particular to the individual penitent who should feel hungry but not debilitated, drowsy, or ill. The penitent should consult a spiritual director, confessor, or, if needed, a physician regarding the amount of food to be eaten.

9. In keeping with section 9 of the Rule:

9a. Penitents are to observe a pre-Christmas fast from November 12, the day after the Feast of St. Martin, until Christmas and a pre-Easter fast from Ash Wednesday until Easter.

9b. Penitents who are guests in the homes of others, or who have been invited out to eat, are permitted to eat what is set before them so as not to embarrass the host unless that day is a day of fast and/or abstinence enjoined by the Church. Penitents might consider not accepting invitations to eat out on Church enjoined days of fast and abstinence.

9c. Sundays are never days of fast or abstinence.

9d. Penitents should not fast or abstain on any of the Church Solemnities. These include the Octave of Christmas, the Feasts of New Year's, Epiphany, Annunciation, the Octave of Easter, the Feasts of the Ascension, Assumption, All Saints, Immaculate Conception, and all other Solemnities of the Church.

9e. Penitents are permitted to celebrate with between meal snacks birthday parties, anniversaries, baptisms, confirmations, marriages, and other special occasions unless these would fall on a fast day enjoined by the Church.

9f. Additional exceptions to the fasting provisions of this Rule are listed under sections 6, 10, and 11 of the Rule and Constitutions and in Appendix A to these Constitutions.

10. In keeping with section 10 of the Rule:

10a. All pregnant and breastfeeding mothers are exempt from fasting and abstinence both by the Church and the Rule.

11. In keeping with section 11 of the Rule:

11a. Fatiguing work may be either physical or mental. If a penitent is unsure whether his or her work classifies as fatiguing, a priest or spiritual director should be consulted.

11b. Those engaged in fatiguing work may eat three times daily on work days if necessary for strength. They are bound to follow, however, the days of fast and abstinence enjoined by the Church and, as a penitent, to observe Friday as a day of fast and abstinence, unless their parish priest, confessor, or spiritual director exempts them.

CHAPTER IV: PRAYER

12. In keeping with section 12 of the Rule:

12a. Prayer is the core of growth in a life with God. Penitents must be committed to a life of prayer as outlined in this Rule. More prayer than what is listed, including daily mental prayer, meditation, and contemplation, is encouraged.

12b. One must adjust one's schedule to make time to pray. Extraneous activities that do not foster prayer life should be dropped. However, prayer must not interfere with daily duties such as caring for family members, keeping house, or earning a living. Penitents may have to pray during the night, while driving, while doing house or yard work, and so on. Playing tapes of spiritual conferences or sacred music and hymns while working or driving may help. A pocket sized New Testament or Psalter may be carried so that the penitent can seize a few moments of prayer and meditation while waiting in line, waiting on hold on the phone, and so on.

12c. While the Liturgy of the Hours is the preferred method of prayer, substitution of the rote prayers (Option Four below) is permissible especially for those times when it is impossible to sit down with a breviary. The penitent should, however, not rely totally on these other prayers as a substitute for the Liturgy of the Hours.

12d. There will arise certain days on which a penitent finds it impossible to say all the required prayers in any form. On such days, the penitent is to raise his or her mind to God at the required prayer times and have the intention to pray even though the opportunity is not available. These days should be rare. If a penitent finds it impossible to pray the hours on most days, he or she must examine his or her life and make proper adjustments so that the prayers can be said.

12e. All should renew the consecration of themselves and the Confraternity to Our Lady. The recommended prayer of consecration of the Confraternity, The Marian Consecration Prayer, is in Appendix B of these Constitutions.

12f. All are to pray a daily formal prayer (office) of some kind. The preferred method is to use the Liturgy of the Hours (breviary).

12g. For those who have no breviary, other offices approved by the Church may be substituted. These include the Little Office of the Blessed Virgin or the Office of the Passion.

12h. For those without breviaries or copies of other offices, certain Psalms may be substituted for each of the hours. These are listed in Appendix C of these Constitutions.

12i. If a penitent cannot read or has no Bible, breviary, or Office book, the penitent may pray Our Father's, Hail Mary's, and Glory Be's in place of each office as directed below under Option Four.

12j. All penitents are to pray daily Morning, Evening, and Night Prayer, preferably using the Liturgy of the Hours. Morning Prayer (Lauds, called Prime in the Primitive Rule) is to be prayed between 6 a.m. and 11 a.m. Evening Prayer (Vespers) is to be prayed between 4 p.m. and 11 p.m. Night Prayer (Compline) is to be prayed right before retiring for bed.

12k. In addition, for Morning Prayer, all are to add the Apostles' Creed and Psalms 51 ("Have mercy on me, O God, according to your steadfast love," etc.) and 54 ("Save me, O God, by your name, and vindicate me by your might," etc.) and 119 ("Happy are those whose way is blameless, who walk in the law of the Lord") up to verse 32. If a penitent cannot read, he or she should endeavor to memorize the psalms. If this is not possible, three additional Our Fathers may be said.

12l. ~~For Night Prayer, right before retiring~~ for bed, all are to add Psalm 51 and the Apostles' Creed. If the penitent cannot read Psalm 51, an Our Father may be substituted.

12m. The Glory Be to the Father is to be prayed after each psalm.

12n. In addition, penitents should, if possible, spend a minimum of fifteen minutes daily in meditative or contemplative prayer.

12o. To complete the daily prayer schedule, the penitent must then choose, with the guidance of a spiritual director, one of the following five options:

OPTION ONE: PRAY THE COMPLETE LITURGY OF THE HOURS AS PRESCRIBED IN THE CURRENT BREVIARY

The Office of Readings (formerly called Matins) was once said around midnight but may now be prayed at any time during the day. The little hours of Terce (Midmorning Prayer-about 9 a.m.), Sext (Midday Prayer-about noon), and None (Midafternoon Prayer-about 3 p.m.) are prayed at approximately the hours described. Penitents may combine some of these prayers and say them at alternate hours if their personal schedules require it. For example, the Office of Readings and Morning Prayer may both be said at dawn if need requires. Midmorning, Midday, and Midafternoon Prayer may be combined at noon and Evening Prayer and Night Prayer combined prior to bedtime. Clerics are to recite the Hours after the manner of the clergy.

OPTION TWO: PRAY A FIFTEEN DECADE ROSARY.[28]

If possible the fifteen decades should be broken up so that the Rosary is prayed, in part, throughout the day to approximately correspond to the times of the minor hours.

OPTION THREE: PRAY AN HOUR OF MENTAL PRAYER DAILY.

This may be broken up into two 30 minute segments or four 15 minute segments. An ideal place to pray would be before the Blessed Sacrament.

OPTION FOUR: PRAY OUR FATHER'S

Those who do not know how to read, who have no Bible or breviary, or who cannot read on a particular day, may say, for the Office of Readings, twelve Our Father's, twelve Hail Mary's, and twelve Glory Be's; for every other one of the hours, seven Our Father's, seven Hail Mary's, and seven Glory Be's.

OPTION FIVE: OTHER SUBSTITUTIONS

Those parenting small children or otherwise suffering continuous distractions or time constraints may, with the permission of their spiritual directors, substitute short pious

---

28   Any fifteen decades may be chosen.

ejaculations for the minor hours. These may be as simple as mentally lifting one's mind to God. Penitents should, however, endeavor to pray Morning, Evening, and Night Prayer unless dispensed from doing so by their spiritual directors. At the minimum, those who choose Option Five must review their prayer schedule at the first meeting of each year with their spiritual directors so that adjustments may be made.

13. In keeping with section 13 of the Rule:

13a. While the sick do not have to say an office, they may do so all or part of the time.

14. In keeping with section 14 of the Rule:

14a. Since attendance at public recitation of Matins (the Office of Readings) is inaccessible to most penitents, the penitent should attend daily Mass unless there is an intervening conflict of obligations. Parenting small children, health concerns, getting children off to school, employment schedules, and so on constitute some of these conflicting obligations. If Mass attendance is impossible or is unwise, the penitent should prayerfully recite one decade of the Rosary at some time during the day.

14b. All are to go to daily Mass in Advent and Lent unless serious inconvenience for persons, business, employment, or duties should threaten. Again, a decade of the Rosary is to be said if Mass is not attended.

14c. At Mass, signs of devotion and reverence before the Real Presence of Christ in the Eucharist should follow the parish priest's or the bishop's directives. Penitents' behavior and clothing should avoid drawing attention away from Christ's Presence in the Eucharist and from the words and ceremonies attendant to its celebration.

CHAPTER V: THE SACRAMENTS, OTHER MATTERS

15. In keeping with section 15 of the Rule:

15a. Penitents should consider confessing their sins twice monthly unless an undue burden is involved with this frequency or unless advised by the spiritual director to confess at another time interval. At a minimum, penitents are to confess monthly and to receive the Eucharist weekly provided the penitent is in the state of grace.

15b. All are to be reconciled in every way possible and to tithe ten percent of their income to their parish, the Catholic Church, or to charitable organizations whose goals are in keeping with the Church hierarchy and Magisterium. The tithe must not be given to any organization that is working in opposition to the Church. If a ten percent tithe seems too high, the penitent should consult the spiritual director or a spiritual assistant of the Confraternity, about the appropriate amount of the tithe and then should follow the advice given. Since the penitent is to financially support their home Chapter or Circle of the Confraternity of Penitents and the work of the international Confraternity, a portion of one's tithe may go to this cause.

16. In keeping with section 16 of this Rule:

    16a. They are not to take up or bear lethal weapons that would be used against other human beings with the exception of participation in a just war with the permission of the penitent's spiritual director, or as part of one's legitimate employment (police officers, for example). If a penitent is living in a dangerous environment in which a weapon may be necessary for self-defense, a spiritual director must approve the penitent's possession of any weapon.

    16b. Hunting and fishing to provide meat for one's family is permitted. One is also permitted to kill animal, bird, or insect pests that may be destroying one's food supply or threatening one's life or goods.

17. In keeping with section 17 of this Rule:

    17a. All are to refrain from formal oaths except where required by law.

18. In keeping with section 18 of this Rule:

    18a. They are not to take oaths in ordinary conversations.

    18b. They are to watch their speech and, should they sin by speaking, they are to say, by evening of that same day, three Our Father's.

    18c. Let each member teach his or her household to love and serve God.

    18d. Let the members lovingly serve others outside their household by participating, as much as obligations, time, finances, and health permit, in the Spiritual and Corporal Works of Mercy, following the guidance of God and their spiritual director. Let them serve all with the charity and mercy of Christ. The spiritual and corporal works of mercy are listed in Appendix D of these Constitutions.

CHAPTER VI: SPECIAL MASS AND MEETING EACH MONTH

19. In keeping with section 19 of this Rule:

    19a. Penitents living in proximity to each other should stay in touch with one another and ideally form a Chapter or Circle to assist each other in this way of life, subject to the Confraternity's guidelines on forming a Chapter or Circle.

    19b. No Chapter or Circle may be formed without a spiritual assistant (Visitor). The spiritual assistant must be a priest, deacon, or male or female religious who upholds all the teachings of the Catholic Church and who fully supports the penitents in living this Rule of Life.

19c. Should a Chapter or Circle lose its spiritual assistant, it must obtain permission from the Confraternity Visitor to continue meeting while a search is made for a replacement. In the meantime, the Confraternity shall assign a temporary spiritual assistant to the group. Permission to continue meeting without a permanent spiritual assistant must be renewed annually.

19d. Chapters and Circles that are temporarily without spiritual assistants may wish to use audio or video tapes to provide formation for their members until a new spiritual assistant is acquired.

19e. All members of this Confraternity are to gather for their monthly Chapter or Circle meeting at a time the local ministers see fit. If possible, they should attend Mass as part of this meeting.

19f. If there is no local Chapter or Circle, a member is permitted to attend an internet Chapter of the CFP, be part of a by-mail Chapter of the CFP, or live this Rule on his or her own under a competent spiritual director. All such members should be in regular contact with the Confraternity by letter, email, or phone call and should obey the spiritual assistant (Visitor) of the Confraternity in all matters that concern the Visitor as stated in the Rule.

20. In keeping with section 20 of this Rule:

20a. Every member shall contribute generously to the treasury of their Chapter or Circle or of the Confraternity.

20b. There are fixed expenses affiliated with running the Confraternity that are part of every member's responsibility and apostolate. These include mail and newsletter costs, formation materials, miscellaneous printing, phone expenses, and the cost of maintaining the Web page. Monies will be used to cover these expenses and occasionally to provide alms for needy members, as approved by the minister and the council, who may be consulted to determine a fitting donation as well.

20c. A report of how this money is being utilized may be requested at any time by any member.

20d. If a Chapter or Circle in the Confraternity requests a visit from the Visitor or someone else, they should reimburse the expenses of the visit.

20e. In the United States of America, all monies donated to the Confraternity of Penitents are tax deductible. The CFP is a bona fide nonprofit, tax exempt organization.

21. In keeping with section 21 of this Rule:

21a. At Mass the penitents should pay particular respectful attention to the Gospel, the homily or sermon, the Consecration of the Eucharist, and its worthy reception.

21b. In their Chapter or Circle meetings they are to listen attentively and to speak charitably.

21c. All members should have the opportunity to faith share about their spiritual experiences and concerns at each meeting.

21d. It is suggested that all penitents make an annual retreat or hermitage experience, unless so exempted by a spiritual director or Chapter minister.

CHAPTER VII: VISITING THE SICK, BURYING THE DEAD

22. In keeping with section 22 of the Rule:

22a. When a Chapter or Circle member falls ill, fellow penitents should visit the person or else send a card or make a phone call to the ailing party, exhorting the ill penitent to penance (personal, ongoing conversion). Weekly contact is encouraged.

22b. If penitents are able to provide help to ill members, they should lovingly do so.

23. In keeping with section 23 of the Rule:

23a. If a Chapter or Circle member should die, those surviving members should gather for the funeral if work and family commitments allow. They are not to leave until Mass is celebrated and the body consigned to burial.

23b. Within eight days of the demise, each member shall say for the soul of the deceased: a Mass, if a priest, fifty Psalms other wise.[29] If a member cannot read the Psalter, he or she may say fifty Our Father's with the words "May the souls of the faithful departed through the Mercy of God rest in peace" following each Our Father.

23c. Penitents may, if they wish, add the ejaculation, "Lord, have mercy on _____'s soul" after praying each psalm, or the Glory be.

---

[29] Any fifty psalms may be said. However, penitents with severe time constraints may wish to know that there are exactly 50 psalms in the Psalter which are 9 lines or less. These are 1, 3, 4. 8, 11, 12, 13, 14, 15, 20, 23, 28, 43, 47, 52, 53, 54, 61, 67, 70, 82, 87, 93, 98, 99, 100, 101, 110, 113, 114, 117, 120, 121, 122, 123, 124, 125, 126, 127, 128, 129, 130, 131, 133, 134, 137, 138, 142, 149, 150

24. In keeping with section 24 of the Rule:

   24a. In addition, every year, for the welfare of the brothers and sisters living and dead, each priest must say three Masses and the other Chapter or Circle members are to recite the entire Psalter from the Bible. The Psalter may be recited all at once, in sections throughout the year, or by praying one psalm or section of psalm daily.

   24b. Those who cannot read shall say one hundred Our Father's with the words "May the souls of the faithful departed through the Mercy of God rest in peace" after each Our Father. These may be said all at once or throughout the year.

25. In keeping with section 25 of the Rule:

   25a. All are to make their last will and testament within three months of their pledging to live the Rule, lest anyone of them die before creating a valid will.

26. In keeping with section 26 of the Rule:

   26a. All are to make peace with members of the Confraternity and all others, seeking, if necessary, the consultation of the Church.

   26b. The penitent must daily pray for all those who refuse to make peace with the penitent and must forgive such people all wrongs done to the penitent.

   26c. The brothers and sisters are always to take the first steps toward reconciliation. Under no circumstances are penitents to hold grudges or wish ill to anyone.

27. In keeping with section 27 of the Rule:

   27a. If contrary to their rights and privileges, trouble is made for the brothers and sisters by those in civil authority of the places where they live, the ministers of the place shall do what they shall find expedient on the advice of their Chapter or Circle's spiritual assistant, their spiritual director, or their parish priest.

28. In keeping with section 28 of the Rule:

   28a. Let each member accept and faithfully exercise the ministry of other offices imposed on him or her, although anyone may retire from office after a year.

   28b. The penitent should follow the consensus of the electing group in determining whether or not to accept an office. If nominated for a position it is prudent to consider if the nomination be the will of God. This holds true for the election as well.

   28c. All nominations and elections must be conducted in absolute charity and honesty. Secret ballot elections are the proper way to elect someone from among those nominated. The person getting the most votes is the one elected. Terms of office are one year.

28d. If a penitent who is nominated for, or elected to, office feels stress over this service, the penitent should prayerfully examine the causes of this stress and discuss these with a spiritual director, the Chapter or Circle minister, and the Chapter or Circle's spiritual assistant.

28e. In elections, only life pledged members shall be eligible to nominate, vote and hold office. If an insufficient number of capable members are life pledged, officers shall be appointed by the Confraternity or chosen by and from the members in formation and/or pledged for a year.

29. In keeping with section 29 of the Rule:

29a. When others wish to enter this Confraternity, the ministers shall carefully inquire into their standing and occupation and should question them thoroughly to ascertain their adherence to the Church's teaching regarding faith, Church authority, and morals. Only those who hold to the views of the Church's Magisterium, or who change their views to adopt those of the Church, shall be considered for admission to the Confraternity.

29b. Moreover, the ministers shall explain to all inquirers the obligations of life under the Rule, especially that of restoring what belongs to others. And if those inquiring are content with that, let them begin to follow the rules of formation as set up by this Confraternity.

29c. Those living this life must at once begin to pay up their debts, are to reconcile with their neighbors, and begin to tithe if they have not been doing so.

30. In keeping with section 30 of the Rule:

30a. After these particulars are complied with and the year of postulancy and three years of novice formation have elapsed, if those novices seem suitable to the ministers of their Chapter or Circles, let them be received on this condition—that they pledge that they will observe everything here written, or to be written or changed on the advice of the ruling body of the Confraternity, unless on occasion there be a valid dispensation by the ministers or Visitors or their own personal spiritual directors; and that they will, when called upon by the ministers, render satisfaction as the Visitor shall ordain if they have done anything contrary to this condition.

30b. Penitents may pledge to live the Rule for life or for a year. Yearly pledges are to be renewed annually and may be changed at any time to a lifetime pledge.

30c. All pledges are to be put in writing then and there and signed by the penitent and also by the minister and the spiritual assistant. Nobody is to be received otherwise.

31. In keeping with section 31 of the Rule:

31a. A penitent who has pledged to live this Rule must have the consent of his or her spiritual director in order to be released from the pledge. The penitent must also petition, in writing, the spiritual assistant, minister, and Visitor for release and shall give the reasons for the request. The minister and spiritual assistant should thoroughly explain the seriousness of asking for release from this promise to God. They may also question the penitent to see if the Confraternity has failed the penitent in some way.

31b. Those who wish to depart from this Confraternity to enter a religious Order should receive not only permission but also the blessing of the entire Confraternity. It is the norm of the Church that individuals should always move towards a greater commitment to Christ and His Church when they leave any lifestyle for another.

32. In keeping with section 32 of the Rule:

32a. No person who does not adhere totally to all that the Catholic Church teaches through its hierarchy and Magisterium, and no person in bad repute for disputing these teachings, shall be admitted. If such persons are under suspicion of this, they may be admitted if otherwise fit, upon being cleared by the bishop.

33. In keeping with section 33 of the Rule:

33a. Those married are not to be received except with the consent of their spouses, provided they are living with said spouse. If separation, annulment, or divorce has occurred, spousal consent is not required.

33b. A divorced penitent should seek to reconcile with their spouse, if possible. One can only apply for an annulment if one believes that their marriage is invalid. There could be circumstances in which, for example, a spouse was unjustly abandoned, had to seek civil divorce for reasons of legitimate protection (financial, physical, etc.), and is not able to reconcile with their spouse.

34. In keeping with section 34 of the Rule:

34a. Brothers and sisters ejected from a Chapter or Circle as incorrigible are not to be received in it again except it please the majority of the Chapter or Circle members.

CHAPTER VIII: CORRECTION, DISPENSATION, OFFICERS

35. In keeping with section 35 of the Rule:

35a. The ministers shall report public faults (manifest grave sins) of any members to the Visitor for disciplinary action. And if anyone proves incorrigible, after consultation with the council, they should be denounced to the Visitor, to be expelled by the Visitor from the Confraternity, and thereupon it should be published in the meeting.

35b. If the manifest grave sin also violates civil law, it ought to be also reported to civil authorities.

36. In keeping with section 36 of the Rule:

36a. If anyone learns that scandal is occurring relative to brothers and sisters in any matter, that person shall report it to the Visitor.

37. In keeping with section 37 of the Rule:

37a. The Visitor has the power to dispense all brothers and sisters in any of these points if the Visitor finds it advisable.

38. In keeping with section 38 of the Rule:

38a. When the year has passed, the ministers, with the counsel of the Chapter or Circle, are to elect a minister, associate minister, and a faithful treasurer who is to provide for the needs of the Chapter or Circle and of the brothers and sisters and other poor; and a secretary who, at the command of the ministers, is to publish what is said and done at meetings.

39. In keeping with section 39 of the Rule:

39a. In all the above mentioned points, no one is to be obligated under guilt, but under penalty; yet so if after being admonished twice by the ministers he or she should fail to discharge the penalty imposed or to be imposed on him by the Visitor, he shall be obligated under guilt as contumacious and so expelled from the Chapter or Circle.

ADDENDUM

Every penitent should have a spiritual director for help in discerning how to grow in the penitential lifestyle and understand the motion of the Holy Spirit. Penitents shall pray for this grace.

Spiritually mature priests, deacons, or other male or female religious can serve as spiritual directors, provided they are supportive of all the teachings of the Roman Catholic Church and are also supportive of the intentions of the penitent to live the Rule. In their absence, other penitents, who are experienced in the "things of God" can serve as spiritual directors if approved by a spiritual assistant of this Association.

It is expected that most penitents will have a spiritual director by the middle of the first year of novice formation and that they will be meeting with their spiritual directors at least monthly. Without a spiritual director, no penitent is permitted to make a permanent commitment to living this Rule.

Spiritual direction is best done face to face, but spiritual direction via computer, phone, and postal mail is permitted. Spiritual directors serve as advisors not military commanders. A good relationship enables penitent and director to discuss points of disagreement. Generally, once discussion is ended, it is safer for penitents to follow the director's advice, wary of pride in one's own opinions and judgment. However, before the tribunal of Christ, each person will have to take full responsibility for every decision. The virtue of prudence requires that penitents not deviate from a director's advice without prayerful consideration of the entire situation.

APPENDIX A

APPENDIX TO CHAPTER II AND CHAPTER III
CURRENT CHURCH REGULATIONS ON FASTING AND ABSTINENCE

Penitents observe all Church prescribed days of fast and abstinence as well as additional days required by the Rule itself. Current Church regulations on fasting and abstinence are these:

Fast: The law of fast prescribes that only one full meal a day be taken; but it does not forbid taking some nourishment at two other times during the day. The two smaller meals should be sufficient to maintain strength according to each one's needs, but together they should not equal another full meal. Eating between meals is not permitted, but liquids, including ordinary, homogenized milk and fruit juices, are allowed. Malted milks, milk shakes, and the like are not included in the term "milk." All those from eighteen years of age to the beginning of their sixtieth year are bound by the law of fast on Ash Wednesday and Good Friday.

Abstinence: The law of abstinence forbids the eating of meat, but not eggs, milk products, nor condiments of any kind, even though made from animal fat. Forbidden are the flesh meat of warm blooded animals and all parts of such animals. This does not include meat juices, broths, soups, lards, gravies, sauces, animal fats, and liquid foods made from meat. Also allowed are fish and all such coldblooded animals such as frogs, shellfish, clams, turtles, oysters, crabs, and lobsters. All those who have completed their fourteenth year are bound to the law of abstinence from meat on Ash Wednesday and on all the Friday's of Lent.

The substantial observance of the laws of fast and abstinence is a serious obligation. When a proportionately serious reason exists, there is surely no sin in departing from these norms. Thus, one may very well be excused by sickness or any infirmity which requires that one eat meat even on Friday during Lent, by the need to take one's meals in common, by travel when it is not possible to obtain readily permissible foods, by great poverty, etc.

(Source: The Pastoral Companion: A Canon Law Handbook for Catholic Ministry, Franciscan Herald Press: Chicago, Illinois, 1995, pp. 292-96).

APPENDIX B

APPENDIX TO CHAPTER IV, 12

Marian Consecration Prayer

To you do we turn, O Holy Mary, glorious and Ever-Virgin Mother of God, Queen of Angels and of Saints, the "Virgin made Church." To you do we cry, O Handmaid of the Lord, Mother of the Suffering Servant, who made the Lord of Majesty our brother. For through you the most exalted Son of God emptied Himself for love of our love, taking the form of a slave in your womb and dying in destitution on a cross as He gave you to us, O Refuge of Sinners. To you do we fly as we beg you to obtain for us the true spirit of the Gospel.

Holy Immaculate Conception, Spouse of the Holy Spirit, taking you into our home, we consecrate and entrust ourselves and our Confraternity totally and forever to your Immaculate Heart. Make us your true sons and daughters and use our Confraternity as an instrument of Christ Our King to convert sinners, to sanctify souls, and to strengthen and renew the One, Holy, Catholic, and Apostolic Church, that God—Father, Son, and Holy Spirit—may be glorified, praised, and adored by all mankind. Amen.

APPENDIX C

APPENDIX TO CHAPTER IV, 12

Those who do not have a breviary may use the following substitutions of Psalms for recitation of the Daily Office (Psalms are numbered according to the New American Bible, Catholic edition, and taken from My Daily Psalm Book, arranged by Rev. Joseph Frey, c. 1947 by the Confraternity of the Most Precious Blood. The entire Psalter is recited in a week's time). Since the hour of Prime has been suppressed, those Psalms listed for Prime may be used as focal points for the period of meditation and mental prayer:

Sunday: Office of Readings1, 2, 3, 8, 9, 10, 11; Morning Prayer 93, 100, 63, Daniel 3: 57-88, 148; Prime 118, 119 v. 1-32; Midmorning Prayer 119 v. 33-80; Midday Prayer 119 v. 81-128; Midafternoon Prayer 119 v.129-176; Evening Prayer 110, 111, 112, 113, 114, 115; Night Prayer 4, 91, 134

Monday: Office of Readings 14, 15, 17, 18, 20, 21, 30; Morning Prayer 47, 5, 29, Canticle of David ("Blessed art thou, O Lord, God of our father Israel, from eternity to eternity. Thine, O Lord, are grandeur and power and splendor and glory and majesty. For all that is in heaven and on earth is Thine; Thine is the kingdom, O Lord, and thou art the ruler who is exalted above all. Wealth and honor are from thee, and by thy power thou rulest all things. And in thy hand are strength and power, and to thy hand it belongs to make everything great and strong. Now therefore, our God, we thank thee and we praise thy glorious name."), 117; Prime 24, 19; Midmorning Prayer 27, 28; Midday Prayer 31; Midafternoon Prayer 32, 33; Evening Prayer 116, 120, 121, 122; Night Prayer 6, 7

Tuesday: Office of Readings 35, 37, 38, 39; Morning Prayer 96, 43, 67, Tobit 13 v. 1-10, 135; Prime 25; Midmorning Prayer 40; Midday Prayer 41, 42; Midafternoon Prayer 44; Evening Prayer 123, 124, 125, 126, 127; Night Prayer 12, 13, 16

Wednesday: Office of Readings 45, 46, 48, 49, 50, 51; Morning Prayer 97, 65, 101, Judith 16 v. 13-17, 146; Prime 26, 52, 53; Midmorning Prayer 54, 55; Midday Prayer 56, 57, 58; Midafternoon Prayer 59, 60; Evening Prayer 128, 129, 130, 131, 132; Night Prayer 34, 61

Thursday: Office of Readings 62, 66, 68, 69; Morning Prayer 98, 90, 36, Jeremiah 31, v. 10-14, 147; Prime 23, 72; Midmorning Prayer 73; Midday Prayer 74; Midafternoon Prayer 75, 76; Evening Prayer 133, 136, 137, 138; Night Prayer 70, 71

Friday: Office of Readings 78, 79, 81, 83; Morning Prayer 99, 143, 85; Prime: Canticle of Isaiah: Isaiah 45: 15-26, Psalm 147 v. 12-20, 22; Midmorning Prayer 80, 82; Midday Prayer 84, 87; Midafternoon Prayer 89; Evening Prayer 139, 140, 141, 142; Night Prayer 77, 86

Saturday Office of Readings 105, 106, 107; Morning Prayer 149, 92, 64, Ecclesiasticus 36 v. 1-16; 150; Prime 94, 108; Midmorning Prayer 102; Midday Prayer 104; Midafternoon Prayer 109; Evening Prayer 144, 145; Night Prayer 88, 103, 95, Canticle of Mary: Luke 1 v. 46-55, Canticle of Zachary: Luke 1 v. 68-79, Canticle of Simeon: Luke 2, 29-32

APPENDIX D

APPENDIX TO CHAPTER V, 18d

The Spiritual Works of Mercy are:
- Instruct the ignorant
- Advise the doubtful
- Correct sinners
- Be patient with those in error or who do wrong
- Forgive offenses
- Comfort the afflicted
- Pray for the living and the dead.

The Corporal Works of Mercy are:

- Feed the hungry
- Give drink to the thirsty
- Clothe the naked
- Shelter the homeless
- Visit the sick and imprisoned

- Ransom the captive
- Bury the dead.

In keeping with the conclusion of the Rule:

Here end the Constitutions of the Continent Confraternity of Penitents, that is those who give up things in fulfillment of the Gospels of our Lord Jesus Christ.

APPENDIX E

Expanded Historical Overview

1994, July: Our human "founder" Madeline Pecora Nugent, inspired by the Holy Spirit, begins, with the approval of her spiritual director Dom Julian Stead, OSB, to "live the Rule of 1221."

1995: Upon the advice of Father Pio Mandato, FPO, the living of the Rule is made known to a Rhode Island, USA, Secular Franciscan fraternity. Six members express interest in living the Rule of 1221 in addition to their Third Order Franciscan Rule. They name the group "The Brothers and Sisters of Penance" (BSP)

1996, March: The Visitor Brother Francis Kelly, FPO, asks that the group disband for a year to discern God's direction.

1997, March: The group reorganizes with Dom Julian Stead, OSB, as Visitor. That December, Rev. Robert Mulvee, the Bishop of the Diocese of Providence, is presented a copy of the Rule and Statutes (now called Constitutions).

1998 January 30: Date of the initial letter of permission to live the Rule and Statutes, signed by Rev. Msgr. William I. Varsanyi, Vicar General of the Diocese of Providence, Rhode Island. The letter contains these words, "Bishop Mulvee concurred with my opinion that this Rule does not contain anything contrary to our faith; therefore it may be safely practiced privately by you or by anyone inclined to do so." In autumn of 1998, under the name of the Brothers and Sisters of Penance and with the permission of Bishop Mulvee, the Confraternity goes on the world-wide web, using space on a friend's website. A formation program with six postulants begins. Formation lessons begin to be written.

1999, Lent: A group from Minnesota, organized as the Franciscan Brothers and Sisters of Penance, finds the Rhode Island group and a merger is effected. Members of that group now enjoy the same legal and tax exempt status as the BSP. After 1999, the resources, including a new website owned by the BSP, membership, and documents of the BSP, expand, but still using the same Statutes as were reviewed by the Diocese of Providence in 1998. Slight additional adaptations to the Constitutions are accepted by the Diocese of Providence in 1999. In April 1999, the BSP is legally incorporated in the State of Rhode Island. In the summer of 1999, the first overnight retreat is held in the Knights of Columbus Hall in Middletown Rhode Island with six attendees. In November of 1999, federal non-profit tax exempt status is granted to the incorporated BSP.

2002 April 7 (Divine Mercy Sunday): Stephanie Natalie Carlson Sullivan and Madeline Pecora Nugent, the first two penitents to complete the four year formation program, pledge to live the Rule for life. They make their pledges at Jesus Savior Church Prayer Chapel, Middletown, Rhode Island, before Father Valerius Messerich, OFM, BSP Visitor. (Dom Julian Stead also continues as Visitor).

2002-2003: After about three and one half years, disagreements among the leaders arise over governance, formation, pledging, and communication procedures. Ten months of communications and discussions can not resolve the disagreements. When the Council of the Association learns of and becomes divided over these issues, the founder, in August 2003, asks advice of the Diocese of Providence. She is advised to sever the merger and refound the Association. The Bishop of the Diocese, Bishop Robert Mulvee, concurs with this advice. Several other leaders of the BSP agree. Legally they must resign from the BSP and start a new Association which legally must receive a new name. The name chosen is the Confraternity of Penitents (CFP). After consulting a lawyer, these leaders turn over the BSP treasury, assets, and material resources of the BSP to the remaining leaders. In addition, the BSP website and passwords, which had been managed from Rhode Island since 1998, are transferred to the remaining leaders. Some of the membership of the BSP also voluntarily leave the BSP and join the Confraternity of Penitents while others stay with the former foundation which also must now incorporate as its own entity. On August 19, 2003, the Confraternity of Penitents is legally incorporated in the state of Rhode Island. On August 22 (the Queenship of Mary), the CFP is refounded in the Church with the formation lessons, pledging procedures, requirements for leadership and voting, and how the Rule is lived (the original Statutes) continuing unchanged, thus effecting a true "refounding" rather than the creation of a different group. In October, the Brothers and Sisters of Penance, incorporated in the State of Rhode Island in 1999, is legally dissolved since no Rhode Island members remain.

2004: With the permission of the Diocese of Providence, her spiritual director, and the CFP Visitor, on March 27, 2004, Elizabeth Hill becomes the first penitent to make a private vow to live the CFP Rule and Constitutions for life. Elizabeth takes the privately vowed name of sr. Bridget Clare of the Eucharist. On May 10, the Confraternity is granted tax exempt status by the federal government. Also in 2004, Bishop Mulvee concurs with the advice of CFP Spiritual Advisor Father John of the Trinity, Erem TOCarm, and with the agreement of CFP Visitor Father Jay Finelli, to grant permission for CFP Members to celebrate the Queenship of Mary yearly as a Solemnity, by following the guidelines in sections 6 and 9 of the CFP Rule and Constitutions.

2005: On May 27, the first death of a pledged member occurs with the death of Stephanie Sullivan. In September, the Council of the Confraternity of Penitents meets with CFP Spiritual Advisor Father Martin Mary Fonte, FI, and Sister Jacqueline Dickey, Vicar for Religious of the Diocese of Providence. The governing structure of the Confraternity is revised to allow the Minister General greater freedom in governance and a set of ordinances is adopted.

2006 July: In order to conform more closely to Church terminology, what had been previously termed "statutes" are renamed "Constitutions" and "ordinances" are renamed the "Directory."

2007 March: The first Life Pledged Chapter of the Confraternity of Penitents, for life pledged members and those planning to pledge for life, is held in Dallas, Texas, with seven members attending, one of whom makes her life pledge at this gathering.

2009 February 11: Bishop Thomas Tobin of the Diocese of Providence, Rhode Island, confirms the canonical status of the Confraternity of Penitents as a "private association of the faithful" and extends to it his "special blessing."

2010: Father Michael Anthony Sisco becomes Visitor of the Confraternity of Penitents. The first community house for the Confraternity of Penitents is established at the main headquarters of the Confraternity in Middletown, Rhode Island with Patrick Hamor being the first resident

2011: With the permission of Father Benedict Groeschel, founder of the Oratory of Divine Love ministry and web site, Father Sisco's homilies are adapted by Confraternity members to provide weekly reflections for an online web site for the Oratory of Divine Love. The Confraternity of Penitents sponsors the web site. Patrick Hamor enters the Franciscan Brothers Minor and will be given the name Brother Fidelis Maria upon entering the Novitiate. In the fall, the second community house, St. Theresa's Residence, is opened in Tiverton, Rhode Island, for two women in the Confraternity of Penitents.

2012 December: With the departure of all its residents, St. Theresa's Residence closes.

2013: On September 26, 2013, at the invitation of Bishop Kevin Rhoades, Bishop of the Diocese of Fort Wayne - South Bend Indiana USA, the Confraternity of Penitents relocates its international headquarters to Fort Wayne, Indiana, USA, to a house, outbuildings and property owned by the Diocese. Madeline Pecora Nugent, Jim Nugent, and Kay-Marie Nugent move to Fort Wayne to manage the CFP office and gift shop and to oversee use of the property. Bishop Rhoades blesses the house and property on November 4, 2013. While retaining a location in Rhode Island, the Confraternity receives from the state of Indiana a Certificate of Authority as Non-Profit Foreign (out of state) Corporation on November 12, 2013.

2014. Bishop Rhoades confirms the canonical status of the Confraternity of Penitents as a private association of the faithful in a letter dated January 3, 2014 and grants the CFP his blessing. He names Father Jacob Meyer as Confraternity of Penitents' Visitor.

CANON LAW

"Our Lord preserved the soul together with the body of the Blessed Virgin in that purity which became her who was to receive God into her womb. For, as God is holy, He reposes only in holy places."

St. John Damascene

Prayer to Mary, Mother of Compassion

O Virgin most pure, wholly unspotted, O Mary, Mother of God, Queen of the universe, you are above all saints, the hope of the elect and the joy of all the blessed. It is you who have reconciled us with God, you are the only refuge of sinners and the safe harbor of those who are shipwrecked; you are the consolation of the world, the ransom of captives, the health of the weak, the joy of the afflicted and the salvation of all who have recourse to you, and we beg you to have pity on us.

O Virgin Immaculate, Mother of God and my Mother, from your sublime heights turn your eyes of compassion upon me. Filled with confidence in your goodness and knowing full well your power, I beg you to extend to me your assistance in the journey of life, which is so full of dangers for my soul.

In order that I may never be a slave of the devil through sin but may ever live with my heart humble and pure, I entrust myself wholly to you. I consecrate my heart to you forever, my only desire being to love your divine Son, Jesus. Mary, none of your devout servants has ever perished; may I, too, be saved. Amen.

CANONS THAT PERTAIN TO THE CONFRATERNITY OF PENITENTS

The Confraternity of Penitents is a private Catholic Association of the Faithful with commendation. Several Canons in the current Code of Canon Law apply to the Confraternity and its place in the Catholic Church. Additional canons apply to the private vow to live the CFP Rule for life, a vow which a pledged member may choose to make.

Those Canons which apply to the Confraternity of Penitents are as follows[30]:

TITLE V.

ASSOCIATIONS OF THE CHRISTIAN FAITHFUL (Cann. 298 - 329)

CHAPTER I.

COMMON NORMS

Can. 298 §1. In the Church there are associations distinct from institutes of consecrated life and societies of apostolic life; in these associations the Christian faithful, whether clerics, lay persons, or clerics and lay persons together, strive in a common endeavor to foster a more perfect life, to promote public worship or Christian doctrine, or to exercise other works of the apostolate such as initiatives of evangelization, works of piety or charity, and those which animate the temporal order with a Christian spirit.

§2. The Christian faithful are to join especially those associations which competent ecclesiastical authority has erected, praised, or commended.

---

30   Translation from the Vatican Website www.vatican.va

Can. 299 §1. By means of a private agreement made among themselves, the Christian faithful are free to establish associations to pursue the purposes mentioned in ⇒ can. 298, §1, without prejudice to the prescript of ⇒ can. 301, §1.

§2. Even if ecclesiastical authority praises or commends them, associations of this type are called private associations.

§3. No private association of the Christian faithful is recognized in the Church unless competent authority reviews its statutes.

Can. 300 No association is to assume the name Catholic without the consent of competent ecclesiastical authority according to the norm of ⇒ can. 312.

Can. 301 §1. It is for the competent ecclesiastical authority alone to erect associations of the Christian faithful which propose to hand on Christian doctrine in the name of the Church or to promote public worship, or which intend other purposes whose pursuit is of its nature reserved to the same ecclesiastical authority.

§2. Competent ecclesiastical authority, if it has judged it expedient, can also erect associations of the Christian faithful to pursue directly or indirectly other spiritual purposes whose accomplishment has not been sufficiently provided for through the initiatives of private persons.

§3. Associations of the Christian faithful which are erected by competent ecclesiastical authority are called public associations.

Can. 302 Those associations of the Christian faithful are called clerical which are under the direction of clerics, assume the exercise of sacred orders, and are recognized as such by competent authority.

Can. 303 Associations whose members share in the spirit of some religious institute while in secular life, lead an apostolic life, and strive for Christian perfection under the higher direction of the same institute are called third orders or some other appropriate name.

Can. 304 §1. All public or private associations of the Christian faithful, by whatever title or name they are called, are to have their own statutes which define the purpose or social objective of the association, its seat, government, and conditions required for membership and which determine the manner of its acting, attentive, however, to the necessity or advantage of time and place.

§2. They are to choose a title or name for themselves adapted to the usage of time and place, selected above all with regard to their intended purpose.

Can. 305 §1. All associations of the Christian faithful are subject to the vigilance of competent ecclesiastical authority which is to take care that the integrity of faith and morals is preserved in them and is to watch so that abuse does not creep into ecclesiastical discipline. This authority therefore has the duty and right to inspect them according to the norm of law and the statutes. These associations are also subject to the governance of this same authority according to the prescripts of the canons which follow.

§2. Associations of any kind are subject to the vigilance of the Holy See; diocesan associations and other associations to the extent that they work in the diocese are subject to the vigilance of the local ordinary.

Can. 306 In order for a person to possess the rights and privileges of an association and the indulgences and other spiritual favors granted to the same association, it is necessary and sufficient that the person has been validly received into it and has not been legitimately dismissed from it according to the prescripts of law and the proper statutes of the association.

Can. 307 §1. The reception of members is to be done according to the norm of law and the statutes of each association.

§2. The same person can be enrolled in several associations.

§3. Members of religious institutes can join associations according to the norm of their proper law with the consent of their superior.

Can. 308 No one legitimately enrolled is to be dismissed from an association except for a just cause according to the norm of law and the statutes.

Can. 309 According to the norm of law and the statutes, legitimately established associations have the right to issue particular norms respecting the association itself, to hold meetings, and to designate moderators, officials, other officers, and administrators of goods.

Can. 310 A private association which has not been established as a juridic person cannot, as such, be a subject of obligations and rights. Nevertheless, the members of the Christian faithful associated together in it can jointly contract obligations and can acquire and possess rights and goods as co-owners and co-possessors; they are able to exercise these rights and obligations through an agent or a proxy.

Can. 311 Members of institutes of consecrated life who preside offer or assist associations in some way united to their institute are to take care that these associations give assistance to the works of the apostolate which already exist in a diocese, especially cooperating, under the direction of the local ordinary, with associations which are ordered to the exercise of the apostolate in the diocese.

CHAPTER III.

PRIVATE ASSOCIATIONS OF THE CHRISTIAN FAITHFUL

Can. 321 The Christian faithful guide and direct private associations according to the prescripts of the statutes.

Can. 322 §1. A private association of the Christian faithful can acquire juridic personality through a formal decree of the competent ecclesiastical authority mentioned in ⇒ can. 312.

§2. No private association of the Christian faithful can acquire juridic personality unless the ecclesiastical authority mentioned in ⇒ can. 312, §1 has approved its statutes. Approval of the statutes, however, does not change the private nature of the association.

Can. 323 §1. Although private associations of the Christian faithful possess autonomy according to the norm of ⇒ can. 321, they are subject to the vigilance of ecclesiastical authority according to the norm of ⇒ can. 305 and even to the governance of the same authority.

§2. It also pertains to ecclesiastical authority, while respecting the autonomy proper to private associations, to be watchful and careful that dissipation of their energies is avoided and that their exercise of the apostolate is ordered to the common good.

Can. 324 §1. A private association of the Christian faithful freely designates its moderator and officials according to the norm of the statutes.

§2. A private association of the Christian faithful can freely choose a spiritual advisor, if it desires one, from among the priests exercising ministry legitimately in the diocese; nevertheless, he needs the confirmation of the local ordinary.

Can. 325 §1. A private association of the Christian faithful freely administers those goods it possesses according to the prescripts of the statutes, without prejudice to the right of competent ecclesiastical authority to exercise vigilance so that the goods are used for the purposes of the association.

§2. A private association is subject to the authority of the local ordinary according to the norm of ⇒ can. 1301 in what pertains to the administration and distribution of goods which have been donated or left to it for pious causes.

Can. 326 §1. A private association of the Christian faithful ceases to exist according to the norm of its statutes. The competent authority can also suppress it if its activity causes grave harm to ecclesiastical doctrine or discipline or is a scandal to the faithful.

§2. The allocation of the goods of an association which has ceased to exist must be determined according to the norm of its statutes, without prejudice to acquired rights and the intention of the donors.

CHAPTER IV.

SPECIAL NORMS FOR ASSOCIATIONS OF THE LAITY

Can. 327 Lay members of the Christian faithful are to hold in esteem associations established for the spiritual purposes mentioned in ⇒ can. 298, especially those which propose to animate the temporal order with the Christian spirit and in this way greatly foster an intimate union between faith and life.

Can. 328 Those who preside offer associations of the laity, even those which have been erected by virtue of apostolic privilege, are to take care that their associations cooperate with other associations of the Christian faithful where it is expedient and willingly assist various Christian works, especially those in the same territory.

Can. 329 Moderators of associations of the laity are to take care that the members of the association are duly formed to exercise the apostolate proper to the laity.

TITLE V.

A VOW AND AN OATH (Cann. 1191 - 1204)

CHAPTER I.

A VOW

Can. 1191 §1. A vow, that is, a deliberate and free promise made to God about a possible and better good, must be fulfilled by reason of the virtue of religion.

§2. Unless they are prohibited by law, all who possess suitable use of reason are capable of making a vow.

§3. A vow made out of grave and unjust fear or malice is null by the law itself.

Can. 1192 §1. A vow is public if a legitimate superior accepts it in the name of the Church; otherwise, it is private.

§2. A vow is solemn if the Church has recognized it as such; otherwise, it is simple.

§3. A vow is personal if the person making the vow promises an action; real if the person making the vow promises some thing; mixed if it shares the nature of a personal and a real vow.

Can. 1193 By its nature a vow obliges only the person who makes it.

Can. 1194 A vow ceases by the lapse of the time designated to fulfill the obligation, by a substantial change of the matter promised, by the absence of a condition on which the vow depends, by the absence of the purpose of the vow, by dispensation, or by commutation.

Can. 1195 The person who has power over the matter of the vow can suspend the obligation of the vow for as long a time as the fulfillment of the vow brings disadvantage to that person.

Can. 1196 In addition to the Roman Pontiff, the following can dispense from private vows for a just cause provided that a dispensation does not injure a right acquired by others:

1/ the local ordinary and the pastor with regard to all their subjects and even travelers;

2/ the superior of a religious institute or society of apostolic life if it is clerical and of pontifical right with regard to members, novices, and persons who live day and night in a house of the institute or society;

3/ those to whom the Apostolic See or the local ordinary has delegated the power of dispensing.

Can. 1197 The person who makes a private vow can commute the work promised by the vow into a better or equal good; however, one who has the power of dispensing according to the norm of ⇒ can. 1196 can commute it into a lesser good.

Can. 1198 Vows made before religious profession are suspended while the person who made the vow remains in the religious institute.

PRAYERS OF CONFRATERNITY PENITENTS

"As a consoler of the human race, Mary never ceases to pour out before her Son her prayer for the salvation of the faithful crushed by the weight of their sins." - *St. Pius V*

Memorare

Remember, O most gracious Virgin Mary, that never was it know that anyone who fled to Your protection, implored Your help, or sought Your intercession was left unaided. Inspired with this confidence, I fly unto You, O virgin of virgins, my Mother. To You I come, before You I stand, sinful and sorrowful. O Mother of the Word Incarnate, despise not my petitions, but in Your mercy, hear and answer me. Amen.

PRAYER FOR OUR CONFRATERNITY MISSION

The following prayer was composed on July 20, 2005, following a three day group discernment among CFP leaders regarding the Holy Spirit's Will for the future of the Confraternity of Penitents.

Lord, help us to reach out and support one another. Help us to teach others by the example of our lives. Help us to trust in the Holy Spirit to do Your Will. Make us living flames of hope for each other and the world. Oh Lord, help us to have faith in each other and faithfulness to the Confraternity and to spread and share this life. Continue to help us to trust and to surrender to Your Will. Help us to grow in holiness by this total surrender and to persevere in our journey to holiness. Help us to evangelize and to cast out nets while protecting us in our fidelity to our Lord through the Catholic Church, to living the Rule and to the original vision for our Confraternity. Amen.

PRAYER FOR THE MORAL RENEWAL OF OUR COUNTRY

The Council of the Confraternity of Penitents agreed, at the annual Council meeting in July 2006, to promote daily prayer to Saint Michael the Archangel, to come against the moral degradation pervading the world. Each one is asked to pray that Saint Michael, accompanied by all the hosts of heaven, will do battle against the forces of evil and will prevail over the moral degradation of their own country. Here is a sample daily prayer. Printed copies of this prayer are available for any donation from the CFP Holy Angels Gift Shop, 1702 Lumbard Street, Fort Wayne IN 46803 USA, website www.cfpholyangels.com

Lord, we ask You to send Saint Michael and all the host of heaven to battle against the forces of evil in our nation. We ask specifically that the moral degradation of our country be reversed and that our nation's inhabitants will turn to you in purity, trust, selflessness, and faith. With this intention in mind, we offer this prayer:

> Saint Michael the Archangel,
> defend us in battle.
> Be our protection against the wickedness and snares of the devil.
> May God rebuke him, we humbly pray;
> and do Thou, O Prince of the Heavenly Host -
> by the Power of God -
> cast into hell, satan and all the evil spirits,
> who roam throughout the world seeking the ruin of souls.
> Amen.

(prayer to St. Michael composed by Pope Leo XIII).
(Permission to distribute the Prayer for the Moral Renewal of Our Country granted by Bishop Thomas Tobin, Bishop of the Diocese of Providence, RI, December 15, 2008)

AFFILIATES' PRAYER FOR THE CONFRATERNITY OF PENITENTS

Affiliates of the Confraternity are asked to pray the following prayer daily:

Blessed Lord, as You made Saint Francis reflective of the image of Christ through a life of humility and penance, so, too, please help us and all of our brothers and sisters to die to the world with You, in order that our hearts may be inflamed with the fire of Your Love, and finally we may be brought to new life. Please have mercy on all those who are burdened with leadership in the Confraternity, especially the Bishop, Visitor, Minister General, Regional Ministers, Ministers, Officers, and Formators. Father of all, please renew the marks of Jesus' Passion on our souls, and bring us to perfection for the sake of Your glory. We ask this through Christ our Lord, Who lives and reigns with You and the Holy Spirit, God, world without end. Amen.

Our Lady of the Angels, pray for us.
Saint Francis, pray for us.
Saint Clare, pray for us.
Saint Anthony, pray for us.
All you saints of God, pray for us. Amen.

CFP PRAYERS PRAYED DAILY

Note: Psalms are numbered differently in different translations. Compare the Psalms in your Bible with those below and use the Psalms whose meaning corresponds to that in the Psalms listed. The translations below are from the New American Bible, St. Joseph Edition.

The Apostles' Creed

I believe in God, the Father Almighty, Creator of heaven and earth, and in Jesus Christ, His only Son, our Lord, Who was conceived by the Holy Spirit, born of the Virgin Mary, suffered under Pontius Pilate, was crucified, died and was buried. He descended into Hell, and on the third day He arose again from the dead. He ascended into Heaven, and is seated at the right hand of God the Father Almighty. From thence He shall come to judge the living and the dead. I believe in the Holy Spirit, the Holy Catholic Church, the Communion of Saints, the forgiveness of sins, the resurrection of the body, and life everlasting. Amen.

Psalm 51

Have mercy on me, O God, in Your goodness; in the greatness of Your compassion, wipe out my offense. Thoroughly wash me of my guilt and of my sin cleanse me. For I acknowledge my offense, and my sin is before me always. "Against You only have I sinned, and done what is evil in Your sight."–That You may be justified in Your sentence, vindicated when You condemn. Indeed, in guilt was I born, and in sin my mother conceived me. Behold, You are pleased with sincerity of heart, and in my inmost being You teach me wisdom.

Cleanse me of sin with hyssop, that I may be purified; wash me, and I shall be whiter than snow. Let me hear the sounds of joy and gladness; then the bones You have crushed shall rejoice. Turn away Your face from my sins, and blot out all my guilt.

A clean heart create for me, O God, and a steadfast spirit renew within me. Cast me not out from Your presence, and Your holy spirit take not from me. Give me back the joy of Your salvation, and a willing spirit sustain in me.

I will teach transgressors your ways, and sinners shall return to You. Free me from blood guilt, O God, my saving God; then my tongue shall revel in Your justice. O Lord, open my lips, and my mouth shall proclaim Your praise. For You are not pleased with sacrifices; should I offer a holocaust, You would not accept it. My sacrifice, O God, is a contrite spirit; a heart contrite and humbled, O God, You will not spurn.

Be bountiful, O Lord, to Zion in Your kindness by rebuilding the walls of Jerusalem; then shall You be pleased with due sacrifices, burnt offerings and holocausts; then shall they offer up bullocks on Your altar.

Glory to the Father and to the Son and to the Holy Spirit, as it was in the beginning, is now, and will be forever. Amen.

Psalm 54

O God, by Your name save me, and by Your might defend my cause. O God, hear my prayer; hearken to the words of my mouth. For haughty men have risen up against me, and fierce men seek my life; they set not God before their eyes.

Behold, God is my helper; the Lord sustains my life. Turn back the evil upon my foes; in Your faithfulness destroy them. Freely will I offer You sacrifice; I will praise Your name, O Lord, for its goodness, because from all distress You have rescued me, and my eyes look down upon my enemies.

Glory to the Father and to the Son and to the Holy Spirit, as it was in the beginning, is now, and will be forever. Amen.

Psalm 119: Verses 1-32

Happy are they whose way is blameless, who walk by the law of the Lord. Happy are they who observe His decrees, who seek Him with all their heart, and do no wrong, but walk in His ways. You have commanded that Your precepts be diligently kept. Oh, that I might be firm in the ways of keeping Your statutes! Then I should not be put to shame when I beheld all Your commands. I will give You thanks with an upright heart, when I have learned Your just ordinances. I will keep Your statutes; do not utterly forsake me.

How shall a young man be faultless in his way? By keeping to Your words. With all my heart I seek You; let me not stray from Your commands. Within my heart I treasure Your promise, that I may not sin against You. Blessed are You, O Lord, teach me Your statutes. With my lips I declare all the ordinances of Your mouth. In the way of Your decrees I rejoice, as much as in all riches. I will meditate on Your precepts and consider Your ways. In Your statutes I will delight; I will not forget Your words.

Be good to Your servant, that I may live and keep Your words. Open my eyes, that I may consider the wonders of Your law. I am a wayfarer of earth; hide not Your commands from me. My soul is consumed with longing for Your ordinances at all times. You rebuke the accursed proud, who turn away from Your commands. Take away from me Your reproach and contempt, for I observe Your decrees. Though princes meet and talk against me, Your servant meditates on Your statutes. Yes, Your decrees are my delight; they are my counselors.

I lie prostrate in the dust; give me life according to Your word. I declared my ways, and You answered me, teach me Your statutes. Make me understand the way of Your precepts, and I will meditate on Your wondrous deeds. My soul weeps for sorrow; strengthen me according to Your words. Remove from me the way of falsehood, and favor me with Your law. The way of truth I have chosen; I have set Your ordinances before me. I cling to Your decrees; O Lord, let me not be put to shame. I will run the way of Your commands when you give me a docile heart.

Glory to the Father and to the Son and to the Holy Spirit as it was in the beginning, is now, and will be forever. Amen.

Marian Consecration Prayer

To you, do we turn, O Holy Mary, glorious and Ever-Virgin Mother of God, Queen of Angels and of Saints, the "Virgin made Church."

To you do we cry, O Handmaid of the Lord, Mother of the Suffering Servant, who made the Lord of Majesty our brother. For through you the most exalted Son of God emptied Himself for love of our love, taking the form of a slave in your womb and dying in destitution on a cross as He gave you to us, O Refuge of Sinners.

To you do we fly, as we beg you to obtain for us the true spirit of the Gospel. Holy Immaculate Conception, Spouse of the Holy Spirit, taking you into our home, we consecrate and entrust our selves and our Confraternity totally and forever to your Immaculate Heart. Make us your true sons and daughters and use our Confraternity as an instrument of Christ our King to convert sinners, to sanctify souls, and to strengthen and renew the One, Holy, Catholic, and Apostolic Church, that God–Father, Son and Holy Spirit–may be glorified, praised and adored by all mankind. Amen.

PRAYERS FOR MONTHLY MEETINGS

AM–Penitents whose last names begin A to M
NZ–Penitents whose last names begin N to Z

When praying on the internet, one leader will be designated for the *AM* group and one for the *NZ* group. Designated leaders will type in the CAPITALIZED WORDS only on line and all others will pray the remainder of the prayer silently at their computers without typing anything. The Leader and All designations are for local Chapter or Circle meetings and should be ignored while praying on line. On line, the AM and NZ designations are to be followed throughout.

In local Chapter or Circle meetings, those in each group will pray out loud the prayers as so indicated. The instructions (such as brief pause for silent meditation) should not be said aloud at a Chapter or Circle meeting but rather should be simply followed by the group. In local meetings, a prayer leader should be designated. This leader will read the prayers marked Leader and all others respond where All is designated. Otherwise, you may organize the recitation of the prayers in any way you wish.

+ + + PRAYERS FOR BEGINNING THE MONTHLY MEETING + + +

AM (or Leader) —IN THE NAME of the Father and of the Son and of the Holy Spirit.

NZ (or All)—AMEN

All — Selected opening hymn, or the following.

All Creatures of Our God and King

All creatures of Our God and King,
Lift up your voice and with us sing,
Alleluiah, Alleluiah!
Thou burning sun with golden beam,
Thou silver moon with softer gleam,

O, Praise Him, O, Praise Him,
Alleluiah, Alleluiah, Alleluiah!

Thou rushing winds that are so strong,
Ye clouds that sail in heaven along,
O praise Him, Alleluiah!
Thou rising morn in praise rejoice,
Ye lights of evening find a voice:

O Praise Him, O Praise Him,
Alleluiah, Alleluiah, Alleluiah!

Psalm 51

AM - HAVE MERCY on me, O God, in Your goodness
in Your great tenderness wipe away my faults;
wash me clean of my guilt,
purify me from my sin.

NZ–FOR I AM well aware of my faults,
I have my sin constantly in mind,
having sinned against none other than You,
having done what You regard as wrong.

AM–YOU ARE JUST when You pass sentence on me,
blameless when You give judgment.
You know I was born guilty,
a sinner from the moment of conception.

NZ–YET, SINCE you love sincerity of heart,
teach me the secrets of wisdom.
Purify me with hyssop until I am clean;
wash me until I am whiter than snow.

AM–INSTILL SOME joy and gladness into me,
let the bones You have crushed rejoice again.
Hide Your face from my sins,
wipe out all my guilt.

NZ–GOD, CREATE a clean heart in me,
put into me a new and constant spirit,
do not banish me from Your presence,
do not deprive me of Your Holy Spirit.

AM—BE MY SAVIOR again, renew my joy,
keep my spirit steady and willing;
and I shall teach transgressors the way to You,
and to You the sinners will return.

NZ–SAVE ME from death, God my savior,
and my tongue will acclaim Your righteousness;
Lord, open my lips,
and my mouth will speak out Your praise.

AM–SACRIFICE gives You no pleasure,
were I to offer holocaust, You would not have it.
My sacrifice is this broken spirit,
You will not scorn this crushed and broken heart.

*NZ–*SHOW YOUR FAVOR graciously to Zion,
rebuild the walls of Jerusalem.
Then there will be proper sacrifice to please You
—holocaust and whole oblation–
and young bulls to be offered on Your altar.

*AM–*GLORY to the Father and to the Son and to the Holy Spirit

*NZ–*AS IT WAS in the beginning, is now, and will be forever. Amen.

NZ (or All)–BRIEF PAUSE FOR SILENT MEDITATION

<u>*Marian Consecration Prayer*</u>

AM (or Leader)–TO YOU do we turn, O Holy Mary, glorious and Ever-Virgin Mother of God, Queen of Angels and of Saints, the "Virgin made Church."

NZ (or All)–TO YOU do we cry, O Handmaid of the Lord, Mother of the Suffering Servant, who made the Lord of Majesty our brother. For through you the most exalted Son of God emptied Himself for love of our love, taking the form of a slave in your womb and dying in destitution on a cross as He gave you to us, O Refuge of Sinners.

AM(or Leader)–TO YOU do we fly, as we beg you to obtain for us the true spirit of the Gospel.

NZ (or All)–HOLY, IMMACULATE Conception, Spouse of the Holy Spirit, taking you into our home, we consecrate and entrust ourselves and our Confraternity totally and forever to your Immaculate Heart. Make us your true sons and daughters and use our Confraternity as an instrument of Christ Our King to convert sinners, to sanctify souls, and to strengthen and renew the One, Holy, Catholic, and Apostolic Church, that God–Father, Son, and Holy Spirit–may be glorified, praised, and adored by all mankind. Amen.

NZ (or All)–BRIEF PAUSE FOR SILENT MEDITATION

<u>Invocation of the Holy Spirit</u>

AM (or Leader)–COME, HOLY SPIRIT, fill the hearts of Your faithful

NZ (or All)–AND KINDLE in them the fire of Your love.

59

AM (or Leader)—SEND FORTH Your Spirit and they shall be created.

NZ (or All)—AND YOU shall renew the face of the earth. Amen.

AM (or Leader)—IN THE NAME of the Father, and of the Son, and of the Holy Spirit.

NZ (or All)—AMEN.

+ + + PRAYERS FOR ENDING THE MONTHLY MEETING + + +

NZ (or Leader)–IN THE NAME of the Father and of the Son and of the Holy Spirit.
AM (or All)–AMEN

<u>Apostles' Creed</u>
(All pray together)

NZ (or All)– I BELIEVE in God, the Father almighty, Creator of heaven and earth, and in Jesus Christ, His only Son, our Lord, Who was conceived by the Holy Spirit, born of the Virgin Mary, suffered under Pontius Pilate, was crucified, died and was buried. He descended into Hell; and on the third day He arose again. He ascended into Heaven, and is seated at the right hand of God the Father Almighty. From thence He shall come to judge the living and the dead. I believe in the Holy Spirit, the Holy Catholic Church, the Communion of Saints, the forgiveness of sins, the resurrection of the body, and life everlasting.
AM (or ALL) – AMEN
ALL – BRIEF PAUSE FOR SILENT MEDITATION

<u>Spontaneous Prayer</u>

NZ (or Leader)– LORD, WE LIFT to you our needs in prayer and supplication. *Here follows then spontaneous, oral prayer for needs of members. At an internet meeting, members type in prayer requests at will. At local Chapter and Circle meetings, prayer requests are to be prayed orally. When prayers seem to be done, then:*
NZ (or Leader)–LORD, WE BRING before You these prayers, asking that Your perfect will be done in every situation here mentioned and in those still remaining in the recesses of our hearts. We ask this in the name of Jesus, Our Lord.
AM (or All)–AMEN

The Our Father

(All pray together)

NZ (or All)–OUR FATHER who art in heaven, hallowed be Thy name. Thy kingdom come. Thy will be done, on earth as it is in heaven. Give us this day our daily bread. And forgive us our trespasses, as we forgive those who trespass against us. And lead us not into temptation, but deliver us from evil. AMEN

Closing Blessing

Blessing by Spiritual Assistant, if present. If not present, end with the following blessing followed by the sign of the Cross led by NZ (or Leader) with AM (or All) responding Amen.

NZ (or All)–MAY THE LORD bless us, protect us from evil, and bring us to everlasting life.

AM (or All)–Amen

Closing Song

(All sing together)

Come, Holy Ghost, Creator Blest, and in our hearts take up thy rest. Come with Thy grace and heavenly aid, to fill the hearts which Thou hast made. To fill the hearts which Thou hast made.

Oh, Comforter, to Thee we cry, Thou heavenly gift of God Most High, Thou font of life and fire of love and sweet anointing from above, And sweet anointing from above.

Praise be to Thee, Father and Son, and Holy Spirit, three in one, and may the Son on us bestow all gifts that from the Spirit flow, all gifts that from the Spirit flow. Amen.

FREQUENTLY ASKED QUESTIONS

"It is true that the voice of God, having once penetrated the heart, becomes strong as the tempest and loud as the thunder. But before reaching the heart it is as weak as a light breath that scarcely agitates the air. It shrinks from noise and is silent amid agitation." – St. Ignatius Loyola

"That I May See"

Oh, Lord, You met a blind man who asked You to see. I come before you now, my God, asking for the same grace. Lord, I am on the threshold of pledging to live the Rule of Life for the Confraternity of Penitents. And I must see clearly, Lord, if You, indeed, are calling me to this holy way of life. Open my heart and my mind to Your Will, my God, so that, in all things, I may please You. Amen."

FREQUENTLY ASKED QUESTIONS

HISTORY

I see in the Rule of 1221 that it was written for the Brothers and Sisters of Penance. Did St. Francis invent the Brothers and Sisters of Penance?

No. Penitents (those who wish to do penance, that is, be converted) have existed since the beginning of the Church. The penitents, following the example of the early Christians, often informally referred to themselves as brothers and sisters. Both St. Francis and St. Clare entered a penitential way of life at the beginning of their conversions.

For whom did Francis write the Rule of 1221?

Francis had written letters of advice to the penitents, but he did not write the Rule of 1221. Cardinal Hugolino dei Conti dei Segni, the Protector of the friars and sisters, wrote the Rule of 1221 at the request of Francis and his lay followers who had entered a penitential life due to the friars' preaching. The Rule was a legal document on how most of the penitents were already living. The Rule was adopted by Francis as the Rule for his lay followers, thus becoming the first Rule of the Third Order of Saint Francis.

Where did the idea of the Confraternity of Penitents originate?

Ultimately from the Holy Spirit, our true Founder, Who, in the late twentieth century, was preparing hearts for this call to holiness through a life of penance. It seems to have been the Holy Spirit's intent to call souls from around the world to live some adaptation of the Rule of 1221. One individual was persistently called to live this Rule and to adapt it to modern life and then to organize into an association for all who were also hearing the call of the Holy Spirit to live the penitential life. Thus, in 1994 this individual answered the personal call and began to live the Rule of 1221. This adaptation of the Rule of 1221 was presented first to a spiritual director for approval, and then, in 1995 to others, and finally to diocesan officials. From this little beginning, the Confraternity of Penitents began.

When was the Rule of the Confraternity written?

The Rule of the Confraternity of Penitents was written in 1221. The Constitutions, which are how we live the Rule in this day and age, were written in the mid 1990's and reviewed and recognized by the Diocese of Providence, RI, USA, in 1998 with a few, slight adaptations in 1999 and additional information from other documents including the Directory added in 2006. These Constitutions and Directory have been accepted by the Bishop of the Fort Wayne - South Bend Diocese and are currently followed in the CFP.

Why did the Rule of 1221 need Constitutions? Why couldn't we just have lived with the original Rule?

The Constitutions enable the Rule to be lived today. The 1221 Rule, for example, mandates specific clothing styles. Our brothers would really look odd if they sewed or laced up the sleeves and necks of their garments, and our sisters would look equally out of place in their petticoats. The Church fasts in 1221 mandated no meat, eggs, cheese, or milk products, an unhealthy diet especially when fasting all of Lent and Advent. The Constitutions adapt the original provisions so that penitents can live the Rule today in healthy, inconspicuous ways.

Why are the initials of the Confraternity of Penitents CFP rather than COP or CP?

COP might be confusing in the United States as cop is an American slang term for a policeman. CP are the initials used by the Congregation of the Passion (the Passionists). At the time of the Confraternity's refounding, a search was made for initials used by religious congregations and lay associations, and no organization found used the initials CFP at that time.

LEGALITIES

What was the original name of the Confraternity of Penitents?

In 1995, the small group of Rhode Island individuals who began living an adaptation of the 1221 Rule were known as the Brothers and Sisters of Penance.

Where was the Association headquartered?

Originally incorporated and headquartered in Rhode Island, USA, the Association is now headquartered at 1702 Lumbard Street, Fort Wayne IN 46803 USA.

What was/is the legal status of the original and subsequent Associations?

On April 5, 1999, as the Brothers and Sisters of Penance, the Association was recognized as an incorporated entity under the state of Rhode Island. National, non-profit, tax exempt status (501c3) was granted to the Brothers and Sisters of Penance on November 8, 1999. The incorporated name was retained until August 19, 2003, when the Association was legally re-incorporated, under the State of Rhode Island, as the Confraternity of Penitents. National, non-profit, tax exempt (501c3) status was granted the Confraternity by the United States Internal Revenue Service on May 10, 2004. The original foundation, the Brothers and Sisters of Penance, was legally dissolved under the State of Rhode Island on October 9, 2003, so acknowledged by the State of Rhode Island on October 21, 2003 and by the Internal Revenue Service on March 8, 2004. The Confraternity of Penitents was granted a Certificate of Authority from the State of Indiana on November 12, 2013, to operate as a Non-Profit Foreign* Corporation within the state.

I found another group whose members are living a similar Rule of Life. Would you ever consider uniting with them?

We would certainly be glad to explore a dialog with any other group whose members are living, as closely as we strive to, the 1221 Rule. Please let us know of such groups. Ultimately we would want our Visitor and Diocese to be favorable toward any merger. We wish every group promoting penance God's blessings and we hold them in our prayers.

REFOUNDING

I understand that the Association was refounded. What does that mean?
Refounding means that the original group was begun again by a different name.

Who told you to refound the Association?

The instruction to refound came from the Diocese of Providence. The CFP began as an Association promoting penance and then, five years after our founder began living the Rule, another similar group joined us. After four and a half years of merger, the Vicar for Canonical Affairs for the Diocese of Providence, RI, USA, reviewed the history of the Association to that point and advised us to refound the organization in the same diocese. Three priests who were advising us concurred with this advice, and so, with the knowledge of Bishop Robert Mulvee, the refounding was completed. The refounding legally necessitated a change of name. However, the Rule, Constitutions (then called Statutes), formation lessons, and structure were maintained without change.

---

* Foreign means out of state. The CFP's original incorporation remains in the State of Rhode Island.

Why was the refounding necessary?

Saint Jerome wrote, "Be obedient to your bishop and welcome him as the parent of your soul." St. Ignatius of Antioch reminds us, "Everyone the Master of the house sends on His business, we ought to receive as the One who sent him. It is clear, then, that we should regard the bishop as the Lord Himself."

Section 26 of the Rule and Constitutions state that certain situations, if unable to be resolved within the Association, are to be brought to the Bishop. On August 12, 2003, the diocese received full disclosure and documentation of a situation which had persisted within the Association for the previous ten months and which the spiritual advisors had been trying to resolve peacefully but without success. The Vicar for Canonical Affairs advised the refounding of the Association as the only way to solve the problem. The Bishop concurred with this solution, and the refounding took place on the Queenship of Mary, August 22, 2003.

The Confraternity of Penitents harbors no ill will or bitter feelings toward those left behind. We pray for them daily and wish them every success in their endeavors to also promote a life of penance in the modern world.

THE CONFRATERNITY AND THE CHURCH

Has the Pope OK'd us living this Rule? Or has my bishop?

Bishop Kevin Rhoades of the Diocese of Fort Wayne - South Bend, Indiana, has confirmed the Confraternity of Penitents' canonical status as a private association of the faithful, supports its efforts, and encourages its growth. The letter of commendation can be read in Appendix U of the Directory. The Pope accepts a bishop's judgment in these matters.

Do I have to ask my bishop's permission to live this Rule since I am in another diocese?

The Confraternity of Penitents is in good standing in its diocese where its Rule and Constitutions have been recognized. Therefore, you do not need your bishop's permission to live according to the CFP Rule of Life. However, you could, if you wish, write your bishop a letter to inform him about the CFP. All Circles and Chapters of the Confraternity, which are local gatherings of penitents, do inform their bishops of their existence within their dioceses.

What does a private Association of the Faithful mean? Is this a closed group?

The Confraternity of Penitents is not a closed group. Any lay Catholic who is in full agreement with the teachings of the Catholic Church may live a life of penance.

Associations in the Church fall into several categories. Two of these are private and public. Private Association status is the first step in establishing a new group within the

Catholic Church. As a Private Association, the Confraternity can work with its Visitor (consulting priest) while keeping the diocese informed.

A Private Association, with diocesan approval, can become a Public Association once it has a sufficient number of stable, permanently committed members. Public Associations are subject to a bishop, and any changes in their structure must be diocesan approved.

How do I find a spiritual director if I don't have one?

Spiritual directors can be priests, deacons, or male or female religious. They can be in your parish, your city, your town, or on the internet or via mail. The Confraternity of Penitents has contacts who will help you find a spiritual director once you need one (during First Year Novice Formation).

FOCUS

I saw another web site (or heard of another group) that is promoting this very same Rule. How is the Confraternity different from that group?

If you investigate the other group carefully, you will see what their particular charism, commitment, and focus is. We refer you to our Constitutions which detail the particular charism of the CFP.

MEMBERSHIP

Who can become a member of the CFP?

Any Catholic who adheres to all the teachings of the Catholic Church and who agrees with the Rule. Non Catholics may become Associates of the Confraternity of Penitents provided they understand that their formation will be Catholic in focus. In the same manner, Catholics who, because of certain situations or choices, are ineligible to pledge may proceed in formation as Associates. So may those who have been in formation previously but who have dropped from formation and who wish to be re-admitted. Associates cannot pledge to live the Rule nor can they become CFP formators, vote or hold office in the Confraternity. If an Associate who had previously dropped from formation persists for several years, or if the impediment that precluded membership is eliminated, the Associate may apply for membership without any loss of formation time.

How will I know if the CFP Rule is suitable for me?

Study the CFP Constitutions. They explain how members live the Rule today. If you join a group, or enter its formation program, you are doing so with the intention of seeing if you will live your life, in whole or in part, by that group's Rule and Constitutions. Members of the Confraternity have pledged, or hope to one day pledge, to permanently live according to the CFP Rule and Constitutions. Does this seem to fit the desires which the Holy Spirit has placed within your soul? Will living this way provide you with the spiritual benefits which you seek?

THIRD ORDERS

<u>Does it hinder or enhance the living of the Rule if one is also a member of a Third Order or a Secular Order in the Church?</u>

Being a member of a lay order in the Church can only enhance the living of this Rule. The Confraternity of Penitents is open to members of other Associations and Orders within the Church as long as they are in agreement with their members living this Rule of Life. If not, a person may become an Associate member of the CFP which means that he or she may enter and proceed with formation but without being pledged or being eligible for office or voting privileges. By permission of CFP leaders, Associates may attend gatherings of CFP members.

<u>What's wrong with the current Third Order (Secular Order) Rules?</u>

Nothing. Christ assures us at our baptism that, if we live out our baptismal promises, we will obtain eternal life. As this Rule assists us to live out the Christian life, so it will assist us toward eternal salvation.

<u>If the pope OK'd the Third Order (Secular) Rule I am living, why become a penitent?</u>

Some people need the discipline provided in the Rule of Life for the Confraternity of Penitents. Maybe you are one of these people.

<u>What if my Third Order says I can't live my Third Order Rule and be a member of the Confraternity at the same time?</u>

We would ask you to contact the Confraternity if this happens. We like to remain in contact with Third Orders to explain our charism to them and to inform them that the Confraternity is a response to the Church's call for a renewal of penance. The Confraternity Rule is not in conflict with Third Order Rules but actually enhances them in the penitential aspect.

If your Third Order is insistent in their decision, then you will have to decide what to do by exploring the spiritual benefits of membership in your Third Order and in the CFP. Prayer will help you determine which group will best provide the spiritual benefits which you seek. If you wish to remain with your Third Order, you can maintain contact with the Confraternity as a friend or Affiliate or go into formation as an Associate. Associates are not members of the CFP nor can they become CFP formators, pledge to live the Rule, hold office, or vote.

<u>Do you have to be in a Third Order to join the Confraternity of Penitents?</u>

Not at all. Most of our members are not Third Order members.

SPECIFICS OF THE RULE

<u>It seems like a lot of rules and regulations. How will all those help me?</u>

Some of us need rules, regulations, and practice in being obedient. We want to follow God, to give Him our total will, to pray, but we have trouble disciplining ourselves to do this. The Rule and Constitutions for the Confraternity of Penitents give us specific ways to begin to break our own wills and to practice obedience to something (the Rule and Constitutions) outside our selves. We give up things we like in order to embrace something we want more, namely a deeper relationship with God and peace with one another. Through obedience to the Rule and Constitutions and through its prayer schedule, we become more attuned to the Holy Spirit, more spiritually pliable, more willing to follow God's lead and to serve others in love.

MONEY MATTERS

<u>Are there dues or fees to pay if I join?</u>

No. The Confraternity is a national, non-profit, tax exempt organization and, as such, all donations to it are tax deductible. It requires no set fee to join but rather survives on freely given donations of its members. We would hope that you support the Confraternity as you are able, as this is asked of you in our section 20 of our Rule and Constitutions. You will be responsible for buying your formation texts and breviary. If this is a difficulty, please contact us.

<u>The Rule says to tithe, but I can't give away 10% of my money. We have debts and are</u>
<u>trying to raise a family. Can I still become a penitent?</u>

Yes, you can still become a penitent. The Rule also states that penitents are to pay up their debts. If you have debts, your first obligation is to pay those off as soon as possible. You can tithe your time to help others and give a smaller than 10% amount of money if necessary. Every penitent, however, should make an effort to give some monetary contribution regularly, to their parish and other charities.

Section 20 of the Rule asks each member to give the treasurer "one ordinary denar." "One ordinary denar" was the smallest coinage minted at that time. Since Section 20 follows Section 19, it appears that this amount was to be given monthly. Modern penitents certainly ought to be able to afford to give as alms "the smallest coin minted." Most ought to be able to give much more.

<u>I want to help financially. Do you have any guidelines?</u>

Our CFP Rule asks us to tithe. A tithe is 10% of our income which should be used, if we can afford it, to support our parishes, charitable groups in line with Church teaching, and the CFP. The following suggested tithe guidelines for the CFP were approved by the CFP Visitor.

The CFP will not mandate any tithe for anyone. We do not feel that people should have to pay to do penance. However, we do have expenses including postage, printing, website and internet fees, utilities, rent, property upkeep, phone expenses, and so on. It is reasonable, of course, to expect that those who benefit from the CFP should support the CFP financially if at all possible. We thank especially those in the Alessandro Ministry who, as prisoners, have very little and yet many of whom send their widow's mite to the CFP. May God bless them for their donations.

The suggested guidelines, approved by the Visitor, should be within reach of most in the CFP. These guidelines are that postulants tithe a minimum of 0.25% of their yearly income to the CFP, Novice 1's tithe a minimum of 0.50%, Novice 2's tithe a minimum of 0.75%, and Novice 3's and above tithe a minimum of 1% of their yearly income.

For example, if a CFP member makes $25,000 per year, the minimum suggested yearly tithe to the CFP would be:

Postulant-- 0.25% of yearly income of $25,000 = $62.50

Novice 1-- 0.50% of yearly income of $25,000= $125.00

Novice 2 -- 0.75% of yearly income of $25,000 = $187.50

Novice 3 and above -- 1% of yearly income of $25,000 = $250.00

We sincerely thank you for considering these suggestions and for whatever you can give, most especially and above all your prayers.

PEACE ISSUES

<u>I see I am supposed to make peace with all. What if I can't?</u>

As a penitent, it's your obligation to try to make peace. If your peace making efforts are rejected, then pray regularly for the offender and ask God to give that person the grace of reconciliation. Be always ready to reconcile if the other becomes ready. Hold no grudges. "Forgive one another, as God has forgiven you."

<u>What does the Confraternity consider a "just war?"</u>

Whatever the Holy Father, the Pope, considers to be one. Penitents who face being sent to battle should discuss this with their spiritual directors.

ENTERTAINMENT

<u>The Rule says I'm not supposed to donate to actors. But there are some good Catholic acting troupes. Can't I donate to them?</u>

Yes, you may donate to good, Catholic acting companies, and please do! In 1221, when the Rule was written, all acting troupes were engaged in presenting bawdy, immoral, or heretical plays. Penitents were not to use their money to foster such activity then nor should they foster such activity today. Modern, good Catholic acting companies, on the contrary, advance the faith and deserve our support.

<u>Constitutions 5a states that penitents are not to attend immodest functions or events, including movies, plays, parties, and so on. Are members allowed to enjoy good forms of entertainment such as wholesome movies and plays, ballet, art museums, opera, and so on?</u>

Of course. Constitutions 5a enjoins the penitent to stay away from anything that would be an occasion of sin. Penitents are encouraged to heartily enjoy all wholesome forms of entertainment. The United States Conference of Catholic Bishops has excellent guidelines and gives favorable reviews to those movies and plays suitable for viewing.

CLOTHING

<u>Why would one have to get rid of certain colors of clothes? What's wrong with colors? What's wrong with patterns?</u>

Nothing is wrong with colors or patterns. A life of penance is designed to give up good but worldly things for the sake of better ones. The 1221 Rule stated that penitents were to wear "undyed cloth of humble quality." All penitents and penitential rules had clothing parameters. The purpose of these are to break the penitent's worldly concern about clothing. Penitents limit their wardrobe as a discipline so that they may grow closer to God through voluntary renunciation.

The colors used by the Confraternity of Penitents are similar to the "undyed cloth" of the first penitents. This undyed cloth was of various neutral shades (no patterns) depending on the natural material that made up the fabric. Blue was added in the modern Rule because it is the color associated with Our Lady to whom the Confraternity and all its members are consecrated. The addition of blue also keeps the penitent's neutral colored wardrobe from resembling a religious habit.

Since a penitent's clothing should not attract attention (good or bad), patterns and colors, generally eye-catching, are avoided. The clothing parameters are also a way to identify with Christ Who divested Himself of His glorious Divinity (we divest ourselves of comely colors and patterns) to clothe Himself in humble human flesh (we clothe ourselves in humble, muted colors).

I dress modestly but I do wear bright colors such as red, plum, purple, and pink. If I stop wearing these colors, my family and friends will notice and comment, and I would like to keep my penances private as Jesus advised and the CFP Rule and Constitutions state. Would it be acceptable to wear these colors on Sundays and Solemnities?

In considering modifications of the CFP way of life, it's important to look at the original Rule and how the Church has always viewed religious dress. While the Church has stated that we ought not fast or abstain on Sunday's and Solemnities, it has never made such a stipulation regarding religious garb. Religious who wear habits wear them year round. The penitents who lived the 1221 Rule in the Middle Ages wore their garb daily. As modern penitents, we follow in their footsteps regarding the clothing colors that we use.

It's almost impossible for most penitents to live according to the CFP Rule and Constitutions without close family members knowing. The penitent's gradual change in eating habits, prayer times, clothing, and outlook on life will eventually become evident to those with whom the penitent has close, daily contact. These people can come to understand the CFP way of life even if they do not embrace it themselves. However, when penitents go into the larger world, they ought not be distinguishable by their garb. It is not necessary to wear colors and patterns outside the stipulations of the Rule and Constitutions to achieve this goal.

What is the purpose of wearing a cross or crucifix?

Penitents should give visible witness to their Catholic faith. The crucifix or cross chosen should be simple, not ostentatious. As opposed to other religious jewelry, a crucifix or cross is a commonly accepted symbol of penance because it shows the supreme sacrifice of Christ.

Are there any restrictions about a penitent belonging to a workout club or gym as a way of exercising and helping to stay healthy? Can penitents go swimming?

Certainly penitents may join these clubs and work out as long as their clothing is modest and in the colors of the Rule and Constitutions. However, if the club has certain "uniforms" that must be worn, the penitent ought to go along with the club colors so as not to call attention to himself or herself. Modest work out clothing may not be suitable for wearing in the mall but it is certainly suitable for the gym. In the same way, penitents may go swimming as long as they wear modest bathing suits which ought to be in the colors stipulated in the Rule and Constitutions if those are available. Enjoy your work-outs and swims and stay healthy!

SACRAMENTS

<u>I can barely make it to confession two times a year. How can I go two times a month?</u>

You should not enter a penitential life unless you are serious about surrendering your entire life to God. Making time for confession on a regular basis is part of this surren-der. Some penitents go to confession weekly, others monthly. The spiritual director has the final say in how often a penitent is to confess. The two times per month is a general guideline.

FASTING AND ABSTINENCE

<u>If the Church has made certain fast and abstinence days binding, why fast and/or abstain on other days, too?</u>

Food is good. The fasting and abstinence requirements of the Rule have the penitent voluntarily give up a good (here, food) for a greater good, namely surrender to God. The food stipulations of the Rule and Constitutions break the penitent's attachment to what is eaten and when. By growing in the self discipline of this daily denial of one's will, the penitent begins to break attachments to other more subtle things like opinions, time, controls, ways of acting, and so on. The fasting and abstinence are also ways to identify with Christ Who fasted. They are effective supports to prayer and ways to atone for past sins of oneself or of others.

<u>The fasting seems too severe for a lay person.</u>

Seems is the proper word here. We fast according to current Church law which indi-cates one full meal, one meal lesser in size than the full one, and a bite to eat at a third time during the day, if necessary. Note that nothing is said about the amount of food to be taken other than that only one meal may be a full one. You must eat enough food at each meal to maintain your strength and clarity of thinking. The fasting is disciplined but not difficult. Many lay people have done, and are doing, this fasting with no problem.

<u>I have so many health constraints. How can I follow the fast and abstinence requirements?</u>

These are to be followed only if they do not adversely affect your health. When in doubt, consult a physician and follow the advice given.

<u>Who was St. Martin and why do penitents begin a pre-Christmas fast on the day after his</u>

feast (fast to begin on November 12)?

November 11 is the Feast of St. Martin. In Medieval times, this was a highly celebrated feast for a popular saint and was, in fact, one of the days mentioned in the 1221 Rule as a day of no fasting or abstinence. To keep the spirit of the original Rule and to prepare spiritually for the Solemnity of Christmas, modern day penitents observe this pre-Christmas fast as did their medieval predecessors.

PRAYER

I have so many time constraints. What if I don't have enough time for all the prayers?

There are five prayer options in the Constitutions. The option chosen for regular use will be agreed upon by the penitent and spiritual director. On busy days, the penitent can switch freely between options.

How can I pray all the prayers if I have children or full care of an elderly relative?

With small children or relatives suffering from dementia, penitents will find difficulty in getting uninterrupted moments to pray. In these situations, penitents should make an effort to begin the prayers at the appointed hours. However, once an interruption from a child or forgetful elder occurs, the penitent should put down the prayers, lift his or her mind to God with resignation and love, and then tend to the need at hand. The penitent should consider that part of the prayer time done for the day and not feel compelled to return to finish it. As time goes on and children age or circumstances change, the prayers will be completed at their appointed times.

STRUCTURE

What are Chapters and Circles of the Confraternity?

Chapters are local groups of penitents consisting of at least five members. Circles are smaller groups.

How does the internet community work?

The internet community for the Confraternity of Penitents meets in a password protected chat room on line for a monthly teaching by one of the leaders of the Confraternity. This gathering is primarily for those who do not live near any local Chapter or Circle of the Confraternity and who have internet access. However, anyone in the Confraternity may attend. The internet community is also connected through various other sites, chats, on-line forums, phone calls, and emails.

<u>If I don't have a computer at home and don't live near a local group, can I still become a penitent?</u>

Yes. You may complete your monthly lessons at home and return them to your formator by postal mail.

<u>Can't I just live this Rule on my own without joining the Confraternity? What is the advantage of joining a group?</u>

Of course, you can live this Rule on your own, but you won't be living all of it on your own because community is a very big part of this way of life. Study Chapters 6, 7, and 8 of the Rule and Constitutions and you'll see. A Chapter or Circle gives you the friendship and counsel, if you need it, of others who are living the same way you are. Our internet and postal mail communities provide the same support. We cherish our relationships with our fellow penitents for we all share a common faith and life style. It is difficult to find laity who understand this unique way of following the Lord's call. Other CFP penitents understand for they are living the same way.

<u>Why do we have to enter formation during Lent or August? Why can't we begin formation at any time?</u>

The life of penance in the CFP is lived within the community of the Confraternity. We like to begin our classes at the same time so that members in each level of formation are part of a "class" whose members are completing the same lessons simultaneously. This makes sharing with others in the CFP more workable as those at the same level of formation are also on the same lesson. Having fixed entry dates also gives aspiring penitents a target at which to aim. It provides penitents in formation an incentive to complete their lessons monthly so that they can move into the next year of formation with the rest of their "class." In addition, two major aspects of the life of penance are obedience and self-control. While it may seem exciting to want to enter formation as soon as you find our website, it's important to remember that, if God has given you a call to live this way of life, that call is going to get stronger over time, not fade away. By waiting to enter formation with your fellow penitents-to-be, you are growing in obedience and self-control. Most of us need these virtues.

LEADERSHIP

<u>How does the Confraternity's leadership work? What is it composed of?</u>

The officers listed in the Rule and Constitutions of the Confraternity of Penitents refer primarily to those in local Chapters and Circles. The government of the entire Confraternity of Penitents consists of a Minister General (president), Ministerial Assistant (vice president), Messenger (secretary), and Treasurer. These are to be life pledged members, whenever possible. Advisors to the Minister General and Regional Ministers complete the leadership structure. Decisions of Confraternity leadership are overseen by the Visitor (a priest) who is ultimately subject to the Bishop of the Diocese of Fort Wayne - South Bend. Spiritual advisors also advise the leadership.

Why is your president called a "minister"? The term sounds like a clergyman.

The term "Minister" is used in the Rule of 1221. It means a person who "ministers" to the others. The Minister (president) is to minister to all in the CFP as a servant.

COMMITMENT

It's a big commitment. I don't know if I can do it.

Most of us didn't know if we could do it either. Many of us were sure we could not. God gives the grace if He gives the call to live this way of life. You will never know what you can or can't do unless you try. Remember, formation takes four years and is worked into gradually. You will have time to make the adjustments.

Most people can't live the Rule and their current lifestyle as well. Penitents end up voluntarily relinquishing good but worldly attachments such as watching the news, reading the paper, or having that second cup of coffee in favor of praying. You should not embark upon this way of life unless you are willing to make some very real but valuable changes in how you are currently living. This is a religious way of life for lay people, and no one enters religious life without giving up many aspects of his or her former, more worldly life.

I don't want people to think I'm nuts.

People should not know that you are living this way of life. It is to be done privately and without fanfare. The clothing is not noticeable and is what everyone is wearing. The food choices are not unusual in this day of vegetarians. Many people eat small meals or skip one. If people think you are nuts, it won't be because you are a penitent because they won't know unless you tell them. We would suggest you not tell them as the value of penance is greatly reduced if it is done to impress others.

I would love to see all live this life, but I don't want to be a zealot.

The penitential life is not for everyone. Many would not understand it. There has never been a time in history when everyone or even most everyone were penitents. You will know with whom you can share your zeal.

Why is the formation period four years? I want to do it all now.

The four years of formation allow the brothers and sisters ample time to make the adjustments in their lives necessary to live according to the Rule and Constitutions. It takes time to discern a true call to a religious way of life. The Church does not approve of the faithful making vows or promises in a state of "novitiate fervor." Sometimes, when the required period is dispensed with, this leads to profound regret afterwards.

One must consider the seriousness of promising to live a Rule of Life and ought to consult one's spiritual advisor or confessor before making a permanent commitment. A man who wishes to build first makes an estimate of what the cost of the entire project will be in order to see if he will have enough for the finished structure. (See Luke 14:28.) So too with a person's vocation in life. No one must make serious commitments unless he has first prayed, consulted, and discerned. St. Francis de Sales tells us that he wishes he did not make the promise so hastily to pray the most Holy Rosary everyday as his schedule sometimes made it rather difficult to do as he so promised. One must pray about his or her vocation, consult an advisor, and then discern before entering. This is why we have the Inquiry time, Postulancy and three years of Novitiate in the Confraternity for discernment. Promising to live according to the Rule and Constitutions is a most joyful but also a most serious step and something not to be taken lightly.

What if I need more time to get through formation?

This is allowed with the permission of your spiritual director.

Can I stay in the inquiry period as long as I need to?

Yes, as long as you are still discerning whether or not to enter formation.

Is this commitment for life?

It can be. Or you can take a promise each year to live the way of life for the next twelve months. The choice is up to you and your spiritual director. Remember that the pledge binds by promise, not vow. A promise is made to God and still a serious matter but does not bind under pain of sin. Only after you pledge to live according to the Rule and Constitutions for life can you consider changing that life pledge into a vow which then does become binding under pain of sin, as long as the vow can be kept.

What should be my mindset if I enter formation?

Members of the Confraternity should enter formation with the intention of pledging to live the CFP Rule and Constitutions in their entirety for life, if the Lord so indicates when their formation is complete. Some begin formation and then move on to other spiritual families, and that is certainly acceptable as it is the way the Spirit moves. Others complete formation and feel comfortable in pledging to live the Rule and Constitutions for a year, one year at a time. This is also acceptable, and the CFP has no stipulations on how many times a year pledge may be renewed. However, the initial intent should be, "This is how I believe God may be calling me to live my life. I will explore this holy way and follow the Spirit's lead, ready to say 'yes' to a life of continuing conversion (penance) if and when the Lord indicates."

Some of your members have taken private vows to live according to the Rule and Constitutions. Why?

A vow is the deepest commitment one can make to live the CFP Rule of Life. Some penitents have come to realize that the Lord was calling them to make a binding, lifetime promise called a vow to live this way. Such a vow can be made only with the permission of the pledged penitent's spiritual director and is made to that director or the one whom the director designates. Special guidelines must be followed to be dispensed from a vow. Many graces come with living a vow, in obedience to another human being, but many responsibilities as well. For these reasons, a vow is taken only following adequate prayer and counsel.

Why do some of your members also have names like "sister or brother So and So?" Are they religious? And why don't you capitalize the "sister" or "brother?"

Following tradition in the Catholic Church, CFP pledged members who have also taken a private vow to live the CFP Rule and Constitutions are given Confraternity names. To humbly indicate the lay status of these members, the "sister" and "brother" is written in lower case. These names are used only within the Confraternity.

What if my spouse won't give me permission to join?

You may become an **Affiliate** of the CFP or, if you wish to enter formation and live as much of the Rule and Constitutions as you can under the circumstances of your marriage, you can enter formation as an Associate. Associates are not members of the CFP nor can they become CFP formators, pledge, vote, or hold office in the Confraternity.

What if I drop out and want to come back?

You can certainly re-apply. Your initial status would be that of Associate. If you persist in formation for several years, you can request membership status.

How many are in the Confraternity of Penitents?

The Confraternity is growing so that, as of this writing, January 2014, there are approximately 120 Members who are pledged, in formation, or inquiring, and approximately 60 Associates who are in formation, inquiring, or who have complete formation. These individuals live mainly in the United States but other countries are also represented as the Confraternity of Penitents is an international Confraternity. We thank the Lord for this phenomenal growth and for His wondrous blessings.

PATH TO HOLINESS

Who in the past history of the Church has been a penitent and recognized for sanctity?

St. Margaret of Cortona, Blessed Angela of Foligno, St. Elizabeth Queen of Hungary, Saint Louis King of France, Blessed Luchesio, Blessed Jacoba de Settisoli, Saint Ferdinand III King of Spain, Saint Elizabeth Queen of Portugal, Saint Rose of Viterbo, Blessed Jane of Signa, and about twenty others have lived this Rule and have been declared venerable, blessed, or saints. There have been countless others whose names have not been recorded.

Why did they chose to live this lifestyle?

They realized that their lives were not as converted as they wished. Many had major conversions, some from very sinful lives. All wanted to surrender themselves in every way to God. They hungered for holiness. They wanted ways to atone for past sins. They saw the Rule as a means to those ends. The purpose of the Rule is never to "do what it says" as an end in itself but to "do what it says" as a discipline, a penance, that enables the penitent to "do what HE says." The Rule is only a means to the ultimate end of total union with the will of God.

So this is why you do all this?

Why we "do all this" is best summed up here:

"Love for creation and grateful recognition that all is a gift from God is the underlying characteristic of the authentic penitent. . . . The joyful experience of giving something to God out of pure love, imitating very poorly the completely gratuitous gift of love God makes to us, is inexplicable for those who have not begun to fall in love with Jesus crucified. . . . (it is) a spiritual experience . . . the fullness of love and freedom."

—Segundo Galilea, Temptation and Discernment, Institute of Carmelite Studies.

INQUIRER REFLECTIONS

"If you want to grow in perfection, you cannot advance by yourselves – you need a guide. Hence, when you go to God, go through Mary and with Mary! - *St. Maximilian Kolbe*

Prayer to Our Lady of Gentle Love

Blessed Virgin Mary, Mother of God, infuse in our hearts the love you have for Jesus, your Divine Son. Help us to understand that love and gentleness go together in our daily life. Intercede for us and bring peace and joy in our families, help our neighbors, the lonely, the sick, the homeless and the hungry. You are the Mother of all humankind, given to us by Almighty God and we turn to you for guidance. Help us to be holy, as you are holy and to love as you love. Our Lady of Gentle Love, pray for all your children. We ask you to implore for us to God the Father, God the Son and God the Holy Spirit, to bless us all and to help us to attain eternal salvation. Amen.

INQUIRER REFLECTIONS

Inquirers do not undergo any specific formation program. They are asked to pray about their decision to enter formation as a postulant.

To assist inquirers in this process, they may wish to consider the following questions. It is suggested that a good period of time be spent on each reflection (perhaps a few weeks) Members of the inquirer's Chapter or Circle or the Regional Minister can assist inquirers in the discernment process. The reflections should be taken in order as written but do not have to be completed in order to enter formation as a postulant.

+ + +

1. REFLECTION ON THE RULE OF LIFE:

Study the Guide to the Form of Life of the Confraternity of Penitents—the Rule and its Constitutions. Ask yourself:

Can I envision myself living this Rule of Life? How does that imaginary vision make me feel? What difficulties do I foresee and how will I deal with them? What joys do I think I will experience? Do I foresee any opposition from others? What adjustments will I have to make to live this Rule? Do I feel that God will give me the grace to make them?

+ + +

2. REFLECTION ON THE CONFRATERNITY PRAYERS:

Look for these in the Rule, Chapter I and in the Appendices. Look up the psalms in a Bible:

Why were these particular psalms used in the original Rule of 1221? What does Psalm 51 say to me personally? Psalm 54? Psalm 119 as penitents pray it? What meaning does the Marian Consecration Prayer have for me? Why will I be asked to pray the

Apostle's Creed twice daily? How do I feel about praying these psalms and prayers every day for the rest of my life? How might they influence my life if I do pray them daily?

+ + +

3. REFLECTION ON A LIFE OF PENANCE

How do I feel about living a medieval Rule in the modern world? Do I see myself as one in a long line of penitents? Do I really want to surrender my life, in every way, to God? How might living this Rule help me to do that? What fruits do I see as forthcoming in my own life if I do embrace a life of penance, as put forth in the CFP Rule?

+ + +

4. REFLECTION ON THE SAN DAMIANO CRUCIFIX:

Read the section on the San Damiano Crucifix. Use a good sized photograph of the cross or, better yet, a replica of the crucifix, for this reflection. Try to pray daily, gazing at this crucifix. Ask yourself:

What "leaps out" at me from this crucifix when I gaze at it prayerfully? Why do I think this is so? What might God be telling me through this? What parts of the crucifix do I not really notice unless I look very closely? Why do I think I miss those parts? Might there be any symbolic spiritual lessons in those parts that I may not want to see? Do I think that praying with this crucifix might impact my spiritual life? How?

+ + +

5. REFLECTION ON BEGINNING THE JOURNEY INTO PENANCE

Why do I want to begin this journey into conversion? What questions do I have? Who might I ask for answers?

+ + +

6. REFLECTION ON THE FRANCISCAN CONNECTION

What is the connection between Saint Francis and the Confraternity of Penitents? Why does the CFP focus on penance rather than on St. Francis per se? How do you feel about this? Do you see yourself living a life of penance?

+ + +

7. REFLECTION ON MOTTO, MISSION, ACTION, PRAYER

Read these sections in the CFP Constitutions. Do you feel called to these four aspects of a life of penance? How might the Lord bring these about in your own life?

+ + +

8. GOALS OF A LIFE OF PENANCE

What goals might living this Rule achieve in your life? How do you feel about these? Which one is most important to you and why?

+ + +

9. FOCUSING ON FORMATION

Formation in the Confraternity of Penitents takes at least four years of prayer, change of life style, and study. You will read the entire Catechism of the Catholic Church over a three year period. You will meditate on certain Scripture passages. You will study the Franciscan Virtues, one per month, and, with the grace of the Holy Spirit, begin to more fully implement them in your life.

What can you hope to learn through this formation program? How do you feel it will help you spiritually? How might your relationship with others benefit? How do you think you will change by the end of formation? What excites you about formation? Is there anything that causes you some concern?

+ + +

10. ONGOING FORMATION

Once you complete formation in the Rule and Constitutions, you are not done! You are only just beginning. You will then continue formation by living the Rule and Constitutions, of course, but also by reading the lives and/or writings of the saints and/or documents of the Church. You will choose which you would like to read and then have an opportunity to share with other penitents whose formation is also complete.

Do you look forward to continuing your formation? What would you like to read? Why? Where will you find appropriate spiritual reading material?

POSTULANT LESSONS

"In danger, anguish, or doubt, think of Mary and call upon her! Following her, you will never lose your way. Praying to her, you will never sink into despair. Contemplating her, you will never go wrong."

St. Bernard.

A Parents Prayer
For Their Children's Return to the Church

Dear God, I come to you with a heart of sorrow over love for my children who have drifted from the practice of the holy Catholic faith. Look upon these children of mine with your loving and forgiving mercy. Bring these children back into the embrace of Holy Mother Church, that soon my children may receive once again forgiveness in you Sacrament of Penance and be nourished with you Body, Blood, Soul, and Divinity in Holy Communion.

Oh patron saints of my children, intercede in heaven for their salvation. Angel guardians of my children, you who were appointed to the charge of my children's souls, intercede constantly before the Heavenly Throne of the Most Holy Trinity. Mary, Queen of the Angels, send forth all the angels of God to inspire my children to return to the path of salvation I have attempted to teach them. I beg my children's guardian angels to go with them and inspire them to return.

Give me the strength to bear this cross and offer to you, O Sacred Heart of Jesus and Immaculate Heart of Mary, the pain that I feel, so that some day my children will return and I may glorify God forever in Heaven with these children whom I love. Amen.

POSTULANT LESSONS

POSTULANT[31]: LESSON ONE

<u>Introduction to the Confraternity of Penitents</u>

In the 1100's and 1200's, a great penitential movement spread across Europe. Lay people began to convert from worldly ways to spiritual ones and adopted certain penitential practices to enable them to do so. These people were called penitents or *conversi* (converted ones). Certain ways of living a more simplified, God and-other centered lifestyle were codified into a Rule for Penitents, written in 1221 and approved by the Pope. A penitent, a *converso*, was, therefore, willing to make adjustments in his or her life in order to more closely follow God's ways. These adjustments were in the areas of prayer, diet, clothing, and works of mercy. The penitential life led to detachment from worldly values and things and attachment to the values and things of God.

In our modern, materialistic, self-centered society, some people feel the need to simplify their lives and to turn more completely to God and neighbor. While the term "penitent" may seem archaic, people who are moving into deeper surrender to God's will for them are, indeed, modern day penitents. The way of life that worked for penitents 800 years ago in the self-centered, materialistic medieval world still works today to bring people into a more disciplined life style that makes more room for God.

Today the Confraternity of Penitents is an association of lay men and women who are following modern Constitutions to the 1221 Rule for Penitents. The Constitutions make the penitential practices of 1221 livable in today's society while effecting the same conversion which the 1221 Rule achieved for centuries. The Rule and the Constitutions

---

31   Note: Keep copies of all lessons turned in to your formator both for sharing in your Chapter or Circle meetings, and in case your formation lessons get lost in the mail or on the internet.

have been reviewed and deemed acceptable to live by the Bishop of the Diocese of Fort Wayne - South Bend, Indiana, USA.

Life as a modern penitent will enhance, not conflict with or replace, any Third Order vocation or membership in any other Catholic lay association. The penitential way of life gives more discipline and direction to a Catholic's life, thus enabling him or her to be more willing to submit to God's will.

Anyone considering this way of life must be a Catholic who agrees with all the teachings of the Catholic Church. A penitent must have a desire to become as holy as God wishes. This desire must be affected by doing God's will.

A penitent will receive guidance from a spiritual director. The spiritual director must agree with all the teachings of the Catholic Church and must be an ordained member of the Catholic clergy (priest or deacon) or a Catholic religious. A penitent will meet with his or her spiritual director regularly, the most common time interval being once monthly. However, the frequency and length of meetings will be determined by the penitent and the spiritual director.

A married penitent must also obtain the consent of the spouse in order to live this Rule. Hopefully, obtaining this consent will not be difficult since living a penitential life does not conflict with spousal, parental, or family obligations and should, in fact, make the penitent a more charitable and compassionate family member.

Over a four year period, the penitent will make adjustments in his or her life style in the three areas of prayer, diet, and clothing. All these areas need attention in our materialistic, self-centered world. The Rule and Constitutions take into account the penitent's health, employment, family, age, and work conditions, allowing exceptions and substitutions when necessary.

Prayer for the average penitent takes about ninety minutes daily when living in full conformity to the Rule and Constitutions. This is a conscious way of making time for God in our society that tends to keep us too busy to have time for God. In a society in which food is plentiful and people can indulge as they wish, the diet adjustments help penitents to control their physical appetites in healthy, yet somewhat sacrificial ways.

Because our modern societies are so clothing conscious and most people have a variety of styles, colors, and patterns from which to choose, the modern penitent limits his or her wardrobe in certain specific but easy to follow ways.

The prayer, diet, and clothing adaptations prepare the penitent to be more open to God's direction and discipline. They prepare the penitent's spirit to become more aware of spiritual and corporal works of mercy that need to be performed. The penitent's spiritual awareness heightens so that he or she can discern what works of mercy God is requesting and how God wishes them to be performed.

These adjustments in life style are made gradually over the period of formation, allowing ample time to discern whether or not an individual is truly called to this way of life.

The goals of formation for the Confraternity of Penitents are as follows:

- To enable the penitent to understand the transitoriness of life and the superfluities of a worldly existence.
- To direct the penitent in surrendering his or her own will to the Rule and to the spiritual director, and thus become more inclined to accept with joy the discipline and direction that God gives.
- To draw the penitent into a deep union with God who wishes all people to surrender everything to Him.
- To enable the penitent to experience in a small way the self emptying willingly embraced by Our Lord Jesus Christ.
- To foster an increase of love in the penitent for God the Father, Son, and Holy Spirit and for human beings who are made in God's image. This love must lead to loving, selfless service of God and of others. True love is to seek the others' good before one's own. The Rule is intended to have the penitent do this.
- To lead the penitent into personal sanctity and eternal life in heaven.
- To grow in the Franciscan Virtues. To this end, the penitent will complete one chapter per month from the book <u>Franciscan Virtues through the Year: 52 Steps to Conversion</u>
- To know Jesus.

If an inquirer desires this way of life but is fearful of being unable to follow it, the following must be remembered: God would not give the desire unless He is willing to grant the means. Those whom God calls to a life of penance will be given the grace to live it. What is needed are patience and trust.

BRIEFLY ANSWER THE FOLLOWING QUESTIONS.

Am I attracted to the idea of a penitential life style? Why or why not?
Do I feel the need for conversion in my life? Where?
Do I believe that God will give me the grace to live this lifestyle? Why?

LESSON ON THE RULE

During the first month of postulancy, look over the entire Rule and Constitutions of the Confraternity. What subjects are covered? How will they impact my life if I continue into formation?

LESSON ON THE FRANCISCAN VIRTUES

In <u>Franciscan Virtues</u>, read Virtue 1: Attentiveness. Spend at least five minutes meditating on the virtue. Answer the questions. Share your answers with your formator.

DAILY GOSPEL READING AND QUESTIONS FROM CHRIST IN THE GOSPEL

Saint Francis of Assisi wanted to follow the Gospel. His whole way of life was based on living the Gospel which meant that he had to know the Gospel. Therefore, penitents begin their formation in the Confraternity of Penitents by daily reading the Gospel.

<u>Christ in the Gospel</u> is a small, illustrated book that combines the four Gospel accounts into one narrative. The entire Gospel is then read in 6 months with the cycle then repeating so that, in one year, the reader will have gone through the Gospels twice. Each day has questions for reflection and recall at the back of the book. Christ in the Gospel is available through the <u>CFP Holy Angels Gift Shop.</u>

Postulants read <u>Christ in the Gospel</u>, starting with the first day of the postulancy, by selecting the appropriate reading for the calendar day, answering the questions mentally, and then continuing to read <u>Christ in the Gospel</u> daily for their entire postulancy. Each month they will be asked to reflect on one of the Gospel readings of their choice.

Therefore, for this month, daily read <u>Christ in the Gospel</u> and answer for yourself the questions on the day's reading, found in the back of the book.

Select one reading or section of the Gospel that particularly resonated with you. Share that passage and your thoughts with your formator.

FIRST MONTH'S ACTIVITIES

- Pray daily in the morning the Apostle's Creed, all of Psalm 51, all of Psalm 54, and verses 1 to 32 of Psalm 119. In the evening, pray daily the Apostle's Creed and all of Psalm 51. Pray the "Glory Be to the Father" after each Psalm.
- Pray daily for the Holy Father, our Bishops, pastor(s), spiritual assistants, and all of the Confraternity of Penitents, all sinners, family members, and yourself.
- Submit your answers to this month's questions to your CFP formator.

POSTULANT: LESSON TWO

<u>Encountering God through Scripture</u>

God is the divine being. He is real. He created you and everything else. He knows you. He loves you. He wants you to know Him and to live eternally with Him. Do you believe this?

Love changes people. Think of how your love of someone has changed you. How has your love changed someone else? When we change for the better, we experience conversion. To the extent that we know and love Our Lord, to that extent we will begin to enter a life of conversion (penance).

How do we get to know someone? By spending time with that person. We will know God better if we spend time learning about Him. To know Him is to love Him. If we love Him, we are already in the process of conversion.

How do we get to know our God? By reading what is sometimes called His "love letter" to us, the Bible. Throughout history, God revealed Himself to the Jewish people, the nation that He had chosen to know Him. The history of the Jewish nation is a history of God intervening in the lives of people whom He claimed as His. What did the Jewish people do to have God choose them instead of other nations as the ones to whom He revealed Himself? They did absolutely nothing to deserve this favor. In fact, a "sensible" God would not have chosen the stubborn, prideful, and often foolish Jewish people as the ones to whom He would promise, "You shall be My people and I will be your God."

Here is the first lesson we can learn from Scripture. God, as St. John tells us, is Love, and Love is not sensible. Love loves the beloved with reckless and unbounded abandon, not because of any good qualities in the beloved but because of the pure qualities of Love. God loves us, not for who we are, but because of Who He is.

Love is loyal but Love is also just. This, too, is seen from the Old Testament where time and again God showed the Jewish people where sin led. It is not Love to allow someone to be less than they can be. God would not tolerate the Jewish nation's stubborn refusal to do His will because toleration is not Love. We may tolerate rudeness or bad behavior in someone else's child, but we will correct and discipline these traits in our own children. Why? Because they are OUR children and we know who they can be. We won't settle for them being any less than their best.

Love is powerful. Time and again God works miracles, manipulating and controlling nature which He Himself created. By reading Scripture we begin to understand that God's will is in every thing that happens. Either He is actively working or He is passively permitting all things.

We see that some of these things are evil, some bring suffering, and we ask why, if God is good, do these bad things happen. Scripture tells us that God made us in His image, as the pinnacle of His creation, even above the angels, and that He gave us charge over creation. What we decided would affect all. What did we decide, not just once in the Garden of Eden, but every day since then? That our will is superior to God's. Since we are inferior, created creatures, that decision has to be pride-fully wrong.

Since we have been placed in charge of creation, our decisions affect that creation much as food coloring dripped into water colors the entire batch. Our turning from God has removed not only our perfection, but that of all creation. Nothing on earth is or ever will be perfect again.

Now we begin to see that we, like the Jewish nation, do not always, or even much of the time, understand God's active and permissive will, but we can, if we delve deeply enough, understand a truth. God, in His mysterious way called grace, is able to bring good out of evil. He did this in Scripture. He does it in our lives.

The God of the Old Testament revealed Himself more fully in the New Testament. God, in His Second Person, came to earth as a human being. We begin to see the great and humbling mystery. God, the Creator of heaven and earth, enters the womb of a virgin upon her acceptance of Him. He does not force Himself upon her. He leaves her free to accept or reject Him, just as He leaves us free to do the same. Then, in total dependence and helplessness, God grows and is born and then depends totally on a man and a woman to care for Him. What humility and trust does this show about God?

All His life, Christ suffered for us, for Love will do anything for the beloved. We see the extent of that love upon the cross where God is destroyed by His creatures and all because He not only permitted it but actually willed it. And then, beyond this supreme act of love, God returns in the Eucharistic bread down through time to our present day. Do we realize, when we take Him in His Eucharistic Presence into our bodies, that our Creator, Redeemer, and Lover is intimately uniting with us? The God Whose tale is told through Scripture and Who manages all that is, comes to dwell within us as He did in the womb of the Virgin. What mystery we begin to touch! The mystery of God Himself!

As a postulant in the Confraternity of Penitents, spend a bit of time daily reading Scripture. This practice will continue throughout your formation and should continue until your death, which is really your entry into eternal life. This said, remember that it is better to read and reflect on a brief Scripture passage than it is to read too much too quickly.

Where should you begin? With the Gospels. Read and savor the words that you have heard again and again at Mass. Only this time, before reading, ask God to give you an insight into the passage you will read. Then read slowly and pause to think about what you read. God will instruct you.

After you have read the Gospels, read the Book of Acts and then the various New Testament letters. Then you may begin to read whatever you wish next. Perhaps you will choose the Book of Revelation or the Old Testament. Nevertheless, return to the Gospels frequently, perhaps alternating your reading of other parts of Scripture with the Gospels. Why the Gospels? Because Jesus is God made man. The more you know of Him, the more you know of God. The more you know of God, the more you will love Him.

BRIEFLY ANSWER THE FOLLOWING QUESTIONS.

1. What do I see as God's greatest act of love? Why?
2. What in Christ's life reveals to me Who He is? Why?
3. What does the Eucharist mean to me?

LESSON ON THE RULE: SECOND MONTH

Look at the FRUITS OF THE COMMITMENT and PURPOSE (CHARISM) sections of the Constitutions of the Confraternity. What are the goals of a penitential life? How do you think following the Rule and Constitutions of the Confraternity can help achieve these?

LESSON ON THE FRANCISCAN VIRTUES

In Franciscan Virtues, read Virtue 2: Confession. Spend at least five minutes meditating on the virtue. Answer the questions. Share your answers with your formator.

DAILY GOSPEL READING AND QUESTIONS FROM CHRIST IN THE GOSPEL

Daily read Christ in the Gospel and answer for yourself the questions on the day's reading, found in the back of the book.

Select one reading or section of the Gospel that particularly resonated with you. Share that passage and your thoughts with your formator.

SECOND MONTH ACTIVITIES

- Continue praying the Apostles' Creed and the psalms introduced last month.
- Add time daily to read and ponder Scripture. Begin with the Gospels. Try to spend fifteen minutes per day if possible. Christ in the Gospel (see below) may be used to achieve this.
- Submit your answers to this month's questions to your CFP formator.

POSTULANT: LESSON THREE

<u>Our Catholic Faith</u>

The first penitents prayed the Apostles' Creed twice daily, and we do the same. The Creed was important in the 1200's when penitents were living their original Rule because heresy was rampant and many so called "faithful" were using Scripture to justify some very unscriptural teachings. Today the Creed is just as important when many, even within the Church, call into question the very truths of our faith as well as some of its moral teachings.

No one can be accepted into the Confraternity of Penitents unless he or she adheres to all the teachings of the Catholic Church. These are found in Scripture, the Creed, and the Catechism of the Catholic Church. Penitents begin to formally study the Catechism when they enter first year formation. As postulants, your study will be confined to the Creed and to Scripture. In this lesson, we will do some comparison between the two.

The Apostles' Creed is a profession of faith that contains twelve fundamental doctrines. Even in apostolic times, those about to be baptized had to express their faith. The Apostles' Creed is so named, not because it was written by the Apostles, but because it is a summary of their teaching. The Apostles' Creed is similar to the Nicene Creed which is a part of the Roman rite of every Mass. The Nicene Creed, which presents the chief doctrines of the Catholic faith, was formulated at the first ecumenical council of Nicaea (325 A.D.). The Nicene Creed authoritatively established the divinity of the Second Person of the Blessed Trinity by pronouncing that the Son is "consubstantial with the Father," a doctrine that had been in dispute in some quarters at that time.

We can see from these definitions that the Creeds express the chief doctrines of our faith, but not ALL the doctrines. All the doctrines are expressed in the Catechism. But those in the Creeds are fundamental, basic to all the rest. We often "rattle off" these prayers without thinking about what we are saying. Let us examine the Apostles' Creed in detail:

"I believe in God, the Father almighty,
Creator of heaven and earth;
And in Jesus Christ, His only Son, Our Lord. Who was conceived by the Holy Spirit,
Born of the Virgin Mary,
Suffered under Pontius Pilate,
Was crucified, died, and was buried.
He descended into hell;
On he third day He rose again from the dead; He ascended into heaven,
Sits at the right hand of God, the Father almighty;
From thence He shall come to judge
The living and the dead.
I believe in the Holy Spirit,
the holy Catholic Church;
the communion of saints,
the forgiveness of sins,
the resurrection of the body,
and life everlasting. Amen."

Now read the Prologue to the Gospel of St. John in the Bible (John 1:1-18). Compare the Prologue to the Creed. What similarities do you notice? Differences? Omissions? The Prologue to John's Gospel is not meant to be a complete Creed, but it is a creed, a statement of faith. It speaks of the union of Christ and the Father and of how God the Father was made manifest in His Word, God the Son. A word, if properly chosen, fully expresses a certain idea. Jesus, the one Word of God, fully expresses the reality of God. To know the Word is to know the reality. That is why we must strive to know Christ. To know Christ is to know the All.

The Apostles' Creed summarizes the life of Christ. It tells us that He was born, lived, died, rose, and will return. It reminds us that we must believe in God the Father and God the Holy Spirit, and that we must adhere to all that the Catholic Church teaches. The Creed affirms our faith in the forgiveness of sins and in our bodily resurrection and tells us that the saints are in "communion" with each other, meaning that we can ask them to pray to God for us and they will do so.

BRIEFLY ANSWER THE FOLLOWING QUESTIONS

1. How does the Creed encapsulate our faith?
2. Can you truly say that you embrace all that it states?
3. If you have difficulty with any part, discuss it with a priest, deacon, or religious.

LESSON ON THE RULE

Look at Chapter I: DAILY LIFE, of the Rule and Constitutions.

Some things for you to ponder at this time are:

Note the clothing provision. All penitential Rules contained clothing parameters because clothing is a worldly concern, and a penitential life is intended to break attachments to worldly concerns.

Why were the particular colors chosen as defined in the Constitutions?

Read section 2 of the Rule and Constitutions.

Note that in Constitutions 2g the penitent is instructed to visibly wear a simple cross or crucifix unless already wearing the habit of a Third Order. Why?

Look over sections 3, 4, and 5 of the Rule and Constitutions. Why do you suppose that section 3b of the Constitutions can be implemented only to the extent that others in the family go along with it?

LESSON ON THE FRANCISCAN VIRTUES

In <u>Franciscan Virtues</u>, read Virtue 3: Courage. Spend at least five minutes meditating on the virtue. Answer the questions. Share your answers with your formator.

DAILY GOSPEL READING AND QUESTIONS FROM CHRIST IN THE GOSPEL

Daily read <u>Christ in the Gospel</u> and answer for yourself the questions on the day's reading, found in the back of the book.

Select one reading or section of the Gospel that particularly resonated with you. Share that passage and your thoughts with your formator

THIRD MONTH'S ACTIVITIES

- Continue your prayer life as you have been doing. Continue to read a portion of Scripture daily and to spend some time pondering it. Unless you are already wearing the habit of a Third Order, obtain a cross or crucifix and wear it visibly always.
- Submit your answers to this month's questions to your CFP formator.

POSTULANT: LESSON FOUR

The Magisterium of the Church

Catholics are supposed to be obedient people. We are to obey the Pope and bishops in all matters of faith and morals. Being human, some of us may disagree with decisions of the hierarchy, but as Catholics we are to follow their directives. Why? Because Christ has ordained it.

The Roman Pontiff and the bishops are "authentic teachers," that is, teachers endowed with the authority of Christ, who preach the faith to the people entrusted to them, the faith to be believed and put into practice. "The ordinary and universal Magisterium of the Pope and the bishops in communion with him teach the faithful the truth to believe, the charity to practice, the beatitude to hope for." (Catechism of the Catholic Church, section 2034).

How do we know that the Church has this power? Scripture tells us of this in Matthew's Gospel, Chapter 28, verses 19-20, where Jesus gives final instructions to His apostles: "Go, then, to all peoples everywhere and make them my disciples: baptize them in the name of the Father, the Son, and the Holy Spirit, and teach them to obey everything I have commanded you. And I will be with you always, to the end of the age."

The Apostles took this directive to heart as even a cursory reading of the Book of Acts will show. Their mission was to teach authoritatively the doctrines which Christ had commissioned them to spread. Using the deposit of faith contained in Scripture, and the oral and written truth called tradition, the Church "formally declares, through councils and infallible definitions, her magisterium" (Catholic Encyclopedia, p. 366).

The authority of the Pope was conferred by Christ Himself on the Apostle Peter as recorded in Matthew 16: 17-19. "Blest are you, Simon, son of Jonah! No mere man has revealed this to you, but my heavenly Father. I for my part declare to you, you are 'Rock', and on this rock I will build my church, and the jaws of death shall not prevail against it. I will entrust to you the keys of the kingdom of heaven. Whatever you declare bound on earth shall be bound in heaven; whatever you declare loosed on earth shall be loosed in heaven."

Note how Christ declares that the truth of faith, given to Peter, was not the result of human reasoning but was directly infused by God Himself. It is this infusion of divine knowledge that enabled Peter to hold the "keys to the Kingdom of heaven." What He permitted and prohibited were not the results of his own logic; rather, the Holy Spirit had instructed him to permit or prohibit those very things.

Jesus chose Peter to be the head of the Apostles and the visible head of the Church on earth. The Book of Acts clearly shows that the Apostles recognized this. Upon Peter's death, St. Linus was chosen as Peter's successor. He was followed by Saints Cletus, Clement, Evaristus, Alexander, and so on to the current Holy Father. Thus, except for a few brief, sad periods of history, the Church has never been without a Pope.

The Magisterium of the Church, evident in the authoritative teaching of the Pope in union with the bishops, makes the Catholic Church unique among all the Christian faiths. Catholics everywhere are to be in obedience to this hierarchy. They are to accept and teach the truths of the faith as found in the Catechism of the Catholic Church. This is not to say that other faiths are "bad" because they are not bad but, generally, quite good. But, good as they may be, other faiths cannot equal the perfection of the Catholic faith which is the fullness of the teaching of Christ. Christ promised to be with Peter and his successors down through time, guiding them without error in the areas of faith and morals.

This does not mean that some pastors of the flock do not sin, sometimes in extreme ways. But when the Pope and bishops expound a teaching of the Church in the area of faith and morals, they are speaking the mind of Christ Himself, unless it is clear that they are only expressing their personal opinion. All penitents must believe and accept this basic truth of the Catholic faith.

The Pope is himself a bishop, the bishop of Rome. By divine law, he also has supreme jurisdiction over the universal Church and over all religious. He may act alone or with a council of bishops in defining Church doctrine. Thus the hierarchy of the Church is formed. First Christ, the head of the "mystical body," then His Vicar on Earth, the Pope, followed by bishops, clergy, religious, and laity.

If a person has difficulty with obedience to the Pope and the bishops, that person has difficulty with obedience to Christ. Many of the saints have put the dilemma this way. "If an angel appeared and told me to do thus and so, but I went to my bishop and he forbade it, I would obey the bishop. I may be deceived by the angel for even a demon can come as an angel of light, but I can see my bishop and cannot be deceived about his directives. If the bishop is right and I am wrong, I am justified by my obedience. If the bishop is wrong and I am right, God will reveal the truth in His time."

A good example of this very thing occurred regarding the Divine mercy messages to Sister Faustina. Spread initially, then repressed by a bishop, the messages are now being spread with the good wishes of the Pope. Moreover, the nun who received the visions has been canonized. A measure of Saint Faustina's holiness was her obedience.

Penitents must be obedient to the faith and moral teachings of the Church. This does not imply that every religious in the Church is without sin or that penitents cannot work to address any injustices or lacks of good judgment that they may notice. It does mean that penitents should study the Catechism of the Catholic Church so that they will know what the Church does teach. Penitents must adhere to all the truths of the Catholic faith as the Church teaches them in the Catechism. Formal study of the Catechism begins in First Year Formation.

BRIEFLY ANSWER THE FOLLOWING QUESTIONS

1. Reread the second paragraph of this lesson. What is the Magisterium? From where derives the doctrine of the Magisterium?
2. Reread Jesus's address to Peter. What insights does it reveal to you?
3. If someone in the hierarchy of the Church sins, how is it possible to separate the sin from the teaching authority of the bishop involved?

LESSONS FROM THE RULE

DAILY MASS

Look at CHAPTER IV: PRAYER in the Rule and Constitutions. Pay particular attention to section 14. The Constitutions 14a and 14b clarify the daily Mass requirement. Study these sections carefully and discuss them with another penitent if possible. Note that penitents do not **HAVE** to attend daily Mass.

The Rule and Constitutions for the Confraternity of Penitents always put concern for the welfare of others above following rules. Therefore, if daily Mass attendance would seriously inconvenience a penitent in fulfilling his or her daily duties, the penitent should stay home. Right?

Should a penitent feel "guilty" if he or she feels that attending daily Mass is a "serious inconvenience?"

COMMUNITY LIFE

Look at Chapter VI, sections 19-21 of the Rule and Constitutions. This chapter discusses many aspects of community life within the Confraternity. Note that penitents are to attend Confraternity meetings, if possible. Note how penitents are to respond if this is not possible. Also note the discussion on the structure of the meetings themselves.

What procedure is to be followed if a Chapter loses its spiritual assistant?

How are members to financially support their Chapters and the Confraternity?

What can you personally do to strengthen fellow penitents?

LESSON ON THE FRANCISCAN VIRTUES

In <u>Franciscan Virtues</u>, read Virtue 4: Courtesy. Spend at least five minutes meditating on the virtue. Answer the questions. Share your answers with your formator.

DAILY GOSPEL READING AND QUESTIONS FROM CHRIST IN THE GOSPEL

Daily read <u>Christ in the Gospel</u> and answer for yourself the questions on the day's reading, found in the back of the book.

Select one reading or section of the Gospel that particularly resonated with you. Share that passage and your thoughts with your formator.

<u>FOURTH MONTH'S ACTIVITIES</u>

- Continue your prayer life, Scripture reading, and meditation.
- Consider attending daily Mass if possible.
- Submit your answers to this month's questions to your CFP formator.

POSTULANT: LESSON FIVE

<u>The Person of Jesus</u>

Penitents should have a love affair with Jesus. Jesus is not to be the spouse of only consecrated religious. He is to be the mystical spouse of every Catholic. There is no doubt that Jesus lived. History, including pagan texts, attests to that. The question is, "Who was He?" This is a question that every penitent should consider and every penitent must answer. It is not enough to give an answer that someone else has given. The penitent's answer must be from the heart.

We can have many different possible relationships with Jesus. We may ignore Him, disbelieve Him, consider Him to be mentally unbalanced. We may think He was a good teacher, a great prophet, a holy man, a miracle worker. But Jesus wants our relationship with Him to be different. He wants us to know that He is Creator, Brother, Spouse, and Redeemer of each of us. All these relationships are possible because Jesus is God and God, as St. John tells us, is Love.

St. Peter Julian Eymard wrote, "What are the proofs of a genuine love? There is only one, its sacrifices: the sacrifices it prompts us to do and those it accepts with joy.

"Love without sacrifice is but an empty name, a self-love in disguise" (The Real Presence: Eucharistic Meditations, Congregation of the Blessed Sacrament, Emmanuel Publications, 5384 Wilson Mills Road, Cleveland OH 44143, p. 59).

We can say with certainty that Jesus loves us because He sacrificed so totally for us. He left eternal bliss to come to earth as a child in a virgin's womb. He Who had the adulation of angels was subjected to ridicule and rejection by His creatures. Giving Himself and His healing to us, He taught us that God is merciful, welcoming, ready to forgive, and yet we crucified Him, all with His consent. Now, in the greatest act of sacrifice, He comes to earth minute by minute in the hands of His priests, uniting through the Eucharist His sinless Body with our sinful one. St. Peter Julian Eymard puts this very clearly. "He (the priest) commands that God be on the altar, and on the instant, God is there. . . . Our Lord has never disobeyed His priest. . . . A weak, mortal creature gives birth to our sacramental Jesus!" (The Real Presence: Eucharistic Mediations, p. 56).

To develop our love of Christ, we should meditate on the roles He has played for us.

<u>Creator</u>: From God the Father, through Christ the Son, by the power of the Holy Spirit, all things came to be and are held in being. All things. That includes us. Do we ever think that we are here only because God willed us? And that we remain alive because of His will? That we will live eternally because of the will of God? What did we ever do to deserve being created? What can we ever do to deserve eternal bliss?

<u>Brother</u>: Christ told us that He is our brother. A brother is one with whom we are utterly familiar. We can joke with our brother and tell him things we wouldn't think of telling someone else, even a close friend. Can we relate to Jesus as brother? What does this mean to you?

<u>Spouse</u>: A union with a spouse is one of intimate and private sharing. A spouse is to know all about us, but even a human spouse may not know the deepest thoughts in our hearts. Yet Jesus wishes to be our Divine Spouse. He desires the most intimate union of love with us. He wishes us to share with Him every part of our spirits including the good, the bad, and the ugly! He knows what we are thinking and feeling anyway. To share these with our Lord is to give Him access to the most intimate recesses of our beings.

<u>Redeemer</u>: To redeem means to buy back, to liberate, to free by force, to ransom. Only something that is in possession of someone else can be redeemed. If we think we are free, then we certainly are not going to be looking for a redeemer because we will think that we don't need one. Only if we realize that we are subject to sin and held prisoner by it can we see the need for our redemption. How can we be freed from the power sin holds over us? Only by the redeeming grace of God.

Jesus is Creator, Brother, Spouse, Redeemer. All these roles involve tremendous Love and hence tremendous sacrifice on God's part. When we see how God has sacrificed for us, we should be moved to imitate Him and sacrifice for Him. As penitents, we are called to imitate Christ. We can only do this if we know Christ, and we can only know Him if we learn about Him.

To learn about Him, we must read about Him in the Gospels and meditate on the messages found there. Then we need to go beyond this and put into practice what we have learned. The Beatitudes, "Blessed are the meek, the pure of heart, those who mourn, the suffering," and so on, are meant to be guidelines for us. We are to be meek and humble before Christ and in the presence of others. We are to be peacemakers. We are to be pure. We are to mourn for our sins and for the sins of the world. We are to hunger and thirst for righteousness, for those who hunger and thirst for anything strive to alleviate their hunger and thirst.

In a word, we are to beg God's grace to subjugate our sinful nature to God's will and to embrace what may be difficult and perhaps even physically harmful if it is for the good of another. By behaving these ways, we are showing love. We love God because He first loved us. Love means sacrifice. It means death of the will to do the will of God. "The measure of love," said one of the saints, "is to love without measure." Love is always willing to die for the beloved.

God, Who is Love, died for us. How much are we willing to die to ourselves for love of Him?

BRIEFLY ANSWER THE FOLLOWING QUESTIONS

1. Describe your relationship with Jesus.
2. What title do you use most often for Christ? Creator? Brother? Spouse? Redeemer? Friend?
3. How far do you think you would go in your love of Christ?

LESSON ON THE RULE

Look at Chapter VII, VISITING THE SICK/BURYING THE DEAD, sections 22 to 24, of the Rule and Constitutions. Why do you think penitents are to exhort their ill brothers and sisters in Christ to penance (conversion)?

If a fellow penitent dies, what obligations does a penitent have regarding the funeral? What prayers are to be said for the soul of the deceased?

LESSON ON THE FRANCISCAN VIRTUES

In Franciscan Virtues, read Virtue 5: Detachment. Spend at least five minutes meditating on the virtue. Answer the questions. Share your answers with your formator.

DAILY GOSPEL READING AND QUESTIONS FROM CHRIST IN THE GOSPEL

Daily read Christ in the Gospel and answer for yourself the questions on the day's reading, found in the back of the book.

Select one reading or section of the Gospel that particularly resonated with you. Share that passage and your thoughts with your formator.

FIFTH MONTH'S ACTIVITIES

- One way to show love for others is to pray for the dead. As penitents, we are to yearly pray the entire Psalter for our deceased Confraternity members. The easiest way to do this is to pray every day one Psalm or a portion of a Psalm with this intention in mind. This month, in addition to the prayers that you are already praying, begin with the first Psalm and pray one Psalm daily (or portion of a larger Psalm) for deceased members, adding a Glory Be after the Psalm and the words, "Eternal rest grant unto them, O Lord, and let perpetual light shine upon them. May their souls and the souls of all the faithful departed rest in peace. Amen."
- Submit your answers to this month's questions to your CFP formator.

POSTULANT: LESSON SIX

<u>The Secret of Sanctity</u>

Some people have misconceptions about saints. They mistakenly believe that saints were extraordinary people who, once converted, never experienced the temptations that the rest of us undergo. The saints were superior in their sanctity, workers of miracles, stigmatists, prophets, superhuman in enduring physical suffering, torture, and death. Saints fasted to extremes, performed severe bodily penances, prayed for hours, slept little. Believing that such heroism is totally beyond their grasp, most people are certain that they could never be saints.

When someone asked Blessed Mother Teresa of Calcutta if she knew that people called her a saint, she replied, "I try to be one. Don't you?" Blessed Teresa had the right idea. We are ALL called to be saints. Everyone in heaven is a saint. Don't we hope to go there?

If we are called to be saints, but we can't pray all night or live on half a roll a day, if we've never performed a miracle or healed anyone, if we are scared stiff of torture, how in the world will we ever be saints? The answer is quite simple. We will be saints by being all that God has called us to be.

You see, God wants us to live with Him eternally in heaven. Since this is His desire, wouldn't it be unjust of Him not to provide the means for us to fulfill His plan? God has given every person the means to become a saint. The secret is that the means is not the same for every person.

The path to sanctity for Saint Francis was not the same path that Saint Dominic or Saint Anne or Saint Gregory the Great took. All the paths led to God, but every path was tailor-made to the saint who was walking it. We make the greatest error when we try to imitate the saints by doing what they did instead of asking God what He wants us to do and then doing that.

The secret of sanctity is not doing miracles or having ecstasies. It is not founding Orders or being martyred for Christ. The secret of sanctity is surrender.

Surrender! Surrender to God's plan for us. Not surrender to God's plan for the woman who prays five rosaries a day or the man who is our parish deacon. Not God's plan for

Father X or Sister Y but God's plan for us. Do we honestly believe that God has a plan for us personally? Not just a general outline, "I want you to know, love, and serve Me in this world so you can be happy with Me in the next", but a very specific plan that God intends to work out in our behalf if only we allow Him to do so.

God's path to sanctity is different for each person. Pray to find the path for you and walk in it. Your path. Your way to holiness. Yours, not someone else's. To be totally conformed to God's will for you is to become a saint because God wills you to be holy, to be a saint. Our prayers should be, not "God, do You want me to be a saint?" but "Lord, let me not 'mess up' Your plan."

How can we know God's plan for us? First, by prayer and by reading and meditating on Scripture. Ask God to reveal His plan to you. Then wait for an answer. If God tarries, it is not because He has no plan for you. It is because you are not yet mature enough to follow it or because the time is not yet right for the next step. We have to be at the level of spiritual maturity that corresponds to each step of the plan. Maybe we have to grow deeper spiritually before God reveals the next step of the plan to us. Maybe God is even now working out the next phase, putting all the pieces together. At the right time, we will know. If we continue to pray, to listen to God's still, small voice within, if we continue to read Scripture and meditate on it, asking God to speak to us through it, God will guide us. Often He is guiding when we least suspect it. We must be patient, trusting, peaceful. We must walk with the plan, not rushing ahead, not lagging behind.

We must also not wish to know more than what God reveals to us at the time. Scripture calls God's word a "lamp to our feet." Think of walking at night with a lantern. A lantern lights up the path before you and around you, but in the distance, everything is dark. God promises to give us enough light to see our way, one step at a time. He never promised to light up the entire path. We will have enough of His light to take one step forward in the path that He has prepared, but what is farther along we must leave to His wisdom and providence. Our job is not to know everything but to trust what we do know and to follow.

God calls us to surrender to His plan for us. We can only do that if we give God ALL of ourselves. Recall the story of the widow's mite (Luke 21: 1-4). Jesus commended the widow for putting into the Temple treasury ALL she had. It didn't seem like a lot but it was more than others gave because it was ALL she had.

We may not have the elaborate spiritual gifts common to some canonized saints. That's because we don't need them to be holy. To be holy, we must give God what we have, i.e., our wills, our lives. God does not want fifty percent or seventy five percent or even ninety percent. He wants 100 percent. God wants ALL of us.

This is total surrender. This is the secret of sanctity. The ultimate purpose of the Rule for the Confraternity of Penitents is to foster in the penitent this attitude of total surrender. When penitents surrender their wills to the daily discipline of the Rule, they are not only glorifying God by their prayers and mortification but they are also practicing surrender to Him. By voluntarily surrendering what is desirable for the sake of greater, spiritual gains, penitents become more docile to the will of God Who, in time, may ask them to surrender far more, i.e., their worldly plans, time, health, possessions, loved ones. We cannot be totally surrendered to God if we are attached to anything else. By practicing detachment through the Rule, penitents should be more likely than others to say, "Lord, Your will, not mine, be done."

To be totally surrendered to God requires moral courage. Penitents will soon discover this if they share the Rule with others who think it is "archaic, medieval". Why would anyone want to do such a thing? Surrounded by all sorts of tantalizing choices and an array of easily accessible foods, clothing, and possessions, those who are not called to this way of life might think that living the Rule seems ridiculously unnecessary, even severe. We must be sure that, if God has called us to this, then it is His will that we embrace it. Living the Rule is part of our path to sanctity and to ultimate union with Our Lord.

BRIEFLY ANSWER THE FOLLOWING QUESTIONS

1. Do I believe that God has a specific plan for my life?
2. How have I seen His hand at work in my life to this point?
3. What does total surrender mean to me?

LESSON ON THE RULE

Look over Chapter V: THE SACRAMENTS, OTHER MATTERS, section 15 of the Rule and Constitutions. What is the spiritual goal of this section?

A tithe is 10% of one's income usually taken from one's gross income. Why do you think tithing is part of this Rule?

Study sections 16, 17, and 18 of the Rule and the Constitutions. Choose one of these sections and discuss it relative to your life.

LESSON ON THE FRANCISCAN VIRTUES

In Franciscan Virtues, read Virtue 6: Discernment. Spend at least five minutes meditating on the virtue. Answer the questions. Share your answers with your formator.

DAILY GOSPEL READING AND QUESTIONS FROM CHRIST IN THE GOSPEL

Daily read Christ in the Gospel and answer for yourself the questions on the day's reading, found in the back of the book.

Select one reading or section of the Gospel that particularly resonated with you. Share that passage and your thoughts with your formator.

SIXTH MONTH'S ACTIVITIES

- Begin receiving the Sacrament of Reconciliation monthly.
- Submit your answers to this month's questions to your CFP formator.

POSTULANT: LESSON SEVEN

A Life of Prayer

People center their lives around an infinite number of things. Family, work, recreation, sports, hobbies, travel, even pets. Penitents are called to center their lives on God. This means that, ultimately, the "work" of a penitent's life is prayer. St. Paul advised the early Christians to "Pray constantly" (1 Thessalonians 5:17). This penitents must do.

How can penitents "pray constantly" when they are living in the world, raising families, holding down jobs, and being involved in a wide range of social issues and charitable works? Praying constantly is possible because every single moment of a penitent's life must be a prayer. The prayer may be one of actual words in praying the Divine Office or reading Scripture. It may be a prayer of silent presence before the Lord at Eucharistic Adoration, or in contemplative prayer. It may be a prayer of sleeping in the arms of God, trusting Him for the night and the morrow. Or it may be a prayer of daily activity in which all that we do is done in the name of Jesus and to and for those in whom we see, sometimes with great difficulty, Christ Himself.

Prayer is the "lifting of the heart and mind to God." A Benedictine aphorism is, "To work is to pray." To work is to pray when we lift our minds and hearts to God as we work, when we know Whom we serve and for Whom we work. As penitents, we must strive to see Christ, not only in the "distressing disguise of the poor," but also in the distressing disguise of the rebellious, the insolent, the rude, the bossy, and the domineering. We need to see Christ in our boss, our spouse, our kids, our neighbors, our clients, and in the driver who cuts us off on the interstate. We are to serve and, if duty requires, obey Christ in all these people. This is not easy! How can we do it?

Our prayer life should help us begin to see Christ in the people whom He has created. We should begin to separate the imperfections and sins from the potential glory of a soul centered on God. No matter how depraved a soul may be, while life exists, the potential exists as well for conversion and holiness. A life of prayer should help us see this potential in others.

During the First Year of Novice Formation as penitents, you will come to spend about ninety minutes daily in vocal and mental prayer, unless you are given other options by your spiritual director whom you will have by that time. Penitents have many choices regarding their prayer lives. Here are a few:

- Pray the complete Divine Office which is the official prayer of the Church, daily prayed by clergy and religious everywhere in the world.
- Pray the Psalms
- Pray another office such as the Little Office of the Blessed Virgin
- Pray a fifteen decade rosary, meditating on all the mysteries of Christ's life as they involved Him and His Mother
- Spend an hour in mental prayer, using Scripture or other spiritual reading as a point of departure for meditating on the attributes and actions of God.
- Spend an hour a day in contemplative prayer, just loving the Lord without words or thoughts in some quiet, restful, place.
- With a spiritual director, devise another workable option such as making brief, pious prayers throughout the day

As postulants, you are not obligated to spend ninety minutes per day in prayer. But you should pray daily. You have already embarked on the prayer life of a penitent by praying certain Psalms in the morning and the evening and by praying the Apostles' Creed. Prayer is critical because it is time spent with God. We must spend time with God if we are to know His plan for our lives. Therefore, for penitents whose goal is to be totally surrendered to God's will for them, prayer must have top priority.

It is through prayer, Scripture reading, and meditation that we come to know God, not just know about Him. Atheists can study about God and know about Him, but they do not know Him. Certainly when we know someone, we know something about that person. But we may not know everything or even many things. Think of your best friend. How much do you know about this person? How much don't you know? Even if there are many details that you don't know, e.g., childhood experiences, favorite colors, your friend's worst trauma, you still love your friend. Why? Because you and your friend have shared thoughts and feelings on the deepest level of your being. You and your friend can talk together, laugh and cry together, and encourage each other. Friendship is much more than knowing about someone. It is knowing the spirit of the friend. Every penitent must strive to know the Spirit of God.

To know God, not just know about Him, means that the penitent will love God because all His traits are lovable. Because we know and love God, we can trust Him, for who can really trust someone whom he does not know or love? We may trust the police officer, the store clerk, and the teacher because we have been taught to trust those who hold those offices. But if we met the police officer, store clerk, or teacher on the street, having never met them before, would we trust them the way we would trust our friends? Love and knowledge spawns trust.

To the degree that we know and love God, to that degree will we surrender to Him. If we do not yet totally trust and totally love God, we will not yet totally surrender to

Him. We will still hold onto some parts of our lives and some parts of our wills. We will give God permission to work when we are fairly sure that the outcome will be favorable. But if we have our doubts, we will take matters back into our own hands. This is how we act when our trust and love are still imperfect.

We must always strive to know, love, and trust God in an ever deeper way. Then we will more deeply surrender our wills, our plans, our lives, our families, our ideas, our possessions to Him. To be totally united to God, we must be totally surrendered to Him. We are to say, "Lord, You may do whatever you want with me and with all that I have and desire. Everything I have and everything I am is Yours. Do with me as You will." This is total surrender. When we are totally surrendered to God, we will know beyond a doubt that His hand is active in all things and His Spirit present in all peoples, even the most distressing. Prayer is to lead to this.

BRIEFLY ANSWER THE FOLLOWING QUESTIONS

1. What place does prayer have in your life right now? What place should it have?
2. Explain how you believe prayer can lead a person to total surrender to God.
3. How is it possible to see God in others?

LESSON ON THE RULE

Look at Chapter IV: PRAYER, of the Rule and Constitutions. Find the paragraphs under section 12 that deal with the specific morning and evening psalms prayed by penitents and the Creed. Are you praying these daily? Do you notice any difference in your spiritual life because of your praying these daily?

The Rule and Constitutions ask that Night Prayer (Compline) be prayed each night. Begin a simple form of Night Prayer this month, if not from the Divine Office, at least perhaps a psalm.

LESSON ON THE FRANCISCAN VIRTUES

In Franciscan Virtues, read Virtue 7: Eagerness. Spend at least five minutes meditating on the virtue. Answer the questions. Share your answers with your formator.

DAILY GOSPEL READING AND QUESTIONS FROM CHRIST IN THE GOSPEL

Daily read Christ in the Gospel and answer for yourself the questions on the day's reading, found in the back of the book.

Select one reading or section of the Gospel that particularly resonated with you. Share that passage and your thoughts with your formator.

SEVENTH MONTH'S ACTIVITIES

- Begin to make a nightly examination of conscience followed by an Act of Contrition.
- Submit your answers to this month's questions to your CFP formator.

POSTULANT: LESSON EIGHT

The Blessed Virgin as a Model

Every day every penitent offers a prayer of consecration to Our Lady. Every Chapter or Circle meeting is to begin the same way. The Marian Consecration prayer dedicates both the community, however great or small, and all its members to the Blessed Mother, using titles for Mary taken from Scripture, from sacred writings, and from the teachings of the saints. The prayer asks Mary to obtain for us the true spirit of the Gospel and to make us instruments of Christ to convert sinners, to sanctify souls, and to strengthen and renew our Church, all goals which Mary herself achieved.

When the angel approached Mary at the annunciation, he addressed her, "Hail, full of grace." Who of us is full of grace? Yet, as penitents, we should pray to be "full of grace." Grace is the undeserved gift of God that enables us to willingly and joyfully conform all our human will to all God's divine will. Mary needed God's grace to do this and so do we. But, unlike us, Mary was "full of grace" from conception, the only person (other than Christ Who was fully both human and divine) who never needed a conversion. Mary's sinless soul was always totally conformed to God's will.

This is why the angel could truthfully say, "the Lord is with you." She was with God and He with her. "Blessed are you among women," indeed among all humanity after Christ. In her humility, Mary did not see herself as being "full of grace" or "blessed" above others nor could she ever possibly imagine that the promised Messiah would come through her. Mary's holiness was hidden from herself.

The saints say that Mary, because of her total conformity to God's will, had already birthed Christ in her heart before she conceived Him in her womb. The saints also tell us that we are to be the mothers of Christ, meaning that we, too, will birth Him spiritually if we totally, joyfully, and trustingly give Him free rein in our lives. If we allow Christ to direct us, He will enable us to evangelize others by our actions, love, and/or words.

Saint Francis is reported to have said, "Preach always. If necessary, use words." God desires that all people know and love Him; if we follow Christ, He will give us opportunities to spread His message.

Mary did not refuse the angel's request nor complain about the hardships it might entail. Nor did she question how it was to come about beyond reminding the angel that she had taken a vow of virginity. When the angel assured her that the conception of the Lord would not harm that virginity, Mary replied, "I am the handmaid of the Lord. Be it done unto me according to thy word." We must make these words ours. We must be the servants of the Lord, allowing Him to freely do with us as He wills. Thus we will grow in holiness; we will move toward union with God, the goal for which we were created.

How fully Mary lived her faith and trust in God! She bore the Lord in a stable, fled with Him to Egypt, and lived in poverty in an obscure town. If she, the holy Mother of Christ, was not spared hardship, should we who are less holy complain about our own sufferings? Scripture states that we must "make up what is lacking in the sufferings of Christ." As penitents, we need to look to Mary to see how to trustingly embrace suffering, knowing that it is one of God's primary means to detach us from worldly attachments.

How empty Mary's life was without the Lord is shown when Jesus was lost in the temple. Upon finding Him, Mary asked Him, "Son, why have You done this to us?" How often have we asked that question when God does something we cannot understand, something that makes us lose sight of God? Then we, too, must search for Christ as Mary did, and we, too, will find Him in His Father's house, the Church. Do we look there for Him? In times of trial, do we turn to prayer, the sacraments, and our spiritual director?

How did Mary deal with problems? She noticed one at the wedding feast in Cana. The wine had run out. Mary did not tell Christ how to solve the problem. She only brought it to His attention. Then she told the servants, "Do whatever He tells you." As penitents, we must curb the impulse to tell God how to run His world or solve its problems. We must instead pray to Him about the difficulties and then we must "do whatever He tells us" about them. In prayer, through reading, and through counsel with our spiritual directors, we will come to know, if we are patient, how God is directing us. Everything in life can be used by God to make someone a saint, that is someone who lives eternally with God. This is God's goal.

Mary was so perfectly united to God's will that she could be, as much as humanly possible, one with her Son in His passion and death. We see her on the way to Calvary and at the foot of the Cross. We see her again in the upper room at Pentecost. Mary's faith in God and acceptance of His will never wavered. Through her fidelity she gave Christ to us; through His fidelity, He redeemed us. Mary shows us that, if we unite ourselves to God's will in the trials of our lives, we will pass through them to God's blessings and to renewed gifts of the Holy Spirit.

Some things in life we learn only by suffering. Some attachments we release only because of suffering. As penitents, we must embrace these sufferings as Mary embraced hers, not always understanding but always trusting the better judgment of God Who sends them our way.

Mary is the Queen of heaven and earth, the one through whom Christ became human. In this sense, she is said to be the Mediatrix of all Graces since God, from Whom all grace comes, was birthed through her. At the foot of the cross, Christ made His own Mother ours. Before her Son, Mary pleads for us, her "adopted" children. We must pray for the grace to become worthy children of so worthy a Mother and faithful images of our Brother the Lord.

BRIEFLY ANSWER THE FOLLOWING QUESTIONS

1. Can I view Mary as a model for penitents? Why?
2. Would I want God to give me the gifts He gave to Mary? Why or Why not?
3. What aspects of Mary's life relate to my own life?

LESSON ON THE RULE

Look at Chapter IV: PRAYER, of the Rule and Constitutions, section 12. Why do you think penitents are to consecrate themselves to Mary daily?

LESSON ON THE FRANCISCAN VIRTUES

In Franciscan Virtues, read Virtue 8: Empathy. Spend at least five minutes meditating on the virtue. Answer the questions. Share your answers with your formator.

DAILY GOSPEL READING AND QUESTIONS FROM CHRIST IN THE GOSPEL

Daily read Christ in the Gospel and answer for yourself the questions on the day's reading, found in the back of the book.

Select one reading or section of the Gospel that particularly resonated with you. Share that passage and your thoughts with your formator.

EIGHTH MONTH'S ACTIVITIES

- Pray the Marian Consecration prayer, or a prayer of consecration of your own choosing, to Our Lady daily.
- If possible, pray at least a five decade Rosary daily. Praying a fifteen decade Rosary is one prayer option that you can choose in First Year Formation. Praying the Rosary is a source of great graces.
- Look over the Corporal and Spiritual Works of Mercy as written in the Constitutions, Appendix D. Embrace one of these as a special apostolate of love for God and others.
- Submit your answers to this month's questions to your CFP formator.

POSTULANT: LESSON NINE

A Spirit of Mortification

Mortification is almost a forgotten word in today's culture. Mortification means giving up what is legitimate, pleasurable, and good for the sake of conversion and union with God. It is any conscious form of self denial done for spiritual ends.

Jesus spoke of mortification when He said, "Whoever wishes to be My follower must deny his very self" (Luke 9:23). This denial of self means denial of things we desire in order to grasp that which we should desire more deeply, namely union with God. St. Anthony used a metaphor to explain this idea. If a glass is full of water, it cannot be full of wine. Wine can be poured into a glass only when the water is poured out. To the extent that water is poured out of the glass, to that extent can wine be poured in. We are like glasses. When we are totally full of ourselves, God cannot fill us with Himself. To the extent that we empty ourselves of ourselves, to that extent can God fill us with Himself. Mortification is the act of emptying the glass.

Mortification is not mortification if done for anything other than spiritual good. To give up sweets in order to diet may be just as difficult as giving them up in order to foster detachment from them. But the ends differ. In the first case, the person wishes to lose physical weight. In the second, the person hopes to drop the baggage of attachment to things of the appetite.

Mortification involves the entire pleasure urge in one's body, mind, and soul. A person craves sweets in his mind, savors them with his tongue, and longs for them in his soul. To give them up for the sake of growing closer with God is to say, "Lord, I want You to take a higher place in my life than chocolate."

Mortification is important, but it must be practiced with discretion. This is one reason why the Constitutions for the Confraternity of Penitents insist that every penitent have a spiritual director. A spiritual director will see that penitents who wish to practice mortification beyond that in the Rule do so wisely. A spiritual director will also be able to help penitents, who have health or other limitations, determine whether the mortification in the Rule should be practiced or modified.

The Rule for the Confraternity of Penitents is grounded on a three-legged stool of mortification. The first leg, worked on during the First Year of Formation, is mortification of time. By requiring the penitent to spend about ninety minutes of the day in prayer, the Rule is saying, "Prayer must have first place in your life. In order to make time for this much prayer, you may have to detach yourself from other legitimate pleasures." Perhaps you must relinquish your favorite news program or newspaper. Perhaps you must turn off the snooze alarm the first time or forgo that extra cup of coffee in order to have the time to pray. For many people, mortification of time is the most difficult and yet most beneficial part of the Rule. In this mortification, penitents model Jesus Who, despite how busy He was, constantly took time to pray.

The second mortification, worked on during the Second Year of Formation, is mortification of the appetite. The days of fast and abstinence in the Rule are intended to detach the penitent from gluttony and desire for foods. Jesus practiced this mortification as well. Recall how He fasted for forty days in the wilderness before beginning His mission and then observed the other days of fast and abstinence common to the Jews.

The mortification involving food has much in common with some aspects of modern culture. Vegetarians eat no meat ever. The penitent is limited to eating meat three days per week. Dieters watch their food intake carefully for weeks and months. Penitents fast daily except Sundays during Lent and Advent and fast throughout the year on Fridays and part of the year on Wednesdays. While vegetarians and dieters are fasting and abstaining for health or other reasons, penitents do so for the sake of spiritual growth. The mortification undertaken is certainly not difficult for penitents, who should be a bit hungry on fast days, but not famished.

In the Third Year of Formation, the penitent begins to practice mortification in the area of clothing. This mortification mirrors that of Christ Who relinquished His heavenly glory to be clothed in human flesh. Moreover, while on this earth, He wore only the plainest, meanest clothes. Penitents are not asked to wear poor clothing but only to limit their wardrobe in specific ways. Such mortification is intended to help the penitent detach from personal possessions and appearance.

A penitent can and should still look attractive, but the wardrobe he or she uses is limited in colors. Thus some penitents will have to give away to others their favorite clothes. Giving away one's favorite clothes can be a penance that will bring great fruit. It may help for a penitent to realize that, at death, all one's clothes will be given away anyway. Better to begin now and reap the spiritual fruit of detachment.

Moreover, the clothing colors permitted in the Rule and Constitutions are varied enough to hide from others what the penitent is doing. Thus, the penitent is spared the satisfaction of having others know how self sacrificing he has been in weeding out his wardrobe. The idea that "I will give up all the things I like and no one will even know" is perhaps the greatest mortification in that it directly attacks the vice of spiritual pride.

Spiritual pride is deadly to anyone, but particularly to a penitent. For this reason, all mortification is to be done without fanfare and without discussion with others outside the Confraternity of Penitents. No penitent should be praised for his or her mortification because no one but other penitents should know about them. Moreover, the penitent must bear in mind that the penance in the Rule is not excessively difficult or restrictive.

Poor people in underdeveloped nations practice such mortification daily because they never have enough to eat or wear. Most penitents have many more things to eat and wear than do the marginalized poor. So penitents have nothing at all of which they can be spiritually proud. If mortification is done in a spirit of humility and surrender to God's will through the Rule, then the fruits of performing them will be great. Penitents will begin to find that they have attained a new degree of trust and peace in whatever befalls them.

BRIEFLY ANSWER THE FOLLOWING QUESTIONS

1. How do you feel about the mortification in the Rule?
2. What can it do for you?
3. Do you believe that God will give you the grace to embrace mortification when the time comes to practice it?

LESSON ON THE RULE

Look at Chapters II: ABSTINENCE, and III: FASTING, of the Rule and Constitutions as well as Appendix A to the Constitutions. Remember that postulants need not embrace the full fasting and abstinence provisions of this way of life until the second year of Novice formation. Postulants, however, should begin to abstain from eating meat on Fridays of the year. Note how the Rule and Constitutions define fasting and abstinence.

What precautions should penitents take when doing fasting and abstinence?

Look at section 7 of the Rule and Constitutions. What prayer is a penitent to pray before and after meals?

Why do you think sections 9 and 11 are in the Rule and Constitutions?

LESSON ON THE FRANCISCAN VIRTUES

In Franciscan Virtues, read Virtue 9: Encouragement. Spend at least five minutes meditating on the virtue. Answer the questions. Share your answers with your formator.

DAILY GOSPEL READING AND QUESTIONS FROM CHRIST IN THE GOSPEL

Daily read Christ in the Gospel and answer for yourself the questions on the day's reading, found in the back of the book.

Select one reading or section of the Gospel that particularly resonated with you. Share that passage and your thoughts with your formator.

NINTH MONTH'S ACTIVITIES

- Begin to abstain from meat on every Friday of the year with the exception of Church Solemnities and special celebrations. Pray an Our Father, or another from of meal blessing, before and after every meal.
- Submit your answers to this month's questions to your CFP formator.

POSTULANT: LESSON TEN

<u>Choosing a Spiritual Director</u>

The Constitutions for the Confraternity of Penitents require that every brother and sister, beginning in the First Year Novitiate, have a spiritual director. All penitents are to have spiritual directors as long as they are living the Rule. Why?

The Rule and Constitutions for the Confraternity of Penitents are intended to foster in the penitent the discipline, faith, and detachment needed to foster total surrender to and union with God's will in prayer, works of mercy, and contemplation. Guidance from a competent director is crucial to this progression. A penitent can encounter many difficulties.

Is the penitent living the penitential life in its spirit or is he or she too lax or too scrupulous? Are the inner promptings and/or revelations that the penitent receives truly from God? Is the penitent being led by the Spirit of God or by his or her own personal desires? What is the best way for the penitent to deal with obstacles and sufferings? Does the penitent have a good balance between prayer, activity, and relaxation? If God begins to draw the penitent into the dark nights of the soul that precede contemplative prayer, what should be the penitent's response to the possible confusion, frustration, and questioning that these dark nights can bring? An experienced spiritual director can give guidance in all these matters.

A penitent must remember that, to grow in sanctity and to reach the highest levels of prayer, he or she is to confide everything to the spiritual director and must obey the director's guidance. Therefore, the penitent must choose a spiritual director with whom he or she feels comfortable, someone the penitent can trust. A spiritual director offers spiritual guidance. He (she) is not a marriage, family, or addiction counselor nor a psychologist. Nor should he (she) be at odds with the Church on any issue. The spiritual director may be a priest, deacon, or a male or female religious, but not generally a lay person. A priest is to be preferred because the penitent can then also go to confession with the spiritual director. However, many people have both a spiritual director and a confessor (someone from whom they regularly receive the Sacrament of Reconciliation). Spiritual direction is best done in person, but spiritual direction by mail, telephone, or private email is also allowed.

The best way to choose a spiritual director is to determine who might be a good first choice and then make an appointment with that person to discuss your prayer life and desire for conversion as a penitent. One logical candidate is the penitent's regular confessor. At this first meeting, be honest. Tell the potential director about your yearning for holiness and your discovery of the Confraternity of Penitents. Share the Rule and Constitutions with the spiritual director. Ask the potential director if he or she might be able to help you progress on this way of penance (conversion) into union with God.

Ask yourself these questions about your spiritual director:

- Am I comfortable with this person?
- Can I understand how this person expresses himself or herself?
- Could I confide my innermost self in confidence to this individual?
- Is this person perceptive? Able to give me concrete guidance?
- Does this person understand contemplation and do they accept the idea that God intends contemplation for everyone, not just for a select few?
- Is he (she) in total communion with the Roman Catholic Church?
- Can he (she) guide me without making me slavishly dependent?
- Can this person understand and accept different spiritual temperaments and prayer styles?
- Does he (she) use the Gospel as the primary mode of guidance? Does he (she) seem accepting of the CFP way of life?

All these questions must be answered with a "yes" before the individual can qualify as a logical spiritual director. If they are, ask the person if he (she) might consent to be your spiritual director. If the answer is affirmative, give the person a copy of the Rule and Constitutions. Request a second appointment.

At the second appointment, discuss the Rule and Constitutions, and ask for spiritual direction. You should be able to confirm that this person is right for you by what they say. Ask how frequently you should meet. Formulate what you would be discussing in your sessions. Bring the matter to prayer as well.

If you would be seeking a spiritual director by mail, phone, or email, it is best to have a phone conversation for these first two meetings. That way you and the possible director can get to know each other and have a sense of who each of you are.

Be prepared to change. A good spiritual director will see the darkness and the light that you may have hidden in yourself. He (she) will not be content to let you be as you are. The spiritual director's job is to help you become who God intends you to fully be. This means change for you, good change, but change nevertheless. You can only surrender to

God's will for you if you are willing to face yourself as you are. This a spiritual director will help you do.

Certainly if you have difficulty with what your spiritual director tells you to do, discuss it. Understand the reasons why your director is guiding you in a certain way. Pray to accept these reasons. A good spiritual director will never tell you to do anything unethical or immoral, but he (she) may have you change certain ways you do things, cut back on certain activities, alter your prayer life, and so on. This you must do if you wish to grow spiritually.

If you are having a great deal of difficulty because it seems that your spiritual director does not understand you, speak to another trustworthy priest or religious for help in discernment. Often the problem lies, not with the director, but with the penitent who does not wish to face the truth. We are often not good judges of ourselves. We need to trust the director's judgment. If you cannot do this, either you need to change yourself or else you need a director whom you can trust.

BRIEFLY ANSWER THE FOLLOWING QUESTIONS

1. Am I eager for spiritual direction?
2. What aspects of my life, especially my prayer life, would I like to discuss with a spiritual director?
3. Can I confide my innermost thoughts to another person?
4. Am I willing to make the changes in my life that I will need in order to grow in sanctity?

LESSON ON THE RULE

Look at the ADDENDUM to the Constitutions of the Confraternity.

Why is a spiritual director necessary to a penitent? What will a good relationship with a spiritual director be like?

Look at Chapter VII: VISITING THE SICK/BURYING THE DEAD, of the Rule and Constitutions, especially sections 25 to 34.

Why do you think each of these are important to the penitential life?

LESSON ON THE FRANCISCAN VIRTUES

In Franciscan Virtues, read Virtue 10: Eucharist. Spend at least five minutes meditating on the virtue. Answer the questions. Share your answers with your formator.

DAILY GOSPEL READING AND QUESTIONS FROM CHRIST IN THE GOSPEL

Daily read Christ in the Gospel and answer for yourself the questions on the day's reading, found in the back of the book.

Select one reading or section of the Gospel that particularly resonated with you. Share that passage and your thoughts with your formator.

TENTH MONTH'S ACTIVITIES

- Continue your prayer life as you have been doing.
- Continue to abstain on Fridays.
- Continue to wear the crucifix or cross.
- Continue to go to Confession monthly.
- Make a list of people who could be possible spiritual directors for you. Go over the list, numbering your choices from one to five with the person you think you'd feel most comfortable with as number one. Feel free to review your list with your Chapter or Circle Minster, Regional Minister, or with any other leader in the Confraternity. They may be able to help guide you. Contact the first person on your list, and see if he or she is comfortable offering you spiritual direction. If not, proceed to your second choice and so on down the list. Remember, you do not need a spiritual director until the first year of the Novitiate.
- Submit your answers to this month's questions to your CFP formator.

POSTULANT: LESSON ELEVEN

A Life of Penance

Penance is defined as conversion, as doing's things God's way instead of our own. When God's way conflicts with ours, we chose His plans. He will let us know His plans when we embark on a penitential life.

Our life is like a garden. A garden is a place where flowers, herbs, fruits, and vegetables are cultivated and grow. To be fruitful, a garden requires work.

First the soil must be tilled, turned over, and the rocks picked out. Clumps of grass must be removed, clods of dirt broken apart. Isn't this how conversion begins? God enters our consciousness and we feel dug into, sifted, pulled apart. What our lives had been, they are no longer. We are like an upturned field, once with its own wild but unkempt beauty but now, to our untrained eye, barren and ugly. What satisfied before now satisfies no longer. But nothing has yet taken its place.

Then God begins to increase the fertility of the garden of our soul. Into us He pours the right amount of grace, making our souls fertile enough to grow the flowers, fruits, and vegetables He intends to plant. At this stage of conversion, we do not see growth nor do we understand grace. We only know that, despite our losing what had thrilled us before, we feel an odd but real peace. We know something is coming. We do not know what.

Into this prepared ground, God plants the seed of what He calls us to do, to be. It is this purpose that He has envisioned for us from all eternity. It was for the growth of this seed that He created us. Now we are ready. We feel something moving within us, something swelling. It is strangely exhilarating, but we don't know what it is.

The seed grows; the plant begins to take form. We begin to sense what it is that God has called us to do. It is wondrously satisfying even though a bit frightening in its power, beauty, and usefulness. We begin to understand, we begin to embrace, this plan. We begin to feel a deep wonder and gratitude to God.

At this stage, as the young growth moves toward maturity, we find the old life, the old ways creeping up on us, crowding us, threatening to suffocate the seed. We may not recognize these desires, options, or busyness as weeds, but weeds they are. At first, we think that we can ignore them because they are small and the beautiful goal that God is growing in us seems so much larger and stronger than the peppering of weeds about us. But the weeds grow quickly, more quickly and wildly than the new growth. They begin to choke the growth. Precisely at this stage conversion often dies, and the garden of the soul becomes once again overgrown with vices and activity that squeeze out thoughts of God.

Here, at this stage, we must work the hardest. We must recognize the weeds of the past for what they are, and we must be ruthless with them. We must uproot, not simply break off, the weeds. We must shake the dirt from their roots and toss these habits onto the fire of God's consuming power. Some weeds will be easy to eliminate. Others will require more effort. A few will be so deeply rooted that we must go after them with shovel or plow. The implements to uproot the weeds are the sacraments of Eucharist and Confession and the virtue of Persistent Prayer. With God's grace, we will overcome and eliminate the forces that threaten the new life within. We will clear the garden of our soul so that God's new growth will push upward toward the Son.

When the weeds are out, the garden again looks barren except for the new growth. But we have learned something. We cannot take for granted that weeds will not again come. We begin now to mulch the plants, piling grass, leaves, and straw about their roots to keep in moisture, add nutrients, and prevent the seeds of any weeds from sprouting again. The mulch is like the friends with whom we associate, new friends who will foster the new growth within us. Their words are like fertilizer to our souls; their friendship keeps us supple with the warm, sweet dew of God. For us, these friends are our brothers and sisters in the Confraternity. They are the mulch that bolsters our spiritual growth.

We now seem to be growing stronger, grander. But then the unexpected happens. Something is plucked from our lives. Then something else. What is happening? God is pruning our lives to make us bear more and better fruit. Too many little shoots on the plant cause a poor yield of small fruits. Better to have a few strong shoots that produce large, abundant crops. We must trust God with the pruning and even help Him with it. He knows what will foster our life with Him and what, although good, must go.

If we are patient, we will eventually see a yield. With some plants, the yield comes quicker than with others. The fruits of all plants are not the same. If God is growing pumpkins in us, we must not yearn to yield tomatoes. We must cooperate with the Master Gardener so that our pumpkins are the best and biggest possible for us. Now we may realize that the fruit we thought God was growing is a bit different from what we actually intended. We need to look at God and answer, "Yes, Lord. This is not what I thought, not even what I wanted. But it is certainly what I needed and exactly what You wished."

We will begin to see now why the fruit God is growing in us is what it is. We will begin to meet those who benefit from this growth. And we will sometimes be humbled into silence by what God is working through us. Truly His plan is perfect, and we have nothing to do with it. We have merely cooperated with His plan and allowed the seed He planted within us to grow. It is not to our credit that it grew well but rather to His planting, tending, and encouraging. Anything good that happens because of us is His doing not ours.

As the fruit or vegetables or flowers that God is growing within us mature, they form seeds that God will plant in others. As we age, we will slow down, shrivel, die. But the seeds fostered in others from our growth will live and God's Will shall continue. The life of conversion does not end with death, for a converted life is an inspiration to those still living. And in God's eternal garden there is a precious place for all those who have been fertile ground for His planting.

BRIEFLY ANSWER THE FOLLOWING QUESTIONS

1. Review the stages of conversion. How am I cooperating with God?
2. What progress do I see in relation to the past?
3. What is meant by the term "ongoing conversion?"

LESSON ON THE RULE

Study CHAPTER VIII: CORRECTION, DISPENSATION, OFFICERS, of the Rule and Constitutions.

What power does this Chapter give to the Visitor (spiritual assistant) of the Confraternity? Why does the Visitor have these powers?

What does section 39 of the Rule and Constitutions say to you? Why do you think the language here is so strong?

LESSON ON THE FRANCISCAN VIRTUES

In Franciscan Virtues, read Virtue 11: Evangelization. Spend at least five minutes meditating on the virtue. Answer the questions. Share your answers with your formator.

DAILY GOSPEL READING AND QUESTIONS FROM CHRIST IN THE GOSPEL

Daily read Christ in the Gospel and answer for yourself the questions on the day's reading, found in the back of the book.

Select one reading or section of the Gospel that particularly resonated with you. Share that passage and your thoughts with your formator.

ELEVENTH MONTH'S ACTIVITIES

- Make appointments with your chosen spiritual director. See how you feel about the first meeting Consult your Chapter or Circle Minister, your Regional Minister, or any other leader in the Confraternity if you have any questions or need assistance.
- Submit your answers to this month's questions to your CFP formator.

POSTULANT: LESSON TWELVE

On the Threshold of Change

Having completed the months of postulancy in the Confraternity of Penitents, you are on the threshold of change. Hopefully God's grace has been active and you are a different person now than you were when you first heard of the Confraternity. You can rest assured that, if you persist in your vocation, one year from now you will be someone far closer to God than you are today.

You are about to embark on a changed existence. To live a Rule of Life is not like changing jobs or changing homes where externals change but the person involved in the change remains essentially the same. No, your external environment is not likely to change this year. What is going to change is your internal, spiritual environment.

During the upcoming year, you will be making a commitment to spend at least ninety minutes daily in prayer (unless you receive special instructions otherwise from your spiritual director). Spending this much time in prayer may require a major adjustment on your part. But if you have come this far, and if you feel that God is leading you on, then be assured that God will reveal to you how you can make time for Him.

In this lesson, we will examine three things.

1. Am I prepared and willing to enter this period of spiritual intensity and growth with the changes it will necessarily entail?
2. Do I have the books that I will need?
3. Can I evaluate my life as it now stands and find the time in my day that I will need?

READINESS TO ENTER FIRST YEAR FORMATION

In order to enter first year formation, you must have completed the Novice 1 Application requesting entrance. The application is reproduced in this Handbook. The application will ultimately be submitted to the Confraternity of Penitents main office. If you have not yet completed the application, make a resolution to do so as soon as possible.

The application contains the following points:

- Why you wish to enter first year of formation as a novice
- Your willingness to obey all the teachings of the Catholic Church and your loyalty to the Pope and bishops, i.e. the Magisterium of the Church
- A brief autobiography and personal history
- Your next of kin

TEXTS NEEDED

In first year formation, you will need a Bible and Rosary. You will also need The Catechism of the Catholic Church, either hardback or paperback, available from most bookstores and from the CFP Holy Angels Gift Shop at www.cfpholyangels.com. Do not get an abridged version. The Catechism is also on the Internet.

An optional text is Difficulties in Mental Prayer by Fr. M. Eugene Boylan which is available from the CFP Holy Angels Gift Shop at www.cfpholyangels.com. This is an excellent guide to developing a deeper prayer life.

All penitents should have a breviary, either the one or four volume variety, also called Christian Prayer. Be sure that yours contains the Divine Office (Liturgy of the Hours) in a Church approved version. Do not get any of the shorter versions which are often used when people travel. Religious communities may have used breviaries that they can give you. For a copy of <u>The Divine Office for Dodos</u>, which is a breviary instruction manual on how to pray the Divine Office, contact the CFP Holy Angels Gift Shop at 1702 Lumbard Street, Fort Wayne Indiana 46803 USA, website www.cfpholyangels.com

If you cannot afford a breviary, you may substitute Psalms or Our Fathers and Glory Be's for the Divine Office, as the Rule and Constitutions state. The Divine Office is also on the Internet.

If you have difficulty paying for texts, please confide in your Chapter or Circle Minister or Regional Minister. They will see that everyone called to this way of life has the materials needed to embrace it. Donations from wealthier members or a fund raiser (bake sale, yard sale, etc.) could raise the funds needed. If a member cannot read, another Confraternity member should read the texts aloud to him or her at some mutually convenient time and place.

EVALUATION OF YOUR LIFESTYLE

You will need to have ninety minutes per day to pray (unless your spiritual director approves of another option). No matter how busy your life may be, now is the time to evaluate it. Here are some things you can consider that may help:

- Can you get awake a half hour earlier?
- Can you go to bed a half hour later?

- Do you watch television or read newspapers? Can you cut back on the time spent on these?
- If you are caring for a house, where can you cut back to save time? Can you do larger loads of laundry? Cook simpler meals? Make fewer foods "from scratch?" Rearrange the house to make for less cleaning? Organize materials to keep them neater? Have a yard sale so there is less to care for? Make other adjustments?
- If you are employed outside the home, can you pray on your way to or from work? Use part of your lunch break to pray?
- Is there a church or quiet spot near your place of employment where you might spend some time in prayer?
- How much time do you spend on hobbies? Recreation? Can you spend some of this time in prayer?
- What clubs, organizations, committees, and so on do you belong to? How much do these mean to you? Should you continue to belong to all of them? Should you curtail your responsibilities in some of them?
- Go through your typical week hour by hour. Where can you make adjustments to find time to pray?

THE LAST MONTH

This last month before entry into First Year Formation should be an intensified time of prayer and reflection. Make a day of recollection some time during this month to really solidify your commitment to embrace the way of life for the Confraternity of Penitents. If your Chapter or Circle can attend this day as a community, all the better. If not, do it on your own. Your spiritual director or local retreat center will certainly help you.

Every day pray this prayer or one like it. "Lord, not my will but Yours be done. I surrender my life to You. Accept me, Lord, as I am and make me, Lord, into who you want me to be. Amen."

LESSON ON THE RULE

- Review the entire Rule and Constitutions.
- Look closely at Chapter IV: PRAYER. This is the part that you will focus on in First Year Novice Formation.
- Do you have a breviary? If not, how will you obtain one?
- What prayer option do you think you will choose? Why?
- What adjustments might you have to make to fit in the prayer time? Are you prepared to make these?
- Do you think you will be able to attend daily Mass?

- What are your thoughts about entering the Novitiate? Are you ready?
- Submit your answers to this month's questions to your CFP formator.

LESSON ON THE FRANCISCAN VIRTUES

In <u>Franciscan Virtues</u>, read Virtue 12: Example. Spend at least five minutes meditating on the virtue. Answer the questions. Share your answers with your formator.

DAILY GOSPEL READING AND QUESTIONS FROM CHRIST IN THE GOSPEL

Daily read <u>Christ in the Gospel</u> and answer for yourself the questions on the day's reading, found in the back of the book.

Select one reading or section of the Gospel that particularly resonated with you. Share that passage and your thoughts with your formator.

NOVICE 1 LESSONS

"Human beings will never comprehend sufficiently the anguish and immensity of Mary's sorrows. Very few Christians partake of those sufferings and even fewer offer any consolation to her."- *St. Bridget of Sweden*

Prayer to Our Lady of Sorrows

O Most holy Virgin, Mother of our Lord Jesus Christ: by the overwhelming grief you experienced when you witnessed the martyrdom, the crucifixion, and the death of your divine Son, look upon me with eyes of compassion and awaken in my heart a tender commiseration for those sufferings, as well as a sincere detestation of my sins, in order that, being disengaged from all undue affections for the passing joys of this earth, I may long for the eternal Jerusalem, and that henceforth all my thoughts and all my actions may be directed toward this one most desirable object.

Honor, glory, and love to our divine Lord Jesus, and to the holy and immaculate Mother of God. Amen

NOVICE 1 LESSONS[32]

FIRST YEAR NOVITIATE: LESSON ONE

STARTING OUT

Welcome to First Year Novice Formation for the Confraternity of Penitents! If you have arrived at this point, you have successfully completed the postulancy of the CFP. Since you wish to continue your formation, this is a good sign that God may be calling you to this way of life. Your spouse, if you are married, should have agreed to your following this Rule.

This will be a year of major changes for you.

First, if you do not yet have a spiritual director, please continue to seek one out. You should have obtained a spiritual director by the sixth month of your first year novice formation.

Secondly, you will increase your prayer time to about ninety minutes daily, unless your spiritual director grants you a special dispensation. This may seem impossible now but it is not. You will be able to do this by daily surrendering your life to God and allowing Him to lead you into the embracing of this way of life.

The attitude toward all of these activities is summed up in the great penitential Psalm, Psalm 51, which, for penitents, both begins and ends the day. "Have mercy on me, O Lord, in Your kindness. In Your compassion, blot out my offense." As penitents, we recognize that God is kind and forgiving, and that we, as sinners, are in need of that forgiveness. We realize that we deserve God's justice, yet we are bold and trusting enough to claim His mercy. The penitential way of life humbly recognizes both the holiness and majesty of God and the sinfulness of our own lives, not with fear of God's just anger but

---

32   Note: Keep copies of all lesson answers turned in to the formator in case your answers are lost in postal or internet mailings. Lesson answers need not be confined to texts discussed.

with trust in His loving kindness to those who turn from their own sins to His ways. As penitents, we know that we have never "arrived" at sanctity. Our conversion does not happen once. It must happen daily, minute by minute, until our wills are always one with His and we can truly say, in peace and joy, "Your will, not mine, be done."

Four texts form the basis of the three years of Novice formation. First, of course, is the Bible. This should be a Catholic edition of Scripture. Penitents should be daily reading a portion of Scripture and meditating on it. This should be done every day of our lives. It is impossible to exhaust the riches of God's holy word.

Secondly, the Catechism of the Catholic Church which contains the teachings of our Church. We are bound to uphold these. A great sin of our time is ignorance of what the Church actually teaches. We must know these teachings so that we can adhere to them ourselves and instruct others in them.

Third, the breviary (the Divine Office) and, for those who do not know how to use the breviary, a breviary instruction manual, The Divine Office for Dodos, available from the Confraternity of Penitents. The breviary is the official prayer book of the Catholic Church. To pray the Divine Office is to join in prayer with Catholics worldwide.

Fourth, the Rule and Constitutions of the Confraternity of Penitents.

The book Difficulties in Mental Prayer is an optional text. Your formator may choose to make this text mandatory.

Each month, reading assignments in Scripture, the Rule and Constitutions, The Divine Office for Dodos, Difficulties in Mental Prayer, and the Catechism will be given. The penitent should do the reading assignment prior to the next month's meeting, should bring the texts to the meeting, and should prepare BRIEF answers (five sentences or less) to the questions marked ANSWER. These answers may be mailed, e mailed, or recorded on audio tape and are to be presented to your formator.

May God bless your walk with Him!

INTRODUCTION TO THE CATECHISM OF THE CATHOLIC CHURCH

Every penitent is to have a Catechism of the Catholic Church. Inexpensive paperback editions as well as the more costly hardback editions are available. The Catechism is also on the internet.

The Catechism of the Catholic Church contains in detail the truths that we must believe as Catholics. In this lesson, we will grow familiar with the Catechism and read certain parts of it.

Let's begin by examining the Table of Contents. Page through this, reading the titles of Parts, Sections, and Articles. What do you notice?[33]

---

[33] In this introductory section, the questions on the Catechism are intended to help Novices learn to use the Catechism. Novices should answer each question and then proceed to the next. Answers need not be written out and presented to the formator.

Following the Table of Contents is the Apostolic Constitution *Fidei Depositum* which tells why the Catechism was published. Read this section which Pope John Paul II wrote. What can you learn?

A book's Prologue gives a general overview of the book and tells you how to use it. Read the Prologue to the Catechism. What do you learn from it? Look at section 25 "Above All—Charity." What is the object of all Christian virtue? What does this mean to you? Compare Section 25 with the Prologue to the Gospel of John. What similarities do you find?

Page through Part One: The Profession of Faith. Note how it is divided into Chapters with subdivisions called "Articles." At the end of each chapter is a summary entitled "In Brief."

Scan the remainder of the Catechism. Notice how this system of Chapters, Articles, and "In Brief" summaries is followed throughout.

Now turn to the Abbreviations section at the back of the Catechism. This section gives the abbreviations for texts cited in the Catechism. How thorough do the Biblical references seem to be? What other references are cited? What does this tell you about the Catechism?

Now look at the Subject Index. Read the Prefatory Note. How are the main entry words printed? Reference is made to "In Brief" texts. What are these? Where in the chapters do you find them?

The first entry under the Subject Index is Abortion. Note the reference—2270-75. Find this subject in the Catechism. Do the numbers refer to pages or to numbered sections of the Catechism?

Turn to the Abortion topic in the Catechism. Next to the paragraph numbered 2270 are two other numbers—1703 and 357. What do you think these are? Find sections 1703 and 357 in the Catechism. Do you see that these two sections support the teaching in section 2270?

Read the section on abortion, noting its content, supporting sections, and footnoted material. Read the supporting sections as well.

Look again under the Abortion heading in the Subject Index. You will note references to sections 2319 and 2322-23 which are in italics. The Prefatory Note states that italicized numbers refer to "In Brief" texts. Read those texts also.

Have you understood better the Church's stand on abortion after reading this section?

Now look through the Subject Index for any subject that interests you. Look up the section references and the supporting section references in the Catechism and read them. Look at the footnotes to the sections you are reading. What are you learning about this subject?

The first part of the Catechism is based on our Profession of Faith. All Catholics, and certainly all penitents, must adhere to this profession. So we must know what the profession is. From now on, part of every formation lesson will include some work with the Catechism of the Catholic Church. We will begin with this first section of the Catechism.

Those who are in Chapters or Circles can discuss the work on the Catechism with their spiritual assistants. Those who are not in Chapters or Circles should spend some time discussing these lessons with their spiritual directors. The lessons will be short enough so that even those with time constraints or complex family obligations should be able to complete the assignments with little trouble.

All the lessons from here on will proceed as follows:

1. Penitents will receive a "reading assignment" of about 80 sections in the Catechism. It is suggested that a penitent read about 4 sections each day and reflect briefly on them. This should take between 5 and 10 minutes daily.
2. Study assignments on the Rule and Constitutions will be given.
3. A brief Scripture study will be conducted monthly on the theme of that year's formation (prayer: year 1; fasting: year 2; external simplicity: year 3).
4. Each assignment will be followed by questions marked ANSWER. Please answer the questions BRIEFLY (five sentences or less) in writing, e mail, or on audio tape and return the answers to your formator.
5. Penitents should already be spending at least fifteen minutes daily in mental prayer. Meditation may be on Scripture, the Catechism, the Rule and Constitutions, the monthly newsletter, or on whatever the Holy Spirit gives as a theme.
6. Penitents should have on hand a Mental Prayer Journal (any notebook will do) to write down any insights gained during the time of mental prayer. Writing in the journal should not be considered a daily task. The journal is available should the penitent wish to use it. Some days the penitent may write much. Other days, he or she may write nothing. The goal is not to fill up the prayer journal but to use it to record any important thoughts.
7. Penitents will discuss their answers to the questions with their Chapter/Circle and formator. Jottings in the Mental Prayer Journal should be shared with the penitent's personal spiritual director. Theological questions should be directed to the spiritual assistant.

CATECHISM LESSON

Read Sections 1-25 and 2558-2606

ANSWER: What is the main function of humanity and how does the Catechism assist in this? List what you feel are the three most important truths taught about prayer in Sections 2558-2606 and tell why you selected these.

SCRIPTURE LESSON

"Again I tell you, if two of you join your voices on earth to pray for anything whatever, it shall be granted to you by My Father in heaven. Where two or three are gathered in My name, there am I in their midst." (Matthew 18: 19-20)

Jesus in Matthew 28:20 promises, "And know that I am with you always, until the end of the world." In verses 19-20 of Matthew 18 we have our Lord's promise in action. Wherever even two of His people are, there He is with them.

Is He not with us when we are alone? Yes, He is. But in Matthew 18: 19-20, Jesus is saying that, when two people agree together on praying for the things of God, we have a quorum. We have Church. We have congregation.

The "marks," or obvious signs of the Catholic faith are the Sacraments. If we have the Sacraments and a Catholic congregation with only two, or three people in the service, do we have Church? Here the Lord answers with a loud, "Yes!" If any two agree together, as we do when we confess our Catholic faith with mutual charity, then He is there with us.

Just think how powerful our prayers are before our Lord's "throne of grace" when we have several of His Holy-Spirit-filled Christians agreeing together! This is especially true when we speak together the "prayer of the Church," the sacred liturgy. We are not only in agreement together in the here and now, but also with every saint who has ever participated in the divine liturgy before us. Prayer, in small groups and at the Mass, is especially blessed by the Lord of the Church.

1. Do you experience the power of agreeing together in your prayer life?
2. Can you see the benefit of having prayer fellowship with a consecrated group, such as the Confraternity of Penitents?
3. Have you experienced the sensation of being connected with all the Christian people throughout the past who have participated in the Mass and liturgy of the Church?
4. Will you seek a partner to pray with you in prayer as you seek God's will in your CFP formation?

ANSWER: Answer question two above and give your reasons in writing.

RULE LESSON

Look over the entire Rule and Constitutions. Study Chapter VI, sections 19 through 21.

ANSWER: Are you supporting the Confraternity of Penitents by your attendance at and participation in meetings and by your financial help (as much as you can)?

Chapter IV. Read section 12. Note all the prayer options in section 12 of the Constitutions.

ANSWER: Am I fulfilling the prayer requirements of the Rule, as expected of me at this point of formation (Constitutions 12, 12l, 12m, 12n)? If I am not, how can I begin to do so?

Addendum to the Constitutions

ANSWER: Do you have a spiritual director? If so, how is your spiritual direction working out? If not, how will you begin to seek one?

LESSON ON THE FRANCISCAN VIRTUES

In <u>Franciscan Virtues</u>, read Virtue 13: Faith. Spend at least five minutes meditating on the virtue. Answer the questions. Share your answers with your formator.

<u>DIVINE OFFICE FOR DODOS</u> (Optional)

Look at Table of Contents. Discuss how each part builds on the other. Look at first two sections in general, noting methods for using breviary instruction. Read Sections 1 and 2.

<u>DIFFICULTIES IN MENTAL PRAYER</u> (Optional)

Read the Preface. ANSWER: What do you hope to get out of reading this book?

<u>ASSIGNMENT</u>

- Submit BRIEF answers to the above questions to your formator.
- Attend all meetings of your CFP Chapter (or Circle). If you must miss, turn in a written excuse to your Chapter's secretary. If you are an isolated CFP member, keep in monthly contact with the by-mail or internet community.
- Having successfully completed your postulancy, you have begun to live the Rule by following certain guidelines which you will continue all your life as a penitent. These are what you should already be doing:

  - Daily praying in the morning the Apostles' Creed, all of Psalm 51, all of Psalm 54, and verses 1 to 32 of Psalm 119 as did the first penitents. The "Glory Be" is prayed after the Psalms.
  - Daily praying in the evening, the Apostles' Creed and all of Psalm 51 as did the first penitents with a "Glory Be" prayed after the Psalm. Making a nightly examination of conscience and praying an Act of Contrition which is part of the Office of Night Prayer.
  - Spending fifteen minutes daily in mental prayer. This might involve reading and pondering Scripture and fulfills the obligation for the Office of Prime.
  - Always wearing a visible cross or crucifix unless you are already wearing the habit of a Third Order.

- Attending daily Mass, if possible.
- Praying the Psalter yearly for deceased penitents.
- Receiving the Sacrament of Reconciliation monthly and Eucharist weekly, at a minimum.
- Praying a Marian Consecration prayer daily.
- Praying a daily five decade Rosary if possible. Praying a fifteen decade Rosary is one prayer option that you can choose.
- Embracing an apostolate from either the spiritual or corporal works of mercy.
- Abstaining from meat on every Friday of the year with the exception of Church Solemnities and special celebrations and praying an Our Father or another prayer before and after every meal.
- Daily asking the Lord to help you surrender your life to Him and praying for the Holy Father, bishops, priests, religious, your spiritual assistant, your spiritual director, all penitents, all sinners, and yourself.

Are you doing these? If not, implement them into your life.

FIRST YEAR NOVITIATE: LESSON TWO

<u>RULE LESSON</u>

Review the Preamble to the Rule and Constitutions and the Object of the Commitment, Fruits of the Commitment, and Purpose (Charism) in the Constitutions.

When was our Primitive Rule written?
What is penance? How is it achieved?
What should the Rule, well lived, achieve for the penitent?
Why should a penitent be careful to avoid spiritual pride?

ANSWER: Choose one of the above questions and submit your written answer to your formator.
Review Constitutions 12a and 12b.
ANSWER: How will you embrace the spirit of Constitutions 12a and 12b?

<u>SCRIPTURE LESSON</u>

"Until now you have not asked for anything in My name. Ask and you shall receive, that your joy may be full." (John 16:24)
There are three main things in this verse:

- Pray in Jesus' Name.
- Ask.
- If you do the previous two, then your "joy may be full."

Jesus became one of us. That is the mystery of the incarnation. The Infinite, personal God of the universe became a flesh and blood human like us "in all ways, except without sin."

Jesus came to earth with a mission–to reconcile fallen mankind with God. He accomplished this mission through His sinless life, His sacrificial death on the cross and His resurrection from the dead.

Jesus says in John 14:6, "no one comes to the Father but through Me." How does this truth apply to our prayer life?

The writer of the book of Hebrews says, "Since, then, we have a great High Priest Who has passed through the heavens, Jesus, the Son of God, let us hold fast to our profession of faith . . . let us confidently approach the throne of grace to receive mercy and favor and to find help in time of need" (Hebrews 4:14-16).

Jesus has opened the Holy of Holies for us, so that our prayers may ascend to God. They ascend to the throne of grace when we pray in the name of Jesus.

Next, we need to ask for what we need or, even better, for what God wants to give us. James the apostle tells us that "You do not obtain because you do not ask (James 4:2). So often we are too busy with the troubles of the world to remember that we have Jesus as our Great High Priest. We need only ask Him for help. Did He not say, "I will never leave you nor forsake you?"

Finally, "you will receive that your joy may be full." Does Jesus promise us whatever material blessing we want? First, of all, He is talking about things that will strengthen our spiritual walk. Jesus also tells us to, "lay not up for yourselves treasures on earth..., but instead lay up treasures in heaven." We are told elsewhere in Scripture (1 John 5:14), "We have this confidence in God: that He hears us whenever we ask for anything according to His will."

God has a plan for our lives. He always answers our prayers. Sometimes it is "no." Other times it is "yes," and sometimes it is "later" or "I have something better for you." We are approaching Christian maturity when we can conform our will to His Divine Will. We live each day one at a time, walking with Him "in the spirit." If we are praying, reading His word, and living a Christian, God centered life, then "our joy will be full."

1) What is so "special" about the Name of Jesus?
2) What is the place of saying, "not My will, but Thy Will be done," in our prayer life?
3) Is there a difference between "joy" and "happiness?"

ANSWER: Submit to your formator a written response to one of the above questions.

CATECHISM LESSON

Read Sections 2607-2682.

ANSWER: List six ways to pray in these sections and give the section number that refers to each way.

LESSON ON THE FRANCISCAN VIRTUES

In <u>Franciscan Virtues</u>, read Virtue 14: Fraternity. Spend at least five minutes meditating on the virtue. Answer the questions. Share your answers with your formator.

DIVINE OFFICE FOR DODOS (Optional)

Read Section 3.

DIFFICULTIES IN MENTAL PRAYER (Optional)

Read Chapters 1 and 2.
ANSWER: Explain how man's being a rational animal relates to prayer.

ASSIGNMENTS

- Use a prayer journal at least once a week to record your spiritual progress. What are your feelings about using this?
- Resolve to be at peace with all from now on.
- Implement anything not yet being done from First Month Assignments.
- If you do not yet have a spiritual director, begin to actively seek one now. The Confraternity through its Chapters and leadership can assist you.
- Return BRIEF answers to questions in this lesson to your formator.

FIRST YEAR NOVITIATE: LESSON THREE

RULE LESSON

Chapter I of the Rule and Constitutions: Daily Life.

Review all the provisions of Chapter I of the Rule and Constitutions. Note that you are expected to live none of them yet with the exception of Constitutions 2g.

ANSWER: What do you suppose is the purpose of Chapter I?

Review Constitutions 12e and Appendix B.

ANSWER: Why do penitents pray a daily Marian Consecration Prayer? Do you feel that praying this has strengthened your commitment to living the CFP way of life?

CATECHISM LESSON

Read Sections 2683-2758.

ANSWER: List three teachings that especially spoke to you from these sections and tell why they were meaningful to you.

SCRIPTURE LESSON

"I give you My word, if you are ready to believe that you will receive whatever you ask for in prayer, it shall be done for you." (Mark 11:24)

Here is another outstanding promise from our God. But you may notice a contingency. What is that contingency? What role do you think it plays? Just in case you aren't getting the point of this verse yet, the topic is; "What role does our faith play in our prayer life?"

Martin Luther, who was once a son of the Church, but later rebelled against her, once said that, "faith is trusting that God will take care of you in the way that's in your best interest." Hebrews 11:6 says, "But without faith it is impossible to please Him...." Faith, or trust and belief in God as our provider and the "lover of our souls," is a pre-requisite for answered prayer.

Does that mean that God will not answer our prayers of desperation on that "dark night of the soul?" Yes, He will answer, but in His purpose and in His time. The process we must go through will mature our walk of faith. That verse in Hebrews ends like this: "Anyone who comes to God must believe that He exists, and that He rewards those who seek Him."

1. Does this verse in Mark mean that if we believe strongly enough we will receive anything we materially want?
2. Does this verse mean that if we have faith "God will supply all of our needs from His riches in Glory?"

ANSWER: Answer the above questions in writing.

LESSON ON THE FRANCISCAN VIRTUES

In <u>Franciscan Virtues</u>, read Virtue 15: Generosity. Spend at least five minutes meditating on the virtue. Answer the questions. Share your answers with your formator.

DIVINE OFFICE FOR DODOS (Optional)

Read Section 4.

DIFFICULTIES IN MENTAL PRAYER (Optional)

Read Chapters 3 and 4.

ANSWER: What is discursive prayer? How may we practice it?

ASSIGNMENT

- Pray Night Prayer every night using the breviary.
- Return BRIEF answers to questions in above lessons to your formator.

FIRST YEAR NOVITIATE: LESSON FOUR

<u>RULE LESSON</u>

Chapters II and III of the Rule and Constitutions and Appendix A of the Constitutions.

Note that at this stage of formation, you are not bound to observe any of these Constitutions with the exception of abstaining from meat on Fridays and to observe the Church appointed days of fast and abstinence.

Why do you suppose the Rule has a fasting/abstinence dimension?
Explain the Church fast and abstinence laws.
Who is exempt from fasting and abstinence?
What days are days of abstinence for the Catholic Church?
What are days of fast and abstinence for the Catholic Church?

ANSWER: Select one of the above questions and submit your answer in writing to your formator.

Read Rule/Constitutions 7.

ANSWER: What does Rule/Constitutions 7 require?

<u>CATECHISM LESSON</u>

Read Sections 2759-2837.
ANSWER: How is God the Father made known in the Lord's Prayer and what is to be our relationship to Him?

<u>SCRIPTURE LESSON</u>

"Rising early the next morning, He went off to a lonely place in the desert; there He was absorbed in prayer." (Mark 1:35)

Isn't this a beautiful model for prayer?

What do we learn from our Lord's "school of prayer?"

The Scriptures say that in this case Christ arose early. It is fine, of course to pray, at any hour of the day, and in fact the apostles prayed the office of the hours throughout the day. However, it is often in the early morning when we have our most uncluttered thoughts and are the most open to hearing the voice of God in our hearts. For many of us, unless we are standing up late at night, prayer is a sure ticket to nodding off to sleep. However, when we awake refreshed we can offer up some quality time for our first office of prayer.

This scripture also says Jesus, "went off to a lonely place in the desert." There is a "time for every purpose under heaven," and this applies to our prayer life as well. There are times when a group prayer is best. Our time at Mass is a special prayer as the whole covenant people of God meet together to offer up the liturgy and receive God's gift in the True Body and Blood of Christ. Yet, there is also a time when contemplative prayer is indicated. That special quiet time alone with our Savior is precious and should be included in our busy day.

1. A prayer closet is a quiet spot within our house where we can go to pray alone. Must we have a "prayer" closet? If we want one, how can we construct one or create one at home?
2. Is it a part of your prayer life to have moments alone with the blessed Trinity?
3. In a quiet and solitary prayer time, what might we gain in our prayers and in the responses we receive from God?

ANSWER: Where do you go at home when you wish to pray alone? How often do you pray alone? If you wish to have more time alone with God, how might you achieve your goal?

LESSON ON THE FRANCISCAN VIRTUES

In <u>Franciscan Virtues</u>, read Virtue 16: Gratitude. Spend at least five minutes meditating on the virtue. Answer the questions. Share your answers with your formator.

<u>DIVINE OFFICE FOR DODOS</u> (Optional)

Read Section 5.

DIFFICULTIES IN MENTAL PRAYER (Optional)

Read Chapters 5 and 6.
ANSWER: Discuss one difficulty in prayer and how to combat it.

ASSIGNMENTS

- Pray Night Prayer nightly using breviary.
- Continue with all prayers and penances up to this point.
- In line with Rule/Constitutions 7, begin to pray an Our Father or other regular meal prayer both before and after meals. If you forget or are fasting completely from food, pray Three Our Father's as stated in Constitutions 7a.
- Return BRIEF answers to questions above to your formator.

FIRST YEAR NOVITIATE:
LESSON FIVE

<u>RULE LESSON</u>

Chapter V, Rule/Constitutions 15.

How often do you receive the Sacrament of Reconciliation?
How often do you receive the Eucharist?
Are you tithing?

ANSWER: Why do you think that the Sacraments of Reconciliation and Eucharist and the admonition to restore what belongs to others and to pay tithes are all combined in section 15 of the Rule and Constitutions?

Rule and Constitutions 12, Constitutions 12c and 12d.

ANSWER: What substitutions are allowed for the Divine Office and when might you use them?

<u>CATECHISM LESSON</u>

Read Sections 2838 to 2865 and Sections 26-53.

ANSWER: How does the ending of the Lord's Prayer fit with what is discussed in Sections 26-53?

SCRIPTURE LESSON

"Then, after singing songs of praise, they walked out to the Mount of Olives." (Matthew 26:30)

Do you ever "sing" the blessing over your family's meal together? It is often a practice in many liturgical traditions to sing some of the church's prayers. For instance, at Mass we often sing the Agnus Dei (Lamb of God you take away the sin of the world), and the Sanctus (Holy, Holy, Holy Lord of Hosts....). Often when we sing a spiritual song, or hymn (by the way, is there a distinction between these?), can we feel our hearts lifting up to God? The Book of Revelation indicates that in heaven we will "sing our praises to God." What better way to lift our hearts to Him?

What if you can't sing like an opera star or a country singer? Take heart. You will not be judged on your vocal prowess. The Bible only says, "Make a joyful noise unto the Lord" but not so as to disturb people around you.

1. Have you ever tried singing a verse of a spiritual song at the dinner table instead of a spoken prayer?
2. What do you think of the idea?
3. Is there a time when your spirit soars to the heavens as you sing in church?
4. Do you ever spontaneously sing your prayers to God?
5. Singing a hymn is part of the Divine Office. Many religious chant or sing the entire Office. Why do you think song is included in this official prayer of the Church?

ANSWER: Choose one of the above questions to answer in writing for your formator.

LESSON ON THE FRANCISCAN VIRTUES

In <u>Franciscan Virtues</u>, read Virtue 17: Honesty. Spend at least five minutes meditating on the virtue. Answer the questions. Share your answers with your formator.

DIVINE OFFICE FOR DODOS (Optional)

Read Section 6.

DIFFICULTIES IN MENTAL PRAYER (Optional)

Read Chapter 7 and 8.

ANSWER: What is affective prayer? How may we practice it if we don't "feel" like praying?

ASSIGNMENTS

- Pray Morning and Evening Prayer every weekday (Monday-Friday), using a breviary.
- Actively seek a spiritual director if needed.
- Submit BRIEF answers to questions above to your formator.

FIRST YEAR NOVITIATE:
LESSON SIX

RULE LESSON

Rule/Constitutions 16-17.

ANSWER: Why do you think these two sections are part of the penitential life?

Chapter IV, Section 12 of the Rule and Constitutions, particularly Constitutions 12f, 12g, 12h, 12i, and Appendix C.

ANSWER: What is the preferred method of formal prayer for the Rule? What can be substituted?

CATECHISM LESSON

Read Sections 54-141.

ANSWER: 1. Name three of the many ways God speaks to us. 2. What is faith and how may it be developed?

SCRIPTURE LESSON

"Rejoice" in the Lord always! I say it again. Rejoice! Everyone should see how unselfish you are. The Lord is near. Dismiss all anxiety from your minds. Present your needs to God in every form of prayer and in petitions, full of gratitude. Then God's own peace, which is beyond all understanding, will stand guard over your hearts and minds, in Christ Jesus." (Philippians 4:4-7)

In this verse we hear once again, "Ask!" But St. Paul makes another connection. He says "Present your needs to God in every form of prayer and in petitions, full of gratitude." Commentator R.C. Lenski says, "Do you first have to inform God? God certainly knows even before we ask (Matthew 6:8), but God bids us ask and promises to give us what we ask. Those, who like the skeptic, refuse to ask, simply do not have." (James 4:2) Why do you think God wants us to ask when He already knows what we need?

Supplications in this case mean "petitioning." We are instructed to make these known in every need or trouble. In what better hands can any trouble rest than God's? Paul assures us that God will attend to all that we ask by either granting our petition, or giving us something better above what we ask or think.

We are told to ask with "thanksgiving." This means constant joy (mind you, not necessarily happiness). And as R. Lenski says, "Only a thankful heart is a joyful heart."

1) Do you take time each day to consciously think how God has blessed you?
2) Do so now.
3) Does our "thankfulness" only flow because God has given to us, or because of our relationship with Him?

ANSWER: Time yourself. For five minutes, write down every blessing you can think of that you have received. Share, in writing, your reflection on this activity with your formator.

LESSON ON THE FRANCISCAN VIRTUES

In <u>Franciscan Virtues</u>, read Virtue 18: Hope. Spend at least five minutes meditating on the virtue. Answer the questions. Share your answers with your formator.

<u>DIVINE OFFICE FOR DODOS</u> (Optional)

Read Section 7.

<u>DIFFICULTIES IN MENTAL PRAYER</u> (Optional)

Read Chapters 9 and 10.
ANSWER: How does mortification support prayer?

<u>ASSIGNMENTS</u>

*   You should have a spiritual director by now and should be having regular, that is at least monthly, appointments with him or her. If you do not yet have a spiritual director, speak with your Chapter's council and spiritual assistant or your Regional Minister and strive to obtain one as soon as possible.
*   If you own any lethal weapons that are not being used for hunting game, discuss with your spiritual director the legitimacy of owning these in light of Rule/Constitutions 16. In certain occupations or certain neighborhoods, possession of such weapons may be necessary.
*   Continue with all practices already being performed as a penitent.
*   Submit BRIEF answers to the questions above to your formator.

FIRST YEAR NOVITIATE: LESSON SEVEN

RULE LESSON

Rule/Constitutions 18, Constitutions 18a-d and Appendix D.

ANSWER: Evaluate yourself on how well you are living each of these provisions.

Chapter IV of the Rule and Constitutions, with attention to Constitutions 12o and Option One.

ANSWER: Does Option One appeal to you as your prayer option under this Rule? Why or why not?

CATECHISM LESSON

Read Sections 142-231.

ANSWER: Write a concise definition for faith, creed, and God.

SCRIPTURE LESSON

"When you stand to pray, forgive anyone against whom you have a grievance so that your heavenly Father may in turn forgive you your faults." (Mark 11:25)

Ouch! Here is another prayer pre-requisite! God more or less tells us not to bother asking Him for anything, including forgiveness, unless we are at least willing to begin the forgiveness process in our own lives.

Think of it—who are we to not forgive a neighbor, friend, or family member, when God forgave us for crucifying His Son? We killed the Son of God, yet God forgives us for the sake of His Son. Are we to forgive some human wrong done to us? Yes. We must forgive "so that your heavenly Father may in turn forgive you your faults."

What if someone has done us a horrendous wrong? What if we have been assaulted physically by an attacker for instance? Does this verse mean we have to instantaneously, wholeheartedly forgive the abuser? It means we must have purpose of amendment. We might have to start out very, very small. We might have to ask God, "Dear Lord, please give me the beginning of the desire to just start the forgiveness." Even from the humble beginning of just asking for the will to begin to forgive, the Triune God can work a powerful change in us.

1) How should our forgiveness mirror God's own forgiveness? Does it?
2) Why does God insist that we pray, "forgive us our trespasses, as we forgive those who trespass against us?"
3) Do you have a "seed of bitterness" in your heart? If so, begin the powerful process today, and let forgiveness reign.

ANSWER: Choose one of the questions above and submit its answer in writing to your formator.

LESSON ON THE FRANCISCAN VIRTUES

In <u>Franciscan Virtues</u>, read Virtue 19: Humility. Spend at least five minutes meditating on the virtue. Answer the questions. Share your answers with your formator.

DIVINE OFFICE FOR DODOS (Optional)

Read Section 8.

DIFFICULTIES IN MENTAL PRAYER (Optional)

Read Chapters 11 and 12.
ANSWER: What are some ways to deal with distractions in prayer?

ASSIGNMENTS

- Return BRIEF answers to above questions to your formator.
- Pray Morning Prayer using the breviary every day.
- Follow the provisions of Constitutions 18a-d.
- If you sin habitually through speech, devise, with your spiritual director, a way to combat this, and be sure to pray three Our Fathers whenever you do sin by speech.
- Determine with your spouse and your spiritual director how better to teach your household to love and serve God. Implement that plan.
- Continue your other penitential practices.

During the ninth month of First Year Novitiate, you will be asked to make a personal evaluation of your journey so far into a life of penance. Is it your intent to complete this year successfully and move into second year novitiate? Between now and the ninth month, please pray about this question. It is very important. If you are behind on a few lessons, strive to catch up. If you need help understanding the lesson or getting through it, let your formator know.

FIRST YEAR NOVITIATE: LESSON EIGHT

RULE LESSON

Chapter VII, Rule/Constitutions 22-24.

ANSWER: Evaluate yourself on your fulfilling of these sections of the Rule and Constitutions.

Chapter IV, Rule/Constitutions 12 with attention to Constitutions 12i and 12o, Options Two, Three, Four, and Five.

ANSWER: Can these options be used at any time as substitutes for Option One? Why do you say this?

CATECHISM LESSON

Read Sections 232-314.

ANSWER: What traits of God show that He is Master of creation?

SCRIPTURE LESSON

"He said to them, 'When you pray, say: Father, hallowed be Your name, Your kingdom come. Give us each day our daily bread. Forgive us our sins for we too forgive all who do us wrong; and subject us not to the trial." (Luke 11:2-4)

Prayer in its purest form, is an act of worship, where we lift up our needs to God and offer Him our praise and thanksgiving! This we owe our Creator, Redeemer and Sanctifier.

Why do we pray the "Our Father" (Lord's Prayer)? It is the prayer that Jesus taught us to pray. It is a perfect model for our prayers. And it is "awesome" (in the words of Mother Angelica)!

The "Our Father" has:
- An introduction
- Seven petitions
- A conclusion

In the introduction (Our Father who art in heaven), God tenderly invites us to believe that He is our true Father and that we are his true children. Thus, like beloved children asking a beloved father, we can, boldly and confidently, ask Him for whatever we need.

It was often said that the early Church's "desert fathers" were so deeply immersed in meditation that when they would start to pray the Lord's Prayer, they often could get no further than, "Our Father, who art in heaven, hallowed be Thy name...."

The thoughts contained in this prayer are so often skimmed over. Perhaps we don't appreciate them as we should. Here are the seven petitions. Meditate briefly on each one, asking what each means to you.

1. Hallowed by Thy name....
2. Thy kingdom come.....
3. Thy will be done on earth as it is in heaven....
4. Give us this day, our daily bread....
5. And forgive us our trespasses, as we forgive those who trespass against us....
6. And lead us not into temptation....
7. But deliver us from evil....

ANSWER: Which of the above petitions means the most to you and why?

LESSON ON THE FRANCISCAN VIRTUES

In <u>Franciscan Virtues</u>, read Virtue 20: Imitation of Jesus. Spend at least five minutes meditating on the virtue. Answer the questions. Share your answers with your formator.

DIVINE OFFICE FOR DODOS (Optional)

Read Section 9.

DIFFICULTIES IN MENTAL PRAYER (Optional)

Read Chapters 13 and 14.

ANSWER: Describe three difficulties besides distractions that one may experience in prayer. How should one deal with them?

<u>ASSIGNMENT</u>

- Add Evening Prayer to your daily prayer schedule. Continue receiving instruction on how to pray Morning and Evening Prayer.
- Submit BRIEF answers to the above questions to your formator.
- Visit, call, or write ill members.
- Attend, if possible, the funerals of deceased members. Pray the fifty psalms within eight days of the demise of any member.
- Pray the Psalter yearly for all living and deceased penitents.

Continue penitential practices of previous months.

FIRST YEAR NOVITIATE: LESSON NINE

RULE LESSON

Chapter VII, Rule/Constitutions with particular attention to sections 28 and 38.

ANSWER: Choose one of these sections and discuss how this might be implemented in your CFP Chapter or Circle.

Chapter IV, Rule/Constitutions 13-14.

ANSWER: Who is dispensed from saying the Hours and attending Mass?

CATECHISM LESSON

Read Sections 315-395.

ANSWER: Compare good and bad angels and humanity, listing similarities and differences.

SCRIPTURE LESSON

"Be on your guard lest your spirits become bloated with indulgence and drunkenness and worldly cares. The great day will suddenly close in on you like a trap. The day I speak of will come upon all who dwell on the face of the earth. So be on the watch. Pray constantly for the strength to escape whatever is in prospect, and to stand secure before the Son of Man." (Luke 21:34-36)

There was a highway patrolman one day, sitting by the side of the road when he noticed something curious. There was a car, full of nuns, creeping ever so slowly down the highway. Cars were racing up behind the nun's car and honking angrily before speeding around them. The officer drove up and stopped them with his flashing lights. When he walked over to their car he noticed an elderly nun was driving.

"Sister", he said, "I stopped you because you were going slower than the legal minimum speed limit. Did you know you can't drive any slower than 45 on this freeway?"

She smiled at him and said, "Officer, I feel so silly, I thought that the speed limit here was 26 miles per hour."

"No, Sister," the officer replied grinning, "that's the highway number sign."

He then looked in the back seat where he saw a strange sight. There were four young nuns, all shivering and gripping the back of their seat in horror. Concerned, he asked the elderly driver, "Sister, why are all those nuns back there so upset?"

"Well, you see," she said, "we just turned off of highway 101."

Jesus warns us to "Be on the watch. Pray constantly for the strength to escape whatever is in prospect and to stand secure before the Son of Man." Do we take for granted that we will be counted among the elect? We may be correct in thinking that we are, but Jesus warns us against complacency. Our number one prayer concern should be our salvation and the salvation of the world. The Bible tells us that it is a "fearful thing to fall into the hands of the living God." (Hebrews 10:31)

This prayer can become a favorite and is often prayed along with the Rosary. "Oh my Jesus, save us from the fires of hell, and lead all souls into heaven, especially those who are most in need of Your mercy. All for the Sacred and Eucharistic Heart of Jesus, all through the Sorrowful and Immaculate Heart of Mary, all in union with Saint Joseph."

ANSWER: The nuns in the earlier joke thought that they were about to meet their Maker. What are your feelings about death? How are you preparing for your own death? Do the prayer requirements of the Rule help?

LESSON ON THE FRANCISCAN VIRTUES

In <u>Franciscan Virtues</u>, read Virtue 21: Joy. Spend at least five minutes meditating on the virtue. Answer the questions. Share your answers with your formator.

<u>DIVINE OFFICE FOR DODOS (Optional)</u>

Read Section 10.

<u>DIFFICULTIES IN MENTAL PRAYER (Optional)</u>

Read Chapters 15 and 16.

ANSWER: What is our union with Christ and how should this influence our prayer life?

<u>SELF-EVALUATION</u>

Am I keeping up with the novice lessons and turning in my answers on time?

Am I incorporating the assignments into my life?

Is it my intent to successfully complete the next months of the formation and move into Second Year Novitiate?

Or do I feel it would be better for me to repeat or continue this year of formation before moving on?

ANSWER: Do you or do you not plan to move into Second Year Novitiate and why?

<u>ASSIGNMENT</u>

- Submit BRIEF answers to the above questions to the formator.
- Begin to pray the Office of Readings daily or make another substitution by choosing one of the prayer options.
- During Lent and Advent, attend Daily Mass unless impossible or a serious inconvenience intervenes.
- Show proper reverence when receiving the Eucharist.

FIRST YEAR NOVITIATE: LESSON TEN

RULE LESSON

Chapter VII, Rule/Constitutions 26-27.

ANSWER: What do these sections say to you about charity (love), forgiveness, and a life of penance?

Chapter VII, Rule/Constitutions 29-31 and 33.

ANSWER: What do these sections say to you about the commitment of living this holy way of life?

CATECHISM LESSON

Read Sections 396-483.

ANSWER: How are the fall of humanity and the redemption of Christ related? How should our faith respond to this?

SCRIPTURE LESSON

"In prayer you call upon a Father who judges each one justly on the basis of his actions. Since this is so, conduct yourselves reverently during your sojourn in a strange land." (1 Peter 1:17)

We are to be imitators of Christ. Holiness is not an option. Perfection this side of heaven is, unfortunately, not an option either. Even the holiest of the saints had to rely on the perfections of Jesus as their source for eternal life.

As you look at verse 17 notice the verbs. But what's more, notice the verbs in the four preceding verses (13-16) and in the two which follow (18-19). Here is the full text: "So gird the loins of your understanding; live soberly; set all your hope on the gift to be conferred on you when Jesus Christ appears. As obedient sons, do not yield to the desires that once shaped you in your ignorance. Rather, become holy yourselves in every aspect of your conduct, after the likeness of the holy One Who called you; remember, Scripture says, 'Be holy, for I am holy.' In prayer you call upon a Father who judges each one justly on the basis of his actions. Since this is so, conduct yourselves reverently during your sojourn in a strange land." Realize that you were delivered from the futile way of life your fathers handed on to you, not by any diminishable sum of silver or gold, but by Christ's blood beyond all price, the blood of a spotless, unblemished lamb chosen before the world's foundation and revealed for your sake in these last days. It is through Him that you are believers in God, the God Who raised Him from the dead and gave Him glory. Your faith and hope, then, are centered in God."

We have action verbs- "do not yield, become, be, conduct, gird, live soberly...." Even though we are promised the help of the Holy Spirit to keep us in the faith from our baptism on, this doesn't mean that we cannot fall away and lose our reward. Be vigilant.

However, if you look at verses 18-19 you will see the source of our hope and all of the grace that is necessary to make it to heaven- Jesus Christ. "Realize that you were delivered from the futile way of life your fathers handed on to you, not by any diminishable sum of silver or gold, but by Christ's blood beyond all price, the blood of a spotless, unblemished lamb chosen before the world's foundation and revealed for your sake in these last days. It is through Him that you are believers in God, the God Who raised Him from the dead and gave Him glory. Your faith and hope, then, are centered in God." If we have sinned, we can turn to Him for our forgiveness.

1 John 1:8-9 says, "If we say, 'We are free of the guilt of sin,' we deceive ourselves; the truth is not to be found in us. But if we acknowledge our sins, He Who is just can be trusted to forgive our sins and cleanse us from every wrong." The promise is ours. This is especially given to us in the Sacrament of Reconciliation (or penance).

1) Are you actively working on becoming holy? How?
2) How often do you frequent the Sacrament of Reconciliation?

ANSWER: Do you see the spiritual life and the pursuit of holiness as active or passive and why?

LESSON ON THE FRANCISCAN VIRTUES

In <u>Franciscan Virtues</u>, read Virtue 22: Justice. Spend at least five minutes meditating on the virtue. Answer the questions. Share your answers with your formator.

<u>DIVINE OFFICE FOR DODOS (Optional)</u>

Read Section 11.

DIFFICULTIES IN MENTAL PRAYER (Optional)

Read Chapters 17 and 18. ANSWER: Briefly describe the journey of prayer. How may Our Lady assist us on this journey?

ASSIGNMENTS

- Submit BRIEF answers to the above questions to your formator.
- Begin to pray the Office of Readings on Feasts, Memorials, and Solemnities or choose and implement another prayer option.
- If you are not at peace with someone, attempt to make peace following section 26 of the Rule and Constitutions. If you are not sure how to do this, seek the advice of your spiritual director. Also make a list of your "enemies" and pray daily for them by name.

FIRST YEAR NOVITIATE: LESSON ELEVEN

RULE LESSON

Chapter VII, Rule/Constitutions 32, 34, 35, 36, 39.

ANSWER: How could scandal among members of the Confraternity harm others and the Church?

Chapter VII, Rule/Constitutions 37.

ANSWER: What power does the Visitor have regarding the penitents' living of this Rule?

CATECHISM LESSON

Read Sections 484-570.

ANSWER: What to you is the most meaningful mystery of Christ's life and why?

SCRIPTURE LESSON

"The Lord said in reply to her: 'Martha, Martha, you are anxious and upset about many things; one thing only is required. Mary has chosen the better portion, and she shall not be deprived of it.'" (Luke 10:41-42)

Did Jesus not say, "let not your heart be troubled," and "be not afraid." This same Jesus says "listen, guys and gals, your lives are not your own. They were purchased at a price. Worry won't get you anywhere, because it is God's world and He has a plan for you."

Okay, okay, I know, that was a paraphrase, but the truth is there somewhere. I saw a sign once that said, "Good Morning! This is God. I will be handling all of your problems today. I will not need your help. So, relax and have a great day!"

This is true. It is also true that we are to "work out our salvation." So while we need not worry, we should balance this by living a life for Christ. Walk in the Spirit and avail yourselves of all of the graces that the Church has to offer, and you will prosper spiritually and eternally. Amen.

1) Find the passage in Luke 10 in which the entire story of Martha and Mary is told. Who would you be in the scene? Martha, Mary, Lazarus, one of the servants, Jesus, one of the disciples?

2) Who would you want to be in this story?

ANSWER: Write out your reflection on the above questions.

LESSON ON THE FRANCISCAN VIRTUES

In <u>Franciscan Virtues</u>, read Virtue 23: Love of Enemy. Spend at least five minutes meditating on the virtue. Answer the questions. Share your answers with your formator.

<u>DIVINE OFFICE FOR DODOS</u> (Optional)

Read Section 12.

<u>DIFFICULTIES IN MENTAL PRAYER</u> (Optional)

Read Chapters 19 and 20.

ANSWER: What is spiritual dryness? How severe can it become? What must one do when experiencing this stage of prayer? What follows this period?

<u>ASSIGNMENT</u>

- Submit BRIEF answers to the above questions to your formator.
- Begin to pray the Little Hours (Midmorning, Midday, and Midafternoon prayer) daily or chose another prayer option with the consent of your spiritual director.
- Evaluate your prayer life with your spiritual director to see if the options you have chosen are the best for you.
- Do you know of anyone who might be interested in living the CFP Rule? If so, invite them to attend next month's meeting or to inquire into this way of life.

FIRST YEAR NOVITIATE: LESSON TWELVE

RULE LESSON

Review the entire Rule and Constitutions with particular attention to all of Chapter IV and also to Rule/Constitutions 7, 15-18, 21-24, 26, and the Addendum and Appendices B, C, and D of the Constitutions.

ANSWER: Evaluate yourself on your living of the prayer and charity requirements of this Rule with particular attention to Chapter IV and the Rule/Constitutions, Addendum, and Appendices mentioned above.

Rule/Constitutions 25.

ANSWER: Why do you think this is in the Rule?

CATECHISM LESSON

Read Sections 571-658.

ANSWER: Pretend that you are Mary Magdalene, Joseph of Arimathea, or anyone else who was present at Christ's Passion. Write your own account of the death and resurrection of Christ as you might have experienced it. What are your thoughts, questions, insights, and emotions? This is a meditative exercise in which you, the penitent, reflect on and prayerfully try to participate in the Passion and death of Christ.

SCRIPTURE LESSON

"He advanced a little and fell prostrate in prayer. 'My Father, if it is possible, let this cup pass Me by. Still, let it be as You would have it, not as I." When He returned to His disciples, He found them asleep. He said to Peter, 'So you could not stay awake with Me even for an hour? Be on guard and pray that you may not undergo the test. The spirit is willing but nature is weak.' Withdrawing a second time, He began to pray, 'Father, if this cannot pass me by without my drinking it, Your will be done!' Once more, on His return, He found them asleep; they could not keep their eyes open. He left them again, withdrew somewhat, and began to pray a third time, saying the same words as before." (Matthew 26:39-44)

"We are here in a dark sanctuary of deep mysteries which we should enter reverently, humbly confessing our ignorance. Although it was impossible for the human nature of Christ to be separated from His divine nature and all this union entails, still in this agony Christ seems in a certain sense to suspend the spiritual support which His human nature normally received from His divinity. He is here the Second Adam, voluntarily undoing by His loving obedience to the Father the sins which the disobedience of the First Adam had brought upon mankind. Therefore, since Jesus acts here as the representative of all mankind, the Man par excellence, He acts, as far as possible, purely according to His human nature, suffering all the natural, though sinless, frailties of human nature, the dread of suffering and death, the shrinking from depredation and revilement, the intense sorrow of being abandoned by His friends and betrayed by His own disciple, the overwhelming grief at the thought of men's black ingratitude in despising the cost and value of His Sacrifice, and perhaps, as far as it would be compatible with His sinless soul, a sense of guilt for all the shameful sins of the world that He was taking upon Himself to atone for." (A Commentary on the New Testament, Catholic Biblical Confraternity, William H. Sadlier, Inc., 1942, p. 180).

1) How did prayer sustain Christ through the Agony in the Garden?
2) Have you ever experienced a time of intense emotional pain?
3) What was your prayer response at that time? Did it help?

ANSWER: How might our prayer be a union with and consolation to Our Lord?

LESSON ON THE FRANCISCAN VIRTUES

In Franciscan Virtues, read Virtue 24: Love of God. Spend at least five minutes meditating on the virtue. Answer the questions. Share your answers with your formator.

DIVINE OFFICE FOR DODOS (Optional)

Read Section 13.

DIFFICULTIES IN MENTAL PRAYER (Optional)

Read Chapter 21.
ANSWER: Has reading this book changed how I view my prayer life? If so, how? If not, why not?

ASSIGNMENT

- Submit BRIEF answers to the above questions to your formator.
- Discuss any concerns you may have about your CFP formation with your formator before proceeding on to second year formation.
- Evaluate the 15 minutes of mental prayer that you are doing daily. This will suffice to observe the Office of Prime. Should you alter how you are spending this time with God?
- Complete the application form requesting admission to Second Year Formation.
- If instructed by your formator, obtain the optional text A Year with the Saints available from the CFP Holy Angels Gift Shop at www.cfpholyangels.com or write to the CFP for a copy..

Make a Day of Recollection prior to entering 2nd year formation. This may be done formally at an established Day of Recollection or informally in the privacy of your home.

NOVICE 2 LESSONS

"So pleasing to God was Mary's humility that He was constrained by His goodness to entrust to her the Word, His only Son. And it was that dearest Mary who gave Him to us." - *St. Catherine of Siena*

Mary, Mother of God

O Mary, Mother of God, as You are above all creatures in Heaven and Earth, more glorious than the Cherubim, more noble than any here below, Christ has given You to His people, firm bulwark and Protectress, to shield and save sinners who fly unto You.

Therefore O Lady, all embracing refuge, we solemnly recall Your sweet protection, and beg Christ forever for His mercy. Amen.

NOVICE 2 LESSONS[34]

SECOND YEAR NOVITIATE: LESSON ONE

CONTINUING YOUR FORMATION

Congratulations! You are about to enter the second year of novice formation for the Confraternity of Penitents. Some of you will feel very comfortable entering upon this year. Others may feel a twinge of dread.

Be assured of one thing. The eating adjustments that you will make this year will be more freeing than restrictive. If you are used to snacking, you will discover that you have more time to do other things when you restrict your food intake. You will also have fewer dishes to wash, a healthier body, and lower food expenses. If you love to eat meat, you will find some interesting and tasty ways to observe the Rule's abstinence provisions. By the end of this year, you will feel healthier physically than you do now.

Nevertheless, the CFP is not a health club that claims to add years to your physical life. The CFP is a Confraternity intended to improve your spiritual health and bring you closer to the Lord. As you discipline yourself in the area of food, especially if you are undisciplined in this area, you will find yourself more readily surrendering to God's guidance in other areas of your life. It is this surrender, not the meatless or fast days, that will ultimately assist in sanctifying you.

In the First Year Novitiate, you learned to give God a great deal of your time in prayer. This year you will learn to give Him a portion of your physical appetites. What

---

34   Note: Keep copies of all lesson answers that you turn in to your formator, in case your answers are lost in either postal or internet mailing. Lesson answers need not be confined to texts discussed.

you learn about Him and yourself in this process will draw both you and Him into a deeper union. With such a worthy goal, let us begin.

The texts we will use are those used in First Year Novitiate: the Bible; the Rule and Constitutions of the Confraternity of Penitents; and <u>Catechism of the Catholic Church.</u>

Each month, reading assignments in Scripture, the Rule and Constitutions, and the Catechism will be given. You should do the reading assignment prior to the next month's meeting. It is suggested that 4 sections of the Catechism lesson be read daily so as to complete the lesson within a month's time. If desired, you may use the assignments as a basis for mental prayer or may jot down any insights into a Mental Prayer Journal which may be shared with your spiritual director.

Your formator may wish to use the optional text <u>A Year with the Saints</u> (available from the CFP Holy Angels Gift Shop and published by TAN Books and Publishers.

Texts should be brought to all Chapter or Circle meetings to aid in discussion. BRIEF answers (five sentences or less) to the questions marked ANSWER should be mailed, emailed, or recorded on audio tape for your formator.

You will also be given monthly assignments in living the Rule and Constitutions by following certain parts of the fasting and abstinence provisions. These practices should be started in the month given and then continued as long as you live this Rule. If, due to age, pregnancy, health, or other reasons, you are dispensed from following these provisions, then implement your dispensation while continuing formation for this second year of novice training.

May God bless you this year as you strive to more closely follow Him!

CATECHISM LESSON

Read Sections 659-747.

ANSWER: What is the mission of the Holy Spirit in the world and the Church? How has the Holy Spirit worked in your life?

SCRIPTURE LESSON

"...When you fast, you are not to look glum as the hypocrites do: They change the appearance of their faces so that others may see they are fasting. I assure you, they are already repaid. When you fast, see to it that you groom your hair and wash your face. In that way no one can see you are fasting but your Father Who is hidden; and your Father Who sees what is hidden will repay you." (Matthew. 6:16-18)

Jesus assumes that we, who are His disciples, will FAST. Some Protestant denominations do practice fasting. Some do it to bolster their supplications. Some fast to help their spiritual discipline. Lutherans used to fast during Lent, but only a handful do these days. Roman Catholics fast on Ash Wednesday and Good Friday. Orthodox Christians fast all during Lent. We living the CFP Rule fast daily during Lent and Advent, except Sundays and Solemnities, as well as on every Friday of the year, and on Wednesdays from the Octave of Christmas until Lent. Some of the brothers and sisters voluntarily keep a continual fast on all days of the year except Sundays, Solemnities, and the Octaves of Easter and Christmas.

There is a right way and a wrong way to fast. Fasting to lose weight, for instance, is not a fast unto God. Fasting to show off how "spiritual" we are immediately causes us to lose any spiritual reward we would have received. Once again we see Jesus reprimanding the Pharisees because they were only practicing their religion outwardly and not seeing the inward spiritual importance. Jesus takes them to task in the Beatitudes and the Woes in Matthew Chapters 5, 6, and 23.

Our darker, more sinful spiritual woes come from within; so also do our reflections of the Divine image when we live our lives in Truth and in Spirit. Anything we offer up to God must come from within and be combined with the outward to be a blessing to God, or to ourselves and neighbors. God promises that our reward for seeking Him through acts of consecration, such as fasting and prayer, will be secret in this world (usually anyway), and outward in the world to come.

1) What was your first impression when you understood that the Rule required fasting?
2) Do you see fasting as a part of your prayer life?
3) How can we fulfill Jesus' commitment, as we live our Rule, to let our fasting be done in secret?

ANSWER: How do you see fasting relating to your relationship with God?

RULE LESSON

Read the Object of the Commitment, Fruits of the Commitment, and Purpose (Charism) of the Constitutions, the Preamble of the Rule and Constitutions, and the Addendum to the Constitutions.

ANSWER: Which of the goals of a penitential life seem to be taking place most strongly in your life? How is your spiritual director assisting in this growth?

Make a general review of Chapters II and III of the Rule and Constitutions. Study Constitutions 6a, 6c, 6g, 6i, 9b, 9c, 9d, 9e, 9f, 10a, 11a, 11b, and Appendix A. These contain exceptions to the fasting and abstinence provisions.

ANSWER: Without looking at the Rule or Constitutions, make a list of all the exceptions you can remember. Go back and check your list. Add any exceptions you forgot. Put an identifying mark by any exceptions that apply to you.

Constitutions 6d.

ANSWER: Do you think you will have difficulty with this section? It will be implemented gradually into your life, beginning this month.

LESSON ON THE FRANCISCAN VIRTUES

In <u>Franciscan Virtues</u>, read Virtue 25: Love of Neighbor. Spend at least five minutes meditating on the virtue. Answer the questions. Share your answers with your formator.

A YEAR WITH THE SAINTS (Optional)

Begin with the reading for Day 1 and then read one reading each day in the order in which they are published in the book. Spend at least one minute reflection on the reading. Do this every day until you have completed the book in a year.

ANSWER: Select one writing of a saint from this month's reading and comment on its relevance to your life.

ASSIGNMENT

- Submit BRIEF answers to the above questions to your formator.
- Eliminate all solid-food snacks between lunch and dinner (afternoon snacks). Beverages may be taken.
- Having successfully completed the First Year Novitiate, you should already be doing the following which you will continue doing all your life as a penitent:
  - Daily praying in the morning the Apostles' Creed, all of Psalm 51, all of Psalm 54, and verses 1 to 32 of Psalm 119 as did the first penitents. The "Glory Be" is prayed after the Psalms.
  - Daily praying in the evening, the Apostles' Creed and all of Psalm 51 as did the first penitents with a "Glory Be" prayed after the Psalm.
  - Daily praying Morning, Evening, and Night Prayer.
  - Using another prayer option taken from the Rule, in consultation with your spiritual director, to bring your total prayer to 90 minutes per day unless your obligation has been excused or adapted.
  - Always wearing a visible cross or crucifix unless you are already wearing the habit of a Third Order.
  - Attending daily Mass, if possible.
  - Praying the Psalter yearly for deceased penitents.
  - Receiving the Sacrament of Reconciliation monthly and Eucharist weekly, at a minimum.
  - Praying a Marian Consecration prayer daily.
  - Embracing an apostolate from either the spiritual or corporal works of mercy.

- Abstaining from meat on every Friday of the year with the exception of Church Solemnities and special celebrations and praying an Our Father or another prayer before and after every meal.
- Daily asking the Lord to help you surrender your life to Him and praying for the Holy Father, our bishops, spiritual assistants, your spiritual director, your pastor(s), all penitents, the intentions of the Confraternity of Penitents, your enemies, all sinners, and yourself.

Are you doing these? If not, implement them into your life.

SECOND YEAR NOVITIATE:
LESSON TWO

RULE LESSON

Chapter VI, Rule/Constitutions 19-21.
ANSWER: Discuss your involvement in Chapter/Circle meetings of the CFP.
Chapter II, Rule/Constitutions 7 and Constitutions 6h.
ANSWER: Are you able to implement these sections in your daily life or do you sometimes forget? If you forget, what can you do to help you remember?

SCRIPTURE LESSON

"I warn you then: do not worry about your livelihood, what you are to eat or drink or use for clothing. Is not life more than food? Is not the body more valuable than clothes?" (Matthew 6:25)

As we train our bodies through the disciplines of fasting and simplicity, we likewise train our spirits. Thus we are heeding this warning of our Lord Jesus. Jesus does not say our bodies are unimportant; He is stating that the whole being, body and soul together, is of the most importance. He is not saying that eating and dressing are not important but that we are more important that what we eat or wear. Our priorities are therefore directed to be put in order: 1) Spirit 2) Body.

It has been said that the "eyes are the windows of the soul." Jesus speaks of the eyes as being the "lamp of the body" in this very chapter of Matthew (verses 22 and 23). If our eyes are full of covetousness, we are thinking that we are being neglected by God because someone else has more material goods than we do. We are breaking the Tenth Commandment, "Thou shalt not covet thy neighbor's goods."

1) Is it ever possible in our modern world to "not worry" about clothes, transportation and money?
2) Is there a connection with self-discipline (such as fasting) and the fulfillment of this verse?
3) What is that connection?
4) Will fasting help you set your priorities on the things of God?

ANSWER: Answer question 4 above in writing.

CATECHISM LESSON – Read Sections 748-829.

ANSWER: Name any five truths about the Catholic Church from this assignment and the Sections of the Catechism that discuss them.

LESSON ON THE FRANCISCAN VIRTUES

In Franciscan Virtues, read Virtue 26: Love of Self. Spend at least five minutes meditating on the virtue. Answer the questions. Share your answers with your formator.

A YEAR WITH THE SAINTS (Optional)

Continue reading one reflection daily, taking them in the order in which they come in the book. Spend at least one minute reflecting on the day's reading.

ANSWER: Select one writing of a saint from this month's reading and comment on its relevance to your life.

ASSIGNMENTS

- Return BRIEF answers to questions in this lesson to your formator.
- Eliminate any solid food snacks eaten between dinner (supper) and bedtime. Beverages may be taken.
- At meals, endeavor to allow all others to be served before you if you can do so without calling attention to yourself.

SECOND YEAR NOVITIATE: LESSON THREE

Chapter I of the Rule and Constitutions. Note especially Constitutions 2g.

ANSWER: In no more than five sentences, discuss the tone and reasons for this Chapter of the Rule and Constitutions. Remember that you are not expected to live these provisions at this stage of formation, with the exception of wearing a visible cross or crucifix.

Appendix A of the Constitutions.

ANSWER: The CFP Rule observes fast and abstinence as defined by the Church. What is the difference between fast and abstinence?

CATECHISM LESSON – Read Sections 830-913.

ANSWER: Draw, type, or otherwise create a simple chart or ladder showing the hierarchy of the Catholic Church and summarizing the duties of those on each step.

SCRIPTURE LESSON

"There was also a certain prophetess, Anna by name, daughter of Phanuel of the tribe of Asher. She had seen many days, having lived seven years with her husband after her marriage and then as a widow until she was eighty-four. She was constantly in the temple, worshiping day and night in fasting and prayer." (Luke 2:36-37)

Do we see here a proto-type of the religious orders for women? We should take great comfort that, over the surface of this globe, thousands of men and women live their lives devoted only to Christ. At any given moment, hundreds are offering up prayers for this sin darkened world. Anna was one of these. Her service to God was her "fasting and prayers." This is to be every Christian's service, but especially of those who seek a great level of consecration.

Those of us who seek to be transformed by the content of the Rule for the Confraternity of Penitents must see that value and connection between the "outward and the inward."

1. Why do you suppose that fasting and prayer are usually linked?
2. Does the link come in the discipline that one affords the other?
3. Does fasting add an element of sincerity to our prayers?
4. As Anna was faithful to fast "night and day," can we sustain our intentions to fast and pray?

ANSWER: Answer question 1 above in writing.

LESSON ON THE FRANCISCAN VIRTUES

In <u>Franciscan Virtues</u>, read Virtue 27: Loyalty to the Church. Spend at least five minutes meditating on the virtue. Answer the questions. Share your answers with your formator.

A YEAR WITH THE SAINTS (Optional)

Continue reading one reflection daily, taking them in the order in which they come in the book. Spend at least one minute reflecting on the day's reading.

ANSWER: Select one writing of a saint from this month's reading and comment on its relevance to your life.

ASSIGNMENT

- Eliminate any snacks you may be eating in the morning. By doing this, you should now have eliminated all between meal snacking.
- Return BRIEF answers to questions in above lessons to your formator.

SECOND YEAR NOVITIATE: LESSON FOUR

RULE LESSON

Chapter IV of the Rule and Constitutions and Appendices B and C of the Constitutions.

ANSWER: Evaluate yourself on your living of Chapter IV. All of the provisions of this Chapter should be fully implemented in your life at this time.

Rule and Constitutions 6 and Constitutions 6a, 6b, 8b, Appendix A.

ANSWER: Who does the Church exempt from fasting and abstinence? What days of fast and abstinence are enjoined on all Catholics with the above exceptions?

CATECHISM LESSON

Read Sections 914-991.

ANSWER: In one sentence each, define these terms:

- Consecrated life
- Communion of saints
- Marian prayer
- Forgiveness of sins

SCRIPTURE LESSON

"Jesus, full of the Holy Spirit, then returned from the Jordan and was conducted by the Spirit into the desert for forty days, where He was tempted by the devil. During that time, He ate nothing and at the end of it He was hungry." (Luke 4:1-2)

Jesus' self-deprivation, we might think, would have made Him weaker and more likely to succumb to the temptations of the devil. But that is not how fasting works. Our sufferings strengthen our spirits. Jesus' fasting and prayer actually fortified Him where it was important–in His spirit.

Jesus told John and James, when they could not stay awake with Him during His agony in the Garden of Gethsemane, "your spirits are willing, but your flesh is weak." If we train our flesh through the discipline of fasting coupled with prayer, our whole being is strengthened to withstand suffering and turn it to good.

1) Do we see the value of fasting as we experience the hunger and deprivation?
2) Is the experience of fasting similar to John of the Cross's "dark night of the soul," where we experience the silence from God, and the agony of working toward our goal, but then the beauty as we "break through to the other side?"
3) Have you ever experienced a temptation where fasting may have helped strengthen you in your spirit?

ANSWER: Select one of the above questions to answer in writing.

LESSON ON THE FRANCISCAN VIRTUES

In <u>Franciscan Virtues</u>, read Virtue 28: Marian Devotion. Spend at least five minutes meditating on the virtue. Answer the questions. Share your answers with your formator.

A YEAR WITH THE SAINTS (Optional)

Continue reading one reflection daily, taking them in the order in which they come in the book. Spend at least one minute reflecting on the day's reading.

ANSWER: Select one writing of a saint from this month's reading and comment on its relevance to your life.

ASSIGNMENTS

- Begin now to observe every Monday as a day of abstinence (that is, no meat is to be eaten on Mondays). This will be in addition to the Friday abstinence which you should already be keeping.
- Return BRIEF answers to questions above to your formator.

SECOND YEAR NOVITIATE: LESSON FIVE

<u>RULE LESSON</u>

Chapter V, Rule/Constitutions 15-16.
ANSWER: Evaluate yourself on the living of these sections. .
Rule and Constitutions 6 with particular attention to Constitutions 6e, 6f.
ANSWER: How are you observing these provisions?

<u>CATECHISM LESSON</u>

Read Sections 992-1076.
ANSWER: What are death and resurrection in our faith and in your own faith journey?

<u>SCRIPTURE LESSON</u>

"Then, raising His eyes to His disciples, He said, "Blest are you poor; the reign of God is yours. Blest are you who hunger; you shall be filled. Blest are you who are weeping; you shall laugh." (Luke 6:20-21)

While it is true that our Lord is speaking of physical deprivation, He is also saying that His words go deeper than material poverty and physical hunger. To say otherwise is to elevate the physical above the spiritual. When combined with Matthew 5:3 ("How blest are the poor in spirit; the reign of God is theirs), we see that Jesus speaks of an acknowledgment of our "poverty in the spirit," and our "hunger for righteousness."

However, it is true that external things can lead us to a deeper focus on internal things. Think of praying before a crucifix and meditating on our Lord on the Cross. The image is physical, but the crucifix helps us focus on our inward need; it helps us participate in the Cross. We must become poor in our selfish inner beings so that the Lord can lift us up into His kingdom. We must become hungry for righteousness in order to desire to be filled with that virtue.

1. Do you "hunger" for Christ and His righteousness to be a part of you? Is this a general feeling or is it related to some area of your life?
2. Do you believe that something physical can truly have an impact on your spirit?
3. Do you think that it is more inherently spiritual to be poor than to be well off?
4. Is it true that poverty can be either a blessing, or a curse depending on one's relationship with God?

ANSWER: Answer in writing either number 2 or number 3 above.

LESSON ON THE FRANCISCAN VIRTUES

In <u>Franciscan Virtues</u>, read Virtue 29: Minority. Spend at least five minutes meditating on the virtue. Answer the questions. Share your answers with your formator.

<u>A YEAR WITH THE SAINTS</u> (Optional)

Continue reading one reflection daily, taking them in the order in which they come in the book. Spend at least one minute reflecting on the day's reading.

ANSWER: Select one writing of a saint from this month's reading and comment on its relevance to your life.

<u>ASSIGNMENTS</u>

- From now on, observe every Wednesday as a day of abstinence from meat. This will be in addition to the Monday and Friday days of abstinence.
- Submit BRIEF answers to questions above to your formator.

SECOND YEAR NOVITIATE: LESSON SIX

RULE LESSON

Rule/Constitutions 17-18 and Appendix D of the Constitutions.
ANSWER: What are you doing to fulfill Constitutions 18d?
Review all of Chapter II in the Rule and Constitutions.
ANSWER: Summarize the abstinence provisions of this way of life.

CATECHISM LESSON

Read Sections 1077-1144.
ANSWER: Find something in this section that you did not know about the liturgy and discuss it. Give the section number in your discussion.

SCRIPTURE LESSON

St. Paul writes: "What I do is discipline my own body and master it, for fear that after having preached to others I myself should be rejected." (1 Corinthians 9:27)

Hell is real. It is separation from God, but since we are going to be physically resurrected it is also a plane of existence. Some people do go to Hell. See Romans 16:18 "Such men serve, not Christ our Lord, but their own bellies, and they deceive the simpleminded with smooth and flattering speech." In Philippians 3:19, St. Paul says, "Such as these will end in disaster! Their god is their belly and their glory is their shame." See also Romans 1: 18-25.

God does not necessarily enjoy it when we are physically hungry, but He certainly doesn't want us to wind up in Hell. We sinners live in a material and spiritual world, but it is so easy for the material to choke out the spiritual. We have so much trouble keeping the First Commandment ("Thou shalt have no other gods before Me"), let alone the rest. "Where your heart is, there your treasure will be also," Jesus tells us.

We can help keep our eyes on the Lord if we join the good company of St. Paul by "disciplining our body," and "bringing it into subjection."

1. Do you see a connection between the Ten Commandments and Paul's words in 1 Corinthians 9:27?
2. Would a hair shirt and flagellum help us to keep our priorities on the kingdom of God?
3. Would the practices in question 2 be excessive?
4. What is the danger of being excessive in our physical discipline?
5. Do most Americans run the risk of too harshly disciplining their bodies for spiritual reasons?

ANSWER: What can you do to maintain balance regarding mortification in your life?

LESSON ON THE FRANCISCAN VIRTUES

In <u>Franciscan Virtues</u>, read Virtue 30: Obedience. Spend at least five minutes meditating on the virtue. Answer the questions. Share your answers with your formator.

A YEAR WITH THE SAINTS (Optional)

Continue reading one reflection daily, taking them in the order in which they come in the book. Spend at least one minute reflecting on the day's reading.

ANSWER: Select one writing of a saint from this month's reading and comment on its relevance to your life.

ASSIGNMENTS

- Begin to observe Saturday as a day of abstinence from meat, adding this to the Monday, Wednesday, and Friday abstinence days.
- Submit BRIEF answers to the questions above to your formator.

SECOND YEAR NOVITIATE: LESSON SEVEN

RULE LESSON

Chapter VII of the Rule and Constitutions with particular attention to section 22.

ANSWER: How have you been able to observe this section?

Chapter III of the Rule and Constitutions with particular attention to section 8, and Appendix A of the Constitutions.

ANSWER: On fast days, how will you determine how much food to eat?

CATECHISM LESSON

Read Sections 1145-1228.

ANSWER: Pretend that a non-Christian friend asked you how the liturgy was celebrated. Write a one paragraph summary to answer this inquiry.

SCRIPTURE LESSON

"The day will come, however, when the groom will be taken away from them; on that day they will fast." (Mark 2:20)

In some places Jesus and the disciples could be distinguished from the Pharisees because they disdained false outward religion as they feasted and drank. On other occasions Jesus taught that the Pharisee's piety was not even close to being pious enough.

"There is a time a purpose for everything under heaven," said wise King Solomon. This is why the Church, in her wisdom, gives us regulations for both fasting and feasting. "In all things equilibrium," though not catchy, might be a worthwhile slogan for us. In this verse Jesus is contrasting the behavior of His disciples with those of John the Baptist (see preceding verses, Mark 2: 18-19). He is not saying that neither He, nor His disciples, ever fasted until after He was crucified. He was indicating that the true purpose of the disciples' fast would center around their Master, a fact which would only become clear to the disciples after the Resurrection.

(Note: In the Mosaic law, only the fast on the Day of Atonement was required. After the Babylonian exile of the Jewish nation, four other yearly fasts were observed. In Jesus' time, the Pharisees fasted twice a week.)

1. How should we offer up our prayers and fasts?
2. Around what or Who should they be offered up?
3. Our prayers can go through to the Father because we pray through Jesus even if in union with Mary or St. Joseph. Is fasting any different?
4. Have you studied the feast and fast days of the Church?

ANSWER: How can we center our fasting around Christ?

LESSON ON THE FRANCISCAN VIRTUES

In <u>Franciscan Virtues</u>, read Virtue 31: Pardon. Spend at least five minutes meditating on the virtue. Answer the questions. Share your answers with your formator.

A YEAR WITH THE SAINTS (Optional)

Continue reading one reflection daily, taking them in the order in which they come in the book. Spend at least one minute reflecting on the day's reading.

ANSWER: Select one writing of a saint from this month's reading and comment on its relevance to your life.

ASSIGNMENTS

- Begin from now on to fast as well as abstain on every Friday of the year except those which are Solemnities or within the Christmas and Easter Octaves.
- Return BRIEF answers to above questions to your formator.

During the ninth month of Second Year Novitiate, you will be asked to make a personal evaluation of your journey so far into a life of penance. Is it your intent to complete this year successfully and move into third year novitiate? Between now and the ninth month, please pray about this question. It is very important. If you are behind on a few lessons, strive to catch up. If you need help understanding the lesson or getting through it, let your formator know.

SECOND YEAR NOVITIATE: LESSON EIGHT

RULE LESSON

Chapter VII of the Rule and Constitutions with particular attention to sections 23-25.
ANSWER: How are you observing these sections?

Rule/Constitutions 6 with attention to Constitutions 6c, 6d, 6g, 6i, as well as Rule/Constitutions 8 and 11, and Appendix A of the Constitutions.

ANSWER: Write from memory how often penitents (who are not dispensed from the fasting and abstinence provisions of the Rule) eat, with the exception of Solemnities and Sundays.

CATECHISM LESSON

Read Sections 1229-1321.
ANSWER: Summarize the sacraments of Baptism and Confirmation.

SCRIPTURE LESSON

"Rather put on the Lord Jesus Christ and make no provision for the desires of the flesh." (Romans 13:14)

"Work out your salvation with fear and trembling" is a verse similar to this one which directly opposes salvation by faith alone without the necessity of works (a Protestant teaching from Luther and the Reformers).

Why can we say that? The verse is filled with verbs. The subjects are understood to be you and me. YOU put on the Lord Jesus. How? Through the Sacraments! Through prayer and fasting! Through daily consecration! Through disciplining your body through periodically depriving it!

"Make no provision for the desires of the flesh." Does this mean don't go to work, feed your families, or buy life insurance? No! It means avoid occasions for sin and temptation. Are there certain television shows and movies that fill our brains with nonsense or propaganda? Yes, and these lead to what someone has called "stinkin' thinkin'". Don't forget that your sanctification is God's will. His Holy Spirit works "in you, both to will and to do His good pleasure." But even our Lord Jesus said, "I work and My Father works." Let us work to stay consecrated to our Lord in union with St. Mary and St. Joseph.

1. Is there a place where we should be the subject of the verbs and not God?
2. Is there a place where we should consider ourselves the object of the verbs and God the subject?
3. Are we saved "by grace through faith?"
4. Do our works have a place in our salvation?

ANSWER: Reflect on this month's Scripture verse and tell what it means to you.

LESSON ON THE FRANCISCAN VIRTUES

In <u>Franciscan Virtues</u>, read Virtue 32: Patience. Spend at least five minutes meditating on the virtue. Answer the questions. Share your answers with your formator.

<u>A YEAR WITH THE SAINTS</u> (Optional)

Continue reading one reflection daily, taking them in the order in which they come in the book. Spend at least one minute reflecting on the day's reading.

ANSWER: Select one writing of a saint from this month's reading and comment on its relevance to your life.

<u>ASSIGNMENT</u>

- Determine how you will reduce your meals to two per day in light of Constitutions 6c. Will you need a bite to eat for a third meal? This month try out different patterns of eating to see which seems to work best for you. You will implement this plan next month.
- Submit BRIEF answers to the above questions to your formator.

SECOND YEAR NOVITIATE: LESSON NINE

RULE LESSON

Rule/Constitutions 26-27.

ANSWER: All of us have offended others. Think of one or two people who most need your apology and write or speak an apology to them. Then submit your response to this activity to your formator.

Chapter II of the Rule and Constitutions with particular attention to section 6. .

ANSWER: Explain how you will observe Constitutions 6c.

CATECHISM LESSON

Read sections 1322-1390.

ANSWER: How do the Eucharist and the Mass support each other? How meaningful is the Eucharist to your faith journey with Christ?

SCRIPTURE LESSON

"The man who will eat anything must not ridicule him who abstains from certain foods; the man who abstains must not sit in judgment on him who eats. After all, God Himself has made him welcome." (Romans 14:3)

Does the CFP Rule indicate that we must follow it strictly even in public where other people might be somehow scandalized? No, it does not. We are to follow a rule of simplicity, but where that would unduly burden our spouses it becomes a scandal to the spouse and we are not to do that. We are not to make a show of our piety by refusing meat in public unless it would not be a problem to those around us.

Do we sin if conformity to the crowd conceals our Christianity? God tells us that we must obey Him and not mankind in those instances in which the Catholic Church has set up certain fasting and abstinence provisions (such as meatless Fridays during Lent). However, where there is a voluntary discipline involved, as there is in the case of the CFP Rule, we run the risk of performing our discipline to be "seen by men" if we are overly rigid in public situations.

We are certainly to never gloat over our discipline of fasting and prayer; to do so would indicate that we are far from understanding its purpose. God, through His Church, is working in us through our Rule. We must not bring scandal upon it by a false public show of rigidity.

1. Is Paul talking only of abstinence here, or could fasting be included as well?
2. Do you understand the difference between fasting and abstinence? (Abstinence is denying ourselves meat at meals; fasting is limiting the amount of food intake).
3. What sin is involved if we gloat over our supposed spiritual superiority?
4. Be sure to read the rest of Chapter 14 to truly understand Paul's full thrust! Once you have done so, decide what are two of the key issues in this passage. Hints: For whom did Christ die? What is the essence of the kingdom of God?

ANSWER: Answer in writing number 4 above.

LESSON ON THE FRANCISCAN VIRTUES

In <u>Franciscan Virtues</u>, read Virtue 33: Peace. Spend at least five minutes meditating on the virtue. Answer the questions. Share your answers with your formator.

<u>A YEAR WITH THE SAINTS</u> (Optional)

Continue reading one reflection daily, taking them in the order in which they come in the book. Spend at least one minute reflecting on the day's reading.

ANSWER: Select one writing of a saint from this month's reading and comment on its relevance to your life.

<u>ASSIGNMENT</u>

- Reduce your meals on every day of the week except Sundays and Solemnities to two per day. If you feel you need a bite to eat at the third meal, decide what that will be in light of Constitutions 6c.
- Submit BRIEF answers to the above questions to the formator.

<u>SELF-EVALUATION</u>

Am I keeping up with the novice lessons and turning in my answers on time?
Am I incorporating the assignments into my life?

Is it my intent to successfully complete the next months of the formation and move into Third Year Novitiate?

Or do I feel it would be better for me to repeat or continue this year of formation before moving on?

ANSWER: Do I, or do I not, plan on entering Third Year Novitiate and why or why not?

SECOND YEAR NOVITIATE: LESSON TEN

RULE LESSON

Rule/Constitutions 28, 38.

ANSWER: How are these sections being observed in your CFP Circle or Chapter?

Rule/Constitutions 8, 9, 10, 11.

ANSWER: Unless you are dispensed, how will you observe the pre-Christmas fast as required by Constitutions 9a and the Wednesday fast between All Saints' Day until Easter, as required by Constitutions 8a?

CATECHISM LESSON

Read Sections 1391-1470.
ANSWER: What is the purpose of the Sacrament of Penance and how may one receive it worthily?

SCRIPTURE LESSON

"They gave Him a drink of wine flavored with gall, which He tasted but refused to drink." (Matthew. 27:34)

Jesus refused to drink this mixture because He wanted to be fully conscious until His death. Gall was used as a numbing agent to somewhat mitigate the suffering, but Jesus had to taste suffering for everyone of us. He had to be conscious until His death. Modern mankind seeks not only to avoid suffering but also to stay numbed for recreational purposes. This makes us who seek to live as penitents stand out at times like sore thumbs.

We, in some small way like our Master, choose to experience suffering and deprivation. Ours is to help us focus on our spiritual life and on the needs of the world around us. We, along with Jesus and Mary, say, "not my will but Thy will be done." God works on us through our surrender. We surrender our wills somewhat, through our voluntary living of the CFP Rule and Constitutions.

1. Do you see that the living of the penitential life must be prayerfully considered and fully voluntary?
2. Is there a self-emptying involved in your life as you fulfill your pledge to live this Rule?
3. Have you grown in your "inner man" through daily spiritual discipline?
4. Have you meditated lately on our Lord's suffering and its voluntary nature?

ANSWER: How does the penitential life and its voluntary nature relate to our dealings with our family, co-workers, friends, and other Catholics?

LESSON ON THE FRANCISCAN VIRTUES

In <u>Franciscan Virtues</u>, read Virtue 34: Perseverance. Spend at least five minutes meditating on the virtue. Answer the questions. Share your answers with your formator.

<u>A YEAR WITH THE SAINTS</u> (Optional)

Continue reading one reflection daily, taking them in the order in which they come in the book. Spend at least one minute reflecting on the day's reading.

ANSWER: Select one writing of a saint from this month's reading and comment on its relevance to your life.

<u>ASSIGNMENTS</u>

- Unless dispensed, observe the fasting provisions during the pre-Christmas fast as discussed under Constitutions 9a.
- Also implement the Wednesday fast from the Feast of All Saints until Easter as stated in Constitutions 8a.
- Submit BRIEF answers to the above questions to your formator.

SECOND YEAR NOVITIATE:
LESSON ELEVEN

RULE LESSON

Rule/Constitutions 32, 34, 35, 36, 39.

ANSWER: What is our obligation as penitents regarding scandal or serious sin involving ourselves or another member of the Confraternity?

Chapters II and III of the Rule and Constitutions..

ANSWER: Of all the stipulations in these two chapters, which one do you feel is most important and why?

CATECHISM LESSON

Read sections 1471-1553.

ANSWER: Define these terms in one sentence each:

- Indulgences
- Anointing of the Sick
- Viaticum
- Holy Orders
- Ministerial Priesthood

SCRIPTURE LESSON

"Jesus said to all: "Whoever wishes to be My follower must deny his very self, take up his cross each day, and follow in My steps." (Luke 9:23)

Dietrich Bonhoeffer, German theologian and Hitler martyr, said, "Cheap grace is the preaching of forgiveness without requiring repentance, baptism without church discipline, Communion without confession, absolution without personal confession. Cheap grace is grace without discipleship, grace without the cross, grace without Jesus Christ, living and incarnate. Costly grace is the treasure hidden in the field....Such grace is costly because it calls us to follow, and it is grace because it calls us to follow Jesus Christ. It is costly because it costs a man his life, and it is grace because it gives a man the only true life. It is costly because it condemns sin and grace because it justifies the sinner. Above all, it is costly because it cost God the life of His Son: 'ye were bought at a price,' and what has cost God much cannot be cheap for us." (The Cost of Discipleship, p. 36-37)

The term "Christians" given to believers in Jesus means "Christ's people" or "belonging to Christ." Do we "belong" to Jesus?

Bonhoeffer also wrote, "When Christ calls a man, He bids Him come and die." (79) "Discipleship means adherence to Christ, and because Christ is the object of that adherence, it must take the form of discipleship." (50)

1. For Bonhoeffer "to deny oneself is to be aware only of Christ." Do you agree, or disagree? Why?
2. Is such a thing possible given our nature? Is it something to strive for?
3. ". . . the wounds and scars we receive in the fray are living tokens of this participation in the cross of our Lord." What does this mean? Have you heard this before? Where?

ANSWER: Reflect on the Scripture passage for this month and tell what it means to you.

LESSON ON THE FRANCISCAN VIRTUES

In Franciscan Virtues, read Virtue 35: Poverty. Spend at least five minutes meditating on the virtue. Answer the questions. Share your answers with your formator.

A YEAR WITH THE SAINTS (Optional)

Continue reading one reflection daily, taking them in the order in which they come in the book. Spend at least one minute reflecting on the day's reading.

ANSWER: Select one writing of a saint from this month's reading and comment on its relevance to your life.

ASSIGNMENT

- When Lent comes, observe the daily fast as stated in Rule and Constitutions 9, with particular attention to Constitutions 9a.
- Submit BRIEF answers to the above questions to your formator.

SECOND YEAR NOVITIATE: LESSON TWELVE

RULE LESSON

Rule/Constitutions 29, 30, 31, 33, 37.

ANSWER: Pretend that you found a ragged copy of the Rule and Constitutions. All you could read were the above sections and no others. What would these sections tell you about the objectives of the Confraternity of Penitents?

Constitutions, Appendix A.

ANSWER: Evaluate yourself on how well you are doing in adjusting the way you fast and abstain under the Rule and Constitutions, with the regulations set down by the Church as delineated in Appendix A.

CATECHISM LESSON

Read Sections 1554-1600.

ANSWER: List five important facts about Holy Orders from this section.

SCRIPTURE LESSON

"Life is more important than food and the body more than clothing." (Luke 12:23)

This is not the prevailing philosophy of today's world, especially as represented in pop culture (movies, T.V., commercials etc...). Public education teaches children that religion is at best a myth and crutch. Many youngsters today look at life as ending at biological death. But the Bible teaches that "life is more than....." that. Jesus says, "Do not fear him who can destroy the body, but Him who can destroy both body and soul." (Matthew 10:28)

Our pledge to live the CFP Rule helps us be mindful of what's truly important and hopefully helps us communicate this lovingly to others. We do not lord our Rule over others but use it as a vehicle to draw nearer to God and to be made more into the image of His only begotten Son. Let us meditate on that in this our second year of living the Rule of the Confraternity of Penitents. May the Love of God, the grace of our Lord Jesus Christ, and the communion of the Holy Spirit be with you now and forever. Amen.

1. Where is your "treasure?"
2. Do you understand that grace can neither be bought nor sold? It is a gift, and, like beggars, we thank the Giver for it. Grace can be "merited" but even the merit is God's gift.
3. If you fail in living your pledge of fasting, do you take this to our Lord and ask for His empowerment to try again?
4. Has your spiritual improvement caused you to look at others in a new light?
5. Are you being "salt" and "light" to those around you?

ANSWER: Answer number 4 above in writing.

LESSON ON THE FRANCISCAN VIRTUES

In <u>Franciscan Virtues</u>, read Virtue 36: Praise. Spend at least five minutes meditating on the virtue. Answer the questions. Share your answers with your formator.

<u>A YEAR WITH THE SAINTS</u> (Optional)

Continue reading one reflection daily, taking them in the order in which they come in the book. Spend at least one minute reflecting on the day's reading.

ANSWER: Select one writing of a saint from this month's reading and comment on its relevance to your life.

<u>ASSIGNMENT</u>

*   You should now be living the full fasting and abstinence requirements of the CFP Rule. Evaluate with your spiritual director how you are doing with these and how you are physically and spiritually feeling. Do you need to make any modifications?
*   Complete the application form requesting admission to Third Year Formation.
*   If your formator wishes, obtain the text <u>Abandonment to Divine Providence</u> (Jean-Pierre de Caussade) which is available from the CFP Holy Angels Gift Shop, to use as part of third year Novice formation.

- Make a Day of Recollection prior to entering 3rd year formation. This may be done formally at an established Day of Recollection or informally in the privacy of your home.
- Submit BRIEF answers to the above questions to your formator.

NOVICE 3 LESSONS

"Some people are so foolish that they think they can go through life without the help of the Blessed Mother." - *St. Pio of Pietrelcina*

"Learning Christ"

Teach me, Lord, to be kind and patient in all the events of daily life; in disappointments, the thoughtlessness of others, in the insincerity of those I trusted, in the unfaithfulness of those on whom I relied. Let me put myself aside, to think of the happiness of others, to hide my little pains and heartaches, so that I may be the only one to suffer from them.

Teach me to profit by the suffering that comes across my path each day. Let me so use it that it may mellow me, not harden or embitter me; that it may make me patient not irritable, that it may make me broad in my forgiveness, not proud and narrow, haughty and overbearing.

May no one be less good for having come within my influence. No one less pure, less true, less kind, less noble for having been a fellow traveler in our journey toward Eternal Life.

As I go my way from one distraction to another, let me whisper from time to time, a word of love to you.. May my life be lived in the super-natural, full of power for good and strong in its purpose of sanctity. Amen.

NOVICE 3 LESSONS

THIRD YEAR NOVITIATE: LESSON ONE[35]

YOUR FINAL YEAR OF FORMATION

May God be praised! You are about to enter your final year of formation for the Confraternity of Penitents. If you have come this far, be assured of one thing. Your persistence is a good indication that God may, indeed, be calling you to live this way of life as your own path toward sanctity.

You may already be living very simply. Some of you will have already made a few or more of the clothing adjustments of this Rule. Others may dread getting rid of that favorite outfit.

Be certain of this. Those who are serious about entering a religious way of life must be unencumbered by attachments to worldly things. This year may be a bit difficult. But it will bear much fruit because it will sever you from externals.

Once your wardrobe and life style are simplified according to the Rule and Constitutions, you will feel a new sense of freedom. Not only will the former worldly attachments have lessened their grip on you but you will also have less clutter in your life. You will have more closet space, more attic space, and less to care for. Very freeing, indeed.

The purpose of this year of formation is not to keep the Salvation Army stocked or to have a less cluttered house. This year will move you a major step away from worldly things and a major step toward a total devotion to spiritual ones. At the end of this year, you will look backward and wonder how you could have been so attached to things that ultimately do not matter. You will find yourself loving things a lot less and people and

---

35   Keep copies of all lesson answers you turn in to your formator as they can be lost in mailing either via postal or email. Lesson answers need not be restricted to the texts discussed.

God a lot more. God willing, you will become so firmly rooted in the Lord that, were He to ask you to give up your life for Him, you would respond, "Yes." And, whether or not you actually die a martyr's death, you will give up your life for Him because following Him in the path He has chosen for you is to be dead to your own will and alive for His.

The texts we will use are those used in the previous years of formation: the Bible; Rule and Constitutions of the Confraternity of Penitents; and Catechism of the Catholic Church.

Each month, reading assignments in Scripture, the Rule and Constitutions, and the Catechism will be given. As in previous years, you should do the reading assignment prior to the next month's meeting. It is suggested that 4 sections of the Catechism lesson be read daily so as to complete the lesson within a month's time. If desired, you may use the assignments as a basis for mental prayer or may jot down any insights into a Mental Prayer Journal which may be shared with your spiritual director.

Your formator may also wish to use the optional text Abandonment to Divine Providence (Jean-Pierre de Caussade), available from the CFP Holy Angels Gift Shop, as part of your formation.

Texts should be brought to all Chapter or Circle meetings to aid in discussion. BRIEF answers (five sentences or less) to the questions marked ANSWER should be mailed, e mailed, or recorded on audio tape for your formator.

You will also be given monthly assignments in living the Rule by following certain parts of the Rule and Constitutions not yet assigned in previous years. These practices should be started in the month given and then continued as long as you live the CFP way of life.

In making the initial clothing adjustments, you may find that you do not have the clothing you need in the colors permitted by the Rule and Constitutions. Remember that you do not need many clothes in order to live this way of life. Four or five at the most of each article of clothing (other than undergarments) should suffice. You will only need one or two coats or jackets at most. The clothes you select should be tasteful and neat. No one, by looking at you, should suspect that you are doing penance in the area of clothing. Only you should know.

If you still do not have enough clothes, do not go out and purchase new items unless your spouse agrees as well as your spiritual director. Instead, make a list of items and colors needed and request them for birthdays, anniversaries, or holidays. Or shop at a second-hand sale or a thrift store or sew your own clothing. Most penitents at this stage of formation can make the clothing switch with little expense and trouble.

May God bless you this final year as you strive to give yourself completely to the Lord in this penitential way of life!

CATECHISM LESSON

Read Sections 1601-1679.

ANSWER: Is marriage a less meritorious sacrament than Holy Orders? Why or why not? What are sacramentals and how are they used?

SCRIPTURE LESSON

"Conscience gives testimony to the boast that in our behavior toward all and especially toward you we have always acted from God given holiness and candor; this has been prompted, not by debased human wisdom, but by God's goodness." (2 Cor. 1:12)

When we discuss living a life of simplicity, we begin where St. Paul does: in "God-given holiness and candor (simplicity)." Apart from these there is no reason to attempt to "simplify" our lives. As we grow in a relationship with God through His Son and with the help of His saints' example, we feel the need for holiness. As we grow in a walk that begins to use the grace God gives us daily, and especially through His Word and Sacraments, we start to "cast off" the time-consuming affairs of this world that choke holiness.

Paul adds that our consciences will guide us in this endeavor, but that is true only insofar as our consciences are formed by God Himself. St. Paul ends this verse with a reminder that we are not to walk in the ways of the world, but to empty ourselves of worldliness by relying on God's goodness (grace).

1. Why does Paul say that his boast consists in his behavior toward all in the world?
2. What are some contrasts between how the world views life and how God's people are instructed to view life?
3. What is the source for your ability to give up any worldly attachments according to the above verse?

ANSWER: What does the above Scripture verse speak to you as someone who wishes to live according to the Rule and Constitutions of the Confraternity of Penitents?

RULE LESSON

Review the Object of the Commitment, Form of the Commitment, and Purpose (Charism) in the Constitutions, the Preamble to the Rule and Constitutions, and the Addendum to the Constitutions. .

ANSWER: How are the goals of the penitential life, under the guidance of your spiritual director, being realized in your own life?

Read Rule/Constitutions 5 and Constitutions 3b.

ANSWER: How do you avoid attending functions at which immoral or sacrilegious behavior is present?

LESSON ON THE FRANCISCAN VIRTUES

In <u>Franciscan Virtues</u>, read Virtue 37: Prayer. Spend at least five minutes meditating on the virtue. Answer the questions. Share your answers with your formator.

<u>ABANDONMENT TO DIVINE PROVIDENCE</u> (Optional)

Read the Preface and Book 1, Chapter 1, sections 1-4.

ANSWER: Select one key sentence from this assignment and explain what it means to you.

<u>ASSIGNMENT</u>

- Reread Constitutions 3b again. Beginning this week, go through your personal items and discard at least one per week that you do not need. Remember that these are to be your personal items, not those belonging to another family member. Discuss with your spiritual director how you are feeling about doing this.
- If you have already weeded through your possessions and have very little to yet discard, discuss with your spiritual director what you might do in order to implement the spirit of this directive.
- Having successfully completed the first two years of novice formation, you should already be following all the provisions of Chapters II, III, IV, V, VI, VII (with the exception of Rule/Constitutions 25), and VIII of the Rule and Constitutions. How are you doing with these?
- Submit BRIEF answers to the above questions to your formator.

THIRD YEAR NOVITIATE: LESSON TWO

RULE LESSON

Review Chapters II and III of the Rule and Constitutions and Appendix A of the Constitutions.

ANSWER: How are you doing with the fasting and abstinence provisions of this way of life? What is easiest? What is most difficult?

Read Constitutions 2g regarding the wearing of the cross or crucifix.

ANSWER: Are you wearing a cross or crucifix regularly? Do you feel that it fits the spirit of the Constitutions? Why or why not? If not, how will you select a style that does fit?

SCRIPTURE LESSON

"What profit does a man show who gains the whole world but destroys himself in the process?" (Mark 8:36)

The previous verses say that each follower of Christ must, "deny his very self, take up his cross, and follow in My steps. Whoever would preserve his life will lose it, but whoever loses his life for My sake and the gospel's will preserve it."

If we are following Christ, then we have to be denying our selves and carrying our crosses. If we are denying self and following our Master, then we will not be caving in to our selfish lusts. The admonition in verse 36 is very direct and even scary. There is a chance that by denying Christ and following only our own inclinations that we could lose our very soul.

The message is clear. It is good for us to use and enjoy the gifts that God gives us in our everyday lives. But there is a dividing line between enjoying good things and living for those that are strictly of this world.

There are, however, spiritual blessings that we ought to live for. Some cannot be lived at the present moment, yet it is good to live in the hope of someday receiving them. For example, in Matthew 25, Christ says, "Come, you blessed of my Father." Now there is a blessing to live for.

Seen in the proper way, we can balance self-denial with gratitude for the gifts of God. Then we will be glorifying and enjoying our Creator and Redeemer from Whom every gift comes.

1) Is there anything that you covet in your mind that could be a stumbling block for you in God's kingdom?
2) What steps could help you to dedicate this area to Christ and be free of the harmful obstruction?
3) What is a proper attitude for enjoyment of God's blessings?

ANSWER: What worldly thing do you covet the most? How can you handle your attitude toward this object, attitude, or person?

CATECHISM LESSON

Read Sections 1680-1761.
ANSWER: How are humanity's dignity, freedom, and happiness related in the vocation given to the human race? How do we observe the death of a human being?

LESSON ON THE FRANCISCAN VIRTUES

In Franciscan Virtues, read Virtue 38: Presence. Spend at least five minutes meditating on the virtue. Answer the questions. Share your answers with your formator.

ABANDONMENT TO DIVINE PROVIDENCE (Optional)

Read Book 1, Chapter 1, sections 5-9.
ANSWER: Select one key sentence from this assignment and explain what it means to you.

ASSIGNMENTS

• Continue to reduce personal belongings by getting rid of one weekly. Why are you doing this?
• Evaluate your personal wardrobe. What articles of clothing do you have that you never or very rarely use? Remove those from your wardrobe and give them away. Discuss with your spiritual director how you feel about doing this.
• Submit BRIEF answers to the above questions to your formator.

THIRD YEAR NOVITIATE: LESSON THREE

RULE LESSON

Review Chapter IV of the Rule and Constitutions and Appendices B and C of the Constitutions.

ANSWER: Are you fulfilling this part of the Rule? Is it time to evaluate your prayer options or are they still working well for you?

Read Rule/Constitutions 1.

ANSWER: Study Rule/Constitutions 1 and then write down, from memory, what colors can be worn and why.

CATECHISM LESSON

Read Sections 1762-1845.

ANSWER: Name and define the virtues. How is conscience related to them?

SCRIPTURE LESSON

"If we have food and clothing we have all that we need." (1 Timothy 6:8)

St. Paul's saying in our material times may strike us as "archaic," or even impossible to live by. Is it really? Are we too conditioned by the world to even conceive of an existence where our joy is full, not through the things we own, but rather through the Holy Spirit, the Scriptures and Sacraments, and the people around us?

Many of the saints, both recent and ancient ones, have fought this battle, and their faith walks and stories can help us on our journey toward simplicity of life and contentment with what God chooses to give us for our daily needs.

1. Can you see how reaching this state of spiritual grace can be an entrance way into complete freedom from worldly bondage?

2. What are the negatives that come with continually seeking "things?"
3. What do you make of the saying popular in the 1980's that "you can separate the men from the boys by the price of their toys?"

ANSWER: What is your reflection on this Scripture verse?

LESSON ON THE FRANCISCAN VIRTUES

In <u>Franciscan Virtues</u>, read Virtue 39: Purity. Spend at least five minutes meditating on the virtue. Answer the questions. Share your answers with your formator.

ABANDONMENT TO DIVINE PROVIDENCE (Optional)

Read Book 1, Chapter 2, sections 1-6.

ANSWER: Select one key sentence from this assignment and explain what it means to you.

ASSIGNMENT

- Go through your entire outerwear wardrobe. Put the clothes that fit the colors of the Rule together in one place in your closet. If you were to only wear these clothes, would you have enough or would you need to supplement your wardrobe?
- How does doing this make you feel? Why are you making these adjustments? Discuss your feelings with your spiritual director.
- Submit BRIEF answers to these questions to your formator.

THIRD YEAR NOVITIATE: LESSON FOUR

RULE LESSON

Review Chapter V in the Rule and Constitutions and Appendix D in the Constitutions.

ANSWER: How are you doing in living Chapter V of the Rule and Constitutions? If you need improvement in an area or two, how can you improve?

Review Rule/Constitutions 1, particularly Constitutions 1b and 1c.

ANSWER: Why do you think it is important for a lay penitent to avoid giving the appearance of wearing a habit?

SCRIPTURE LESSON

"...Anyone among you who aspires to greatness must serve the rest, and whoever wants to rank first among you must serve the needs of all. Such is the case with the Son of Man Who has come, not to be served by others, but to serve, to give His Own life as a ransom for the many." (Matthew 20:26-28)

Here Jesus is giving Himself as an example. He served others, giving His life, for no reward to Himself, but to ransom others. The reward of His service went to us.

Sometimes this happens in the world as well. Those who are in the line of duty as military, police, or firefighters serve the nation or the public by sacrificing their lives. They at least knowingly risk their lives in these occupations. Even worldly service professions consist in providing service to others, and in these there are rewards for those who serve and those who are being served.

In God's economy, we are not forbidden to hope for the rewards that He has promised. There is an element of self-seeking that can be present in both, and is expected to be more present in worldly service, but it would be an excessive "perfectionism" to rule this out in spiritual service. After all, Jesus told us to "lay up for yourselves treasure in heaven." What other motive is there in wanting to follow the Rule of the CFP? Even if we are living this life as a means of prayer and sacrifice for the conversion of others, we still hope that God will reward our efforts with eternal life for us.

However, in Matthew 20: 26-28, Our Lord is not talking about seeking rewards but about aspiring to greatness and wanting to be first. We might paraphrase it today by saying, "If you're a priest, and you want to rank first among priests, and be the greatest in God's eyes, don't aspire to be a bishop, or if you're a monk, don't aspire to become abbot. Aspire to serve, to be of benefit to others." The humblest priest or most obscure lay brother may rank first in God's eyes. Elsewhere Christ speaks of not lording it over others, but of serving. Surely in God's economy the service of others brings spiritual rewards.

The world sometimes will do good works because God's image, though greatly damaged, is still present in humankind. Sometimes the works are done out of self-seeking, or merely to have a tax deduction. These are not works done, "...in Jesus' name."

St. Paul says, "Esteem others as greater than yourselves." He doesn't mean, "Have a poor self-image." He also doesn't mean be someone who is purposely trodden under people's feet. If we don't sometimes help people know right from wrong then we aren't truly loving them, as we would be guilty of helping to keep them in their sins. However, we are to not be "self-seeking." Not seeking our glory above other's and God's. Do good and God will lift you up at the appropriate time.

1. Does Matthew think that it's better to be impoverished, or that poverty is necessarily glorifying to God?
2. Can poverty be turned into a glory unto God?
3. What does Matthew mean by "must serve the needs of all?"

ANSWER: How does this passage foster poverty of spirit and how does poverty of spirit lead to poverty of possessions?

CATECHISM LESSON

Read Sections 1846-1927.
ANSWER: Define these terms in one sentence each:

* Mortal sin
* Venial sin
* Society
* Subsidiarity
* Authority
* The Common Good

LESSON ON THE FRANCISCAN VIRTUES

In <u>Franciscan Virtues</u>, read Virtue 40: Reverence for Creation. Spend at least five minutes meditating on the virtue. Answer the questions. Share your answers with your formator.

<u>ABANDONMENT TO DIVINE PROVIDENCE (Optional)</u>

Read Book 1, Chapter 2, sections 7-12. ANSWER: Select one key sentence from this assignment and explain what it means to you.

<u>ASSIGNMENTS</u>

- Go through your wardrobe and remove all patterned outerwear. Give these away. Why are you doing this? Discuss with your spiritual director how doing this makes you feel.
- Submit BRIEF answers to the above questions to your formator.

THIRD YEAR NOVITIATE: LESSON FIVE

<u>RULE LESSON</u>

Review Chapter VI of the Rule and Constitutions.

ANSWER: How important do you think your Confraternity membership will become as you reduce your wardrobe this year? Why do you feel this way?

Read Rule/Constitutions 2 with particular attention to Constitutions 2a, 2b, 2e, 2f.

ANSWER: Discuss how each of these are to fit the Rule and Constitutions:

- Visible undergarments
- Men's ties
- Perfumes and after shave lotions
- Cosmetics

<u>SCRIPTURE LESSON</u>

"Thus the last shall be first and the first shall be last." (Matthew 20:16)

Have you ever heard the expression, "There goes so-and-so; he's a legend in his own mind." If we are seeking to empty our selves and to be filled with the Holy Spirit, Who always does the work of transforming us into the image of Christ, then we will not be seeking "firstness." Christ Himself, Paul says, "emptied Himself, even to the point of becoming a servant who died on a cross."

1. If Christ is our example, how does emptying oneself fit into His statement that the "last will be first?"
2. Have you yet attempted to esteem others before yourself, in your family, work, and other environments?

3. Honestly take inventory and see if any of your possessions lead you to think that you are somehow "better" than anyone else for having them.

ANSWER: How can you foster the desire to be last in yourself?

CATECHISM LESSON

Read Sections 1928-2005.
ANSWER: Define these terms in one sentence each:

*   Social justice
*   Human solidarity
*   Natural moral law
*   Old law
*   New law
*   Justification
*   Grace

LESSON ON THE FRANCISCAN VIRTUES

In Franciscan Virtues, read Virtue 41: Sacrifice. Spend at least five minutes meditating on the virtue. Answer the questions. Share your answers with your formator.

ABANDONMENT TO DIVINE PROVIDENCE (Optional)

Read Book 2, Chapter 1, sections 1-4.
ANSWER: Select one key sentence from this assignment and explain what it means to you.

ASSIGNMENTS

*   Implement parts of Rule/Constitutions 2 and Constitutions 2a, 2b, 2e, and 2f in your life. No longer use scented lotions, sprays, perfumes, after shave, and so on. Go through your visible undergarments and ties and give away those that do not fit the Rule. Why are you doing this?
*   Discuss with your spiritual director how this makes you feel.
*   Submit BRIEF answers to the above questions to your formator.

THIRD YEAR NOVITIATE: LESSON SIX

<u>RULE LESSON</u>

Review Rule/Constitutions 22-24.

ANSWER: How are you doing following these sections of the Rule and Constitutions? Are you having difficulty with any part?

Read Rule/Constitutions 3 with particular attention to Constitutions 3a.

ANSWER: Do your clothes fall into the simple, inexpensive category or do you feel that a dispensation is necessary in some cases?

<u>SCRIPTURE LESSON</u>

"He instructed them to take nothing on the journey but a walking stick—no food, no traveling bag, not a coin in their purses in their belts. They were, however, to wear sandals. 'Do not bring a second tunic,' He said." (Mark 6:8-9)

Can you imagine the disciples' faces when they learn they must go on their first missionary journey without their credit cards, their new cars, and their designer jeans? What a break with the world it must have been to have to rely on the Creator and Sustainer of the universe! Can we relate? How do we come to the point where we can serve self last and rely on our Creator from day to day for all of our needs?

The Bible says that God will "give us what we need from His riches in glory." The Bible also says, "Cast all your cares upon Him for He cares for you." God will supply what He wants you to have!

However, we must be prudent. This quotation is a good example of the kind of words of Christ which are not to be taken literally in all circumstances by all disciples. It was to be taken literally (most probably) for that particular journey. But St. Joseph most likely didn't take the Holy Family to Egypt under a Rule like that, and St. Paul definitely didn't follow this exactly on his missionary journeys.

We must be careful not to take every word of the Scriptures out of the context of the whole New Testament. People ought not to go on extended trips with no traveling bag, money, credit cards, or extra clothing these days. The lesson seems to be simply "Cast your care upon the Lord." Don't worry over your plans. You'll have to adapt them to circumstances as they arise. But you won't even get to where you want to go unless you adapt this admonition in light of what is necessary and what is not.

1. Do you believe that God will supply your needs?
2. Can you "let go and let God?"
3. How have your first two years of spiritual formation helped to bring you to the point of "self-emptying?"

ANSWER: Make a list of ten things that you have (your possessions, not those of other family members) that you don't really NEED. Ought you to get rid of them? Why or why not?

CATECHISM LESSON

Read Sections 2006-2082.
ANSWER: How does merit help Christians advance in holiness? How do the Church and the Ten Commandments assist in this development?

LESSON ON THE FRANCISCAN VIRTUES

In <u>Franciscan Virtues</u>, read Virtue 42: Self-knowledge. Spend at least five minutes meditating on the virtue. Answer the questions. Share your answers with your formator.

ABANDONMENT TO DIVINE PROVIDENCE (Optional)

Read Book 2, Chapter 1, sections 5-8.
ANSWER: Select one key sentence from this assignment and explain what it means to you.

ASSIGNMENTS

- Go through your wardrobe. Give away all clothing that is red, orange, or yellow. Remember, however, the dispensation that goes with Rule 3 and Constitutions 3a. Fancier clothes are permitted in certain occupations and for certain social occasions.
- How do you feel about doing this? Discuss this with your spiritual director.
- Submit BRIEF answers to the above questions to your formator.

THIRD YEAR NOVITIATE: LESSON SEVEN

<u>RULE LESSON</u>

Review Chapter VII of the Rule and Constitutions with particular attention to sections 25-27.

ANSWER: Do you have a will? If not, how can you begin to make one?

Review Chapter I of the Rule and Constitutions, with particular attention to sections 1, 2, and 3.

ANSWER: Do you notice anything in these sections that you had not seen before? If so, what?

<u>SCRIPTURE LESSON</u>

"Have no love for the world or things that the world affords. If anyone loves the world, the Father's love has no place in him." (1 John 2:15)

What in the world does the beloved disciple mean, "Have no love for the world?" Aren't we supposed to love everyone? Yes, indeed, but you do not love the world's system of thinking. We do not love the world's ideology that keeps our young people thinking about self-gratification and pre-marital sex. We do not love the world's way of thinking that bigger, richer and more fleshly beautiful is always better. We must, if we will be followers of the Incarnate YHWH, be able and ready to renounce the darkness that keeps our world from seeing the light that comes from above. We must share the truth with others, but always winsomely and spoken in love.

1. Do you agree that lust for the world chokes out the life of the spirit?
2. Read the rest of the passage, including verses 16-17. How does that strike you?

3.   Boasting of our accomplishments is mentioned and so is lust of our eyes. How do these two go against the revealed will of our Father? Can you think of examples from Scripture?

ANSWER: Suppose an angel came to you and offered you fame, joy, success, wealth, and health in this world and a long time in Purgatory in the world to come, or humiliation, grief, failure, poverty, and illness in this world and a quick entry into heaven upon death. Which would you choose and why?

CATECHISM LESSON

Read Sections 2083-2167.
ANSWER: What do the first and second commandments mean to you?

LESSON ON THE FRANCISCAN VIRTUES

In <u>Franciscan Virtues</u>, read Virtue 43: Service. Spend at least five minutes meditating on the virtue. Answer the questions. Share your answers with your formator.

ABANDONMENT TO DIVINE PROVIDENCE (Optional)

Read Book 2, Chapter 2, sections 1-4.
ANSWER: Select one key sentence from this assignment and explain what it means to you.

ASSIGNMENTS

*   Go through your wardrobe. Give away clothing of green, pink, and purple. How does this make you feel? Discuss this with your spiritual director.
*   If you do not have an updated will, make an appointment with a lawyer to update your will or make a will.
*   Submit BRIEF answers to the above questions to your formator.

During the ninth month of Third Year Novitiate, you will be asked to make a personal evaluation of your journey so far into a life of penance. Is it your intent to complete this year successfully and pledge to live the Rule and Constitutions for life? Or would you prefer to take a promise to live the Rule and Constitutions for a year? Perhaps you are considering a private vow to live the Rule and Constitutions for life. Between now and the ninth month, please pray about your future as a penitent. It is very important. If you are behind on a few lessons, strive to catch up. If you need help understanding the lesson or getting through it, let your formator know.

THIRD YEAR NOVITIATE: LESSON EIGHT

RULE LESSON

Review Chapter VIII of the Rule and Constitutions with particular attention to sections 35-37.

ANSWER: Summarize the tone of these three sections.

Review Rule/Constitutions 4 with particular attention to Constitutions 4a.

ANSWER: Do you have any outer winter garments? Do they fit the Rule and Constitutions?

SCRIPTURE LESSON

"Sell what you have and give alms. Get purses for yourselves that do not wear out, a never-failing treasure with the Lord which no thief comes near nor moth destroys. Wherever your treasure lies, there your heart will be." (Luke 12:33-34)

Does Jesus instruct us to have nothing but to give all to the poor? Our Lord seeks balance in our lives. St. Paul in 1 Corinthians 13 says that, "though we sell all we have to give to the poor, but have not love, we have nothing." So it isn't only the outward acts of penance, but also the accompanying love that goes with them that counts before our God. He does want us to use our resources for others. We are not to deprive our families, over which we, as our God given duty, are to be good stewards. The first of the neighbors to whom we should give are the parents and children whom God has given us. That is our duty in justice as well as in charity. If we do this, then selling and giving away beyond caring for our families and relatives are good things.

The key point is, "Where is your heart?" Is it fixed on things above where the treasure is incorruptible, or below where the treasure is fleeting and transient?

1. To whom is Jesus speaking in this passage?
2. Are you a disciple of Jesus?
3. Have you inventoried how you might lay up treasures in heaven by giving away and selling things that you don't need?

ANSWER: What we think most about is where our heart is. If you made a graph of the things you think about, what would have the longest column? What does this tell you about your priorities?

CATECHISM LESSON

Read Sections 2168-2257.

ANSWER: If a teen asked you why the third and fourth commandments are so important, what would you answer?

LESSON ON THE FRANCISCAN VIRTUES

In Franciscan Virtues, read Virtue 44: Silence. Spend at least five minutes meditating on the virtue. Answer the questions. Share your answers with your formator.

ABANDONMENT TO DIVINE PROVIDENCE (Optional)

Read Book 2, Chapter 2, sections 5-8.

ANSWER: Select one key sentence from this assignment and explain what it means to you.

ASSIGNMENTS

- Submit BRIEF answers to the above questions to your formator.
- Look at your outer weather-wear. Do your clothes fit the Rule and Constitutions? If you can give away those that do not and still have clothing to wear, then do so this month. If you would have to purchase items because nothing you have fits the Rule and Constitutions, then wait for a yard sale or visit a thrift shop to see if you can make the clothing transition with little expense or trouble. Or ask for these items as a holiday or birthday gift.
- Discuss how you feel about doing this with your spiritual director.

THIRD YEAR NOVITIATE: LESSON NINE

<u>RULE LESSON</u>

Review Rule/Constitutions 39.

ANSWER: What does this say to you in light of the adjustments you are now making in your wardrobe?

Review all of Chapter I of the Rule and Constitutions.

ANSWER: What adjustments are going smoothly for you? Which are not? Have you any idea why?

<u>SCRIPTURE LESSON</u>

"Lazarus longed to eat the scraps that fell from the rich man's table. The dogs even came and licked his sores." (Luke 16:21)

What a travesty of God's will for His creation! A rich man, blessed with goods by God, shows utter contempt for God and God's people by not sharing with and caring for Lazarus. It is very likely that this rich man fancied himself religious. We see people every day in need. We also see the world's well-off every day, with haughty appearance, not only not helping the disadvantaged, but even laughing at them and saying, "Those people get what they deserve." We all need to remember, "There but for the grace of God go I."

1. Do we have some crumbs to share that we are hoarding?
2. Is it a sin, necessarily, to be rich?
3. Who has the "gift of benevolence" that St. Paul mentions in 1 Corinthians 12:28?

ANSWER: How do you assist the poor? Do you think you are doing as good a job as possible given your circumstances?

CATECHISM LESSON

Read Sections 2258-2330.

ANSWER: Make as extensive a list as possible of all the circumstances covered by the fifth commandment.

LESSON ON THE FRANCISCAN VIRTUES

In <u>Franciscan Virtues</u>, read Virtue 45: Simplicity. Spend at least five minutes meditating on the virtue. Answer the questions. Share your answers with your formator.

ABANDONMENT TO DIVINE PROVIDENCE (Optional)

Read Book 2, Chapter 3, sections 1-3.

ANSWER: Select one key sentence from this assignment and explain what it means to you.

ASSIGNMENTS

- Go through your outerwear wardrobe. Remove any colors or clothing that still do not fit the Rule and Constitutions. How does this make you feel? Discuss this with your spiritual director.
- Submit BRIEF answers to the above questions to your formator.

SELF-EVALUATION

Am I keeping up with my novice lessons and turning in my answers on time?

Am I incorporating the assignments into my life?

Is it my intent to successfully complete the next months of the Third Year Novitiate and pledge to live the Rule and Constitutions for life or take a promise to live it for a year? Am I considering a private vow to live the Rule and Constitutions for life?

Or do I feel it would be better for me to repeat or continue this year of formation before pledging?

ANSWER: Do I, or do I not, plan on completing the Third Year Novitiate and why or why not?

THIRD YEAR NOVITIATE: LESSON TEN

RULE LESSON

Review Rule/Constitutions 28 and 38.

ANSWER: Are you willing to accept an office in your Chapter or Circle of the Confraternity or in the larger organization? Why or why not?

Look at Rule/Constitutions 2 with particular attention to Constitutions 2c and 2d.

ANSWER: Why should colorful ornamentation and jewelry be avoided? What jewelry is permitted?

SCRIPTURE LESSON

"The affectation of an elaborate hairdress, the wearing of golden jewelry, or the donning of rich robes is not for you. Your adornment is rather the hidden character of the heart, expressed in the unfading beauty of a calm and gentle disposition. This is precious in God's eyes." (1 Peter 3:3-4)

Proverbs says, "Like a fine gold ring in a pig's snout is a beautiful woman who lacks discretion." A Christian with a beautiful spirit who lacks outward beauty radiates far more loveliness than a crass pagan, who revels in the things of the world and neglects the spirit. Which should Christ's disciples seek? Outward beauty that can distract and lead astray, or inward beauty which attracts others to the light of Christ within us? Embracing the attitude of Christ can be a very difficult thing for those of us seeking to live as penitents, especially in this current age which puts shallow outward beauty and wealth at so much more of a premium than any kind of self-sacrifice or inward beauty.

1. Can you see yourself, with the help of God, being able to do away with excess outward adornment?
2. Will you be self-conscious around friends or co-workers without your usual trappings? Can you see yourself dwelling in God's Spirit to an extent where this no longer bothers you?
3. Can freedom from outward trappings actually become a source of freedom for you?

ANSWER: Select one of the above questions to answer in writing.

CATECHISM LESSON

Read Sections 2331-2400.

ANSWER: Summarize the positive and negative aspects of the sixth commandment. In other words, what is not only permitted but encouraged and what is sinful under this commandment?

LESSON ON THE FRANCISCAN VIRTUES

In Franciscan Virtues, read Virtue 46: Surrender. Spend at least five minutes meditating on the virtue. Answer the questions. Share your answers with your formator.

ABANDONMENT TO DIVINE PROVIDENCE (Optional)

Read Book 2, Chapter 3, sections 4-5.

ANSWER: Select one key sentence from this assignment and explain what it means to you.

ASSIGNMENTS

- Go through your jewelry. Put jewelry aside or give it away. Use cosmetics tastefully if at all. How does doing this make you feel? Discuss this with your spiritual director.
- Meet with a lawyer about your will and complete the work on it.
- Submit BRIEF answers to the above questions to your formator.

THIRD YEAR NOVITIATE: LESSON ELEVEN

RULE LESSON

Review Rule/Constitutions 29-34.

ANSWER: Do you meet the qualifications for pledging in the Confraternity? Are you prepared to pledge to live the Rule for life or for a year? Are you considering making a private vow to live the Rule for life?

Review Rule/Constitutions 4 with particular attention to Constitutions 4b.

ANSWER: Do you think this section will be difficult to implement? Why or why not?

SCRIPTURE LESSON

"Trust Me when I tell you that whoever does not accept the kingdom of God as a child will not enter into it." (Luke 18:17)

How does a little child approach a great and awesome spectacle? With a degree of timidity and humility yet trust in those adults who have taken him or her there.

Little children have an innate trust that our God loves to see in all of His people. We must live in this world, yet not be a party to this world's warped ways of thinking. This can only be done if we trust our Father in a childlike way, each and every day of our lives. We can show humility and yet still be strong in our faith and in how we "seize each day" for our Lord.

1) How do you see a correlation between a little child and how our Father wants us to approach Him?
2) Have you ever seen a 9 month old baby play with her mother or father? The pure joy and security is truly a wonder to behold. Can we have that kind of innocent and pure glee in our relationship with the infinite, personal God?
3) What do you think the kingdom of God means (or is)?

ANSWER: How much of a child are you before God? How can you foster the child-like attitude called for by Christ?

CATECHISM LESSON

Read Sections 2401-2463.

ANSWER: List five types of action that are covered by the seventh commandment.

LESSON ON THE FRANCISCAN VIRTUES

In <u>Franciscan Virtues</u>, read Virtue 47: Trust. Spend at least five minutes meditating on the virtue. Answer the questions. Share your answers with your formator.

ABANDONMENT TO DIVINE PROVIDENCE (Optional)

Read Book 2, Chapter 4, sections 1-6.

ANSWER: Select one key sentence from this assignment and explain what it means to you.

ASSIGNMENTS

- Examine your purses and carry bags in light of Rule/Constitutions 4 and Constitutions 4b. If you can switch to the CFP colors without expense, do so. If not, wait until an inexpensive opportunity presents itself.
- Determine to complete any work on your will before pledging to live the Rule and Constitutions, if possible.
- Submit BRIEF answers to the above questions to your formator.

THIRD YEAR NOVITIATE: LESSON TWELVE

<u>RULE LESSON</u>

Review the entire Rule and Constitutions.

ANSWER: Are you ready to embrace this Rule and Constitutions in their entirety? Why or why not?

Review Chapter I of the Rule and Constitutions.

ANSWER: How are you doing in implementing this Chapter? Are you seeing the fruit of it in your life? How?

<u>SCRIPTURE LESSON</u>

"Say 'Yes' when you mean 'Yes' and 'No' when you mean 'No.' Anything beyond that is from the evil one." (Matthew 5:37)

In the book of James it is said that, "With the tongue we praise our Lord and Father, and with it we curse men, who have been made in the image of God. ....My brothers, this should not be."

With this tongue we break the Eighth Commandment when we do not put the best construction on things we hear about others. With it we also pray to Our Father. The tongue is a member that needs taming. We need self-denial to overcome our sinful tendencies, including those sparked by the lust of the eyes, the "pride of life," and our judging nature. The good news is that "God's grace is sufficient for you." Seek Him on yours knees. Discipline your flesh and exercise your spiritual inner man. Build up your spirit with the ministry of Word and Sacrament. Receive the Body and Blood of the Lord often. Sin can be conquered but not without effort on our parts. Together, brothers and sisters, let us strive to "reach for the high calling in Jesus Christ." Amen.

1. Go and sin no more! When our Lord says this, does He mean sins of an outward and an inward nature?
2. What are some instances in your life where too many words, or unkind words spoken by you, or others around you, had a profound effect?
3. Can you see where a tongue that is consumed in prayer and praise would be less likely to sin against its Maker?

ANSWER: How might you combat your sins of the tongue?

CATECHISM LESSON

Read Sections 2464-2557.
ANSWER: How do the last three commandments relate to purity of motive and thought?

LESSON ON THE FRANCISCAN VIRTUES

In <u>Franciscan Virtues</u>, read Virtue 48: Vigilance. Spend at least five minutes meditating on the virtue. Answer the questions. Share your answers with your formator.

ABANDONMENT TO DIVINE PROVIDENCE (Optional)

Read Book 2, Chapter 4, sections 7-12.
ANSWER: Select one key sentence from this assignment and explain what it means to you.

ASSIGNMENTS

- Make any adjustments needed, that you can make without undue expense or trouble, to fully implement the living of Chapter I of the CFP Rule and Constitutions.
- Finalize your will with your lawyer.
- Complete the Three Lessons Prior to Pledging.
- Make a Day of Recollection either with your Chapter or Circle or on your own. Spend time in prayer to discern your call to pledge to live the CFP Rule for life or for a year's time. If you are considering a private vow, spend additional time in prayer, reflecting on this commitment.
- Complete the Pledging Application Form.
- Submit BRIEF answers to the above questions to your formator.

<u>May God bless you as you embrace this life of penance, and may it lead you into the very heart and mind of Christ! May He, and He alone be your joy and consolation, and give you the strength to endure anything, now and throughout your life, for the Love of God.</u>

THREE LESSONS PRIOR TO PLEDGING

"In heaven Mary remains always in the presence of her Divine Son. There she is continually praying on behalf of sinners." - *St. Bede*

Prayer for Respect for all Human Life

Heavenly Father, your cosmic gaze focused on dust and you fashioned in your image and likeness every man and women: give us, we beg you, a keen eye to recognize that image so that respect for all human life becomes our way of life. Grant this through Christ our Lord. Amen.

LESSONS FOR MEMBERS
ABOUT TO BE PLEDGED

INTRODUCTION

"We have to serve God in His way, not in ours." – St. Teresa of Avila

"You cannot choose God and mammon." (Luke 16:13)

Pledging to live the CFP Rule and Constitutions will be one of the most important and life changing things you will ever do. It is vital that you understand what you are undertaking. To help you in this regard, you will be assigned a mentor or you may request the mentor. The mentor will be someone already pledged for life in the Confraternity of Penitents other than your formator. This experienced penitent will be available to you for support, prayer, and guidance during this time of preparation for pledging.

The following three lessons are intended to help you review the pledging commitment and to understand what you are undertaking. The lessons may be done in any order and in any time frame. They must, however, be completed successfully before pledging and your answers shared with your mentor.

Those who pledge to live the Rule of Life for a year must complete these lessons yearly with new answers submitted to their mentor. The last time the lessons must be completed is the year in which a penitent pledges to live the Rule for Life.

The lessons are meant to be not only read and answered but also prayed over and through. The call to live a life of penance comes from the Holy Spirit, and He is the One Whose guidance you must seek. Ask God to reveal His Will to you regarding your pledging to live the CFP Rule and Constitutions. Then "do whatever He tells you." The CFP promises prayers for you as you prepare for pledging. Your mentor especially, who will work with you through these lessons, will hold you in prayer as will your formator who has reviewed your lessons up until this point.

Take time to do the lessons thoroughly and well. Not only your own spiritual life but also the lives of your fellow penitents in the CFP depends on your upcoming decision regarding pledging. May the Lord bless you as you move forward in love of Him, through a life of penance.

PREPARATION FOR PLEDGING—LESSON 1

The Seriousness of the Pledge

"A good vocation is simply a firm and constant will in which the person who is called must serve God in the way and in the places to which almighty God has called him." – St. Francis de Sales

"Not everyone who says to me, 'Lord, Lord,' will enter the kingdom of heaven, but only the one who does the will of my Father in heaven." (Matthew 7:21)

Congratulations! You have completed all four years of formation in the Confraternity of Penitents and are now on the threshold of pledging to live the Rule. Pledging is not automatic, however. Some penitents may complete formation and then discern that they ought not pledge, or at least not pledge right now. It is vitally important that you clearly and deeply consider what you are planning to do.

Whether you pledge to live the Rule and Constitutions for a year or for life, you are making a very serious promise to God that you will do what you are pledging. You are also making a very serious commitment to the Confraternity of Penitents.

Here are the words that you will be writing out[36] and then saying and signing before a Roman Catholic priest or deacon who will also sign as having witnessed your pledge:

I (NAME) promise that I will strive to live, to the best of my means and ability, (for all of my life) (FOR ONE YEAR), according to the Rule and Constitutions of the Confraternity of Penitents in fulfillment of the Gospel and for the Love of God. As part of my commitment I promise to live the Gospel more fully and to pursue more fervently the virtues of poverty, chastity, and humility, which the Saints all loved and promoted. On this journey, I ask the support and prayers of my brothers and sisters in the Confraternity and God's blessing.

The priest or deacon will receive your pledge in these words:

---

36   These may be slightly adapted or added to with the permission of your Spiritual Director. The Minister General and CFP Visitor must approve the wording of any pledge that differs from the one shown.

With my blessing, I accept your promise, (NAME), to Christ, and encourage you to strive to live it joyfully for the Love of God and the good of the Church. This promise of yours is binding, though never under pain of sin, because it carries with it the binding promise of eternal life to you on the part of the Lord, if you do as you say, and is a true gesture of love for the Lord and His Gospel, as given to us by the Saints. May you, by the grace of God, persevere in your promise until the day of your death so as to join the Lord and His Saints in heaven.

I accept and acknowledge you as a (brother or sister) in the Confraternity of Penitents with joy, and ask God's blessing on us and on your commitment.

You will note that your pledge is not binding under pain of sin. But it is binding. Remaining faithful to the Constitutions and this way of life, as one has promised, is a way in which God continues to grow the life of grace and charity in a person, leading them to eternal life.

WHY SHOULD A PERSON PLEDGE?

The pledge to live the Rule and Constitutions of the Confraternity of Penitents must be made because the penitent has a true love of God and His Gospel. Saying how much you love God is not enough. Actions speak much louder than words. Those who truly love God and His Gospel are willing to follow the dictates of God, given by Christ through His Church, whatever they say, wherever they lead. Of course, those dictates extend to you, as a penitent in the Confraternity of Penitents. In addition to following those dictates, your pledge includes your faithful adherence to all of the CFP Rule and Constitutions as well as our Directory. As a Catholic, you cannot pick and choose or water down what you will follow in the Gospel and in the teachings of the Church. Moreover, as a pledged penitent, you cannot pick and choose or water down what you will follow in the Rule, Constitutions, and Directory of the Confraternity of Penitents—they are to be followed as written. Any exceptions regarding the CFP life must be confirmed for you by your spiritual director who has the authority to adjust the penitential life in certain particulars for penitents who, because of physical needs or other inescapable conditions, are unable to live the Rule and Constitutions as written.

The pledge is also to be kept for as long as you have stated–for one year (for a year pledge) or until you die (for a life pledge). The Confraternity is not a club, association, or prayer group where folks can come in, stay as long as things work out for them, and then drop out when they get busy or their interest wanes. You are to remain in the Confraternity for as long as you pledge to do so. For some people, this might mean living the Rule for fifty or sixty or even more years.

SERIOUSNESS OF THE PLEDGE

The Confraternity of Penitents has a Rule of Life which very clearly states the seriousness of the pledge. Here is what the Rule and Constitutions say about departing from the CFP once a pledge has been made:

RULE:

> *31. No one is to depart from this brotherhood and from what is contained herein, except to enter a religious Order.*

CONSTITUTIONS:

> *31a. A penitent who has pledged to live this Rule must have the consent of his or her spiritual director in order to be released from the pledge. The penitent must also petition, in writing, the spiritual assistant, minister, and Visitor for release and shall give the reasons for the request. The minister and spiritual assistant should thoroughly explain the seriousness of asking for release from this promise to God. They may also question the penitent to see if the Confraternity has failed the penitent in some way.*
>
> *31b. Those who wish to depart from this Confraternity to enter a religious Order should receive not only permission but also the blessing of the entire Confraternity. It is the norm of the Church that individuals should always move towards a greater commitment to Christ and His Church when they leave any lifestyle for another.*

In the Original Rule, once their formation in a life of penance was completed, penitents were in the Brothers and Sisters of Penance (as the group was then called) for life. They could not leave except to join a religious Order, which would certainly be a valid reason to ask to be dispensed from a pledge.

A penitent who wishes to leave the Confraternity after pledging cannot simply depart. His or her spiritual director must, first of all, consent to the relinquishing of the pledge. Then the penitent must petition the spiritual assistant of any local group, the minister of that group, and the Visitor of the CFP for release and must state the reasons. The penitent can expect a "lecture" on the seriousness of asking for release and may also be asked to reveal if the CFP caused the penitent to make this request.

Therefore, the penitent should not undertake the pledge lightly, with the intention of rescinding the pledge or dropping out of the Confraternity if one's ardor cools or if living the Rule becomes more difficult or inconvenient due to changes in one's health, family, employment, or other circumstances. You are promising God that you will live the Rule and Constitutions and all promises, especially those to our Lord, should be given much thought and then made with firm purpose and love.

COMMITMENT TO A FAMILY IN THE CHURCH

Is your pledge really THAT serious or is this all exaggeration? It really is THAT serious. Why? Because you are making a promise to God that you will do what you say, for as long as you say, and within the family of the Confraternity of Penitents. Just as spouses marry into families and create their own family by having children, you are coming into a family in the Church and will have contact with and influence on others in your spiritual family. As in any family, you may not like all the members, and you may not see eye to eye with everyone, but you still have a commitment to them and are bound to treat them with love and respect. This is always true, even if you disagree with them, reprimand them, or disapprove of some of the things they do.

You see, it is impossible to live the Rule for the Confraternity of Penitents on your own. Why? Because community is built so firmly into the Rule. The Rule and Constitutions speak about meeting with sisters and brothers, being at their funerals, praying for them, exhorting them to penance, supporting them with alms, and serving them in office. Although a person may say that they are going to "live the Rule on their own," they simply cannot do it outside of a community of brothers and sisters who are living it also. Trying to live the Rule on one's own is like trying to make soup without liquid. We talk about beef soup, vegetable soup, chicken soup, and so on. Those are the main ingredients in the soup, just as Our Lord and His Will are the main ingredients in the Confraternity of Penitents. Nevertheless, ingredients without liquid make a casserole, not a soup, and penitential acts without community make good Lenten discipline, not a Confraternity.

DISCERNING YOUR CALL

At this stage of your spiritual journey, when you have completed formation in the Confraternity of Penitents, go back over the Rule and Constitutions with an open mind and with an open hand. Read each section carefully and honestly ask yourself. "Am I willing to follow this for as long as I promise to do so (for life or for a year)?"

Then take a good bit of time to review the CFP Directory which details the government, legalities, formation details, and so on for the Confraternity. Can you accept and live by these regulations?

Truthfully share the results of this activity with your mentor and spiritual director.

Do not fret about remembering every detail and sometimes forgetting some. You will have to go back often to review details in the Rule, Constitutions, and Directory. Forgetting is not the same as remembering and refusing to do what is required. You can certainly live the Rule and abide by the procedures and ordinances, even if you forget parts from time to time. But you cannot live those parts you refuse to live.

Do not fret about any modifications your spiritual director may have made. These are fine. They are your way to live the Rule. Review them yearly with your spiritual director to see if they still apply and be at peace.

Do not fret because you feel that you are not living this life as well as you could or as well as another penitent. Are you willing to try to do better? That is all that counts. You can pledge to live the Rule and keep striving to improve on the living of it. Even St.

Francis of Assisi, when he was dying, confessed to the brothers that he did not live his own Rule perfectly. He knew that the ideal of any Rule may well be beyond most human beings. The important thing is not perfection but the genuine, honest seeking of it.

Ask yourself why you want to embrace this life. Is it to give God glory, to surrender to Him, to do reparation for your sins and those of others, to grow more disciplined in the spiritual life, to bind yourself more closely to God, to become more Christ like? Any of those are excellent reasons to pledge.

If, however, you are primarily looking for a group of like minded people, then seriously consider whether joining a club or an association might be a better choice. While like minded people are vital to the CFP, you are pledging to live a Rule of Life, not to fellowship with others. If communications disappeared and you were stranded in a city of people who thought penance was a joke, you would still be bound to live the Rule even if you could not find any community to support you in it.

If you are aiming at leadership and power, please look elsewhere as the CFP is meant to foster in you a spirit of humility and servanthood. CFP leaders are to adhere to the original vision of the Confraternity, to share leadership, and to listen. They are to disavow any craving for power.

If you feel that you have come this far and what would be the point if you didn't pledge, take time to consider whether the four years you have spent in formation is worth being uneasily involved with a group to which you pledged because you thought you had to, to avoid embarrassment or an awkward situation.

If you feel you need to pledge now, right away, before you change your mind, give yourself enough time to become firm in your desire to pledge. Take as long as you need to be sure. Being sure does not mean you won't feel some doubts. Before this sounds contradictory, consider that living the CFP Rule, for those called to do so, is truly a path to a greater holiness and a fuller surrender to God. Certainly the evil one is not going to want you to experience those graces. He is going to present all manner of doubts to your mind to dissuade you from going forward. How do you deal with these? Prayer to the Holy Spirit will enable you to sift through the fog, to understand if the doubts are from God, from yourself, or from the evil one. If God wants you to hold off pledging, by all means follow His promptings. But if the doubts are from satan or from your own sense of inadequacy, yet you feel that God really wants you to pledge, then take a leap of faith and trust the Lord. He will not ask you to do something for which He will not give you the graces. The very fact that you are questioning your pledge means that you are taking it as seriously as it deserves. Questioning is a good sign. But jumping into something to avoid the questioning is very dangerous. Work through your doubts and questions before making any decision.

If you feel proud that you can live all the tenets of the Rule while others are self indulgent and spiritually lazy, please refrain from pledging until you understand that those who live this Rule have no reason for any pride as it is a Rule for babies in the spiritual life. No one needs more rules than little children who would certainly be in many unsafe situations if adults didn't have rules for them. The CFP Rule and Constitutions have many prescriptions precisely because penitents need them. Others who are more mature in the faith do not.

The Confraternity of Penitents involves a Rule of Life and a group of people, all trying to get closer to God. Are you willing to live that Rule of Life as it is written and to the very best of your ability? Are you willing to be a brother and sister to all fellow penitents, now and in the future, whether or not you always like every one of them? Are you able to make a promise to God and to keep it, no matter what comes? At this time in your spiritual journey, these questions are critical. Pray about them. Talk over any concerns with your spiritual director and your CFP mentor. Take the time to discern well. And then "Do whatever He tells you." May the Lord bless you no matter what you decide.

QUESTIONS

1. Why do I want to pledge to live the Rule and Constitutions of the CFP? Do my reasons seem to be valid reasons for this desire?
2. Do I understand that pledging is like a marriage between God, the CFP, and me? How do I feel about that?
3. Think of the very worst situation you can, involving you and your family. Are you willing to keep your pledge while dealing with that situation and suffering the consequences of it?
4. Can you honestly say that you will try to treat everyone with love and respect, even those you dislike, and most especially those you dislike who happen to be in leadership?

Share your answers to these questions with your mentor and spiritual director.

LESSON ON THE FRANCISCAN VIRTUES

In <u>Franciscan Virtues</u>, read Virtues 49 and 50: Vulnerability and Wisdom. Spend at least five minutes meditating on each virtue. Answer the questions. Share your answers with your mentor.

PREPARATION FOR PLEDGING – LESSON 2

Becoming a CFP Leader

"Those who are put in charge of others should be no prouder of their office than if they had been appointed to wash the feet of their comrades. They should be no more upset at the loss of their authority than they would be if they were deprived of the task of washing feet. The more they are upset, the greater the risk they incur to their souls." – St. Francis of Assisi

"I am among you as one who serves." (Luke 22:27)

LEADERSHIP IN THE CONFRATERNITY OF PENITENTS

Congratulations on completing the four years of formation in the Confraternity of Penitents Rule of Life! You may have weathered many spiritual storms to get to this point, but God's grace has seen you through. Now you are on the threshold of pledging to live the Rule and Constitutions for life or for a year.

By now, you may have exercised some leadership in the Confraternity. Perhaps you have been a formator or a Chapter or Circle officer. You may have helped at our annual CFP Retreat/Reunion/Conference or you may have given talks or presentations to others. Maybe you even began a CFP Circle or Chapter. All of these, and any others ways you have exercised leadership, have been wonderful means of helping others on their spiritual journey.

Or maybe you have not exercised any leadership in the Confraternity to this point. That is fine, too.

You need to be aware, however, that, upon pledging, you automatically become a leader in the CFP. How can that be if you are not elected or appointed to office?

Leadership in the Confraternity exists on two levels. The more obvious one is holding office. We'll discuss that later. The less obvious mode of leadership is in setting a good example to the other members of the CFP.

THE LEADERSHIP OF GOOD EXAMPLE

CFP members in formation rightly hold in high regard those who have completed formation and who have pledged to live the CFP Rule and Constitutions. Those pledged members have weathered the trials of four years of formation. They have persisted, despite setbacks, to freely answer God's call to live a life of penance for His glory, for the service of others, and for their own sanctity. Pledged members are the ones whose maturity and wisdom are sought by those beginning or journeying along the way. This does not necessarily mean that pledged members have attained the heights of holiness or acquired tremendous spiritual insights. However, pledged members do generally know more about the Rule, the CFP, and a life of penance than those just starting out. Your expertise, even if it's not very expert, will be sought by others. Are you prepared for this?

How vital it is that every pledged member set a good example to others in the Confraternity! So far, you have been incorporating into your life the tenets of the Rule in the first five Chapters. These mainly deal with how you live the Rule privately in your own home, in the areas of prayer, fasting, abstinence, and simplicity of life. Chapters 6, 7, and 8, however, deal with how to live the Rule in a community of fellow penitents. Let's look at those chapters more closely.

What is expected of you as a pledged penitent? The Rule and Constitutions make it clear that you are to set a good example in many areas. Go through Chapters 6, 7, and 8. Please answer these questions, jotting down as well which sections of the Rule and Constitutions provide the answers. Share your answers with your mentor:

What do the Rule and Constitutions say about:

1. Attending CFP gatherings?
2. Supporting the CFP monetarily?
3. Growing in the spiritual life?
4. Caring for the sick?
5. Caring for the dead?
6. Dealing with your own death?
7. Making peace with all?
8. Causing scandal?
9. Discovering scandal?
10. Obtaining spousal consent?
11. Readmitting someone accused of scandal?

Are you willing to try to provide good example in all of these areas?
What will be easiest?
What will be most difficult?
How can you observe the most difficult parts?

By trying to live the sections of the Rule and Constitutions that deal with the above topics, you will be providing a good example to fellow penitents. Upon pledging, you will become an automatic role model. If you live the Rule and Constitutions as they are written, you will be a good role model to all because you will be a good servant of Christ!

CFP OFFICERS AND OTHER LEADERS

The CFP Rule also has prescriptions regarding officers. These officers primarily refer to those in local Chapters and Circles.

Study Chapters 6, 7, and 8 of the Rule and Constitutions.

List the officers mentioned therein and also list their duties.

How long is their term of office?

How are officers elected?

Share your answers to these questions with your mentor.

The CFP utilizes a Directory which details how the CFP, as an international group, is to be governed. The Directory adds governing details to those in the Rule and Constitutions. These additional details are due to the global nature of the Confraternity, the requirements for maintaining its non profit, tax exempt status, the necessity to stay in touch with members world wide, and the methods of managing its various apostolates, ministries, web pages, and gift shop. Those elected or appointed to CFP leadership are required to read the Directory and to refer to it as needed. The Rule, Constitutions, and Directory are the governing manuals for the Confraternity.

The governing structure of the entire Confraternity of Penitents consists of certain officers and other leaders. The CFP Officers consist of the Minister General (president) who has the authority, with the advice of the other CFP Officers, to make virtually all decisions in the CFP; the Ministerial Assistant (vice president) who assists the Minister General, the Messenger (secretary) who records minutes at meetings of the Officers, and the Treasurer who is responsible for managing the CFP funds. The Minister General must be a life pledged member. The other CFP Officers must be pledged members elected by pledged members. (Note: This assumes that there are sufficient qualified pledged members to hold office. If not, non-pledged members may be elected.) Other leaders include all Regional Ministers and other regional officers as well as Advisors to the Minister General. The CFP Visitor and diocesan officials all have roles to play regarding CFP affairs. These roles are delineated in the CFP Rule, Constitutions, and Directory.

CFP leaders keep in touch by electronic means, phone, and at least one yearly in person meeting. As a pledged member, you will be eligible to be elected or appointed to CFP leadership. Do you have the time to be of service to your fellow penitents?

Leadership terms for all leaders, other than the Minister General and formators, are one year in length. If an emergency arises and a leader cannot complete a term, the Minister General will appoint another penitent to fill the slot. However, the position of leadership in the CFP is one of great responsibility and is not to be shrugged off lightly. It is better not to accept a leadership position than to accept with the idea of resigning if your life gets too complicated to continue.

Leaders in the CFP are making a commitment to their fellow penitents. Just as parents, when going through a tough time, can't simply walk out on a family, so CFP leaders ought not just walk out on their CFP family. Obligations to others come with parenting and with leadership. When at all possible, any leader who feels compelled to resign must give a minimum of three weeks notice before the resignation takes place. This allows ample time to obtain and train a replacement.

The Holy Spirit may well call you into leadership in the Confraternity of Penitents. Ask Him to help you discern your answers to the following questions, and then discuss the questions and your responses with your mentor and spiritual director.

1. Do I see myself as a leader? Why or why not?
2. What are my strong points regarding leadership?
3. What are my weak points?
4. How do I respond to criticism?
5. How do I work with others?
6. Can I accept the authority of others above me in leadership, provided that their leadership is morally right? Why or why not?
7. Would I be willing to serve if elected or appointed? Why or why not?
8. Is my life such that I can serve the CFP in a leadership position? Why or why not?
9. What positions do I feel I am capable of doing well and why?
10. What positions do I feel I am incapable of holding and why?
11. Am I willing to accept and abide by everything in the CFP Rule, Constitutions, and Directory?
12. Do I accept the governing structure of the Confraternity of Penitents and the roles, duties, responsibilities, and authority of each person in it?

Review again Chapters 6, 7, and 8 of the CFP Rule and Constitutions. Can you see that the CFP is a family in the Church and that, as a pledged member, you are being called to serve that family in prayer and action? Are you willing to say yes to this commitment, in humility and love?

LESSON ON THE FRANCISCAN VIRTUES

In <u>Franciscan Virtues</u>, read Virtues 51 and 52: Witness and Work. Spend at least five minutes meditating on each virtue. Answer the questions. Share your answers with your mentor.

PREPARATION FOR PLEDGING–LESSON 3

Living the Rule, No Matter What Comes

"Well and good if all things change, Lord God, provided we are rooted in You." – St. John of the Cross

"Amen, amen, I say to you, unless a grain of wheat falls to the ground and dies, it remains just a grain of wheat; but if it dies, it produces much fruit. Whoever loves his life loses it, and whoever hates his life in this world will preserve it for eternal life. Whoever serves me must follow me, and where I am, there also will my servant be. The Father will honor whoever serves me." (John 12:24-26)

Congratulations on getting this far in your formation with the Confraternity of Penitents! Very few who begin make it to this point. The grace of the Holy Spirit has brought you here, to the brink of entering upon a very important promise to live the CFP Rule and Constitutions With the guidance of the Holy Spirit and the advice of your spiritual director and mentor, you will answer the following questions:

Will you promise to live the Rule and Constitutions for a year?

Will you promise to live them for life?

Will you privately vow to live them for life?

What will your pledge or vow mean for you?

DIFFERENT TYPES OF COMMITMENT

The three types of commitment in the CFP are the year pledge, the life pledge, and the private vow. Pray about which of these the Lord is asking of you at this time.

A year pledge means that you will pledge to live the complete Rule and Constitutions, to the best of your ability, for one year. This could be the best course of action if you are not sure if you can or wish to make a life long commitment. The year pledge may be renewed yearly for as many years as you wish. This is why the CFP does not recommend pledging for three years or six months or any other interval of time other than a year. With a year pledge, you will be living the Rule and Constitutions just as fully as you would if you pledged to live them for life, but you may feel more comfortable knowing that you could "get out" of the commitment after a year with no penalties attached.

A life pledge is very serious. It means that you are pledging to live the Rule and Constitutions until you die. Can you really do this? Lesson 1 addresses this very topic with some in depth considerations.

Only those first pledged for life are permitted to turn that pledge into a private vow. The life pledge and life vow may take place on the same day, or may be years apart, but always the life pledge must precede the vow. Usually, unless no one other than CFP members and Church representatives are present, the vow must be taken in private, generally with one's spiritual director. The person receiving the vow is usually the one who will direct the penitent and see that the vow is kept.

A life pledge is binding but not under pain of sin. A vow is binding and under pain of sin. Thus a vow is far more serious than a life pledge. Let's take an example. If you pledge to live the Rule and Constitutions for life and one night just don't feel like praying Evening Prayer, you commit no sin if you skip praying it. However, if you have vowed to live the CFP Rule and Constitutions for life and skip praying Evening Prayer just because you don't feel like it, you commit at least a venial sin.

A vow is binding as long as it can be kept. Suppose that you had an emergency in your family and spent the day in the hospital between concerned doctors and the bedside of a seriously ill relative. Late at night, you come home, hoping that you don't fall asleep at the wheel of your car. You get into the house and collapse into bed, not even bothering to undress. If you had vowed to live the CFP Rule and Constitutions for life and did not pray Evening Prayer on this night, you would not incur any sin. In fact, you may have gained merit for your charity to your very ill relative. In the same way, if you grow old, infirm, and mentally deficient, and have vowed for life, you commit no sin if you cannot even remember the Rule or what you are to do. You are not bound by something you are unable to keep. Likewise, for a greater or equal good, a vow can be commuted by the spiritual director, confessor, parish priest, the CFP Visitor, or the bishop.

Why would anyone vow?

Certainly the reason ought to be, "Because they feel that God is asking it of them." A private vow, which is recognized by Canon Law (Canons 1191-1198), carries with it not only obligations but also graces. Those who make a private vow are giving themselves totally to God through living a penitential life, that is, a life of ongoing conversion. They are saying that they are willing to make the Rule and Constitutions into commandments of sorts for them. They give God, through the Rule, that supreme authority over their lives. The Confraternity recognizes this commitment by allowing vowed members to take a religious name which they can use in the Confraternity only, but with lower case letters for the sister and brother address, to indicate both our lay status and our littleness in God's plan. Because vowed members give themselves totally to God through their living of a life of penance (conversion), they can anticipate great graces from the Holy Spirit. These may not be what one might expect, for vowed members are frequently made perfect through suffering. The living of a penitential life prepares them for this purgation and purification. God's penances are always far superior to any we can devise for ourselves.

Through prayer to the Holy Spirit you will discern whether to pledge to live the Rule and Constitutions for life or for a year. If you choose the life pledge, you will then discern whether or not to vow. Bathe these decisions in prayer and discuss them with your spiritual director and mentor. So much depends on your decision.

ONGOING FORMATION

At this point, you have completed 48 formation lessons in the postulant and novice years of the Confraternity of Penitents. You are now completing these three lessons prior to pledging. And then you are done with formation! Yipee!

Whoops! Don't celebrate too soon. Maybe when you graduate from high school or college, you are done with studying, but that doesn't happen in the CFP. Why? Because the CFP is a school of ongoing spiritual growth. As penitents, we are to keep growing in the spiritual life. Our formation is to be on going.

Once you pledge, however, the formation which you will continue to do is between you and your spiritual director and other CFP members with whom you will be sharing in some way. Certainly invite the Lord to be the ultimate guide for this study, reflection, and sharing.

What will you study? The Confraternity of Penitents asks that pledged members continue their formation by reading the Documents of the Church or the lives or writings of the saints. What you choose within these categories is up to you to discern through prayer, with input from your spiritual director. But it's not up to you to decide whether or not to choose at all.

We all have to "feed our souls," so to speak. Certainly attending Mass, praying, and receiving the sacraments does that the best. But spiritual reading provides good "soul food," too. A little time spent daily or weekly in good spiritual reading will give you insights and support which you won't find anywhere else. Discern carefully what you would like to study as your ongoing formation. The Holy Spirit will direct you to different texts as you need them. Follow His guidance and let Him speak to you through those texts.

By sharing your ongoing formation with someone else (your spiritual director, other pledged penitents, other members of the CFP, prayer group members), you will gain even more insights and help spread the wealth of what you are learning.

If you get to the point where you simply cannot study any longer due to physical or age limitations, then ask your spiritual director how you might fulfill the ongoing formation requirements of our way of life. Perhaps someone can read to you or you can listen to tapes or watch religious programming. If those things become too complex for waning mental faculties or physical abilities, then you can pray some rote prayers or just be still with a crucifix and study the lessons gleaned from gazing at or even "holding" our Lord. However you can, keep growing in the spiritual life, even to the point where all you can offer to the Lord are your inadequacies and sufferings. From those you will learn the final lessons of life.

SUPPORTING THE CONFRATERNITY AND ITS MEMBERS

People today, especially Catholics, don't like to talk about money. But our CFP Rule is not that way. Your pledging to live the CFP way of life brings with it a commitment to support the Confraternity and its members monetarily. What do the Rule and Constitutions say?

RULE:

20. *And every member is to give the treasurer one ordinary denar. The treasurer is to collect this money and distribute it on the advice of the ministers among the poor brothers and sisters, especially the sick and those who may have nothing for their funeral services, and thereupon among the poor; and they are to offer something of the money to the aforesaid church.*

CONSTITUTIONS:

20a. *Every member shall contribute generously to the treasury of their Chapter or Circle or to the Confraternity in general.*

20b. *There are fixed expenses affiliated with running the Confraternity that are part of every member's responsibility and apostolate. These include mail and newsletter costs, formation materials, miscellaneous printing, phone expenses, and the cost of maintaining the Web page. Monies will be used to cover these expenses and occasionally to provide alms for needy members, as approved by the minister and the council, who may be consulted to determine a fitting donation as well.*

20c. *A report of how this money is being utilized may be requested at any time by any member.*

20d. *If a Chapter or Circle in the Confraternity requests a visit from the Visitor or someone else, they should reimburse the expenses of the visit.*

20e. *In the United States of America, all monies donated to the Confraternity of Penitents are tax deductible. The CFP is a bona fide non-profit, tax exempt organization.*

You may be on a fixed income or have debts to pay. You may be barely managing to live on the money you do have. How can you monetarily support the Confraternity?

This section of the Rule was never intended to be burdensome. An "ordinary denar" was the smallest denomination of coin minted at the time the Rule was written. Cardinal Hugolino, who wrote this Rule for the penitents, no doubt knew that many of them were destitute. Still, this section indicates that he also knew that others are even more destitute (they had no money for funeral services, for example). The requirement of giving monthly "one ordinary denar" was probably intended to be the widow's mite. Anyone desirous of giving oneself totally to God ought to be able to give the smallest possible amount of money monthly to help others.

Use this section of the Rule and Constitutions as a guideline for what your monthly contribution might be. Certainly if you monthly give the smallest coin minted in your nation as your donation, that would fit the Rule. Maybe you can give more. Pray about your contribution and then follow the Holy Spirit's lead. Your donation can be given at a Chapter or Circle gathering or mailed monthly or yearly to the Confraternity Treasurer. Or you may prefer to spend your monthly "ordinary denar" on materials which can be offered through the Confraternity of Penitents Holy Angels Gift Shop, thus increasing the value of your contribution. However you monetarily support the Confraternity and its members, may the Lord reward you for your generosity and support.

LIVING THE RULE AND CONSTITUTIONS IN FULL

Living the CFP Rule and Constitutions in their richness and fullness is an ongoing journey into perfection and adjustment. As you embark on this way of life, you will be living the penitential life in one way. However, circumstances or health issues may, down the line, force you to evaluate how you are living the Rule and Constitutions and may necessitate changes. At that point, danger enters in for penitents who have not focused on the flexibility present in our governing documents. They may think that, because they cannot live the Rule and Constitutions as they had been living them up to that point, then they cannot live them well and ought not live them at all. This is a totally erroneous way of thinking. Options and flexibility are built into the CFP Rule and Constitutions. The Rule was never intended to be rigid. If your life changes, find the parts of the Rule and the Constitutions that deal with those changes and adjust your practices accordingly.

Study the Rule and Constitutions very carefully. Then consider these scenarios. For each situation, consider the section(s) of the Rule and Constitutions which address that situation. Pray about the situation, then answer the question, "Can I live the Rule and Constitutions as a pledged penitent if this situation happens to me? What will I have to do to be able to keep my pledge in this situation?" Discuss your answers with your mentor.

1. Suppose you get a job and have to wear a uniform that does not fit the Rule colors. Can you take that job as a penitent? (Refer to Rule and Constitutions 1 and 1c)

2. Suppose you are in a serious accident and suffer horrible facial scarring. In order to conceal the disfigurement so as not to horrify others, your doctor recommends concealing makeup. Can you use the makeup? (Refer to Rule and Constitutions 2 and 2f)

3. You marry (or remarry) and your spouse is much more materialistic than you. Your simple house becomes full of nifty appliances and latest gadgets. As a penitent, what is your response? (Refer to Rule and Constitutions 3 and 3b)

4. You develop an illness. As part of your treatment, your doctor tells you to eat six times a day with red meat every day at one meal at least. Can you do what the doctor requires and still live the CFP life? (Refer to Rule and Constitutions 6, 6a and 6c; 8, 8b; 9; and Appendix A)

5. You move to a region where people are extremely hostile to religion. Everyone with any visible sign of faith is persecuted and their families hounded. What should you do? (Refer to Rule and Constitutions 2 and 2g)

6. You get pregnant. How do you observe the Rule? (Refer to Rule and Constitutions 10 and 10a)

7. You have been praying the full Liturgy of the Hours. Then your parent gets Alzheimer's and needs round the clock care. You are selected as the caregiver. Your parent needs continual watching and your time is constantly interrupted. What should you do? (Refer to Rule and Constitutions 12, 12o, Option 5)

8. You are used to eating only lunch and supper. Suddenly you lose your office job and, after many months of searching, the only job you can land is a brick layer. The work is hot and strenuous and you find yourself getting faint by mid morning. Should you quit your job in order to keep your pledge to live the Rule? (Refer to Rule and Constitutions 11, 11a, and 11b)

9. You have been attending daily Mass, but now you have consented to babysit your fifteen month old granddaughter while her parents are at work. If you take her to Mass, she fusses and insists on being put down, but then proceeds to run around the church. There is no cry room and only one Mass anywhere nearby. What should you do? (Refer to Rule and Constitutions 14, 14a, and 14b)

10. You had been giving $25 per month to the CFP, but then you lose your job. What should you do? (Refer to Rule and Constitutions 15 and 15b)

11. You had been joyfully attending a local monthly CFP gathering. Then your family moves to an area where you are the only CFP member within 100 miles. Your car is unreliable. How can you fulfill the obligation to attend gatherings of the CFP? (Refer to Rule and Constitutions 19 and 19f)

12. You are elected to office in the CFP but, when you have served six months of your term, you are diagnosed with cancer and need chemo treatments which leave you ill and tired. You can no longer fulfill your duties and can barely get

through the day. What should you do? (Refer to Rule and Constitutions 28 and 28d, and 37 and 37a)

13. You have been faithfully keeping up with spiritual reading and on going formation. But now your eyesight is going. The doctor says that this is a progressive, irreversible condition and you will be totally blind in two years. How can you continue your ongoing formation? (Refer to Rule and Constitutions 13 and 13a, and 37 and 37a)

14. You have tremendous debts which you ran up before even knowing about the CFP. Much as you have tried to pay them off, you have only made a dent in them. You want to tithe but you want to pay your debts, too. What should you do? (Refer to Rule and Constitutions 29 and 29c and 15 and 15b)

15. You've been living the Rule as a life pledged member for two years and then meet a lovely person with whom you fall in love. It appears that you are headed for marriage, but this wonderful other is not in favor of your living the penitential life. What should you do? (Refer to Rule and Constitutions 33 and 33a. Note that the clue to this answer is in the word RECEIVED which means "enter formation and then be pledged." You are already pledged in this scenario.)

16. You are pledged member of the CFP when you discover that the treasurer of your local CFP chapter has been pocketing some of the funds. You are dismayed that someone who seemed so pious and trustworthy could do such a thing and now you question the whole CFP. What should you do? (Refer to Rule and Constitutions 36 and 36a)

17. You lose your spiritual director. How will you find a new one? (Refer to the Addendum to the Constitutions)

If you have carefully studied the Rule and Constitutions and prayerfully completed the above exercise, you will have learned that, in every one of these situations and in many more, you can continue to live your pledge. The Rule and Constitutions are not strait jackets but rather elastic garments that will fit your situation. Elasticity does not mean that our way of life is a chameleon, changing appearances for this penitent or that one. Nor is it ball of clay that can be molded into any shape anyone desires. But there is enough elasticity in the Rule and Constitutions to help you to live the penitential life to the end of your days, if the Lord so calls you to do. Your job now is to pray about what He wants. Then "do whatever He tells you."

LESSON ON THE FRANCISCAN VIRTUES

Review the entire book <u>Franciscan Virtues.</u> Prayerfully spend at least thirty minutes of mental prayer and meditation on a review of all 52 virtues. Ask yourself:

Am I living all of these to the best of my ability?

If not, which ones need prayer and work?

What shall my resolution be to more fully implement these virtues into my life as a penitent?

Share your answers with your mentor.

SAMPLES OF ON GOING FORMATION

"Those who burn with the fire of Divine Love are children of the Immaculate Heart of Mary, and wherever they go they enkindle that flame. Nothing distresses them; they rejoice in poverty, labor strenuously, welcome hardships, laugh off false accusations, and rejoice in anguish." - *St. Anthony Claret*

Prayer to the Immaculate Heart of Mary

Mary Immaculate, Mother of God and perfect Christian, you treasured the word of God, in faith you pondered it in your heart and acted on it in charity and service.

We know that as children of God and believing Christians, God's love is given to us, "...the love of God has been poured into our hearts by the Holy Spirit which has been given to us." (Romans 5:5) Your heart as symbol of your love for God, for us, and for all creation, reminds us that "as long as we love one another God will Live in us and His Love will be complete in us." (John 4:12). Amen.

SUGGESTIONS FOR
ON-GOING FORMATION FOR
PLEDGED PENITENTS

Formation continues after one pledges to live the Rule of the Confraternity of Penitents. Pledged members gather at Chapter and Circle meetings to continually discuss and grow in the spiritual life.

Pledged members of the Confraternity of Penitents are to continue their formation by reading the lives or writings of the saints and blesseds of the Roman Catholic Church as well as official documents of the Church and discuss these with other penitents or with their spiritual directors. This section provides a very small sampling of selected writings of a few saints, to give the penitent an idea of the richness available for study. May the saints intercede for us all!

THE CROSS

From Sermons 75 and 88 of Saint Augustine

All those who belong to Jesus Christ are fastened with Him to the cross. A Christian during the whole course of his life should, like unto Jesus, be on the cross. It would be an act of rashness to descend therefrom, since Jesus Christ did not descend, even when the Jews offered to believe in Him. The time for driving out the nails of His cross was only after death; there is, then, no time to extract the nails whilst we live,—we must wait until our sacrifice is consummated: Non est tempus evellendi clavos (Aug. 205).

This cross to which the servant of God is attached, is his glory, as the apostle said, "But God forbid that I should glory, save in the cross of our Lord Jesus Christ" (Gal. 6:14).

This cross, I say, to which the servant of God should be fastened, not for forty days, but for life; therefore he who looks piously upon it should consider it as a treasure, because it teaches him Christ crucified, and he will despise everything to acquire a knowledge which is only to be learned in the school of the cross.

Formerly, it was looked upon as an object of horror, but Jesus Christ has made it so worthy of respect and veneration, that kings and princes have forbidden the punishment of crucifixion to be continued, in order to do honor to those faithful servants, who gloried in a punishment which our Lord and Savior has so ennobled. And this wood to which the Jews had nailed our Lord, accompanied as it was by so many outrages and insults, has become so worthy of honor, that kings have imprinted it on their foreheads, and in union with the lowest of their subjects they look upon the cross of Jesus Christ as the ship which will guide and carry them safely into harbor.

So strong sometimes are the storms of life that strength of arm is of no avail, and there is no other means to save us from shipwreck than trusting in the cross of Jesus Christ by which we are consecrated.

MEEKNESS

From the Writings of Saint Ambrose

"Blessed are the meek: for they shall possess the land." (Matthew 5: 4)

We must accustom ourselves to perform all our actions with quiet serenity; force of habit can correct or subdue the most obstinate bad temper. But because some are naturally so impetuous and violent that it is difficult to effect an immediate cure, it would be as well to reflect on the motives which engender impatience, in order to induce us to effect a gradual cure.

When ebullitions of passion come upon us so suddenly that there is no time for reflection, we must at least try to soothe them, if we cannot immediately master them. It is sometimes proper to make a desperate effort; but we must always try to conquer by degrees, more especially when the first bursts of impatience or anger assail us. It is recommended in Holy writ; give time for anger to evaporate, and- then extinguish it entirely. We must not only do what we can to prevent our getting into a passion, but we must use greater efforts to subdue it when it does come on. Those little outbursts of petulance, which are more amusing than bitter, are innocent in children; they fire up and are appeased in a moment, and all is soon forgotten. Let us not be ashamed to imitate them in this; for does not our Savior say, "If you do not become as little children, you cannot enter into the kingdom of heaven?"

Never answer an angry person with a haughty haste; if he be ill-tempered, why fall into the same fault? When two flinty stones are quickly rubbed together, sparks will fly out.

If you cannot cure anger by those means which a calmer judgment would suggest, you must have recourse to stratagem. Patience is a great assistant; for time softens the most violent passion. If we should be exposed to the provocations of a person who is continually having recourse to sharp, impertinent answers, and we feel that we have not sufficient command over our own temper, we can, at least, moderate our tongue by keeping silent. Holy Scripture gives us this advice: "Suffer in silence, and do not have recourse to sharp retorts"; you can then seek reconciliation, and do your best to make it lasting.

We have a noble example in the conduct of Jacob. His first care was to keep his mind free from any temptation to break the precept of meekness.

If you have not the strength of mind to do this, at any rate you can bridle your tongue, and allow no bitter reply to escape your lips. When you have taken all such precautions, you will find that more is to be done to secure a mild and even temper.

Would you wish to know how to act when any injury or affront is imposed on you? Above all, do not return evil for evil; pay no attention to the malice of another; there is no occasion to be wicked, because another is wicked. Take care to preserve self-respect, and do nothing which might be a reproach for you afterwards.

The heathens have often quoted a sensible reply of one of their philosophers. One of his attendants had greatly displeased him by an act of gross injustice. Go! unhappy man, said he, how severely would I punish you, were I not angry?

King David acted in a similar way; at a time when he was tempted to inflict vengeance, he gained a complete victory over his temper, by not uttering a single word to those who had wronged him. Abigail, by her entreaties, calmed that gentle prince, who was at the head of his soldiers, and who was on his road to avenge the insults of Nabal.

It is a sure sign of a noble disposition if you listen to sincere petitions, and grant what is demanded of you. David always felt rejoiced when he forgave his enemies, and he praised the cleverness of that woman, who so well knew his tenderness of heart, that she obtained all she sought for. That royal prophet was not insensible to injury, for he cries out,— I am hurt at what evil-disposed persons have said; had I consulted my evil genius, I should have rejoiced to inflict vengeance. But this glorious and pacific king, on second thoughts, continues to say – Oh ! who will give me the wings of the dove, that I may seek peace in flight?

And notwithstanding all their insults and outrages, he preferred to remain in peace.

He says in another place: "Be angry, but sin not." This is a moral precept, which teaches us to allay any little asperity which we cannot altogether stifle.

ON COURAGE

From the Writings of Saint Teresa of Avila

This is what I want us to strive for, my Sister, and let us desire and be occupied in prayer not for the sake of our enjoyment but so as to have this strength to serve. . . . Believe me, Martha and Mary must join together in order to show hospitality to the Lord and have Him always present and not host Him badly by failing to give Him something to eat. How would Mary, always seated at His feet, provide Him with food if her sister did not help her? His food is that in every way possible we draw souls that they may be saved and praise Him always.

You will make two objections: one: that He said that Mary had chosen the better part. The answer is that she had already performed the task of Martha, pleasing the Lord by washing His feet and drying them with her hair. Do you think it would be a small mortification for a woman of nobility like her to wander through these streets (and perhaps alone because her fervent love made her unaware of what she was doing) and enter a house she had never entered before and afterward suffer the criticism of the Pharisee and the very many other things she must have suffered? The people saw a woman like her change so much - and, as we know, she was among such malicious people - and they saw her friendship with the Lord whom they vehemently abhorred, and that she wanted to become a saint since obviously she would have changed her manner of dress and everything else. All of that was enough to cause them comment on the life she had formerly lived. If nowadays there is so much gossip against persons who are not so notorious; what would have been said then? I tell you, Sisters, the better part came after many trials and much mortification, for even if there were no other trial that to see His Majesty abhorred, that would be an intolerable one. Moreover, the many trials that afterward she suffered at the death of the Lord and in the years that she subsequently lived in His absence must have been a terrible torment. You see she wasn't always in the delight of contemplation at the feet of the Lord. (Interior Castle, PP. 448-449)

FRIENDSHIP

Taken from the Devout Life by Saint Francis de Sales

"Blessed is he that finds a true friend." (Proverbs 25:12)

Friendship requires great communication between friends otherwise it can neither grow nor subsist. Wherefore it often happens, that with this communication of friendship other communications insensibly glide from one heart to another, by a mutual infusion and reciprocal intercourse of affections, inclinations, and impressions.

But this happens especially when we have a high esteem for him whom we love; for then we open our heart in such a manner to his friendship, that with it his inclinations and impressions enter rapidly in their full stream, be they good or bad. Certainly the bees that gather the honey of Heraclea, seek nothing but honey; but yet, with the honey they insensibly suck the poisonous qualities of the aconite, from which they gather it Good God, Philotheo, on these occasions we must carefully put what the Savior of our souls was accustomed to say, in practice: Be ye good bankers or changers of money; that is to say, receive not bad money with the good, nor base gold with the fine; separate that which is precious from that which is vile, for there is scarcely any person that has not some imperfection. For why should we receive promiscuously the spots and imperfections of a friend, together with his friendship? We must love him, indeed, notwithstanding his imperfections, but we must neither. love nor receive his imperfections; for friendship requires a communication of good, not of evil.

True and living friendship cannot subsist in the midst of sins. As the salamander extinguishes the fire in which he lies, so sin destroys the friendship in which it lodges. If it be but a transient sin, friendship will presently put it to flight by correction; but if it be habitual, and take up its lodging, friendship immediately perishes, for it cannot subsist but on the solid foundation of virtue. We must never, then, commit sin for friendship's sake.

A friend becomes an enemy when he would lead us to sin, and he deserves to lose his friend when he would destroy his soul.

It is an infallible mark of false friendship to see it exercised towards a vicious person, be his sins of whatsoever kind; for if he whom we love be vicious, without doubt our friendship is also vicious, since, seeing it cannot regard true virtue, it must needs be grounded on some frivolous virtue or sensual quality. Society, formed for traffic among merchants, is but a shadow of true friendship, since it is not made for the love of the persons, but for the love of gain. Finally, the two following divine sentences are two main pillars to secure a Christian life. The one is that of the wise man: He that feareth God shall likewise have a true friendship. The other is that of the apostle St. James: The friendship of this world is the enemy of God.

SUFFERING

From a Letter of Saint Agnes of Assisi to her Sister Saint Clare (1230)

To her venerable mother and the woman beloved in Christ beyond all others, to the Lady Clare and her whole community, Agnes, the lowly and least of Christ's servants, humbly presents herself with all obedience and devotion with best wishes for her and them for whatever is sweet and precious in the eyes of the most High King.

The lot of all has been so established that one can never remain in the same state or condition. When someone thinks that she is doing well, it is then that she is plunged into adversity. Therefore, you should know, Mother, that my soul and body suffer great distress and immense sadness, that I am burdened and tormented beyond measure and am almost incapable of speaking, because I have been physically separated from you and my other sisters with whom I had hoped to live and die in this world. This distress has a beginning, but it knows no end. It never seems to diminish; it always gets worse. It came to me recently, but it tends to ease off very little. It is always with me and never wants to leave me. I believed that our life and death would be one, just as our manner of life in heaven would be one, and that we who have one and the same flesh and blood would be buried in the same grave. But I see that I have been deceived. I have been restrained; I have been abandoned; I have been afflicted on every side.

My dearest sisters, sympathize with me, I beg you, and mourn with me so that you may never suffer such things and see whether there is any suffering like my suffering (cf. Lam 1:12) This sorrow is always afflicting me, this emotional tenderness is always torturing me, this ardent desire is always consuming me. As a result, distress utterly possesses me and I do not know what to do (Ph 1:22), what I should say, since I do not expect to see you and my sisters again in this life.

O if only I could lay bare for you on this page the continuing sorrow that I anticipate and that is always before me. My soul burns within me, and I am tormented by the fires of innumerable tribulation. My heart groans within me, and my eyes do not cease to pour out a flood of tears. Filled with every kind of sorrow and spiritless, I am pining away entirely. *Even though I seek consolation, I do not find it (cf. Lam 1:2).* I conceive sorrow upon sorrow, when I ponder within me with fear that I will never see you and my sisters again. Under such distress I am totally disheartened.

Saint Agnes of Assisi

Clare of Assisi Early Documents

Pg 109

SPOUSAL LOVE OF GOD

By Saint Clare of Assisi in Her Fourth Letter to Saint Agnes of Prague

Happy, indeed, is she to whom it is given to share in this sacred banquet so that she might cling with all her heart to Him

Whose beauty all the blessed hosts of heaven unceasingly admire,

Whose affection excites,

Whose contemplation refreshes,

Whose kindness fulfills,

Whose delight replenishes,

Whose remembrance delightfully shines,

By Whose fragrance the dead are revived,

Whose glorious vision will bless all the citizens of the heavenly Jerusalem:

Which, since it is the splendor of eternal glory, is the brilliance of eternal light and the mirror without blemish.

Gaze upon that mirror each day, O Queen and Spouse of Jesus Christ, and continually study your face within it, that you may adorn yourself within and without with beautiful robes, covered, as is becoming the daughter and most chaste bride of the Most High King, with the flowers and garments of all the virtues. Indeed, blessed poverty, holy humility, and inexpressible charity are reflected in that mirror, as, with the grace of God, you can contemplate them throughout the entire mirror.

Look at the border of this mirror, that is, the poverty of Him Who was placed in a manger and wrapped in swaddling clothes.

O marvelous humility!

O astonishing poverty!

The King of angels,

The Lord of heaven and earth,

Is laid in a manger!

Then, at the surface of the mirror, consider the holy humility, the blessed poverty, the untold labors and burdens that He endured for the redemption of the whole human race. Then, in the depth of this same mirror, contemplate the ineffable charity that led Him to suffer on the wood of the Cross and to die there the most shameful kind of death.

Therefore, that Mirror, suspended on the wood of the Cross, urged those who passed by to consider, saying: *"All you who pass by the way, look and see if there is any suffering like my suffering!"* Let us respond with one voice, with one spirit, to Him crying and grieving Who said: *"Remembering this over and over leaves my soul downcast within Me!"*

AN ACT OF HOPE AND CONFIDENCE IN GOD

By Saint Claude de la Colombiere

My God, I believe most firmly that Thou watchest over all who hope in Thee, and that we can want for nothing when we rely upon Thee in all things; therefore I am resolved for the future to have no anxieties, and to cast all my cares upon Thee.

People may deprive me of worldly goods and of honors; sickness may take from me my strength and the means of serving Thee; I may even lose Thy grace by sin; but my trust shall never leave me. I will preserve it to the last moment of my life, and the powers of hell shall seek in vain to wrestle it from me.

Let others seek happiness in their wealth, in their talents; let them trust to the purity of their lives, the severity of their mortifications, to the number of their good works, the fervor of their prayers; as for me, O my God, in my very confidence lies all my hope. "For Thou, O Lord, singularly has settled me in hope." This confidence can never be in vain. "No one has hoped in the Lord and has been confounded."

I am assured, therefore, of my eternal happiness, for I firmly hope for it, and all my hope is in Thee. "In Thee, O Lord, I have hoped; let me never be confounded."

I know, alas! I know but too well that I am frail and changeable; I know the power of temptation against the strongest virtue. I have seen stars fall from heaven, and pillars of firmament totter; but these things alarm me not. While I hope in Thee I am sheltered from all misfortune, and I am sure that my trust shall endure, for I rely upon Thee to sustain this unfailing hope.

Finally, I know that my confidence cannot exceed Thy bounty, and that I shall never receive less than I have hoped for from Thee. Therefore I hope that Thou wilt sustain me against my evil inclinations; that Thou wilt protect me against the most furious assaults of the evil one, and that Thou wilt cause my weakness to triumph over my most powerful enemies. I hope that Thou wilt never cease to love me, and that I shall love Thee unceasingly. "In Thee, O Lord, have I hoped; let me never be confounded."

AGAINST HERESIES

From the writings of Saint Ireaneus, Bishop of Lyons

Book I

Preface.

Inasmuch as certain men have set the truth aside, and bring in lying words and vain genealogies, which, as the apostle says, "minister questions rather than godly edifying which is in faith," and by means of their craftily-constructed plausibilities draw away the minds of the inexperienced and take them captive, [I have felt constrained, my dear friend, to compose the following treatise in order to expose and counteract their machinations.] These men falsify the oracles of God, and prove themselves evil interpreters of the good word of revelation. They also overthrow the faith of many, by drawing them away, under a pretence of [superior] knowledge, from Him who rounded and adorned the universe; as if, forsooth, they had something more excellent and sublime to reveal, than that God who created the heaven and the earth, and all things that are therein. By means of specious and plausible words, they cunningly allure the simple-minded to inquire into their system; but they nevertheless clumsily destroy them, while they initiate them into their blasphemous and impious opinions respecting the Demiurge; and these simple ones are unable, even in such a matter, to distinguish falsehood from truth.

Error, indeed, is never set forth in its naked deformity, lest, being thus exposed, it should at once be detected. But it is craftily decked out in an attractive dress, so as, by its outward form, to make it appear to the inexperienced (ridiculous as the expression may seem) more true than the truth itself. One far superior to me has well said, in reference to this point, "A clever imitation in glass casts contempt, as it were, on that precious jewel the emerald (which is most highly esteemed by some), unless it come under the eye of one able to test and expose the counterfeit. Or, again, what inexperienced person can with ease detect the presence of brass when it has been mixed up with silver?" Lest, therefore, through my neglect, some should be carried off, even as sheep are by wolves, while they perceive not the true character of these men, -because they outwardly are covered with sheep's clothing (against whom the Lord has enjoined us to be on our guard), and because their language resembles ours, while their sentiments are very different,-I have deemed it my duty (after reading some of the *Commentaries*, as they call them, of the disciples of Valentinus, and after making myself acquainted with their tenets through personal intercourse with some of them) to unfold to thee, my friend, these portentous and pro-found mysteries, which do not fall within the range of every intellect, because all have not sufficiently purged their brains. I do this, in order that thou, obtaining an acquain-tance with these things, mayest in turn explain them to all those with whom thou art connected, and exhort them to avoid such an abyss of madness and of blasphemy against Christ. I intend, then, to the best of my ability, with brevity and clearness to set forth the opinions of those who are now promulgating heresy. I refer especially to the disciples of Ptolemaeus, whose school may be described as a bud from that of Valentinus. I shall also endeavor, according to my moderate ability, to furnish the means of overthrowing them, by showing how absurd and inconsistent with the truth are their statements. Not that I am practiced either in composition or eloquence; but my feeling of affection prompts me to make known to thee and all thy companions those doctrines which have been kept in concealment until now, but which are at last, through the goodness of God, brought to light. "For there is nothing hidden which shall not be revealed, nor secret that shall not be made known."

Thou wilt not expect from me, who am resident among the Keltae, and am accus-tomed for the most part to use a barbarous dialect, any display of rhetoric, which I have never learned, or any excellence of composition, which I have never practiced, or any beauty and persuasiveness of style, to which I make no pretensions. But thou wilt accept in a kindly spirit what I in a like spirit write to thee simply, truthfully, and in my own homely way; whilst thou thyself (as being more capable than I am) wilt expand those ideas of which I send thee, as it were, only the seminal principles; and in the compre-hensiveness of thy understanding, wilt develop to their full extent the points on which I briefly touch, so as to set with power before thy companions those things which I have uttered in weakness. In fine, as I (to gratify thy long-cherished desire for information regarding the tenets of these persons) have spared no pains, not only to make these doc-trines known to thee, but also to furnish the means of showing their falsity; so shalt thou, according to the grace given to thee by the Lord, prove an earnest and efficient minister to others, that men may no longer be drawn away by the plausible system of these heretics, which I now proceed to describe.

LOVE OF ONE'S NEIGHBOR

From the Thoughts and Sayings of Saint Margaret Mary Alacoque

While at prayer, I begged our Lord to make known to me by what means I could satisfy the desire that I had to love Him. He gave me to understand, that one cannot better show one's love for Him than by loving one's neighbor for love of Him; and that I must work for the salvation of others, forgetting my own interests in order to espouse those of my neighbor, both in my prayers and in all the good I might be able to do by the mercy of God.

+ + +

Bear patiently the little vexations caused by your neighbor's being of a disposition contrary to your own; do not show your resentment, for that displeases the Sacred Heart of our Lord.

+ + +

Our Lord wishes us to have great charity for our neighbor, for whom we should pray as for ourselves; it is one of the characteristic effects of this devotion to reconcile hearts and to bring peace to souls.

+ + +

Work courageously and untiringly in the vineyard of the Lord, for this is the price of your crown; you must forget yourself and all you own interests and think only of increasing His glory in the work He has confided to you.

+ + +

You see plainly that I do not mean to advise you to perform great austerities, but rather generously to mortify your passions and inclinations, detaching your heart and emptying it of all that is earthly, and exercising charity towards your neighbor and liberality towards the poor.

+ + +

You should never find fault with, accuse or judge anyone but yourself, so that your tongue on which the Sacred Hose so often rests, may not serve Satan as instrument to sully your soul.

+ + +

Never keep up any coldness towards your neighbor, or else the Sacred Heart of Jesus Christ will keep aloof from you. When you resentfully call to mind former slights that you have received, you oblige our Lord to recall you past sins which His mercy had made Him forget.

EXHORTATION TO FAITH AND REPENTANCE

By Saint Francis of Assisi in His Letter to All the Faithful

To all Christians, religious, clerics and layfolk, men and women; to everyone in the whole world, Brother Francis, their servant and subject, sends his humble respects, imploring for them true peace from heaven and sincere love in God.

I am the servant of all and so I am bound to wait upon everyone and make known to them the fragrant words of my Lord. Realizing, however, that because of my sickness and ill-health I cannot personally visit each one individually, I decided to send you a letter bringing a message with the words of our Lord Jesus Christ, who is the Word of the Father, and of the Holy Spirit, whose words are *spirit and life* (Jn 6:64).

Our Lord Jesus Christ is the glorious Word of the Father, so holy and exalted, whose coming the Father made known by St. Gabriel the Archangel to the glorious and blessed Virgin Mary, in whose womb he took on our weak human nature, He was rich beyond measure and yet his holy Mother chose poverty.

Then, as his passion drew near, he celebrated the Pasch with his disciples and, taking bread, he *blessed and broke, and gave to his disciples, and said, Take and eat; this is my body. And taking a cup, he gave thanks and gave it to them, saying, This is my blood of the new covenant, which is being shed for many unto the forgiveness of sins* (Mt. 26: 26-29). And he prayed to his Father, too, saying, *Father, if it is possible, let this cup pass away from me* (Mt. 26:39); and his sweat fell to the ground like thick drops of blood (cf. Lk. 22:44). Yet he bowed to his Father's will and said, *Father, thy will be done: yet not as I will, but as thou willest* (Mt. 26:42 and 39). And it was the Father's will that his blessed and glorious Son, whom he gave to us and who was born for our sake, should offer himself by his own blood as a sacrifice and victim on the altar of the cross; and this, not for himself, through whom *all things were made* (Jn 1:3), but for our sins, *leaving us an example that we may follow in his steps* (1 Pet. 2:21). It is the Father's will that we should all be saved by the Son, and that we should receive him with a pure heart and chaste body. But very few are anxious to receive him, or want to be saved by him, although his *yoke is easy, and his burden light* (Mt. 11:30).

All those who refuse to *taste and see how good the Lord is* (Ps. 33:9) and who love *the darkness rather than the light* (Jn. 3:19) are under a curse. It is God's commandments they refuse to obey and so it is of them the Prophet says, *You rebuke the accursed proud who turn away from you commands* (Ps. 118:21). On the other hand, those who love God are happy and blessed. They do as our Lord himself tells us in the Gospel: Thou shalt love the Lord thy God with thy whole heart, and with thy whole soul, . . .and thy neighbor as thyself (Mt. 22:37-39). We must love God, then, and adore him with a pure heart and mind, because this is what he seeks above all else, as he tells us, *True worshippers will worship the Father in spirit and in truth* (Jn 4:23). All *who worship him must worship him in spirit and in truth* (Jn 4:24). We should praise him and pray to him day and night, saying, *Our Father, who art in Heaven* (Mt. 6:9), because we must always pray and not lose heart (Lk. 18:1).

And moreover, we should confess all our sins to a priest and receive from him the Body and Blood of our Lord Jesus Christ. The man who does not eat his flesh and drink his blood cannot enter into the kingdom of God (cf. Jn 6:54). Only he must eat and drink worthily because *he who eats and drinks unworthily, without distinguishing the body, eats and drinks judgment to himself* (1Cor. 11:29); that is, if he sees no difference between it and other food.

Besides this, we must *bring forth therefore fruits befitting repentance* (Lk. 3:8) and love our neighbors as ourselves. Anyone who will not or cannot love his neighbor as himself should at least do him good and not do him any harm.

St. Francis of Assisi, Omnibus of Sources, Pg. 93

THE NEED FOR SPIRITUAL DIRECTION

By Saint M. Faustina Kowalska

120. I have wandered onto the subject of silence. But this is not what I wanted to speak about, but rather about the soul's life with God and about its response to grace. When a soul has been cleansed, and the Lord is on intimate terms with it, it begins to apply all its inner force in striving after God. Yet the soul cannot do anything of itself. God alone arranges everything. The soul knows this and is mindful of it. It is still in exile and understands well that there may yet come cloudy and rainy days, but it must now look upon things differently from what it had up to now. It does not seek reassurance in a false peace, but makes ready for battle. It knows it comes from a warrior race. It is now much more aware of everything. It knows that it is of royal stock. It is concerned with all that is great and holy.

121. There is a series of graces, which God pours into the soul after these trials by fire. The soul enjoys intimate union with God. It has many visions, both corporeal and intellectual. It hears many supernatural words, and sometimes, distinct orders. But despite these graces, it is not self-sufficient. In fact it is even less so as a result of God's graces, because it is now open to many dangers and can easily fall prey to illusions. It ought to ask God for a spiritual director; but not only must it pray for one, it must also make every effort to find a leader who is an expert in these things, just as a military leader must know the ways along which he will lead his followers into battle. A soul that is united with God must be prepared for great and hard-fought battles.

After these purifications and tears, God abides in the soul in a special way, but their soul does not always cooperate with these graces. Not that the soul itself is not willing to work, but it encounters so many interior and exterior difficulties that it really takes a miracle to sustain the soul on these summits. In this, it absolutely needs a director. People have often sown doubt in my soul, and I myself have sometimes become frightened at the thought that I was, after all, an ignorant person and did not have knowledge of many things, above all, spiritual things. But when my doubts increased, I sought light from my confessor and my superiors.

Diary - Divine Mercy in My Soul
St. M. Faustina Kowalska
Notebook 1, Pg 67

UNION WITH GOD

By Saint John of the Cross

In our previous discussion, we have already given some indication of the meaning of the phrase "union of the soul with God." Thus our teaching here about the nature of this union will be more understandable.

It is not my intention now to discuss the divisions and parts of the union. Indeed, I would never finish were I to begin explaining the union of the intellect, or that of the will or the memory, or trying to expound the nature of the transitory and the permanent union in each of these faculties, or the significance of the total, the transitory, or the permanent union wrought in these three faculties together. We will discuss all this frequently in the course of our treatise. But such an exposition is unnecessary for an understanding of what we now wish to state about these different unions. A better explanation of them will be given in sections dealing with the subject, and then we shall have a concrete example to go with the actual teaching. In those sections the reader will note and understand the union being discussed and will for a better judgment of it.

Here I intend to discuss only this total and permanent union in the substance and faculties of the soul. And I shall be speaking of the obscure habit of union, for we will explain later, with God's help, how a permanent actual union of the faculties in this life is impossible; such a union can only be transitory. (1)

To understand the nature of this union, one should first know that God sustains every soul and dwells in it substantially, even though it may be that of the greatest sinner in the world. This union between God and creatures always exists. By it he conserves their being so that if the union should end they would immediately be annihilated and cease to exist. Consequently, in discussing union with God we are not discussing the substantial union that always exists, but the soul's union with and transformation in God that does not always exist, except when there is likeness of love. We will call it the union of likeness; and the former, the essential or substantial union. The union of likeness is supernatural; the other, natural. The supernatural union exists when God's will and the soul's are in conformity, so that nothing in the one is repugnant to the other. When the soul rids itself completely of what is repugnant and unconformed to the divine will, it rests transformed in God through love.

The Ascent of Mount Carmel
Book 2, Chapter 5, P162

A LETTER TO A SPIRITUAL BROTHER

By Saint Therese of Lisieux

My dear little Brother,

My pen, or rather my heart, refuses to call you "Monsieur l;Abbe," and our good Mother has told me that from now on, in writing you I may use the name I always use when I speak of you to Jesus. It seems to me that this Divine Savior has wanted to unite our souls so that we might work for the salvation of sinners, as He once united those of the Venerable Father de la Colombiere and Blessed Margaret Mary. Recently I read in the Life of that Saint: "One day when I was approaching Our Saviour to receive Him in Holy Communion, He showed me His Sacred Heart as a burning furnace and two other hearts (her own and that of Pere Colombiere) which were about to be united and plunged into it, and He said to me: 'It is in this way that My pure love unites these three hearts forever.' He made me understand again that this union was entirely for His glory, and that for the reason He wanted us to be like brother and sister, equally sharing in spiritual benefits. When I pointed out to Our Lord my poverty and the inequality that existed between a priest of such great virtue and a poor sinner like me, He said to me: 'The infinite riches of my Heart will make up for everything and make you completely equal.'".

Perhaps, my Brother, the comparison doesn't seem right to you? It is true that as yet you are no Father de la Colombiere, but I don't doubt that like him you will one day be a real apostle of Christ. For me, the thought doesn't even enter my head to compare myself to Blessed Margaret Mary. I'm only saying that Jesus has chosen me to be the sister of one of His apostles, and the words which this holy lover of His Heart spoke to Him out of humility, I repeat to Him about myself in all truth. Moreover, I'm hoping that His infinite riches will supply for everything I lack in order to achieve the work He has entrusted to me.

I am happy if the Good God makes use of my poor verses to do you a little good. I would have been embarrassed to send them to you if I had not recalled that a sister should hide nothing from her brother. It is surely with a brother's heart that you have welcomed and judged them. No doubt you were surprised to receive "Vivre d'Amour" again. I had no intention of sending it to you twice. I had started to copy it when I remembered that you already had it and it was too late to stop.

Maurice & Therese
The Story of a Love
P. 103

KINGSHIP OF CHRIST

By Saint Anthony of Padua from a Sermon on Palm Sunday

(translated by Paul Spilsbury)

All this was done that it might be fulfilled what was spoken by the prophet (Zechariah) *saying: Tell ye the daughter of Sion: Behold, thy king cometh to thee, meek, and sitting upon an ass and a colt, the foal of her that is used to the yoke.* [Mt 21.4-5]

The actual words of Zechariah are: *Rejoice greatly, O daughter of Sion; shout for joy, O daughter of Jerusalem. Behold, thy king will come to thee, the just and saviour. He is poor and riding upon an ass and upon a colt, the foal of an ass. And I will destroy the chariot out of Ephraim and the horse out of Jerusalem; and the bow of war shall be broken.* [Zech 9.9-10]

Sion and Jerusalem are the same city, Sion being the citadel of Jerusalem. They stand for the heavenly Jerusalem, in which is the sight of eternity and the vision of lasting peace. Her daughter is Holy Church, and to her, you preachers, say: "Rejoice greatly by your works, and shout for joy in your mind." This joy is conceived as being of such great and heartfelt happiness that words cannot express it. Behold the king, of whom Jeremiah says: *There is none like to thee, O Lord: thou art great, and great is thy name in might. Who shall not fear thee, O king of nations?* [Jer 10.6-7]

He, as is told in the Apocalypse, *hath on his garment and upon his thigh written: King of kings and Lord of lords* [Apoc 19.16]. The swaddling-clothes are his garment, and his 'thigh' is his flesh. At Nazareth he was crowned with flesh as with a diadem; at Bethlehem he was wrapped in swaddling clothes as his purple. These were the first insignia of his reign. At each, the Jews raged, like people wanting to deprive him of his kingdom. In his Passion he was stripped by them of his garments, and pierced with nails. There his kingdom was completely fulfilled, for after crown and purple he lacked only a sceptre; and this he took when he went out, bearing his cross, to the place called Calvary [cf. Jn 19.17]. Isaiah says: *The government was laid upon his shoulder* [Is 9.6], and the Apostle: *We see Jesus, through suffering death, crowned with glory and honour.* [cf. Heb 2.9]

Behold, then, *thy King*, coming to you for your benefit; meek, that he may be loved rather than feared for his power; *sitting upon an ass*. Zechariah calls him, *Just and saviour, poor and riding upon an ass*. There are two proper virtues for a king, justice and piety. Your king is just, in respect of justice, rendering to each according to his works. He is meek, and a redeemer, with respect to piety. He is poor, as the Apostle says in today's Epistle: *He emptied himself, taking the form of a servant*. [Phil 2.7] Because Adam, in Paradise, would not serve the Lord, the Lord took the form of a servant, to serve the servant, so that henceforward the servant might not be ashamed to serve the Lord. *Being made in the likeness of man, and in habit found as a man*. [Phil, loc. cit.] So Baruch says: *Afterwards, he was seen upon earth and conversed with men*. [Bar 3.38] 'As man' expresses the reality of his manhood; he was not just 'like' a man. *He humbled himself, becoming obedient unto death, even to the death of the cross*. [Phil 2.8] St Augustine[2] says: "Our Redeemer spread before our captor the mouse-trap of the cross; he placed his own blood as bait. The devil shed the blood of one who was not a debtor, and by doing so retreated from those who were debtors." St Bernard[3] says of Christ: "So great was his obedience, that he was ready to lose life itself; being made obedient to the Father even to death, death on the cross." He had nowhere to lay his head [cf. Mt 8.20; Lk 9.58], except that place where, bowing his head, he gave up his spirit [Jn 19.30].

ON THE MEANS NECESSARY FOR SALVATION

By Saint Alphonsus Liguori

"I am the voice of one crying in the wilderness: Make straight the way of the Lord" - *John 1:23*

All would wish to be saved and to enjoy the glory of Paradise; but to gain Heaven, it is necessary to walk in the straight road that leads to eternal bliss. This road is the observance of the divine commands. Hence, in his preaching, the Baptist exclaimed: "Make straight the way of the Lord." In order to be able to walk always in the way of the Lord, without turning to the right or to the left, it is necessary to adopt the proper means. These means are, first, diffidence in ourselves; secondly, confidence in God; thirdly, resistance to temptations.

"With fear and trembling", says the apostle, "work out your salvation" - Phil. 2:12.

To secure eternal life, we must be always penetrated with fear; we must be always afraid of ourselves (*with fear and trembling*), and distrust altogether our own strength; for, without the divine grace we can do nothing. "Without me," says Jesus Christ, "you can do nothing.": We can do nothing for the salvation of our own souls. St. Paul tells us, that of ourselves we are not capable of even a good thought. "Not that we are sufficient to think anything of ourselves, as of ourselves, but our sufficiency is from God" - II Cor. 3:5. Without the aid of the Holy Ghost, we cannot even pronounce the name of Jesus so as to deserve a reward. "And no one can say the Lord Jesus, but by the Holy Ghost" - I Cor. 12:3 2.

Miserable the man who trusts to himself in the way of God. St. Peter experienced the sad effect of self-confidence. Jesus Christ said to him: "In this night, before cock-crow, thou wilt deny me thrice" - Mat. 26: 34. Trusting in his own strength and in his good will, the Apostle replies: "Yea, though I should die with Thee, I will not deny Thee" - 5:35. What was the result? On the night on which Jesus Christ had been taken, Peter was reproached in the court of Caiphas with being one of the disciples of the Savior. The reproach filled him with fear: he thrice denied his Master, and swore that he had never known Him.

Humility and diffidence in ourselves are so necessary for us, that God permits us sometimes to fall into sin, that, by our fall, we may acquire humility and a knowledge of our own weakness. Through want of humility David also fell: hence, after his sin, he said: "Before I was humbled, I offended" - Ps. 18:67. 3. Hence the Holy Ghost pronounces blessed the man who is always in fear: "Blessed is the man who is always fearful" - Prov. 28:14. He who is afraid of falling, distrusts his own strength, avoids as much as possible all dangerous occasions, and recommends himself often to God, and thus preserves his soul from sin. But the man who is not fearful, but full of self-confidence, easily exposes himself to the danger of sin: he seldom recommends himself to God, and thus he falls.

Let us imagine a person suspended over a great precipice by a cord held by another. Surely he would constantly cry out to the person who supports him: *Hold fast, hold fast; for God's sake, do not let go.* We are all in danger of falling into the abyss of all crime, if God does not support us. Hence we should constantly beseech Him to keep His hands over us, and to help us in all dangers.

In rising from bed, St. Philip Neri used to say every morning: O Lord, keep Thy hand this day over Philip; if Thou do not, Philip will betray Thee. And one day, as he walked through the city, reflecting on his own misery, he frequently said, *I despair, I despair.* A certain religious who heard him, believing that the saint was really tempted to despair, corrected him, and encouraged him to hope in the divine mercy. But the saint replied: "I despair of myself, but I trust in God, hence, during this life in which we are exposed to so many dangers of losing God, it is necessary for us to live always in great distrust in ourselves, and full of confidence in God."

ON GRACE

By Saint Angela of Foligno

In this felt experience wherein the soul finds the certitude that God is within it, the soul is given the grace of wanting God so perfectly that everything in it is in true and not false harmony. False harmony exists when the soul says that it wants God but does not really mean it, because its desire for God is not true in everything, in every way, or in every respect. Its desire for God is true when all the members of the body are in harmony with the soul, and the soul in turn is in such harmony with the heart and with the entire body that it becomes one with them and responds as one for all of them. Then the soul truly wants God, and this desire is granted to it through grace.

Hence when the soul is told: "What do you want?" it can respond: "I want God." God then tells it, "I am the one making you feel that desire." Until it reaches this point, the soul's desire is not true or integral. This form of desire is granted to the soul by a grace by which it knows that God is within it, and that it is in companionship with God. This gift is to have a desire, now a unified one, in which it feels that it loves God in a way analogous to the true love with which God has loved us. The soul feels God merging with it and becoming its companion.

(pp. 188-189)

ON OBEDIENCE

From His Writings on the Devout Life by Saint Francis de Sales

"Let every soul be subject to higher powers; for there is no power but from God." (Romans 13: 1)

There are two sorts of obedience, the one necessary, the other voluntary. By that which is necessary, you must obey your ecclesiastical superiors, as the Pope, the bishop, the parish priest, and such as are commissioned by them; as also your civil superiors, such as your Queen and the magistrates she has established for administering justice; and, finally, your domestic superiors, namely, your father and mother, master and mistress.

Now this obedience is called necessary, because no man can exempt himself from the duty of obeying his superiors, God having placed them in authority to command and govern, each in the department that is assigned to him. You must then of necessity obey their commands; but, to be perfect, follow their counsels also, nay, even their desires and inclinations, so far as charity and discretion will permit. Obey them when they order that which is agreeable, such as to eat, or to take recreation; for though there seems no great virtue to obey on such occasions, yet it would be a great sin to disobey. Obey them in matters indifferent, as to wear this or that dress, to go one way or another, to sing or to be silent, and this will be a very commendable obedience. Obey them in things hard, troublesome, or disagreeable, and this will be a perfect obedience. Obey, in fine, meekly, without reply; readily, without delay; cheerfully, without repining; and above all, lovingly, for the love of Him who, through His love for us, made Himself obedient unto death, even to the death of the cross, and who, as St. Bernard says, rather chose to part with His life than His obedience.

We call that obedience voluntary, to which we oblige ourselves by our own choice, and which is not imposed upon us by another. We do not commonly choose our prince, our bishop, our father and mother, nor do even wives, many times, choose their husbands, but we choose our confessor and director; if, then, in choosing, we make a vow to obey, as the holy St. Teresa did, who, besides her obedience solemnly vowed to the superior of her order, bound herself by a simple vow to obey Father Gratian.

We must obey every one of our superiors, according to the charge he has over us. In political matters, we must obey our Queen; in ecclesiastical matters, our prelates; in our domestic circle, father, master, or husband; and in what regards the private conduct of the soul, our ghostly father or director.

ON VAINGLORY

From the Writings of Saint John Chrysostom

"Let us not be made desirous of vainglory, provoking one another." –Galatians 5: 26

The yearning after glory is a strange passion. It displays itself in a hundred different ways. Some wish to be honored, some wish to be in regal power, some aspire to be rich and others sigh to be strong and robust. This tyrannic passion, passing still further on, induces some to seek for glory by their alms-deeds, others by their fasts and mortifications, some by their ostentatious prayers, others by their learning and science; so various are the forms of this monster vice.

One need not be astonished that men seek after the emoluments and grandeur of this world but what is more astonishing (and what more blamable), that any one can be found who is proud and vain of his good works, of his fasts, his prayers, and of his alms. I confess that I am pierced to the heart when I see such holy actions tarnished by secret vanity. I feel as much grieved as I should be if I heard of an illustrious princess, of whom much was expected, giving herself up to all sorts of debauchery and vice.

Men soon find that there is no one more importunate than he who, filled with vainglory, praises himself, gives himself airs, and places on his head a wreath of incense. He is laughed at for his vanity, and the more they notice that he boasts of himself, the more they endeavor to humiliate him. In fact, the more you try to attract the praise of the world by your own vanity and vainglory, the more will people either avoid you or laugh at you.

Thus it happens that the result is contrary to our expectations; we are anxious that the world should praise us, and exclaim, "What a good man! how charitable he is!" But people will say, "What a vain man! how easy to see that he wishes to please men, rather than please God."

If, on the other hand, you hide the good you do, it is then that God will praise you; He even will not allow any holy action to remain long concealed. You may try to suppress the performance of good deeds; He will take care to make them known, aye, better known than you could possibly have intended. You see, then, that there is nothing more antagonistic to glory and honor, when you seek to do good merely for the purpose of being seen, known and admired. It is the way of doing quite the contrary to what you intended, since, instead of showing off your goodness, you will only cause your vanity to be known to all men, and punished by Almighty God.

This vice seems, as it were, to smother all our reasoning faculties, so much so, that one would say that he who is a slave to vainglory had lost his senses. You would look upon that man as a madman who, being short of stature, would really believe that he was growing so tall that he would soon be able to look down on the highest mountain. After this extravagance, you would need no further proof of his insanity.

So, in like manner, when you see a man who considers himself to be above all his fellow creatures, and would be offended were he compelled to mix with the common herd of men, you would seek for no other proof of his madness. He is even more ridiculous than those who have lost the use of reason, for he voluntarily reduces himself to that pitiable state of extravagant folly.

Fifty-eight on St. Matthew

APPLICATIONS

"Ask Mary for the grace to love our Lord as she loves Him and to remain faithful to Him in life and in death." - *St. Bernadette*

Prayer to Our Lady, Assumed into Heaven

Immaculate Virgin, Mother of Jesus and our Mother, we believe in your triumphant assumption into haven where the angels and saints acclaim you as Queen. We join them in praising you and bless the Lord who raised you above all creatures. With them we offer you our devotion and love. We are confident that you watch over our daily efforts and needs, and we take comfort from the faith in the coming resurrection. We look to you, our life, our sweetness, and our hope. After this earthly life, show us Jesus, the blest fruit of your womb, O kind, O loving, O sweet Virgin Mary. Amen.

APPLICATION TO FORM A CHAPTER OR CIRCLE OF THE CONFRATERNITY OF PENITENTS

Name of the group_____

Date of Application: _____ (day) _____ (month) _____(year)

Total No. of Members _____

Current Number of the Members: Inquirer____ Postulant ____ Novice ____ Pledged ____

Desire to Form: Circle Chapter (please circle one)

Minister (chairperson) (Name):_____

Postal Address of Minister _____

_____

Email Address of Minister:_____

Phone of Minister_____

FAX of Minister_____

Spiritual Assistant (Name):_____

Address of Spiritual Assistant:_____

_____

Phone of Spiritual Assistant:_____

E Mail of Spiritual Assistant:_____

FAX of Spiritual Assistant:_____

Signature of Minister:_____

Signature of Spiritual Assistant:_____

Make two copies of the completed application.

Keep one copy for your Chapter or Circle.

Mail the one copy to your Regional Minister.

Mail the original copy to the Confraternity of Penitents, 1702 Lumbard Street, Fort Wayne Indiana 46803 USA.

INQUIRER APPLICATION FOR THE CONFRATERNITY OF PENITENTS

To enter the Confraternity as an Inquirer, please complete this application at any time of the year and postal mail or email it us. Please keep a copy of your completed application. If you do not hear back from the Confraternity within a week of mailing in your application, please contact us again. We may never have received your application.

Inquirers who have already completed an inquirer application in the previous year but who do not feel ready to enter formation by Ash Wednesday, are asked to resubmit the Inquirer Application each year before Ash Wednesday, until they enter formation.

Inquirer applications must be received before January 1 in order to enter the Lenten Postulancy and before June 1 in order to enter the August Postulancy.

Please check:

_____ New Inquirer for year _____ (write in year)

_____ Continuing to Inquire for year _____ (write in year)

Date of application: _____ Month _____ Day _____ Year

Mr./Mrs./Ms./Miss _____

            (last name)   (first name)   (middle name)

Address _____

City _____ State _____ Nation _____ Zip _____

Telephone Number (____)_____ E-mail _____

Date of Birth ____ (day) _____ (month) ____(year)

Please Circle: Married____Single____Div_____ Sep_____ Annul_____

Where baptized_____ Where confirmed_____

(A copy of your updated Baptismal Certificate will be required before you can enter the Novitiate of the Confraternity.)

Your Parish _____

           (name)   (city and state)

Parish Telephone Number (_____)_____

This is a Confraternity for penitents and sinners. No one will be denied membership due to past values, lifestyles, or serious sins. No one is expected to be perfect upon entering the Confraternity but rather ought to hope to become more conformed to Christ through living this Rule. Therefore, please provide a brief response to the following questions, recognizing, however, that membership in the Confraternity is not automatic. Applications may be rejected, or membership terminated, by a consensus vote of the Council of the Confraternity where the PRESENT conduct or values of the individual involved are deemed to be in conflict with the desire for conversion, reconciliation, and surrender to God which are the spirit and intent of the Rule.

How and when did you first hear of the Confraternity of Penitents (CFP)?

Prior to completing this application, all inquirers are required to read the Rule and Constitutions of the Confraternity of Penitents. On-line inquirers should also read the CFP internet home page. Have you read these?_____ Do you understand them?_____

Do you understand that only Catholics who accept all the teachings of the Roman Catholic Church and remain in union with the Pope and Magesterium of the Catholic Church can become official members of this Confraternity? _____

Do you understand and accept that lessons of formation will be Catholic in orientation? ____.

Do you have spousal approval to begin the inquirer process? _____

Are you currently involved in any apostolates and or religious organizations? If yes, please list them. (i.e.. Third Orders, parish associations, Knights of Columbus, Religious Education, Legion of Mary, etc.)

Have you been convicted of any crime? _____ If so, please explain:

_____

_____

Have you made restitution or are you trying to make restitution for crimes, sins committed?_____

The Confraternity of Penitents is consecrated to Mary, the Mother of Jesus. What are your thoughts about this?

Do you have any questions about the Confraternity?

Within two weeks of receipt of your application, your Regional Minister will generally request a short interview via phone. When is a good time to call you?

_____

If you do not hear from your Regional Minister within two weeks of submitting your inquirer application, please contact the CFP Office at the address below. We do want to speak with you.

SITUATIONS WHICH PRECLUDE FULL MEMBERSHIP IN THE CONFRATERNITY OF PENITENTS (please check if applicable)

____ You are a member of a Third Order which disallows dual membership in that Order and the CFP. These include, among others, the Secular Franciscan Order, Tau Maria, and Third Order Carmelites. Please circle your Order or write it here:_____

____You had previously been an inquirer or member of the CFP but then dropped.

____You are a non-Catholic.

____You are a Catholic in an irregular marital situation (that is, you had been married, then obtained a civil divorce but not an annulment, and have since remarried. Or you have been married by a Justice of the Peace or are in a "common law" marriage.)

____Your spouse has not given approval to enter the inquirer phase.

____You are a non-practicing Catholic.

____You have another condition which may preclude full membership. Please name _____.

If you meet one of these conditions, you may be accepted as an Associate of the Confraternity and then proceed in formation with members. With permission, you may attend all CFP on line and other gatherings. You will live as much of the Rule as possible.

Associates are not members of the CFP nor may they pledge to live the Rule. They cannot hold office, vote, or conduct formation in the CFP.

If the situation which caused an individual to be accepted as an Associate is rectified, or if an Associate who previously dropped from the CFP persists as an Associate for several years, the Associate may then apply for full membership without losing any formation time. The CFP Council will make a decision on all such applications.

If Associate status interests or applies to you, please share why you would like to enter formation as a CFP Associate.

Prisoners currently serving time in prison can participate in formation as part of the CFP's Alesandro Ministry. Upon release, they will become Associates. They can apply for Membership after two years of completing formation and living the Rule outside of prison. Prisoners serving life sentences without parole will be evaluated on their status on an individual basis.

Mail completed application by postal mail or by pasting the application into an email (do not email as an attachment as our email servers randomly delete emails with attachments and we may never receive your application) to:

Confraternity of Penitents, 1702 Lumbard Street, Fort Wayne, Indiana 46803 USA Phone: (260) 739-6882 email: bspenance@hotmail.com AND copenitents@yahoo.com (Please put the words "INQUIRER APPLICATION" into the subject line of your email. Then please email to both addresses to be sure that we receive at least one of copies. We do want to reply to you.)

Someone will be in touch with you as soon as possible regarding your application. If you do not hear from us within a few days, please contact us again. No response most likely means that we did not receive your application.

Upon receipt of this application, you will be added to our daily prayer list. Please continue to pray about this way of life and for our Confraternity as we will pray for you.

God bless!

POSTULANT APPLICATION FOR THE CONFRATERNITY OF PENITENTS

We ask that an application be completed yearly in February, to be submitted before Ash Wednesday.

Date of Application:_____Day _____Month _____Year

(Note: A copy of your updated Baptismal Certificate will be required to enter Novice formation.)

If you are applying to enter the postulancy, please check here_____

If you are applying to continue the postulancy, please check here _____

Would you do formation via ____ internet _____ postal mail _____ in local CFP Circle or Chapter?

Mr./Mrs./Ms./Miss_____

              (last name)   (first name)   (middle name)

Address _____

City_____State_____Zip_____

Telephone Number (area code first)_____

e mail address_____

Date of Birth ___(day) ___(month) ___(year) Circle: Married – Single – Div. – Sep. – Annul

Your Parish_____

           (name)   (city and state)

Check here if applying for Associate Status _____

On another sheet of paper, please tell us a bit about your personal and family background (personal history, family, work, children, faith journey, etc.).

Have you read and understood the Rule and Constitutions of the Confraternity of Penitents?_____ Are you in agreement with these?_____

Do you wish to live this way of life?_____

Do you feel that God is calling you to become a penitent by living according to the Rule and Constitutions for the Confraternity of Penitents? _____

Are you willing to surrender yourself, everything, and everyone in your life to God?_____

Do you seek union with God's will in every aspect of your life?_____

On another sheet of paper, please explain why you would like to enter the postulancy of the Confraternity of Penitents.

Only Catholics who accept all the teachings of the Roman Catholic Church, and who are in union with the Pope in communion with the bishops, can be accepted into this Confraternity. These include all the teachings on marriage, birth control, abortion, euthanasia, assisted suicide, the death penalty, war, chastity according to your state in life, the sacramental priesthood, the Church's stance on ordaining women, Eucharist, Penance, dogmas on the saints, Mary, etc. Do you accept all these teachings in their entirety as well as the authority of the Holy Father in communion with the bishops?_____

If you do not agree, read further.

    a. If you are a Catholic but are unsure as to what these teachings are, are you willing to accept them because the Church, established by Christ Himself, so teaches?_____

    b. If you are of another faith, you may be accepted as an Associate member of the Confraternity of Penitents on the condition that you understand that lessons of formation will be Catholic in orientation. Are you willing to accept this?_____

Married applicants must have their spouse's consent to live this Rule. If the couple is separated, then spousal consent is not necessary. Do you have your spouse's consent to live this Rule?_____ Explain:

SITUATIONS WHICH PRECLUDE FULL MEMBERSHIP IN THE CONFRATERNITY OF PENITENTS (please check if applicable)

____ You are a member of a Third Order which disallows dual membership in that Order and the CFP. These include the Secular Franciscan Order, Third Order Carmelites, and Tau Maria. Please circle your Order or write it here:_____

____You had previously been a member of the CFP but then dropped from either the inquiry stage or formation.

____You are a non-Catholic.

____You are a Catholic in an irregular marital situation (that is, you had been married, then obtained a civil divorce but not an annulment, and have since remarried. Or you have been married by a Justice of the Peace or are in a "common law" marriage.).

____You do not have spousal approval.

____You are a non-practicing Catholic.

____You have another condition which may preclude full membership. Please name:

If you meet one of these conditions, you may be accepted into formation as an Associate of the Confraternity. With permission, you may attend all CFP on line and other gatherings. You will live as much of the Rule and Constitutions as possible. Associates are not members of the CFP nor may they pledge to live the Rule. They cannot hold office, vote, or conduct formation in the CFP. If the situation which caused an individual to be accepted as an Associate is rectified, or if an Associate who previously dropped from the CFP persists as an Associate for several years, the Associate may then apply for full membership without losing any formation time. If Associate status interests or applies to you, please share on another sheet of paper why you would like to enter formation as a CFP Associate.

My next of kin/good friend is:

Name: _____

Address:_____Phone:_____

I have asked them to contact my Chapter or Circle of the CFP for me should I be unable to do so, and they may be contacted for information on me.

Your Signature _____Date_____

Attached to this are my brief biography and an explanation of why I would like to enter formation in the Confraternity of Penitents.

Make two copies of this application. Keep one copy yourself. Give one copy to your Chapter or Circle Minister, if you are in a Chapter or Circle. If not, then mail a copy to your Regional Minister. Mail the original to the Confraternity of Penitents, 1702 Lumbard Street, Fort Wayne Indiana 46803 USA. Thanks and God bless!

NOVICE AND PLEDGED APPLICATION FOR THE CONFRATERNITY OF PENITENTS

WE ASK THAT AN APPLICATION BE COMPLETED YEARLY IN FEBRUARY, TO BE SUBMITTED BEFORE ASH WEDNESDAY, UNTIL A PERSON PLEDGES FOR LIFE.

Date of Application: Day _____ Month _____ Year _____

I will do my formation via _____ internet _____ postal mail _____ in my local CFP Chapter or Circle.

Your updated baptismal certificate is needed to pledge in the CFP. This certificate should be submitted upon entry into Novice formation.

_____ My updated Baptismal Certificate is enclosed

_____ My updated Baptismal Certificate is already on file with the Confraternity of Penitents

_____ I will mail my updated Baptismal Certificate to you as soon as possible.

Application for (please check):

_____1st Year Novitiate (___entering or __continuing)

_____2nd Year Novitiate (___entering or ___continuing)

_____3rd Year Novitiate (___entering or _____continuing)

_____Pledge for a Year (_____first time pledge or _____renewing a year pledge)

_____Pledge for Life

_____Pledge and Vow for Life

_____Vow for Life (Suitable only for members who have previously pledged for life.)

Associate Section:

If you meet one of the following conditions, you may be accepted as an Associate of the Confraternity and then proceed in formation with members. With permission, you may attend all CFP on line and other gatherings. You will live as much of the Rule and Constitutions as possible.

Associates are not members of the CFP nor may they pledge to live the Rule. They cannot hold office, vote, or conduct formation in the CFP.

- If you are applying as an Associate of the CFP, please check the appropriate reason below:

____ You are a member of a Third Order which disallows dual membership in that Order and the CFP. These include the Secular Franciscan Order, Third Order Carmelites, and Tau Maria. Please circle your Order or write it here:_____

____You had previously been a member of the CFP but then dropped.

____You are a non-Catholic. Are you willing to accept that the formation will be totally Catholic in orientation?_____

____You are a Catholic in an irregular marital situation (that is, you had been married, then obtained a civil divorce but not an annulment, and have since remarried. Or you have been married by a Justice of the Peace or are in a "common law" marriage.).

____You do not have spousal approval.

____You are a non-practicing Catholic.

____You have another condition which may preclude full membership. Please name:_____

If the situation which caused an individual to be accepted as an Associate is rectified, or if an Associate who previously dropped from the CFP persists as an Associate for several years, the Associate may then apply for full membership without losing any formation time. The CFP Council will make a decision on all such applications.

Associates and members, please complete the remainder of the application:
Mr./Mrs./Ms./Miss_____
(last name) (first name) (middle name) Address _____
City_____State_____Zip_____
Telephone Number (area code first)_____
email address_____
Date of Birth ____(day) _____(month) _____(year) Circle: Married Single Sep. Div. Annul.
Your Parish_____
(name, city, state)
Spiritual Director (name) _____

Address_____

Next of Kin _____

(name) (address, city, state, zip)

Next of Kin Phone Number_____

Are you loyal to all the teachings of the Catholic Church, the Pope, and bishops? _____

Do you agree to follow Catholic instruction in this way of life?_____

Do you have your spouse's approval to live the Rule?_____

Do you have an apostolate? _____ Explain:

First year novices: Are you willing and able to live the prescriptions for prayer in the Rule and Constitutions? _____

Comments:

Second year novices: Are you willing and able to continue with the prayer requirements of this way of life, as agreed upon between you and your spiritual director, and to embrace the fasting and abstinence requirements of the Rule and Constitutions as they suit your age and state of health?_____

Comments:

Third year novices: Are you willing to make the external adjustments in clothing and simplified lifestyle as stated in the Rule and Constitutions?_____

Comments:

Pledged: Are you willing to live according to the entire Rule and Constitutions for the Confraternity of Penitents under your spiritual director for all of your life?_____ or for the period of one year?_____

Comments:

Pledged and Vowed for Life: Are you willing to take a private vow to live according to the CFP Rule and Constitutions for the rest of your life? _____ A private vow is made to your spiritual director and is binding under pain of sin as long as the vow can be kept.

Comments:

Why do you wish to enter this stage of membership?

I, as spiritual director of _____, consent to having the above named directee continue in the Confraternity of Penitents as requested above.

Signed:_____ Date: _____

Applicant's Signature_____ Date:_____

　　Please make three copies of your completed application. Keep one copy yourself.

　　a. Give one copy to your formator (the person going over your lessons).

　　b. Give one copy to your Chapter or Circle Minister. If you are not in a local group, mail a copy of the application to your Regional Minister.

　　c. Mail the original to the Confraternity of Penitents, 1702 Lumbard Street, Fort Wayne Indiana 46803 USA, copenitents@yahoo.com Thank you and may God bless you on your spiritual journey!

YEARLY ADDRESS UPDATE FORM FOR CFP MEMBERS WHOSE FORMATION IS COMPLETE

This yearly form is to be used ONLY by those penitents who are either Associates who have completed formation or who are pledged (and possibly privately vowed) for life in the Confraternity of Penitents. Please complete and return this form to your Circle or Chapter minister who will approve it and then forward it to the Confraternity Records Center. If you have no Circle or Chapter, mail the application directly to the Confraternity Records Center address at the bottom of this form.

Please complete this form EVEN IF YOU THINK YOU HAD NO CHANGES FROM LAST YEAR. THANK YOU!

UPDATED INFORMATION FOR THE YEAR _____

Mr./Mrs./Ms./Miss_____
(last name) (first name) (middle name)

Address_____

City_____State_____ Zip_____

Telephone Number (area code first)_____

e mail address_____

Date of Birth_____Married_____ Single___Div___Sep____Annul___
Widow/Widower_____

Your Parish_____
(name) (city and state)

My next of kin/good friend is:
Name: _____

Address:_____

Phone:_____

I have asked them to contact my chapter or circle of the CFP for me should I be unable to do so, and they may be contacted for information on me.

Your Signature_____Date _____

Please make three copies of this completed form.

a. Give one copy to your local chapter or circle minister.
b. Mail one copy to your Regional Minister.
c. Mail one copy to the Confraternity of Penitents Records Center, 1702 Lumbard Street, Fort Wayne IN 46803, 260-739-6882, copenitents@yahoo.com

Thank you and may God bless you on your spiritual journey!

AFFILIATE APPLICATION FOR THE CONFRATERNITY OF PENITENTS

The following obligations must be fulfilled for Affiliate status:

* Completion of the Application for Affiliation and on the web site.
* Promotion of penance (conversion) in ways suitable to the Affiliate's vocation.
* Offering attendance at one Mass per year for deceased penitents.
* Fully living section 26 of the Rule and Constitutions which enjoins peace with all.
* Being consecrated to Our Lady and praying a daily Marian Consecration prayer of their choice.
* Praying daily the Affiliates' Prayer:

Blessed Lord, as You made Saint Francis reflective of the image of Christ through a life of humility and penance, so, too, please help us and all of our brothers and sisters to die to the world with You, in order that our hearts may be inflamed with the fire of Your Love, and finally we may be brought to new life. Please have mercy on all those who are burdened with leadership in the Confraternity, especially the Bishop, Visitor, Minister General, Regional Ministers, Ministers, Officers, and Formators. Father of all, please renew the marks of Jesus' Passion on our souls, and bring us to perfection for the sake of Your glory. We ask this through Christ our Lord, Who lives and reigns with You and the Holy Spirit, God, world without end. Amen.

Our Lady of the Angels, pray for us.
Saint Francis, pray for us.
Saint Clare, pray for us.
Saint Anthony, pray for us.
All you saints of God, pray for us. Amen.

Priests, Deacons, and Religious Affiliates are also asked consider becoming Spiritual Assistants for CFP Chapters or Circles and/or Spiritual Directors for CFP Members and Associates as their time, wishes, and obligations permit. Priest Affiliates are asked to celebrate one Mass yearly for all deceased penitents.

With the permission of the CFP leadership sponsoring the event, Affiliates may attend CFP functions and meetings. CFP leaders retain contact with Affiliates as they wish. The Confraternity of Penitents is most grateful for its Affiliates and prays daily for them.

Affiliates are not Members of the Confraternity of Penitents because they do not wish to participate in formation which is a requirement for Membership. However, Affiliates do support and pray for the CFP. Affiliates may become Members at any time by completing the Inquirer Application and then proceeding, after the time of inquiry, into formation as postulants.

Those who wish to become Affiliates of the Confraternity of Penitents are asked to please complete the following application.

Name_____

Church or Religious House (if applicable) _____

Address (Street)_____City_____State _____Zip _____

Nation_____Diocese _____

Religious Order (if applicable) _____

Your phone number _____ Your email: _____

Are you a member of the Roman Catholic faith?_____ If not, please explain your religious affiliation.

Why do you wish to become an Affiliate of the Confraternity of Penitents?

Have you read the requirements for Affiliate status? _____ Do you agree to fulfill them to the best of your ability?_____

For Roman Catholics, are you totally in agreement with all the teachings of the Roman Catholic Church and the Magisterium?_____

Applicant's Signature:_____

Date: _____(day) _____(month) _____(year)

_____

If you are a member of a Religious Order, your superior must support your Application for Affiliation.
I, as the religious superior of _____ agree to his (her) seeking Affiliate Status with the Confraternity of Penitents. Date_____

Superior's Name_____
Superior's Address _____

_____

Superior's Signature:_____

Please mail completed application to:
Confraternity of Penitents, 520 Oliphant Lane, Middletown Rhode Island 02842-4600 USA
Questions? Phone 401/849-5421 or email copenitents@yahoo.com Thank you for your interest in becoming an Affiliate. May God bless you and please pray for us! We promise prayer for all our Affiliates.

CEREMONIES OF INDUCTION AND MASS OF PLEDGING

"Joseph do not be afraid to take Mary into your home...for she will bear a Son and you will name Him Jesus."

Novena to St. Joseph, Over 1900 Years Old

O St. Joseph whose protection is so great, so strong, so prompt before the Throne of God, I place in you all my interests and desires. O St. Joseph do assist me by your powerful intercession and obtain for me from your Divine Son all spiritual blessings through Jesus Christ, Our Lord; so that having engaged here below your Heavenly power I may offer my Thanksgiving and Homage to the most Loving of Fathers. O St. Joseph, I never weary contemplating you and Jesus asleep in your arms. I dare not approach while He reposes near your heart. Press Him in my name and kiss His fine Head for me, and ask Him to return the Kiss when I draw my dying breath. St. Joseph, Patron of departing souls, pray for us. Amen

CEREMONY OF INDUCTION FOR POSTULANT AND NOVICE MEMBERS AND ASSOCIATES OF THE CONFRATERNITY OF PENITENTS

The following ceremony can be performed as part of Mass, following the Homily, if desired. Members and Associates are inducted together according to year of formation. It is best to practice this ceremony beforehand so that penitents and Presider are comfortable with it.

THOSE IN FORMATION

Presider (Priest, Deacon or Religious):
Would those being inducted into formation in the Confraternity of Penitents please come forward?

Postulants should assemble to far left of the altar, Novice 1's next to them, then Novice 2's, and Novice 3's to far right of altar.

When all are assembled, Presider asks:
Postulants, what do you ask?

Postulants (all together reply):
I, <u>name</u>, of my own will do ask to be allowed to commit myself to live according to the Rule and Constitutions of the Confraternity of Penitents, at the postulancy level for the next year in fulfillment of the Gospel and for the Love of God. In this first year of my journey into formation, I ask the prayers and support of my brothers and sisters in the Confraternity, and your blessing.

Presider (Priest, Deacon or Religious):
Novice 1's, what do you ask?

First Year Novices (all together reply):
I, <u>name</u>, of my own will do ask to be allowed to commit myself to live according to the Rule and Constitutions of the Confraternity of Penitents, at the Novice 1 level for the next year in fulfillment of the Gospel and for the Love of God. In this second year of my journey into formation, I ask the prayers and support of my brothers and sisters in the Confraternity, and your blessing.

Presider (Priest, Deacon or Religious):
Novice 2's, what do you ask?

Second Year Novices (all together reply):
I, <u>name</u>, of my own will do ask to be allowed to commit myself to live according to the Rule and Constitutions of the Confraternity of Penitents, at the Novice 2 level for the next year in fulfillment of the Gospel and for the Love of God. In this third year of my journey into formation, I ask the prayers and support of my brothers and sisters in the Confraternity, and your blessing.

Presider (Priest, Deacon or Religious):
Novice 3's, what do you ask?

Third Year Novices (all together reply):
I, <u>name</u>, of my own will do ask to be allowed to commit myself to live according to the Rule and Constitutions of the Confraternity of Penitents, at the Novice 3 level for the next year, as I further discern my ability and willingness to live this life for the rest of my life in the world, in fulfillment of the Gospel and for the Love of God. In this last year of my journey in formation, I ask the prayers and support of my brothers and sisters in the Confraternity, and your blessing.

Presider:
With my blessing, I accept your commitment, and encourage you to strive to live it joyfully for the Love of God and development of your own spirituality. This commitment of yours is as binding as you make it during this time, never under pain of sin, and is a true gesture of love for the Lord and His Gospel as given to us by the Saints of old. May you, by the grace of God, persevere in your commitment. I accept you as a member in formation in the Confraternity of Penitents with joy, and ask that the Lord grant you every grace necessary to keep your commitment.

Would all those in formation assembled here please hold forth the cross or crucifix which you are wearing for a blessing.

When this is done, the Presider continues:
As a sign of your commitment to live the Gospel more fully through this holy lifestyle, I bless these crosses and crucifixes. Wear them always as visible sign of your commitment, and may Mary, our Mother and advocate, bless and preserve your Love for her Son and His Gospel, as well as your vocation to His service in the Confraternity of Penitents, and always, for the Love of God.

(Postulants and Novices return to their seats.)

THOSE WHOSE FORMATION IS COMPLETE

ASSOCIATES:

Presider:
Would all Associates who have completed formation please come forward?

When Associates have assembled, Presider continues:
As Associates of the Confraternity of Penitents, you have completed formation and live the Rule and Constitutions as much as possible according to your state in life. While you are unable to pledge to live the Rule and Constitutions at this time, the Confraternity of Penitents wishes to acknowledge your support of and commitment to the penitential life and affirms you as sisters and brothers in Christ. May the Lord bless you abundantly, in the Name of the Father and of the Son and of the Holy Spirit. Amen.

(Associates who have complete formation step to the left of the Presider).

PLEDGED MEMBERS

Presider:
Would all those pledged Members of the Confraternity of Penitents please come forward?

When all are assembled, Presider continues:

By your free choice, you have successfully completed formation in the way of life of the Confraternity of Penitents and have chosen to pledge to follow its Rule and Constitutions. In your spiritual journey, you have continued to read the lives and writings of the saints and the documents of the Church as ways to learn more deeply about the love of God. You are participating in one or more of the spiritual or corporal works of mercy and are thus bringing the love of Christ to others. You are supporting the Confraternity by your prayers, tithes, and good works. The Confraternity of Penitents is your family in the Church, and you are all brothers and sisters to one another and to all of us. We thank and praise God for your commitment and love. May God abundantly bless you and may His graces continue to grow in your souls. In the Name of the Father and of the Son and of the Holy Spirit. Amen.

Presider:
Would all those who have completed formation, assembled here, please hold forth the cross or crucifix which you are wearing for a blessing.

When this is done, the Presider continues:
As a sign of your commitment to live the Gospel more fully through this holy lifestyle, I bless these crosses and crucifixes. Wear them always as visible sign of your commitment, and may Mary, our Mother and advocate, bless and preserve your Love for her Son and His Gospel, as well as your vocation to His service in the Confraternity of Penitents, and always, for the Love of God.

(Those who have completed formation return to their seats.)

AFFILIATE BLESSING

Presider:
Would Affiliates of the Confraternity please come forward?

When Affiliates have assembled, Presider continues:
As Affiliates you have agreed to support the Confraternity of Penitents most especially by your prayers as well as in other ways. The Confraternity is most grateful for your support. May God bless you always in the Name of the Father and of the Son and of the Holy Spirit. Amen.

(Affiliates return to their seats).

INQUIRERS, GUESTS, THOSE PREPARING TO PLEDGE, AND OTHERS

Presider:
And may God bless all those inquiring, those preparing to pledge to live the CFP Rule, and all guests, relatives, and friends who are present at this ceremony. In the Name of the Father and of the Son and of the Holy Spirit. Amen.

Presider:
Following all the inductions and blessings, the Presider delivers a brief message to the gathering unless this has been done previously as the Mass homily.

CEREMONY FOR ONE YEAR PLEDGE IN THE CONFRATERNITY OF PENITENTS

This ceremony to be used only for those pledging to live the Confraternity of Penitents Rule of Life for one year. Those pledging will have their pledge already hand written on a sheet of paper. This hand written document is deemed the Formula of Pledging. Each Formula should be dated with the date of the commitment. The year pledge may be made in a private or a public setting.

The Mass ought to be the Mass of the day. Appropriate hymns may be selected. Intercessions and Creed are omitted due to the Rite of Pledging.

Those making pledges outside of Mass make their pledges in a Roman Catholic Church, before the altar and tabernacle. They follow the format below, although the Liturgy of the Eucharist will be omitted. The Liturgy of the Word consists of the Readings of the day.

The **Celebrant** is a Roman Catholic priest. The **Presider** (Roman Catholic Priest, Deacon, or Religious) is the person receiving the pledge, either the penitent's spiritual director or someone else designated to act as the spiritual director's proxy. The **Celebrant** may also act as the **Presider**.

It is recommended that this ceremony be printed out beforehand and the appropriate parts highlighted for the **Presider** and **Celebrant**. The highlighted copy should be reviewed with the **Presider** and **Celebrant** and then given to them to use during the ceremony.

In advance of the ceremony, the penitent about to be pledged selects the **CFP Representative** and **witness** from among the life pledged CFP Members who can be present. If no life pledged Members can be present, the penitent may choose any other CFP Members to fill the roles. If the penitent about to be pledged is the only CFP Member who will be present, the Visitor will have had to approve in advance two others who will stand in as the **CFP Representative** and **witness**. If the Minister General is present, he or she will automatically be the **CFP Representative**.

The Formula of Pledging is the actual pledge which the penitent has written out on a paper. After being signed by the penitent, the Formula of Pledging is kept in the CFP office in the penitent's file.

The Certificate of Pledging is a certificate produced by the Confraternity of Penitents which records the details of the pledge. The of Pledging is then given to the penitent to keep as a remembrance of the pledge.

The San Damiano crucifix, symbol of the Confraternity, may be used as the processional cross.

The cross or crucifix to be blessed during the ceremony is the one the penitent already wears as a sign of membership in the Confraternity. The penitent should remove this prior to the Ceremony and have it readily available. The penitent will also receive a San Damiano Crucifix during the ceremony. These should be within easy reach of the **Presider**.

All those pledging will receive a Certificate of Pledging which will have been signed by the Visitor of the Confraternity. These should also be easily available.

A pen ought to be available at the altar for the penitent to sign, during the Mass, the Formula of Pledging and the Certificate of Pledging.

Before pledging, it is wise for the penitent to practice this ceremony with the **Celebrant, Presider, CFP Representative,** and **witness** and to have in place all the items needed, as listed below.

CHECKLIST:

Penitents about to be pledged should have ready:

____Pledge written out in advance by the penitent. This, deemed the Formula of Pledging, is carried by the penitent to the Ceremony.

____Handbook open to Year Pledging Ceremony

____Pen on the altar or near altar for signing pledge

____Certificate of Pledging filled out, signed by **Visitor**, and ready to be signed by penitent, **Celebrant, CFP Representative,** and **witness.** Prior to the ceremony, these are placed on or near the altar[37] or in another easily accessible location.

____San Damiano Processional Crucifix[38] if desired for procession

____San Damiano Crucifix, placed on a tray or plate, which will be presented to penitent upon pledging[39]

---

37   Available from the Confraternity Office.
38   Available from CFP Holy Angels Gift Shop.
39   Available from the Confraternity Office.

____Cross or crucifix which the penitent wears, placed on a tray or plate, ready to be blessed by **Celebrant**.

ENTRANCE RITE

The entrance hymn is sung as the **Celebrant, Presider,** and those to be pledged enter in procession.

LITURGY OF THE WORD

The Mass proceeds.

After the Gospel, the **Celebrant, Presider,** and congregation sit. The **CFP Representative** comes forward and stands at the lectern.

RITE OF PLEDGING

A. NAMING OF THOSE TO BE PLEDGED

CFP Representative:
Would the brothers and sisters about to make a pledge to live the Rule of the Confraternity of Penitents for one year please rise?

The **CFP Representative** then calls the names of each penitent.

Each penitent, when called, responds:
Present.

CFP Representative:
NAME(S), what do you ask?

REQUEST

ALL THOSE MAKING A YEAR PLEDGE REQUEST IN UNISON: I (NAME), after serious prayer and discernment, freely ask to pledge to live for one year the Rule and Constitutions of the Confraternity of Penitents, in full consecration to the Blessed Virgin Mary as Mother of the Confraternity. I ask the prayers of the Confraternity in this regard.

CFP Representative:
The Confraternity accepts your request and is united with you in prayer. May the Holy Spirit confirm in you the good work He has begun.

The penitents sit and the **CFP Representative** returns to his or her seat.

B. HOMILY

The homily, given by the **Celebrant**, follows and ought to reflect the seriousness of the occasion.

Following the homily, while the congregation is seated, the **CFP Representative** and **Presider** come forward and stand at the lectern while the **Celebrant** stands behind the altar, facing the congregation.

CEREMONY OF YEARLY PLEDGE

Celebrant:

Would those about to be pledged for one year please come forward?

Each penitent comes forward, accompanied by the witness.

When all are standing, the Celebrant continues:

My dear penitent(s), although you have already been consecrated to God and have died to sin through baptism, are you now resolved to consecrate yourself (ves) more closely to God by living for the next year, to the best of your ability, the Rule and Constitutions of the Confraternity of Penitents?

Penitents to be pledged reply together:

I am resolved.

CFP Representative

The Confraternity of Penitents rejoices at your willingness to serve God in the coming year though a life of penance. May God grant you the grace to live your commitment.

All about to be pledged reply.

Amen.

Celebrant:

Please feel free to make your pledge.

Penitents will make their pledge alphabetically by last name and individually, one after the other.

Penitent reads the Formula of Pledging which he or she has written out by hand beforehand. This may be in his or her own words or using the formula below.

I (NAME) promise that I will strive to live, to the best of my means and ability, for one year according to the Rule and Constitutions of the Confraternity of

Penitents in fulfillment of the Gospel and for the Love of God. As part of my commitment I promise to live the Gospel more fully and to pursue more fervently the virtues of poverty, chastity, and humility, which the Saints all loved and promoted. On this journey, I ask the support and prayers of my brothers and sisters in the Confraternity and God's blessing.

Presider:

With my blessing, (NAME), I accept your promise to Christ, and encourage you to strive to live it joyfully for the Love of God and the good of the Church and as a true gesture of love for the Lord and His Gospel, as given to us by the Saints. May you, by the grace of God, persevere in your promise for the duration of this year so as to receive all the blessings of God which are associated with your generosity.

I joyfully accept and acknowledge you as a year pledged (brother or sister) in the Confraternity of Penitents and ask God's blessing on us and on your commitment.

Penitent then proceeds around the altar and places on it the Formula of Pledging, signing and dating it at the altar. At this time, the penitent also signs the Certificate of Pledging, which will shortly be given to the pledged penitent to keep. The witness also signs both of these documents at this time.

Following the signing of the Formula and Certificate, the penitent stands to one side of the altar if other penitents are to be pledged. Following the pledging of every penitent, the **Presider** and **the CFP Representative** sign all the formula(s) and the Certificate(s).

Celebrant

From behind the altar, the **Celebrant** delivers a brief message of support and acceptance and gives a blessing to all.

Penitents return to front of the altar.

BLESSING OF THE HOLY OBJECTS

CRUCIFIX (CROSS)

An **altar server or another individual chosen beforehand** holds the tray with the cross(es) and/or crucifix(es) which the penitent(s) wear(s).

Celebrant
As a sign of your commitment to live the Gospel more fully through this holy lifestyle, I bless this (these) cross(es) (crucifixes). Wear it (them) as a visible sign of your commitment, and may Mary, our Mother and advocate, bless and preserve your Love for her Son and His Gospel, as well as your vocation to His service this year as a member of the Confraternity of Penitents.

The **CFP Representative** clothes each penitent in his or her cross or crucifix.

SAN DAMIANO CRUCIFIX

An **altar server or another individual chosen beforehand** holds the tray with the San Damiano Crucifix(es). This is done with penitents pledging to live the Rule for the first time. Those who have previously pledged to live the Rule for a year will not receive a San Damiano crucifix as they will have received it when they first pledged.

The **Celebrant** then blesses the San Damiano Crucifix(es), sprinkling them with holy water:

Celebrant:
May the Lord bless this (these) crucifixes. May you display it (them) lovingly and learn by meditating on it (them) the message of God's love and sacrifice thereon portrayed.

The **CFP Representative** hands each new penitent a San Damiano Crucifix.

CERTIFICATES

The **Presider** takes the Certificate(s) of Pledging from the altar and says:

Presider:
(NAME), for the next year you shall be a penitent in the service of Christ. Receive this Certificate of Pledging. May it remind you of your promise to God.

When all have received Certificates, they return to their seats while a song expressing joy and thanksgiving may be sung.

The handwritten and signed Formulas of Pledging are kept at the altar.

LITURGY OF THE EUCHARIST

The Liturgy of the Eucharist now follows. The newly pledged may bring forth the gifts.

For Holy Communion, the newly pledged ought to receive first, preferably under both species, with the others following.

Following the final blessing, the newly pledged process out following the altar servers and then the reader, **Presider, Celebrant**.

A collation may now take place in thanksgiving for the newly pledged members of the Confraternity.

The handwritten and signed Formulas of Pledging mailed to Confraternity Office to be kept on file.

LIFE PLEDGING CEREMONY (INCLUDES OPTION FOR PRIVATE VOW) FOR THE CONFRATERNITY OF PENITENTS

This ceremony to be used only for those making a life pledge to live the Rule of the Confraternity of Penitents or for those who have already made a life pledge and are now making a private vow to live the CFP Rule for life. In all cases, the life pledge must precede the private vow.

Those pledging for life will have their pledge already hand written on a sheet of paper. Those pledging for life, and also taking a private vow to live the Rule for life on the same day, will have both their life pledge and their vow written out on two different sheets of paper. Those who have pledged for life on a previous occasion need have only their private vow written out. These hand written documents are deemed the Formula of Pledging (Vowing). Each Formula should be dated with the date of the commitment.

Unless the gathering consists primarily of CFP members only, the private vow must be made in private, out of public view. This may be done at the appropriate place in the ceremony with the Presider, penitent, CFP Representative, and witness retiring to a location out of view of the general public. In this case, a pen for signing the Formula of Vowing and the Certificate of Vowing should be readily accessible in the private location. For those remaining behind, appropriate hymns or meditations may fill in the time until the penitent and others return.

The Mass ought to be the Mass of the day. Appropriate hymns may be selected. Intercessions and Creed are omitted due to the Rite of Pledging.

Those making pledges outside of Mass make their pledges in a Roman Catholic Church, before the altar and tabernacle. They follow the format below, although the Liturgy of the Eucharist will be omitted. The Liturgy of the Word consists of the Readings of the day.

The **Celebrant** is a Roman Catholic priest. The **Presider** (Roman Catholic Priest, Deacon, or Religious) is the person receiving the pledge, either the penitent's spiritual director or someone else designated to act as the spiritual director's proxy. The **Celebrant** may also act as the **Presider**.

It is recommended that this ceremony be printed out beforehand and the appropriate parts highlighted for the **Presider** and **Celebrant**. The highlighted copy should be reviewed with the **Presider** and **Celebrant** and then given to them to use during the ceremony.

In advance of the ceremony, the penitent about to be pledged selects the **CFP Representative** and **witness** from among the life pledged CFP Members who can be present. If no life pledged Members can be present, the penitent may choose any other CFP Members to fill the roles. If the penitent about to be pledged is the only CFP Member who will be present, the Visitor will have had to approve in advance two others who will stand in as the **CFP Representative** and **witness**. If the Minister General is present, he or she will automatically be the **CFP Representative**, but the penitent about to be pledged may select two other life pledged members (such as the penitent's formator and mentor) to act as **witnesses** to the CFP Pledge. These **witnesses**, or the **CFP Representative** and one **witness**, stand on either side of the penitent while the pledge is being made. The **witnesses** sign both the Certificate of Pledging (Vowing) and the pledge. The Minister General, if present, may also sign these documents.

The Formula of Pledging (Vowing) is the actual pledge (private vow) which the penitent has written out on a paper. After being signed by the penitent, the Formula of Pledging (Vowing) is kept in the CFP office in the penitent's file.

The Certificate of Pledging (Vowing) is a certificate produced by the Confraternity of Penitents which records the details of the pledge (private vow). The Certificate of Pledging (Vowing) is then given to the penitent to keep as a remembrance of their pledge (private vow).

Penitents may wish to enter the church, carrying one item symbolic of their lives of penance. Items so carried may be placed in a prominent spot so that they can be seen during the Mass. For example, purple flowers, symbols of penance, could be placed in a vase at the altar. A large rosary could be laid on the altar. And so on.

Each life pledge will carry an unlit candle into the church and place it in a candle holder at the foot of the Blessed Mother's statue or image.

The San Damiano crucifix, symbol of the Confraternity, may be used as the processional cross.

The cross or crucifix to be blessed during the ceremony is the one the penitent already wears as a sign of membership in the Confraternity. The penitent should remove this prior to the Ceremony and have it readily available.

Penitents whose life pledge is the first pledge made in the Confraternity of Penitents will receive a San Damiano Crucifix, brown scapular, and cord during the ceremony.

Penitents who have previously pledged to live the Rule for a year, but who will be making a life pledge during this ceremony, will have already received the San Damiano Crucifix at the time of the year pledge. Therefore, at this ceremony, they will receive only a cord and scapular.

Life pledged members who have already received the San Damiano Crucifix, cord, and scapular during previous pledging ceremonies but who, during this ceremony, will be taking a private vow to live the Rule for life, will simply receive their vowed name by which they can be known in the Confraternity only.

All penitents will receive a Certificate of Pledging (Vowing) which will have been signed by the Visitor of the Confraternity. These should also be easily available.

A pen ought to be available at the altar for the penitent to sign, during the Mass, the Formula of Pledging (Vowing) and the Certificate of Pledging (Vowing).

Before pledging, it is wise for the penitent to practice this ceremony with the **Celebrant**, **Presider**, **CFP Representative**, and **witness** and to have in place all the items needed, as listed below.

CHECKLIST:

Penitents about to be pledged should have ready:

___Pledge and, if applicable, private vow written out in advance by the penitent. These, deemed the Formula of Pledging (Vowing), are carried by the penitent to the Ceremony.

___Handbook open to Pledging Ceremony

___Pen on the altar or near altar for signing pledge and, if applicable, vow

___Certificate of Pledging and a second one of vowing (if applicable), filled out, signed by **Visitor**, and ready to be signed by penitent, **Celebrant**, **CFP Representative**, and **witness**. Prior to the ceremony, these are placed on or near the altar[40] or in another easily accessible location.

___Candle for each life pledgee, candle holder, and matches

___ Statue or image of the Blessed Mother

___San Damiano Processional Crucifix[41] if desired for procession

___Any symbol or memento the penitent wishes to carry in and place at altar

---

40   Available from the Confraternity Office.
41   Available from CFP Holy Angels Gift Shop.

____If not previously received, a San Damiano Crucifix, placed on a tray or plate, which will be presented to penitent upon pledging[42]

____Cross or crucifix which the penitent wears, placed on a tray or plate, ready to be blessed by **Celebrant**.

____If not previously received, a scapular and cord[43] placed on a tray or plate

____Chair to place before altar for **Presider** and any chairs needed by penitents who cannot kneel for the ceremony. An **altar server or another person** chosen beforehand should take care of this responsibility. This same individual will hold the tray(s) with the objects to be blessed and given to the new penitents.

____List of additional saints for the Litany of the Saints. These could be the penitent's patron saint, favorite saint, and/or saint of the name taken with a private vow. The list of saints should be given in advance to the cantor or other person responsible for the Litany of the Saints during the ceremony.

BEFORE MASS BEGINS

Before Mass begins, the **CFP Representative** may give an exhortation regarding the meaning of the act of pledging. This text can serve as an outline:

We are assembled today to take part in the Holy Sacrifice of the Mass. During this Mass, NAME(S) intend to make a pledge (<u>private vow</u>) to live, for the rest of their lives, the Rule and Constitutions of the Confraternity of Penitents. The desire to make this pledge (<u>private vow</u>) is a grace from God, given to the penitent but also to the rest of us who will benefit from the prayers, love, and actions of our brother/sister(s). May God grant NAME(S) the gift of total surrender to and union with the Lord, from this moment and forever.

ENTRANCE RITE

The entrance hymn is sung as the **Celebrant**, **Presider**, and those to be pledged enter in procession. Each about to be life pledged carries an unlit candle. Candles are placed in a candle holder in front of a statue or image of the Blessed Mother. Any other symbolic item is placed by the penitent in a pre-determined spot visible to the congregation.

LITURGY OF THE WORD

The Mass proceeds.

After the Gospel, the **Celebrant**, **Presider**, and congregation sit. The **CFP Representative** comes forward and stands at the lectern.

---

42   Available from the Confraternity Office.
43   Available from the Confraternity Office.

RITE OF PLEDGING

A. NAMING OF THOSE TO BE PLEDGED (VOWED)

CFP Representative:

Would the brothers and sisters about to be pledged (privately vowed) in living the Rule and Constitutions of the Confraternity of Penitents please rise?

The **CFP Representative** then calls the names of each penitent.

Each penitent, when called, responds:

Present.

CFP Representative:

NAME(S), as (a) member(s) of God's Church, God has consecrated you, through the sacraments, with water and the Holy Spirit. What do you now ask of God and of the Confraternity of Penitents?

REQUEST

ALL THOSE MAKING A LIFE PLEDGE ONLY REQUEST IN UNISON: I (NAME) ask to pledge to live for the rest of my life the Rule and Constitutions of the Confraternity of Penitents, in full consecration to the Blessed Virgin Mary as Mother of the Confraternity. I do this freely, believing that God has given me the call to live this holy way of life and knowing that He will provide the grace to do so. May this be for the glory of Christ Crucified and the service of the Church. I ask the prayers of the Confraternity in this regard.

ALL THOSE MAKING, IN THIS CEREMONY, A LIFE PLEDGE FOL-LOWED BY A PRIVATE VOW TO LIVE THE RULE FOR LIFE, REQUEST IN UNISON: I (NAME) ask to pledge and to privately vow to live for the rest of my life the Rule and Constitutions of the Confraternity of Penitents, in full consecration to the Blessed Virgin Mary as Mother of the Confraternity. I do this freely, believing that God has given me the call to live this holy way of life and knowing that He will provide the grace to do so. May this be for the glory of Christ Crucified and the service of the Church. I ask the prayers of the Confraternity in this regard.

ALL THOSE PREVIOUSLY LIFE PLEDGED, WHO HAVE NOW ELECTED TO TAKE A PRIVATE VOW TO LIVE THE RULE FOR LIFE, REQUEST IN UNISON: I (NAME), being a life-pledged member of the Confraternity of Penitents, do ask to privately vow to live for the rest of my life the Rule and Constitutions of the Confraternity of Penitents, in full consecration to the Blessed Virgin Mary as Mother of the Confraternity. I do this freely, believing that God has given me the call to live this holy way of life and knowing that He will provide the grace to do so. May this be for the glory of Christ Crucified and the service of the Church. I ask the prayers of the Confraternity in this regard.

CFP Representative:

The Confraternity accepts your request and is united with you in prayer. May the Holy Spirit confirm in you the good work He has begun.

The penitents sit and the **CFP Representative** returns to his or her seat.

B. HOMILY

The homily, given by the **Celebrant,** follows and ought to reflect the seriousness of the occasion.

Following the homily, while the congregation is seated, the **CFP Representative** and **Presider** come forward and stand at the lectern while the **Celebrant** stands behind the altar, facing the congregation.

C1. EXAMINATION FOR THOSE WHO WILL BE TAKING A LIFE PLEDGE IN THE CONFRATERNITY OF PENITENTS

Celebrant:
Would those about to be pledged for life please stand?

When all are standing, the Celebrant continues:
My dear penitent(s), although you have already been consecrated to God and have died to sin through baptism, are you now resolved to consecrate yourself (ves) more closely to God by living for the rest of your lives, to the best of your ability, the Rule and Constitutions of the Confraternity of Penitents?

Penitents to be pledged reply together:
I am resolved.

Celebrant:
Are you resolved to devote a generous portion of your day to God in prayer, as stated in the Rule and Constitutions of the Confraternity of Penitents, so as to foster surrender of your life to God, so long as you shall live and are able to do so?

Penitents to be pledged:
With God's grace, I am resolved to this surrender.

Celebrant:
Are you resolved to embrace a life of fasting and abstinence, according to the Rule and Constitutions of the Confraternity of Penitents, as a continual prayer of the body, to the best of your abilities within your physical limitations, for as long as you shall live and are able to do so?

Penitents to be pledged:
With God's grace, I am resolved to embrace this life of bodily prayer.

Celebrant:
Are you resolved to live a life of humility and simplicity, as much as is possible for your state in life, as a witness to the transitory nature of this world's goods and the permanence of spiritual realities, for as long as you shall live and are able to do so?

Penitents to be pledged:
With God's grace, I am resolved to live this sort of life.

Celebrant:
Are you resolved to embrace an apostolate from either the Spiritual or Corporal Works of Mercy, doing good to your fellows, in deed or prayer, for as long as you shall live and are able to do so?

Penitents to be pledged:
With God's grace, I am resolved to embrace such an apostolate.

Celebrant:
Are you resolved to be part of the Confraternity of Penitents, serving God through it, and praying for it and its members always, for as long as you shall live and are able to do so?

Penitents about to be pledged:
With God's grace, I am resolved to so serve God through the Confraternity of Penitents.

CFP Representative
The Confraternity of Penitents rejoices at your willingness to serve God though a life of penance, which is a life of conversion. May all that you pray for be granted for the salvation of your soul and the good of the world.

Celebrant:
May God Who has begun this good work in you bring it to fulfillment.

All about to be pledged reply.
Amen.

C2: EXAMINATION FOR THOSE WHO HAVE, AT ANOTHER CEREMONY, BEEN PLEDGED FOR LIFE BUT WHO ARE NOW TAKING A PRIVATE VOW TO LIVE THE CFP RULE FOR LIFE. THIS WILL BE OMITTED IF NO ONE FALLS INTO THIS CATEGORY:

Celebrant:
(NAME[S]), you have already pledged to live the Rule of the Confraternity of Penitents for life and have been living this way for some time. You now request to deepen your commitment by taking a private vow to live the Rule and Constitutions of the Confraternity of Penitents for life. This private vow will be binding on you under pain of sin, as long as the vow can be kept. Do you understand the seriousness of the commitment which you are requesting?

Penitent(s):
With God's grace, I do.

Celebrant:
Are you freely and without constraint making this request to privately vow to live for the rest of your life the Rule and Constitutions of the Confraternity of Penitents?

Penitent(s):
With God's grace, I am.

> *CFP Representative:*
> The Confraternity of Penitents rejoices at your willingness to bind yourself to serve God though a life devoted to penance, which is a life of conversion. May all that you pray for be granted for the salvation of your soul and the good of the world.
>
> *Celebrant:*
> May God Who has begun this good work in you bring it to fulfillment.
>
> *Penitent(s).*
> Amen.

Celebrant:

Let us stand. My dear brothers and sisters, let us pray to God the Almighty Father that through the intercession of those saints who have lived the Rule which you are living as a penitent, and all the saints, God may in His love bless with His grace these penitents whom He has called to a more perfect following of Christ and with loving kindness may strengthen them in their holy purpose.

Let us kneel.

Those to be pledged (privately vowed) approach the altar and kneel before it. All others kneel in their places.

The Litany may be sung with all making the responses. If it is not sung it may be recited.

D. LITANY OF THE SAINTS

Cantor:

With all the saints, the holy men and women of ages past, let us pray:

Lord, have mercy. <u>Lord, have mercy</u>.

Christ, have mercy <u>Christ, have mercy</u>.

Lord, have mercy. <u>Lord, have mercy</u>.

Holy Mary, Mother of God, <u>Pray for us</u>.

Saint Michael, <u>Pray for us</u>.

Holy angels of God, <u>Pray for us</u>.

Saint John the Baptist, <u>Pray for us</u>.

Saint Joseph, <u>Pray for us</u>.

Saint Peter and Saint Paul, <u>Pray for us</u>.

Saint Andrew, <u>Pray for us</u>.

Saint John, <u>Pray for us</u>.
Saint Mary Magdalene, <u>Pray for us</u>.
Saint Stephen, <u>Pray for us</u>.
Saint Ignatius of Antioch, <u>Pray for us</u>.
Saint Lawrence, <u>Pray for us</u>.
Saint Perpetua and Saint Felicity, <u>Pray for us</u>.
Saint Agnes, <u>Pray for us</u>.
Saint Gregory, <u>Pray for us</u>.
Saint Augustine, <u>Pray for us</u>.
Saint Athanasius, <u>Pray for us</u>.
Saint Basil, <u>Pray for us</u>.
Saint Martin, <u>Pray for us</u>.
St. Benedict, <u>Pray for us</u>.
Saint Francis and Saint Dominic, <u>Pray for us</u>.
St. Francis Xavier, <u>Pray for us</u>.
St. John Vianney, <u>Pray for us</u>.
St. Catherine of Siena, <u>Pray for us</u>.
St. Teresa of Jesus, <u>Pray for us</u>.
Saint Elizabeth of Hungary, <u>Pray for us</u>.
King Saint Louis IX, <u>Pray for us</u>.
Blessed Luchesio and Blessed Buonadonna, <u>Pray for us</u>.
Saint Virdiana, <u>Pray for us</u>.
Saint Angela of Foligno, <u>Pray for us</u>.
Saint Elzear and Blessed Delphina, <u>Pray for us</u>.
Blessed Umiliana Cerchi, <u>Pray for us</u>.
Saint Rose of Viterbo, <u>Pray for us</u>.
Blessed Torello of Poppi, <u>Pray for us</u>.
Blessed Peter of Siena, <u>Pray for us</u>.
Saint Margaret of Cortona, <u>Pray for us</u>.
Blessed Jane of Signa, <u>Pray for us</u>.
Saint Roch of Montpellier, <u>Pray for us</u>.
Saint Elizabeth of Portugal, <u>Pray for us</u>.
Saint Conrad of Piacenza, <u>Pray for us</u>.
Blessed Thomas of Foligno, <u>Pray for us</u>.
Blessed Robert Malatesta, <u>Pray for us</u>.
Saint Frances of Rome, <u>Pray for us</u>.
Saint Jeanne of Valois, <u>Pray for us</u>.
Blessed Paula Gambara, <u>Pray for us</u>.
Blessed Luisa Albertoni, <u>Pray for us</u>.
Blessed Pedro de San Jose de Betancur, <u>Pray for us</u>.

(Patron saints of those about to be pledged may be added)

All you saints who lived this penitential rule of life, <u>Pray for us</u>.

All holy men and women, <u>Pray for us</u>.

Lord, be merciful. <u>Lord, deliver us, we pray</u>.

From all evil, <u>Lord, deliver us, we pray</u>.

From every sin, <u>Lord, deliver us, we pray</u>.

From everlasting death, <u>Lord, deliver us, we pray</u>.

By your incarnation. <u>Lord, deliver us, we pray</u>.

By your death and resurrection, <u>Lord, deliver us, we pray</u>.

By the outpouring of the Holy Spirit, <u>Lord, deliver us, we pray</u>.

Be merciful to us sinners. <u>Lord, we ask you, hear our prayer</u>.

Guide and protect Your Holy Church. <u>Lord, we ask you, hear our prayer</u>.

Keep our Pope and all the clergy in faithful service to Your Church. <u>Lord, we ask you, hear our prayer</u>.

Bring all people together in trust and peace. <u>Lord, we ask you, hear our prayer</u>.

Strengthen us in Your service. <u>Lord, we ask you, hear our prayer</u>.

By the self offering of Your servants and their apostolic work, make the life of Your Church ever more fruitful. <u>Lord, we ask you, hear our prayer</u>.

Give in greater abundance the gifts of the Holy Spirit to Your servant Pope N and to all his brother Bishops. <u>Lord, we ask you, hear our prayer</u>.

By life and labor of all penitents, promote the welfare of all people. <u>Lord, we ask you, hear our prayer</u>.

Join more fully to the work of redemption all who live a life of penance. <u>Lord, we ask you, hear our prayer</u>.

Reward the parents, spouses, and friends of these servants with blessings from heaven for the gift they are sharing with You. <u>Lord, we ask you, hear our prayer</u>.

Make these, your servants, more and more like Christ, the first born of many brothers and sisters. <u>Lord, we ask you, hear our prayer</u>.

Jesus, Son of the Living God, <u>Lord, we ask you, hear our prayer</u>.

Christ, hear us, <u>Christ, hear us</u>.

Christ, graciously hear us. <u>Christ, graciously hear us</u>.

The Celebrant then rises and says with hands joined:

Almighty, Eternal, Just, and Merciful God, grant to these brothers and sisters to do for Your sake what they know to be Your Will and ever to will what is pleasing to You, so that purified and enlightened interiorly, and enkindled by the fire of the Holy Spirit, they may be able to follow until death in the footsteps of Your Son, Our Lord Jesus Christ, and, by Your grace alone, come to You, Most High, Who live and reign in perfect Trinity and simple Unity, and dwell in glory, Almighty God, forever and ever.

All respond.
Amen.

Celebrant:
Let us rise.

All stand. Mass servers place a chair in front of the altar.

The **Presider** sits in the chair. The two **witnesses** selected by the penitent stand on either side. One of these **witnesses** may be the **CFP Representative**. However, two other life pledged members may be chosen as **witnesses**.

E. PLEDGING (PRIVATELY VOWING)

Those to be pledged (privately vowed) come one by one before the **Presider** and kneel, folding their hands and placing them between the palms of the **Presider** who will receive the pledge (private vow). Those making a life pledge go first, one by one. Once they are done, those making a private vow come forward. The Presider repeats this part of the ceremony for each penitent until all have completed making their pledges (private vows).

LIFE PLEDGE

Presider:
What do you ask?

Penitent:
I (NAME)_of my own will do ask to be allowed to profess my intention to be bound by the Rule and Constitutions of the Confraternity of Penitents for the rest of my life as my way of living the Gospel more fully for the Love of God.

Presider:
So be it then for that is a holy and good thing. (NAME),_feel free to make your pledge.

Penitent then reads the Formula of Pledging which he or she has written out by hand beforehand. This may be in his or her own words or using the formula below. The CFP Representative may hold this for the penitent to read:

I (NAME) promise that I will strive to live, to the best of my means and ability, for all of my life, according to the Rule and Constitutions of the Confraternity of Penitents in fulfillment of the Gospel and for the Love of God. As part of my commitment I promise to live the Gospel more fully and to pursue more fervently the virtues of poverty, chastity, and humility, which the Saints all loved and promoted. On this journey, I ask the support and prayers of my brothers and sisters in the Confraternity and God's blessing.

Presider:

With my blessing, (NAME), I accept your promise to Christ, and encourage you to strive to live it joyfully for the Love of God and the good of the Church. This promise of yours is binding, though never under pain of sin, because it carries with it the binding promise of eternal life to you on the part of the Lord, if you do as you say, and is a true gesture of love for the Lord and His Gospel, as given to us by the Saints. May you, by the grace of God, persevere in your promise until the day of your death so as to join the Lord and His Saints in heaven.

I accept and acknowledge you as a life pledged (brother or sister) in the Confraternity of Penitents with joy, and ask God's blessing on us and on your commitment.

Penitent then proceeds around the altar and places on it the Formula of Pledging, signing and dating it at the altar. At this time, the penitent also signs the Certificate of Pledging which will shortly be given to the pledged penitent to keep. The witness(es) also sign both of these documents at this time.

Following the signing of the Formula and Certificate, the penitent kneels at one side of the altar if other penitents have been or are to be pledged. If the penitent is the only one pledging, he or she kneels in front of the altar.

PRIVATE VOW[44]

Presider:
What do you ask?

Penitent:
I (NAME) of my own will do ask to be allowed to privately vow to be bound by the Rule and Constitutions of the Confraternity of Penitents for the rest of my life as my way of living the Gospel more fully for the Love of God.

Presider:
So be it then for that is a holy and good thing. (NAME), feel free to make your <u>vow</u>.

Penitent then reads the Formula of the Private Vow which he or she has written out by hand beforehand. This may be in his or her own words or using the formula below. The CFP Representative may hold this for the penitent to read:
I <u>(BAPTISMAL NAME FOLLOWED BY PRIVATELY VOWED NAME TO BE USED IN THE CONFRATERNITY ONLY)</u> vow that I will strive to live, to the best of my means and ability, for all of my life, according to the Rule and Constitutions of the Confraternity of Penitents in fulfillment of the Gospel and for the Love of God. As part of my commitment I vow to live the Gospel more fully and to pursue more fervently the virtues of poverty, chastity, and humility, which the Saints all loved and promoted. On this journey, I ask the support and prayers of my brothers and sisters in the Confraternity and God's blessing.

Presider:
<u>(BAPTISMAL NAME FOLLOWED BY PRIVATELY VOWED NAME)</u>, with my blessing, I accept your private vow to Christ, and encourage you to strive to live it joyfully for the Love of God and the good of the Church. As long as it can be kept, this private vow of yours is binding under pain of sin because it carries with it the binding promise of eternal life to you on the part of the Lord, if you do as you say, and is a true gesture of love for the Lord and His Gospel, as given to us by the Saints. May you, by the grace of God, persevere in

---

44   The private vow must be taken out of public view if the ceremony is being observed by the general public. If the ceremony is done in the presence of other penitents only, the private vow may be taken at the altar or wherever else the pledges have been taken.

your promise until the day of your death so as to join the Lord and His Saints in heaven.

I accept and acknowledge you as a privately vowed (brother or sister) in the Confraternity of Penitents with joy, and ask God's blessing on us and on your commitment.

Penitent then proceeds around the altar and places on it the Formula of the Private Vow, signing and dating it at the altar. At this time, the penitent also signs the Certificate of Vowing, which will shortly be given to the pledged penitent to keep. The witness(es) also sign both of these documents at this time. If the private vow is made in a location out of view of the general public, the signing of these documents is completed in that location. They are brought back with the penitent upon return to the public ceremony.

Following the signing of the Formula and Certificate, the penitent kneels at one side of the altar if other penitents have been or are to be pledged or privately vowed. If the penitent is the only one in this ceremony, he or she kneels in front of the altar.

The **Presider** and **the CFP Representative** now sign all the formula(s) and the Certificate(s).

Following the signing, each penitent lights the candle which he or she carried in. Lights are taken from the candles already lit on the altar. Penitents then kneel before the altar.

Celebrant

From behind the altar, the **Celebrant** delivers a brief message of support and acceptance and gives a blessing to all.

Penitents rise and stand in place.

G. BLESSING OF THE HOLY OBJECTS

G1: CRUCIFIX (CROSS)

An **altar server or another individual chosen beforehand** (perhaps one of the witnesses) holds the tray with the cross(es) and/or crucifix(es) which the penitent(s) wear(s). This is done in every ceremony.

Celebrant

As a sign of your commitment to live the Gospel more fully through this holy lifestyle, I bless this (these) cross(es) (crucifixes). Wear it (them) as a visible sign of your commitment, and may Mary, our Mother and advocate, bless and preserve your Love for her Son and His Gospel, as well as your vocation to His service in your life as a member of the Confraternity of Penitents, and, always, for the Love of God.

The **CFP Representative** clothes each penitent in his or her cross or crucifix.

G2: SAN DAMIANO CRUCIFIX

An **altar server or another individual chosen beforehand** (perhaps one of the witnesses) holds the tray with the San Damiano Crucifix(es). This is done with penitents pledging to live the Rule for the first time. Those who have previously pledged to live the Rule for a year will not receive a San Damiano crucifix as they will have received it when they first pledged.

The **Celebrant** then blesses the San Damiano Crucifix(es), sprinkling them with holy water:

Celebrant:

May the Lord bless this (these) crucifixes. May you display it (them) lovingly and learn by meditating on it (them) the message of God's love and sacrifice thereon portrayed.

The **CFP Representative** hands each new penitent a San Damiano Crucifix.

G3: THE CORD AND SCAPULAR

New life pledged members will be clothed with a cord and a scapular. An **altar server or another individual chosen beforehand (perhaps one of the witnesses)** holds the tray containing these. Penitents who made a life pledge at a previous ceremony will not receive a cord and scapular at this ceremony.

The **Celebrant** now blesses these with holy water while praying:

May the Lord bless these cords whose four knots represent your life pledges of poverty, chastity, and humility according to your state in life and your promise of life time consecration to Our Lady. May He bless this brown scapular which indicates your devotion to His Blessed Mother and your desire to serve her Son with her love and faith. You may wear these beneath your garments as reminders of your life pledge to God to live according to the Rule and Constitutions of the Confraternity of Penitents.

The **CFP Representative** then clothes the life pledged member(s) in the cord and scapular.

G4: CERTIFICATES

The **Presider** takes the Certificate(s) of Pledging (<u>Vowing</u>) from the altar and says (tailoring the presentation to each penitent's level of commitment):

Presider:
(NAME), you are now a penitent in the service of Christ. Receive this Certificate of Pledging (Vowing). May it remind you always of your promise to God.

When all have received Certificates, they return to their seats while a song expressing joy and thanksgiving may be sung.

The handwritten and signed Formulas of Pledging (Vowing) are kept at the altar.

H. CEREMONY OF WELCOME

All life pledged members of the CFP process forward to give a welcoming embrace to the new life pledged member(s). When all have returned to their seats, the Mass proceeds.

LITURGY OF THE EUCHARIST

The Liturgy of the Eucharist now follows. The newly pledged (privately vowed) may bring forth the gifts.

For Holy Communion, the newly pledged (privately vowed) ought to receive first, preferably under both species, with the others following.

Following the final blessing, the newly pledged (privately vowed) process out following the altar servers and then the reader, **Presider, Celebrant**.

A collation may now take place in thanksgiving for the newly pledged (*privately vowed*) members of the Confraternity.

The handwritten and signed Formulas of Pledging (Vowing) are mailed to Confraternity Office to be kept on file.

BROCHURE AND HANDOUTS

"Let not your heart be disturbed. Do not fear that sickness, nor any other sickness or anguish. Am I not here, who is your Mother? Are you not under my protection? Am I not your health? Are you not happily within my fold? What else do you wish? Do not grieve nor be disturbed by anything."

(Words of Our Lady of Guadalupe to Juan Diego)

Prayer to Our Lady of Guadalupe (Feast Day: December 12)

Our Lady of Guadalupe, who blessed Mexico and all the Americas by your appearance to Juan Diego, intercede for the holy Church, protect the pope, and help everyone who invokes you in their necessities.

O mystical rose, hear our prayers and our petitions, especially for the particular one we are praying for at this moment (mention your request).

Since you are the ever Virgin Mary and Mother of the true God, obtain for us from your most holy Son the grace of keeping our faith, sweet hope in the midst of the bitterness of life, burning charity, and the precious gift of final perseverance. Amen.

BROCHURE AND HANDOUTS

This section contains three double sided handouts and one double sided brochure, which may be folded. These may be reproduced and distributed to let others know about the Confraternity of Penitents.

If you would like color copies of these to reproduce, please contact the Confraternity of Penitents at 1702 Lumbard Street, Fort Wayne Indiana 46803 USA, phone 260/739-6882, email copenitents@yahoo.com

Please do not leave any Confraternity material in any places of worship without the consent of the pastor.

HANDOUT 1: PENANCE AND LOVE: TWO SIDES OF THE SAME COIN

The following handout should be printed on two sides of the same paper with the section on PENANCE on one side of the paper and that on LOVE on the other side.

PENANCE AND LOVE: TWO SIDES OF THE SAME COIN: PENANCE

Penance (repentance) means conversion, a turning away from human sinfulness to doing things God's way. Jesus came to call us to repentance.

After John had been arrested, Jesus came to Galilee proclaiming the gospel of God: "This is the time of fulfillment. The kingdom of God is at hand. Repent, and believe in the gospel." (Mark 1:14-15)

"I have not come to call the righteous to repentance but sinners." (Jesus' words as recorded in Luke 5:32)

And he said to them, "Thus it is written that the Messiah would suffer and rise from the dead on the third day and that repentance, for the forgiveness of sins, would be preached in his name to all the nations, beginning from Jerusalem. You are witnesses of these things." (Jesus' words in Luke 24:46-48)

Repentance requires discipline, sacrifice, hard work, and constant prayer. The Roman Catholic Church has always called for penance (conversion) and is renewing that call today.

"The parish is to be a community that calls others to a deeper conversion of life from sin to the light of Jesus. That, in my judgment, should lead us to a further exploration of a restoration of the "Ordo Poenitentium" – the Order of Penitents – that was present in the patristic Church. . . .(Cardinal J. Francis, Stafford, president of the Pontifical Council on the Laity, Interview, August 8, 2003 with the Pilot, diocesan paper for the Archdiocese of Boston)

"To speak of RECONCILIATION and PENANCE is, for the men and women of our time, an invitation to rediscover, translated into their own way of speaking, the very words with which our Savior and Teacher Jesus Christ began his preaching: "Repent, and believe in the gospel" that is to say, accept the good news of love, of adoption as children of God and hence of brotherhood." (Pope John Paul II, On Reconciliation and Penance, 2 December 1984)

"On the occasion of the Great Jubilee, Pope John Paul II frequently exhorted Christians to do penance for infidelities of the past. We believe that the Church is holy, but that there are sinners among her members. We need to reject the desire to identify only with those who are sinless. How could the Church have excluded sinners from her ranks? It is for their salvation that Jesus took flesh, died and rose again. We must therefore learn to live Christian penance with sincerity. By practising it, we confess individual sins in union with others, before them and before God." (Pope Benedict XVI to the Clergy of Warsaw, May 25, 2006)

"Christian life is a never-ending combat in which the 'weapons' of prayer, fasting and penance are used. Fighting against evil, against every form of selfishness and hate, and dying to oneself to live in God is the ascetic journey that every disciple of Jesus is called to make with humility and patience, with generosity and perseverance." (Pope Benedict XVI, March 1, 2006)

FOR CATHOLIC LAITY, RESPONDING TO THE CALL TO PENANCE WITH LOVE:

Confraternity of Penitents, 1702 Lumbard Street, Fort Wayne Indiana 46803 USA, Phone: 260/739-6882

E-mail: copenitents@yahoo.com http://www.penitents.org

PENANCE AND LOVE: TWO SIDES OF THE SAME COIN: LOVE

Penance (conversion) requires love if it's to endure.

"You shall love the Lord your God with your whole heart, with your whole soul, and with all your mind, (and) you shall love your neighbor as yourself." (Jesus words as recorded in Matthew 22:37-38)

"But I say to you, love your enemies, and pray for those who persecute you." (Jesus' words in Matthew 5:44)

"If you keep my commandments, you will remain in my love, just as I have kept my Father's commandments and remain in his love. I have told you this so that my joy may be in you and your joy may be complete. This is my commandment: love one another as I love you. No one has greater love than this, to lay down one's life for one's friends. You are my friends if you do what I command you." (Jesus' words in John 15:10-14)

The Roman Catholic Church emphasizes the connection between penance (conversion) and love.

"Whatever you make of your life, let it be something that reflects the love of Christ. The whole people of God will be the richer because of the diversity of your commitments. And whatever you do, remember that Christ is calling you, in one way or the other, to the service of love: the love of God and of your neighbor." (Pope John Paul II, "To Youth," Boston Common, 1979)

"Love must thus enliven every sector of human life and extend to the international order. Only a humanity in which there reigns the 'civilization of love' will be able to enjoy authentic and lasting peace. . . . 'Omnia vincit amor' (Love conquers all). Yes, dear Brothers and Sisters throughout the world, in the end love will be victorious! Let everyone be committed to hastening this victory. For it is the deepest hope of every human heart. (Pope John Paul II, 8 December 2003)

Love of neighbour is thus shown to be possible in the way proclaimed by the Bible, by Jesus. It consists in the very fact that, in God and with God, I love even the person whom I do not like or even know. This can only take place on the basis of an intimate encounter with God, an encounter which has become a communion of will, even affecting my feelings. . . . Seeing with the eyes of Christ, I can give to others much more than their outward necessities; I can give them the look of love which they crave. (Pope Benedict XVI, Deus Caritas Est 18, 25 December 2005)

The CONFRATERNITY OF PENITENTS is worldwide, private Catholic lay association of the faithful whose Rule of Life has been commended by Bishop Kevin Rhoades of the Diocese of Fort Wayne - South Bend, Indiana, USA, in these words: "I am happy to grant my recognition and approval of the Confraternity of Penitents, a private association of the Christian faithful according to the norms of Code of Canon Law. It is a blessing to have the Confraternity of Penitents now headquartered in the Diocese of Fort Wayne-South Bend. I am grateful for your witness to the Holy Gospel according to the teaching, example, and spirit of Saint Francis of Assisi. . . May God bless you! May the Blessed Virgin Mary, Saint Francis, and Saint Clare intercede for you always!" (3 January 2014)

FOR CATHOLIC LAITY, RESPONDING TO THE CALL TO PENANCE WITH LOVE:

Confraternity of Penitents, 1702 Lumbard Street, Fort Wayne IN 46803 USA
Phone: 260-739-6882
E-mail: copenitents@yahoo.com http://www.penitents.org

HANDOUT 2: THE JOYFUL CALL TO PENANCE IN THE MODERN WORLD

THE JOYFUL CALL TO PENANCE is intended to be printed on one side of this handout and LIVING A LIFE OF PENANCE on the other side of the handout.

THE JOYFUL CALL TO PENANCE IN THE MODERN WORLD

Penance means conversion to doing things God's way.

It also means making the daily sacrifices necessary to reach this type of conversion.

Fasting, going without sleep, and performing other mortifications do not make a person holy. As a devil told one of the desert fathers, "I never sleep so what makes you better than me? I never eat so what makes you better than me?" The devil could mouth the words of prayers or do any sort of mortification and it would not make him holy.

Fasting makes one holy to the degree that one willingly shares in Christ's fasting. It is not to starve us but to remind us that Christ fasted for love of us.

Praying makes one holy to the degree that one willingly prays in union with Christ. It is not simply taking up one's time for God but to remind us that Christ intercedes always for us.

Simplifying one's life makes one holy to the degree that one willingly wishes to participate in Christ's simple way of living. It is not just having a neater house but rather deemphasizing earthly clutter so as to fill our lives with spiritual freedom.

The purpose of penance is to open oneself to selfless love, to God's grace, to turn our mind to God, to unite oneself with God, to open our spirits and to invite God to replace self in them. Penance then goes beyond being open to God to being open to one another. The penitent does not live for himself or herself alone but wishes to give service and render love to others, because they, like the penitent, are children of a loving, eternal Father.

God wishes us to be happy with Him in eternity. Those who are truly penitential are the happiest of all for they know where God's Will lies. The call to penance is a call to joyful union with Christ and to service to others. It is a call to live for and serve the Lord within our homes, our families, our workplace.

WHO ARE THE CONFRATERNITY OF PENITENTS (CFP)?

The CONFRATERNITY OF PENITENTS is a private Catholic lay association of the faithful, whose Rule of Life has been commended by the Bishop of the Diocese of Fort Wayne - South Bend, Indiana, USA. The CFP lifestyle is based on a primitive rule for penitents, written in 1221. The Rule and Constitutions can be found on the Web page of the Confraternity at www.penitents.org. All Catholics who agree with all of the teachings of the Catholic Church may enter upon this way of life.

WHAT IS THE GOAL OF THE CFP?

The goal of the Confraternity of Penitents is to have its members love and serve God. This leads to personal sanctification evidenced in choosing God's Will above one's own. Service to God and others naturally follows. The means of this surrender is through the living of a time tested, penitential Rule and its Constitutions. At the time of the original Rule (1221), history records that: "Many of the people, nobles and commoners alike, were touched by divine inspiration and began to imitate (Saint) Francis' (of Assisi) way of life, and to follow in his steps. They abandoned the cares and pomp of the world, desiring to live under his direction, guidance, and discipline." (Legend of Three Companions - XIII). THE CONFRATERNITY OF PENITENTS joyfully joins those who, down through the centuries, have embraced a life of penance (conversion) as a path to personal holiness and service to others.

Confraternity of Penitents, 1702 Lumbard Street, Fort Wayne IN 46803 USA, 260/739-6882, bspenance@ hotmail.com copenitents@yahoo.com http://www. penitents.org

LIVING A LIFE OF PENANCE

WHAT IS THE PARADOX OF A LIFE OF PENANCE?

What begins as outer discipline becomes a means of interior conversion. What appears difficult grows easy. What seems confining results in freedom. What sounds somber produces great joy. God gives abundant graces to those called to embrace a penitential life or ever deepening conversion to His ways. If you feel at all called to this lifestyle, say, "I'll try!" You might be blessed beyond all imagining.

SYMBOL OF PENITENTS: THE SAN DAMIANO CRUCIFIX

The San Damiano Crucifix is a large, almost life sized painted icon of the Crucified. The crucifix is a visual essay on the spiritual life and a tool of conversion. It was one of the primary instruments which God used to cement in St. Francis of Assisi a firmer change of heart. The rich symbolism of the crucifix speaks to anyone who gazes upon it in faith, but most especially to penitents.

VISION OF THE CONFRATERNITY OF PENITENTS

The Vision of the Confraternity of Penitents is this: To give glory to God and surrender to His Will through the living of a medieval, penitential Rule of Life, the Rule of 1221. This Rule is lived as closely as possible to its original intent, and in one's own home, in peace with all others, and in obedience to the Roman Catholic Church, its Pope, and its Magisterium.

The Prayer, Motto, Mission, and Action of Penitents, as stated below, complete the Vision of the Confraternity:

PRAYER OF PENITENTS

"Most High, Glorious God, enlighten the darkness of my mind, give me right faith, a firm hope and perfect charity, so that I may always and in all things act according to Your Holy Will. Amen." (Saint Francis's prayer before the San Damiano Crucifix)

MISSION OF PENITENTS

"Go and repair My House which, as you can see, is falling into ruin." (The message given to St. Francis in a voice from the San Damiano Crucifix.)

ACTION OF PENITENTS

To pray for God's specific direction in one's life so that, through humbly living our Rule of Life, each penitent may help to rebuild the house of God by bringing love of God and neighbor to his or her own corner of the world.

HIGHLIGHTS OF THE RULE OF LIFE OF THE CONFRATERNITY OF PENITENTS

Daily Prayer and Meditation + Modest Clothing in Subdued Colors + Fast and Abstinence as Heath Allows + Spiritual and Corporal Works of Mercy + Local Gatherings + Internet Community and Formation + By-Mail and Phone Contact + Loyalty to All Teachings of the Roman Catholic Church + Peace and Reconciliation + Consecration to Our Lady + Wearing of Visible Cross or Crucifix + Twice Monthly Confession + Liturgy of the Hours + Almsgiving + Daily Mass if Possible + Teaching Household to Love and Serve God + Acceptance of God's Divine Will +

HOW DO I BECOME A PENITENT?

All Catholics, 14 years of age and older who are loyal to all the teachings of the Roman Catholic Church, are invited to join the Confraternity. Members enter a four-year period of formation before making a pledge to live the lifestyle. Formation is provided via internet, postal mail and in local groups worldwide.

Confraternity of Penitents, 1702 Lumbard Street, Fort Wayne Indiana 46803, phone: 260/739-6882

bspenance@hotmail.com copenitents@yahoo.com http://www.penitents.org

HANDOUT 3: CONFRATERNITY OF PENITENTS: A QUICK OVERVIEW

This is a two sided handout that begins the overview on the first page and continues it on the second page.

CONFRATERNITY OF PENITENTS: A QUICK OVERVIEW

Are you seeking a way to draw closer to God and to surrender all you have and are to Him? Do you want to become a more loving person? Might you desire a faith that is strong enough to carry you through adversity?

Many laity who answer "yes" to these questions find their answers in lay associations and lay orders. Each of these is designed to help a person advance on the spiritual journey. Each has unique qualities. Each is, hopefully, the result of the Holy Spirit's inspiration and in operation under the Holy Spirit's guidance.

To discern what association or order will be best for you, you must research their charisms, Rules of Life, and obligations for membership, and then pray about what you discover. Which one or ones seem able to achieve for you the spiritual goals you seek? Once you know the unique qualities of the organization and pray about your decisions, you will be better able to understand if it might be attractive to you.

Here are some of the unique qualities about the Confraternity of Penitents:

+ The **Bishop** of the Diocese of Fort Wayne - South Bend has recognized the Confraternity of Penitents and affirmed its canonical status as a 'private association of the faithful.' The CFP is in regular contact with diocesan officials.

+ The Confraternity of Penitents is completely **obedient** to the Pope and the Magisterium.

+ Members of the Confraternity of Penitents are at **peace** with all and love God, neighbor, and themselves, with joy.

+ The Confraternity of Penitents and its members are consecrated to the **Blessed Mother**.

+ The Confraternity of Penitents is an **international** association, effectively utilizing internet, postal mail, and person to person contact.

+ The Confraternity of Penitents subsists on freely given **donations** and requires no dues.

+ The Confraternity of Penitents has a Visitor, who is a **priest** assigned by the Bishop of the Diocese of Fort Wayne - South Bend and who has final say on matters within the Confraternity.

+ The Confraternity of Penitents has lay and **spiritual advisors** who assist in spiritual matters.

+ The charism of the Confraternity of Penitents is penance, that is, ongoing, joyful **conversion,** as called for by Christ and evidenced by the saints.

+ The Confraternity symbol is the **Crucifix of San Damiano,** which is the crucifix of penance (conversion).

+ CFP Membership is open to married and single **laity** and to **clergy and religious.**

+ **Entry** into the Confraternity is on three levels: Members who complete formation and pledge to live the Rule; Associates who complete formation but do not pledge to live the Rule; Affiliates who do not complete formation but who support the Confraternity through prayer.

+ Members of the Confraternity of Penitents live modern Constitutions to the Rule of 1221, a Rule given to the laity at the request of **St. Francis of Assisi.**

+ The Confraternity of Penitents fosters slow, **gradual** incorporation of the lifestyle into the penitent's life.

+ The CFP Rule has days of **fast and abstinence** every week (penance in the area of food).

+ The CFP Rule requires daily **prayer** from the psalms and the Liturgy of the Hours (penance in the area of time given to God).

+ The CFP Rule has a **clothing** requirement to which members adhere daily (penance in the area of clothing).

+ The CFP Rule requires **simplification** of possessions (penance in the area of worldly goods).

+ The CFP **apostolate** is participation in the spiritual and/or corporal works of mercy (penance in the area of service).

+ CFP Members wear a visible **cross or crucifix** in a style of their choice.

+ The Confraternity of Penitents fosters **community**. Every member has at least one other CFP Member in close contact with him or her.

+ The Confraternity of Penitents requires a **spiritual director** and will help members find one.

+ The Confraternity of Penitents has 51 specific formation lessons for a **four year formation program**. These cover Scripture, the Catechism of the Catholic Church, and the CFP Rule and Constitutions.

+ All CFP Members must complete the formation program successfully before **pledging**.

+ Members who pledge to live the Rule and Constitutions for life may take **private vows** to live the lifestyle and may receive a Confraternity name.
+ Only CFP Members are assigned as **formators** for those in formation.
+ Only CFP Members may vote and be elected as **Officers**.
+ The Confraternity of Penitents has **local groups** in which Members can meet in person.
+ The Confraternity of Penitents sponsors **Days of Recollection** and a yearly **Reunion, Conference, and Retreat**.
+ The Confraternity of Penitents publishes an optional **Handbook** which contains everything needed to complete the CFP formation program.
+ The Confraternity of Penitents operates an on line **Gift Shop** with materials that promote penance (conversion).
+ **CFP Regional Ministers** are in touch with all new applicants.

Do you want to learn more about the Confraternity of Penitents?
Visit our web site at **www.penitents.org** — Email the Confraternity at **bspenance@hotmail.com** or at **copenitents@yahoo.com** — Write to us at **Confraternity of Penitents, 1702 Lumbard Street, Fort Wayne Indiana 46803 USA** — Phone us at **260/739-6882**

Pray about where God is calling you, then "**Do whatever He tells you.**"

God bless you on your journey into Our Lord's eternal love!

THREE FOLD BROCHURE

The front and back of this three fold brochure are reproduced on the following pages. The brochure should be folded in three parts.

CONFRATERNITY OF PENITENTS

Married and Single Lay People Living a Life of Ongoing Conversion

CONFRATERNITY OF PENITENTS
1702 Lumbard Street
Fort Wayne IN 46803 USA

More about Us

The Confraternity of Penitents meets in local groups as well as via the internet and through postal mail.

Formation in the lifestyle is four years. All lessons are on line as well as in the Handbook published by the Confraternity.

Membership is open to all Roman Catholics ages 14 and up. Non-Catholics may enter formation as Associates.

Affiliates live the CFP Rule as best they can. They pray for the Confraternity daily and are held in prayer by Confraternity members but do not complete formation.

There are no dues or fees.

Contact Us

Phone: 260-739-6882
Email: copenitents@yahoo.com
Web: www.penitents.org
Locally Contact:

Saint Francis of Assisi

Recognition

The Rule and Constitutions of the Confraternity of Penitents have been recognized and approved by the Bishop of the Diocese of Fort Wayne-South Bend, IN USA, in these words:

"I am happy to grant my recognition and approval of the Confraternity of Penitents, a private association of the Christian faithful according to the norms of the Code of Canon Law. It is a blessing to have the Confraternity of Penitents now headquartered in the Diocese of Fort Wayne-South Bend. I am grateful for your witness to the Holy Gospel according to the teaching, example, and spirit of St. Francis of Assisi.... May God bless you! And may the Blessed Virgin Mary, Saint Francis, and Saint Clare intercede for you always!" – Bishop Kevin Rhoades, Diocese of Fort Wayne-South Bend, January 3, 2014

Saint Francis as a layman, praying before the San Damiano Crucifix

Location

Confraternity members live in most of the United States and also internationally.

Governance

Governance is through our Minister General and International Council, subject to our Visitor, a priest appointed by the Bishop of the Diocese of Fort Wayne-South Bend.

Why Penance?

Jesus called all people to repentance:

Jesus came to Galilee proclaiming the gospel of God: "This is the time of fulfillment. The kingdom of God is at hand. Repent, and believe in the gospel." (Mark 1:14-15)

Penance means conversion, a turning away from sinful ways to doing things God's way. With God's grace, we are able to do this through our Rule of Life.

Prayer

Most High, Glorious God, enlighten the darkness of my mind; give me right faith, a firm hope, and perfect charity, so that I may always and in all things act according to Your Holy Will. Amen. (Prayer of Saint Francis before the San Damiano Crucifix)

Motto

You shall the love the Lord your God with your whole heart, with your whole soul, and with all your mind (and) you shall love your neighbor as yourself. (Jesus' words as recorded in Matthew 22:37-38)

Mission

Go and repair My House which, as you can see, is falling into ruin. (The message given to St. Francis in a voice from the San Damiano Crucifix)

Action

To pray for God's specific direction in one's life so that, through humbly living our Rule of Life, each penitent may help to rebuild the house of God by bringing love of God and neighbor to his or her own corner of the world.

Orthodoxy

The Confraternity of Penitents is completely loyal to the Pope, the Magesterium, and Catholic Church doctrine.

What is the Confraternity of Penitents?

The Confraternity of Penitents is a private Catholic Association of the faithful whose members live, in their own homes, a modern adaptation of the Rule of Life given by St. Francis of Assisi to married and single lay people of his time.

Through a life of prayer, simplicity, fasting, abstinence, and works of mercy, these men and women are daily fulfilling the Catholic Church's call to penance (conversion).

ARTICLES ON THE PENITENTIAL LIFE

"When the Holy Spirit finds Mary in a soul, He flies to it. He enters therein and communicates Himself to that soul in abundance." - *St. Louis de Montfort*

Hail Mary of Gold

Hail Mary, White Lily of the Glorious and always-serene Trinity.

Hail brilliant Rose of the Garden of heavenly delights:

O you, by whom God wanted to be born and by whose milk the King of Heaven wanted to be nourished!

Nourish our souls with effusions of divine grace. Amen!

At the hour when the soul which has thus greeted my quits the body I'll appear to them in such splendid beauty that they'll taste, to their great consolation, something of the joys of Paradise.

The Blessed Virgin Mary to St. Gertrude the Great (Revelations book III, chapter XVIII

PENANCE AS VOCATION

"Prayer and fasting are our hope, Penance our vocation." So goes a song often sung during Lent.

The dictionary defines vocation as "a divine call to the religious life." Does God give such a divine call only to the unmarried? Is the religious life possible only to those who live in monasteries, convents, or rectories? Could penance be a vocation, not just for Lent but for always? If it so, why would anyone in his or her right mind embrace such a vocation?

To say that God can give a vocation only to those who are unmarried is to limit God and His Providence. To say that the religious life is not possible for those who live in the world is to say that following God with one's whole being is not possible for the married and for those holding down jobs in the secular world. While the popular mind may not recognize a religious vocation as being possible for those in the world, the Catholic Church certainly disagrees. From the very beginning, the Church has recognized and encouraged the laity to embrace "a divine call to the religious life." In fact, every lay person is called to live "the religious life" as a lay person. How else are we to be converted?

The question really becomes, "What sort of religious life are laity called to embrace?" The sacraments, certainly. Chastity according to one's state in life. Adherence to all ten commandments, in all their nuances. Unmeasured love for God and for all people. Finding and serving Jesus in the least of humanity. If Catholics follow what the Church teaches, they will be living a religious vocation. Their faith and behavior will sanctify whatever state of life God has called them to. They will become holy.

God has, however, called some people to live in a more radical way. It shouldn't be the individual's choice about whether or not to enter religious life or the seminary. God calls the person to do so. Those who have heard the call—who have felt God's prodding—know that their choice was about following God's choice for them. It involved their free will to say "no" to what God wanted them to do, much more than their choosing between getting a PhD in chemistry or becoming a priest or a religious.

350

Is it any surprise that God calls some laity to live in a more spiritually radical way? Maybe they need the discipline of a more radical life. Maybe they are to offer up their so-called fanaticism as prayers for others. Maybe they are to be examples of self-discipline and sacrifice in a world that focuses on self-fulfillment, power, and possession. Maybe they are to show what it means to put God first, others second, and themselves last instead of in the reverse order.

Penance means ongoing conversion. Those called to penance as a vocation are called to witness to the truth that they, at least, can always improve. They've never "made it" spiritually. They don't go around broadcasting what they are doing, but the way they act is broadcast enough. Lay penitents wear the "habit" of humility, patience, simplicity, service, and love, and those virtues ought to make them stand out just as much as a religious veil or a collar would. If penitent doesn't seem any different from others in behavior, he or she isn't embracing the call to penance.

The vocation to penance is a divine call. You don't choose to embrace a penitential life. God calls you to do so. Your choice is whether or not you are going to listen to Him. Why would anyone embrace a vocation to penance? Because God wants them to. To refuse is to say "no" to God. Wise people don't do that, not because they fear God's judgment but because they want to "grab all the grace" He wants to give them. The Rule God calls one to live is that person's means of grace and sanctification. It's that person's surest pathway to eternal life because God set them on that pathway to bring them to Himself. It's just not wise to tell God that you have a better plan for your sanctification than He does.

Many religious Rules of Life for the laity exist. Some focus on prayer, others on community, others on poverty, or evangelization, or sanctifying one's work or family. Each has its own particular charism. All are penitential to some degree. God calls certain people to live certain Rules of Life. Why so many Rules? Because there are so many types of people. In His great love, God made a way for everyone to follow Him more closely. What works best for one person won't work best for another. You can think of a religious Rule of Life as being similar to a suit or a dress. One size doesn't fit all bodies, and one Rule doesn't fit all temperaments. You buy the clothes that fit you, and you look for and embrace a Rule that fits you, too.

The Rule for the Confraternity of Penitents focuses on penance, that is, personal conversion, with the intention that the penitent will then embrace whatever else God is calling him or her to—be it deeper prayer, fostering a more wholesome community, practicing greater poverty, evangelizing, and/or bringing God in a new way into the workplace or family. To live the Rule for the Confraternity of Penitents is to say "yes" to God's divine call. It is to say, "I agree to be continually converted by You, my God, to follow You wherever You lead and to do whatever You tell me. I'm not going to make any plans or have any ideas about what You want next year of me. I am available for whatever it is, whenever it is, wherever it is, however it is. I am totally Yours."

A person can embrace this attitude without living the CFP way of life. But living according to the CFP Rule and Constitutions makes it easier to maintain such an attitude because the way of life reminds you every day that you are to be converted. A vocation is for always. God does not give a divine call to live a religious life and then rescind that call five years later. It is true that many people enter religious life and then leave. The reasons for their departure are many. Perhaps they were not really called. Maybe God wanted them to embrace the Rule for a time because they were to grown spiritually through it, but He then intended them to leave. But everyone is called to a religious vocation of some sort. The question is not if but how.

How will you know if penance is your vocation? Chances are, you won't know unless you begin to embrace it. Embracing it will teach you this, at least. That you do have a religious vocation. It may be to live according to the CFP Rule and Constitutions. It may be to live according another Rule of life. It may be to live "your own rule," that is, to live a faithful, converted life in your own home as you believe, through prayer, is best for you. The important point is to pray about your vocation and then "do whatever God tells you." He does have a plan for your life. Only when you embrace it will you be happy. Be certain that, no matter who you are, you do have a religious vocation. May God show you its exact nature!

Madeline Pecora Nugent, CFP

THE SAN DAMIANO CRUCIFIX

The San Damiano Crucifix is a visual essay on the spiritual life and a tool of conversion. It was one of the primary instruments which God used to cement in St. Francis of Assisi a firmer change of heart. The rich symbolism of the crucifix speaks to anyone who gazes upon it in faith, but most especially to penitents.

No one knows the identification of the artist who, probably sometime in the twelfth century, painted this icon. Quite possibly a Syrian monk was the unknown craftsman, for the Crucifix is an icon in the Syrian vein. The anonymity of the artisan reminds us penitents that we, too, ought to go about unknown and unnoticed to the world. Instead of the world noticing and acclaiming us, others should see instead the fruit of our works and of our prayers which hopefully and humbly proclaim the goodness and glory of God.

Saint Francis and the Crucifix of San Damiano

Sometime during the summer of 1206, Francis Bernardone, a young, playboy merchant of Assisi, Italy, began to experience conversion. He had always possessed a generous heart for others and for God, but now he began to see that his father's obsession with money, his mother's concerns for his health, and his own desires for sumptuous foods, lavish clothes, and extravagant parties were but dead end streets in the city of life. He yearned for more than money, health, recognition, and a good time. Life was too short and too bitter for acquisition of these transitory goods to be its ultimate aim.

Francis had lived, although barely, through war and imprisonment. He'd been nursed back from the brink of death by his mother's loving care. He'd come through a period of physical weakness and spiritual confusion. He knew that there had to be more to life than what he'd been seeking. If he gave himself enough time, if he gave God enough emotional space, Francis sensed that he would find whatever it was he sought. Thus, just recovered from illness, Francis began to spend many hours wandering through the woods and visiting the chapels around Assisi, thinking, praying, being before the One Who could tell him all, whenever He Who is All was ready to speak.

One of the places Francis frequented was the church of San Damiano, a tumbling down., deserted chapel half way down a steep hill outside the walls of the city. In this decrepit place hung a large, almost life size painted icon of the Crucified. This summer day in 1206, Francis was walking in the vicinity of San Damiano when he felt an interior tug of the Spirit that he should go within to pray. Obeying the inner voice, Francis descended the worn staircase into the dark, smoke blackened vault and fell on his knees before the familiar icon, his own spirit alert to what the Lord might wish to convey.

In eager anticipation, Francis looked up into the serene face of the Crucified Lord, the icon's eyes closed in death. "Most High glorious God," he prayed, "enlighten the darkness of my heart. Give me, Lord, a correct faith, a certain hope, a perfect charity, sense and knowledge, so that I may carry out Your holy and true command." Ever more quietly he repeated the prayer until the only words spoken were the unspoken ones in his heart.

Almost imperceptibly, the eyes of the icon opened and the head nodded forward toward Francis. Somehow the movements seemed not startling but rather perfectly natural. From the Crucified spoke a tender, kind voice, a voice a parent might use in addressing an obedient but rather uncomprehending child. "Francis, don't you see that my house is being destroyed? Go, then, and rebuild it for me."

So this was his mission! God be praised! "I will do so gladly, Lord," Francis joyfully exclaimed. Oh, to finally be given direction, after all these months! To rebuild this crumbling edifice and make it fit again for worship! What a glorious task! Francis leaped to his feet and, with an exultant bow to the Crucified, whirled to leave the vault. He would begin at once.

The San Damiano Cross and Its Message to Penitents

Francis began his mission as a penitent, that is, a person converted to the Lord. He adopted the garb and lifestyle of the penitents of his day and went about begging stones to rebuild San Damiano. Folks thought that the playboy merchant had become a madman, but to their taunts and mud slinging, Francis simply offered his thanks and a blessing. As he lugged stones down the steep hill to San Damiano, he would sing. His singing rang out as he repaired the decaying walls. He sang as he trudged uphill, back to Assisi, to beg more rocks and to meet with more verbal and physical mockery. Nothing destroyed his joy. Francis knew that a life of penance is a life of joy or else it is not worthy of the name "conversion."

Only with the passage of time did Francis slowly come to realize that the message to rebuild God's house went beyond the three Assisian chapels which Francis repaired. God was calling Francis to rebuild the Church itself, by becoming a unique and radical witness for Christ, in poverty, simplicity, and humility. In the same vein, Christ calls all penitents to rebuild the Catholic Church. Rebuild it by witnessing to the truth of the faith, by living lives centered on God and devoted to neighbor, by being people of prayer and selflessness. Not easy goals but the San Damiano cross portrays pictorial guideposts on how to do these very things.

When one gazes at the Crucifix of San Damiano, one is immediately captured by the wide open eyes and serene face of the Lord. The eyes seem to gaze gently into the penitent's soul, beckoning, "Come, follow Me." The face pleads but does not cajole. The invitation to become the Lord's is made with love yet freedom. Christ calls, but He does not force assent.

On the cross, Christ is both crucified and glorified, showing that the penitential life of joyful and voluntary self surrender for the sake of others is a humble self emptying that leads to our eternal glory. A small figure of a cock, alongside Christ's lower legs, recalls Peter's denial of Christ, a bitter reminder to penitents of our own sinfulness, which we offer to God as part of our own self-emptying. "Lord, have mercy on me for I am a sinner." On the opposite side, is a very faint creature almost impossible to see. The figure, intentionally nearly invisible, is that of a cat or a fox, both symbols of secretive, sly acts of treachery and deceit. The towering, glowing figure of Christ overshadows both the rooster and the fox/cat. Christ has overcome both public sins like that of Peter and private, hidden sins that lurk in the dens of our souls. We can be forgiven of all if we gaze into the eyes of that Crucified God-Man and call out, "I believe. Forgive me. I give myself to You."

Behind Christ's outstretched arms is a long, black band that represents the empty tomb. Above Him radiate the glories of heaven. The Father's Hand at the top of the icon blesses us who venerate the image as well as the Ascended Christ who enters glory, surrounded by welcoming angels and saints. The Father's two extended fingers, in granting the blessing, grant the Holy Spirit as well, coming from the Father to be with us forever. Thus we have hope that, because of our voluntary giving of self to God and to neighbor, we, too, will overcome eternal death and enter eternal life, won for us by the Sinless One Who took our sins upon Himself and Who died voluntarily for us so that we might live for Him.

Christ stands on a solid black mass which represents the Rock of the Catholic Church. On the foundation of the Church, which, in the Pope and Magisterium support Christ, we penitents can feel secure.

Below this Rock, almost obliterated by thousands of kisses placed at the foot of this cross, are haloed saints whom we cannot identify. Scholars postulate that these may be patron saints of the churches of Assisi: Saints Damian, Rufinus, Michael, John the Baptist, Peter, and Paul. Others believe that this may be representation of the Last Supper. However, no one is certain who these saints are. Because we cannot identify them, these saints remind us of the unknown multitudes who were washed in the Blood of Christ, who remained solidly within the Church, and who reign with Christ in heaven. They are humbly placed beneath the feet of Christ for they recognize that He is their Lord and Master. So must we realize the same.

Around the cross are clustered holy followers of Christ who are models for penitents. First stands Our Lady, the sinless Virgin whose only response to God's Will was always a "yes." To her the Confraternity and all its members are dedicated. May we honor her daily as she intercedes for us.

Next to her, sharing a smile for they know that Our Lord lives, is St. John the Evangelist, Christ's beloved apostle who spoke so eloquently of the divinity and of the love of Christ. It's wise for penitents to read his Gospel frequently and to meditate well on it. The blood from Christ's pierced heart is spurting on John, who is representative of all humanity. We are all bathed in the living, ever flowing sacrificial love of Christ, a love so profoundly intense that it led to His incarnation, life on earth, Passion, and death.

On the opposite side of the Crucifix stands Mary Magdalene, she who loved the Lord so sincerely that she would not even abandon Him at His grave. Her hand is to her mouth, as is Our Lady's Hand. The two women, who loved Christ best, are sharing the deepest feelings of their hearts with those who listen to them. What can these two women teach us about a pure and total love of the Lord? If only we could hear what they are saying! Perhaps if we pray, the Holy Spirit will grant our hearts insights into their selfless and pure love.

Listening intently to Mary Magdalene is Mary Clopas, another woman who came to the tomb with Mary Magdalene, to anoint the dead body of the Lord. These two women typify the intense and courageous devotion which penitents ought to have for Christ, a devotion that persists no matter how difficult life may become.

Last in line, as the last to believe in Christ, is a centurion, oblivious to the crowd at the foot of the cross. His gaze is fixed on Christ, indicating that he is likely the centurion whose conversion came about because he witnessed the crucifixion. The wood which he holds in his hand could be symbolic of his role in erecting the cross or in fastening the inscription over it which reads "Jesus the Nazarene, the King of the Jews." It may also indicate the centurion who, outside of the city of Capernaum, asked Christ to heal his servant and who had built, in his town, a Jewish synagogue. (Matthew 8: 5-13, Luke 7: 1-10). The centurion is holding up three fingers which indicate the Trinity. He now knows, "Truly this man was the Son of God." As the circumstances of the centurion's conversion point out, the past makes no difference and the future does not count where conversion is concerned. The right time for conversion is always now.

Behind the centurion are the heads of many others. These may be the centurion's servant and his whole household who came to believe in Christ following Christ's healing miracle. If this is the case, the frown on the face of the first figure would indicate grief at Christ's death. On the other hand, the heads, with the frowning one in front, may indicate those multitudes who witnessed the crucifixion and who mocked Christ, taunting Him to come down from the cross and save Himself. The grumpy looking man and the heads behind him remind us that we have a choice—we can believe and smile as the other major figures are doing, or we can reject Christ and be devoid of spiritual happiness.

Two small Roman figures are on either side of the cross as well. One seems to signify the soldier who offered Jesus a taste of sour wine. The other could possibly be the centurion who pierced the side of Christ with a lance. These men are sad symbols of those who are just "doing their jobs," without regarding the moral nature of their work. As penitents we need to beware of engaging in any activity that is not morally sound.

In the red border around the cross are scrolls that recall tendrils of vines. They bring to mind Christ's admonition that He is the vine while we are but branches. To bear fruit, we must remain in Him. A life of penance, conversion, must be rooted in Christ.

The Crucifix is bordered with golden scallop shells, ancient symbols of baptism. In baptism, we are made new, our sins removed by the grace of the God-Man Who died for us in agony. Penitents must daily renew their baptismal promises to reject satan and embrace the fullness of the faith. This we do by twice daily praying both the Apostle's Creed and Psalm 51.

The wounds of Christ are spurting blood which pours down upon the figures under the cross and upon us. The crucifixion is not something that happened once and can be thought of as a past event. The crucifixion is timeless in the mind of God to Whom all time is now. Christ's agony is real and immediate. He suffers now for our sins and for the sins of all. His fresh and flowing wounds call us to give our life blood for the sake of others, as He did, in loving service to all.

The loincloth that girds the figure is white for purity and chastity, virtues to which all penitents are called, yet bordered in gold, the garb of a king. The cloth is tied with three knots, reflecting the purity and kingly nature of the Trinity. The cloth reminds us that pure and holy lives are the only lives worthy of penitents, and the only lives that will lead to glory.

The hair that cascades down Christ's shoulders plaits into three locks on His left shoulder and three on His right, with Christ's head in the center. The six locks of hair recall the six days of Creation, while the head of Christ indicates the Lord of that creation and the Commandment that He be honored on the seventh day. Penitents are to honor the Solemnity of the Sabbath and keep it holy for the Lord and, likewise, to keep holy all other Solemnities of the Church.

The halo behind Christ's head is radiant and huge. It portrays a cross, too, yet a glorified one, reminding us that holiness is possible only through embracing of the cross of Christ. The way of the cross leads to glory.

The primary colors of the crucifix are black, gold, and red. Black for sin and penance, red for sacrifice and love, and gold for glory. The colors alone are a sermon on conversion. May we repent of our sins, be willing to sacrifice for and love others and the Lord, and be rewarded with eternal glory.

Madeline Pecora Nugent, CFP

THE FRANCISCAN CONNECTION

Penance means conversion from doing things in human ways to doing things God's way. In the 1100's and early 1200's, a great penitential movement was sweeping Europe. In response to an ever growing materialistic society, pervasive sin and injustice, and the persistent spread of heresy, many lay Catholics were turning more completely to conversion. These people were called penitents or *conversi*, a word meaning "converted ones." They expressed their conversion by greatly simplifying and disciplining their lives in the three areas of prayer, fasting, and clothing. These penitents soon found that their desire to follow God's guiding led them into many different types of spiritual and corporal works of mercy.

SAINT FRANCIS AND SAINT CLARE

When Francis Bernardone experienced his conversion, he adopted the garb and life style of the penitents who were numerous in the vicinity of his hometown of Assisi, Italy. Those men who joined him also called themselves penitents. On their way to see the Pope about their way of life, Francis and his little band were often asked who they were. They replied, "We are penitents from Assisi." Eventually Francis wrote a religious Rule for the men whom he called his "brothers." This became the Rule for the Friars Minor.

In 1212, Clare Offreduccio, who had been secretly meeting for spiritual direction with Francis for a year or more, embraced a penitential life and sought refuge from her angry family in a Benedictine monastery. Soon she moved to another community and finally to San Damiano where she and the women who had joined her in a penitential but enclosed life became the first members of the Second Order, the Poor Clares.

SAINT FRANCIS AND THE PENITENTS

As the influence of Francis and his friars and Clare and her sisters spread, many lay people began to hunger for a deeper union with God. Francis directed these people to the already established groups of penitents who peopled every part of Europe. When the penitents began to ask Francis for more direction, he wrote them letters and eventually, at their request, a Rule which was put into final form by Cardinal Hugolino dei Conti dei Segni, the future Pope Gregory IX. The Rule, written in 1221, committed to writing the way the penitents were already living.

THE FRANCISCAN THIRD ORDER

Laity who wished to align themselves with Francis and his friars adopted the Rule of 1221 as the Rule for a lay Franciscan Order. Soon after Francis's death, this Order became known as the Third Order of Saint Francis. In 1289, Pope Nicholas IV made the 1221 Rule more uniform by removing from it many local statutes that had been appended. For all practical purposes, however, the codified 1289 Rule was the same as the primitive 1221 Rule even to the point of having almost exactly the same wording. The major difference was that the 1289 Rule placed the penitents directly under the Friars Minor. The 1289 Rule was in effect for all Third Order Franciscans until Pope Leo XIII radically modified the Rule in 1883. Pope Leo XIII believed that every Catholic would do well to become a Franciscan, and he foresaw vast spiritual growth if they did. His intent in relaxing and changing the original Rule was to make it more livable for masses of people. Indeed, within years after the Leonine Rule's promulgation, many did join the Third Order of Saint Francis.

After Vatican II, all the Orders within the Catholic Church were asked to reexamine their Rules and return to their original intent. The Third Order of Saint Francis, using the 1883 Rule as a basis, rewrote its Rule. In 1978, Pope Paul VI ratified the new Rule. This Pauline Rule is the current Rule of what is now known as the Secular Franciscan Order. All Rules previous to the 1978 Rule have been abrogated (that is, abolished) for the Secular Franciscan Order. This means that members of the Secular Franciscan Order are not obligated to live the tenets of the Rules of 1221, 1289, or 1883. Rather, Secular Franciscans now promise to live the Rule of 1978, the Pauline Rule, which has some, but not all, of the tenets of the previous Rules. Hence, the Primitive Rule of the Confraternity of Penitents is called simply the Rule of 1221.

WHY A CONFRATERNITY?

In canon law, a confraternity is a voluntary association, usually of laity, which is established under Church authority for the promotion of some work of devotion, charity, or instruction undertaken for the love of God. Confraternities are subject to the assent of the bishop and their Constitutions subject to his approval.

Confraternities of Penitents were common during the Middle Ages with over a hundred such confraternities existing in Rome alone. Members met together, often in their own churches, for support and prayer. The confraternities were distinguished from each other by a specific garb, which concealed the identity of the wearer, by their spiritual and corporal works of mercy, and by different penitential and prayer practices. Each confraternity took a name for itself, often selecting the name of a saint, a title of Our Lady or of Christ, or a specific devotion of the Church. Many confraternities were under the specific patronage of individuals who later were recognized by the Church as saints.

The modern Confraternity of Penitents is in a direct line with those of the Middle Ages. Its Rule is to be lived privately and quietly in one's own home. The clothing colors and styles are modern yet without being flashy or colorful so that the general public is unable to identify who is a member of the Confraternity. The Rule has specific penitential and prayer practices. Penitents participate in spiritual and corporal works of mercy of their own choosing. The Rule is intended to be lived in a supportive community environment, whether in a local gathering or through email or postal mail and telephone support. The local groups take names for themselves, selecting either the name of a saint, a title of Our Lady or of Christ, or a specific devotion of the Church.

A RETURN TO THE ORIGINAL CHARISM

Christ called all people to penance (conversion). "In His (Jesus's) name, penance for the remission of sins is to be preached to all the nations." (Luke 24:47). By living according to the CFP Rule and Constitutions, penitents embrace a means for penance to occur. Thus, the Confraternity of Penitents is a prayerful return to the original charism of the 1221 Rule.

Jesus stated, "Whoever wishes to be My follower must deny his very self, take up his cross, and follow in My steps," (Luke 9:23). Living a penitential life helps to foster a continual and complete surrender to God. This means that penitents are not content with simply overcoming their tendencies to sin. They also desire to embrace the good. By living according to the CFP Rule and Constitutions and participating in spiritual and corporal works of mercy, penitents do good for the love of God and love of all.

Madeline Pecora Nugent, CFP

FINDING A SPIRITUAL DIRECTOR

Each penitent must have a spiritual director. There is good reason for this. Modern society is essentially pagan and unsupportive of conversion to the things of God. A spiritual director is essential to men and women who are trying to live a disciplined spirituality that will ultimately draw them into deeper surrender to and union with God. The spiritual director gives the modern penitent the encouragement and guidance to continue on the route that will lead to eternal life.

All penitents are required to have a spiritual director by the middle of first year novice formation. The first step to finding one is to pray for one. Here is a prayer composed by Karen Sadock, penitent:

"Lord, if you want me to pursue this penitential way of life, please send me the director I need – and the director who needs me. Make sure we recognize one another when we meet. In your good time. Amen."

A spiritual director may be any priest, deacon, or male or female religious who agrees with all the teachings of the Roman Catholic Church and who is supportive of your desire to live according to the Rule and Constitutions of the Confraternity of Penitents.

In approaching any potential spiritual director, assume that he or she has never heard of the Confraternity of Penitents. While you can explain the Confraternity briefly to the individual, it is always imperative that you give the person a copy of the Rule and Constitutions, and, better yet, the CFP Handbook, to review. Also share the CFP web site at http://www.penitents.org Any spiritual director needs to understand what the Confraternity is before making any valid decision regarding spiritual direction in your regard.

Remember that the Confraternity of Penitents is a private Catholic Association of the Faithful. In contacting anyone about spiritual direction or about any other matter regarding the Confraternity, be sure to use the words "private Catholic Association of the Faithful" and not Third Order or any other term in referring to the CFP.

If a potential spiritual director has questions regarding the Confraternity of Penitents, please have him or her contact the Confraternity for information. We can provide them with copies of letters from the Diocese of Fort Wayne - South Bend and other information that they may need.

Be charitable in all your dealings with anyone. Remember that we are all called to follow Christ in certain ways. Those who do not now understand your call to a life of penance may understand later. They may even be called to a life of penance themselves, someday! If you meet with misunderstanding, be loving and kind. If your potential spiritual director is not supportive, look elsewhere. The Confraternity can provide you with referral if you are unsuccessful in your search for spiritual direction.

Madeline Pecora Nugent, CFP

BEING INCONSPICUOUS
AS A PENITENT

Jesus told us that, when we do penance, we are not to try to be conspicuous as the hypocrites are, but are to wash our faces, comb our hair, and not appear to be fasting. Then God, Who alone sees us fasting, will reward us.

As penitents, our penitential practices ought to remain hidden. We are to blend in with the crowd even as we live lives of penance (conversion). A few matters come to mind in this regard.

TO LIVE THE RULE OF 1221

The call from the Holy Spirit, and hopefully we trust that call, was to "live the Rule of 1221 and to pray that more people will live the Rule of 1221 nationwide and worldwide." When we look at the Rule of 1221, we read about the clothing requirements right there in Chapter One. Penitents at the time the Rule was written were to dress in "undyed cloth of humble quality." This was in contrast to the rich and colorful clothes the nobility, clergy, and bishops were wearing. So penitents did stand out from the nobility and clergy, although they could have blended in with the poor who often wore undyed cloth of humble quality. I say often because frequently the poor were given cast off, dyed clothing from the rich. We can assume, however, that this clothing was in poor condition.

So why were penitents instructed to wear "undyed cloth" when even the poor often wore dyed cloth? Because wearing undyed cloth keeps one's life simple and is truly a penance, especially if you like bright colors. It also keeps a person more inconspicuous than bright colors or patterns do. In a crowd, folks generally notice pink more than white, green more than brown, and stripes or polka dots more than solids.

So in 1221, penitents were not totally inconspicuous. Those who knew them would have been aware that there were changes in their dress. If they were asked about those changes, we can imagine that they may have said, "I'm living a Rule of Life in my own home and clothing is part of the Rule."

Penitents today, who have dealings with the same folks day in and day out, might be asked similar questions. "Why I don't see you in red anymore? I thought red was your favorite color." Today's penitent can answer just like those 1221 penitents did. "I'm living a Rule of Life in my own home and clothing is part of that Rule."

HEAD COVERINGS

Some female penitents have asked about using head coverings at Mass. St. Paul asked that women cover their heads at Mass, and this was because those who didn't stood out from the other women and were distracting, calling attention to their uncovered heads. In other words, in Paul's day, women with uncovered heads at Mass were the exception. The 1917 Code of Canon Law mandated head coverings for women (1917 Canon 1262, No. 2). It also said that it was desirable that men and women be separated in church (1917 Canon 1262, No. 1). However, the 1983 Code of Canon Law, which is now in effect and which did not mention head coverings, abrogated (that is, abolished) the 1917 Code (1983 Canon 6, No. 1, Section 1).

Thus, the 1917 Code is no longer in effect. The Code of 1983 does not address the issue. Therefore, canonically, wearing head coverings in a Catholic church is a matter outside the law. The old Code has no effect in the Church today. Since the Catholic Church currently has no obligation that women's heads be covered in church, most women do not wear head coverings, although some do. Suppose a penitent wishes to wear a head covering in a Catholic Church? Certainly that would be fine, as long as she understands that it's her choice and not mandated by the CFP Rule or Constitutions or by the Church. She needs to know, too, that those who don't wear head coverings and those who do are both showing respect for Our Lord in the Blessed Sacrament. If she believes otherwise, she is in opposition to the teachings of the Catholic Church and, therefore, in opposition to what our Rule and Constitutions enjoin.

The head covering, however, ought not be worn all the time, as part of the penitent's day in and day out dress. This is because it then resembles a veil, and the penitent can be confused with a religious, or with someone who is trying to look like a religious (someone once called lay women who wore head coverings indoors and out "wannabe nuns"). Constant use of a head covering can also make others think that wearing head coverings make a woman holier. Or wearing them is or ought to be part of the CFP way of life. All of these are misconceptions, and we, as penitents, need to avoid fostering misconceptions.

Suppose a penitent wants to wear a head covering while at prayer while not in the presence of the Blessed Sacrament? Certainly a penitent can wear a head covering while praying in private. She can also kiss the floor or prostrate herself while at prayer or even, with the approval of the spiritual director, do additional penances and mortifications, when no one sees them but the Lord. But these things should not be done in public as they call attention to the penitent, and that attention can be a matter of spiritual pride. In the case of the CFP, it can also be a matter of confusion for others. If a person knows that someone is in the Confraternity of Penitents, and always sees that person praying with a head covering outside of a Catholic Church, the assumption is that a head covering is necessary for penitents while praying. The penitent may say that praying puts one in the Presence of God and one acknowledges God's Presence with the head covering. This is an idea adopted by some other religions as part of their religious practices. But it is not part of the Catholic faith, as we know that we are always in God's Presence, whether we are conversing with Him or not. Therefore, ought we wear head coverings all the time because God is always with us? What the Church has not mandated, we ought not mandate for ourselves.

SINGULARITY

Penitents who want to continually wear head coverings in public are really being asked by the Holy Spirit to strip themselves of their personal desire for the sake of the community. Putting the community before one's personal preferences is part of religious life. A religious sister or brother, for example, may have to give up many of his or her religious practices or prayers to fit in with the religious community. The purpose of entering religious life is to give up one's will for the sake of God. The CFP is a community of lay people who are living a religious Rule of Life in our own homes. We, too, need to give up our wills for the sake of God, and living our Rule while being mindful of the community and the public are part of giving up that will. All that we do must reflect accurately what the community expects of its members and must be done out of obedience to our Rule and Constitutions, just like those who take religious vows.

Just as those in religious life are not to appear singular to others in their community, so, too, penitents ought not appear singular to other penitents. Singularity causes confusion and spiritual competition. If, for example, a religious brother decided to wear visibly a medal which is not part of his religious habit, another brother might see this and decide to wear one as well. Or maybe two. One can imagine a community of brothers who now are following their own spiritual bent, competing in who looks holier by the number, size, or type of medals he sports.

Similarly, women who always wear head coverings can make other penitents think that, in order to be really humble and holy, they, too, ought to wear head coverings. Or male penitents who always wear a white shirt and black pants can make other penitents feel less mortified if they have a more varied wardrobe. As penitents, our focus ought to be on change of heart, not on appearing singularly holy by our dress.

PROPER ATTITUDE

One woman who inquired with us a few years ago owned a pink flowered dress that she liked very much. She said, "No way am I giving up my pink flowered dress." And she didn't give it up. She gave up being in what was then the Brothers and Sisters of Penance. That woman joined the Benedictine oblates, who have no clothing requirements. Recently, she sat next to me at Mass, and she was wearing her pink flowered dress and her Benedictine oblate name tag. A head covering or a certain style of clothing can be like a pink flowered dress. Certainly there is nothing wrong with it. However, for the sake of our Rule, we may have to relinquish it, and maybe we don't want to. We may feel that we are holier wearing a certain garb, but the Church does not say that we are. To consider certain clothes necessary for ourselves is to go beyond the teachings of the Church. It is to say that we know better than the Church what ought to be worn.

Penitents certainly can wear hats and scarves if the weather warrants their use. I nearly always wear a scarf outdoors because my head gets cold and, if it's windy, I'm subject to ear aches. When it's really cold, I wear a warm hood indoors because my head is cold since we keep our heat low. But I don't wear the hood indoors in public (if I have to answer the doorbell, I take it off, or if a repair man is working in the house, I keep it off unless I tell him, "Please excuse this but my head is cold.").

Penitents might prefer certain styles of dress. But they ought to vary the colors so that they don't appear to be wearing a habit. Some women, for example, feel more comfortable in jumpers than in slacks. They can wear jumpers all the time, as long as they aren't all the same color of jumper. If they are the same, the jumper has become a habit.

That said, penitents must always be sure to do God's Will. Certainly God's Will is above any written Rule. The CFP does not want to stand in the way of how God is calling an individual to serve Him. Saints were sometimes called to extreme styles of dress or unusual mortifications and penances. If a penitent feels that the Lord is calling him or her to any garb, mortification, or penance beyond what our Rule and Constitutions enjoin, he or she must pray intensely to determine if the penitent is really hearing the voice of the Holy Spirit. If the penitent feels that is the case, he or she must share these inspirations with the spiritual director, reminding him or her that penitents are not to appear to be religious, not to stand out, and to dress as the Rule asks. If the spiritual director feels that the penitent is, indeed, dealing with a prompting of God, and if obedience to this prompting would involve a visible variation from our Rule of Life, the penitent's spiritual director should contact the Visitor and Minister General of the Confraternity and discuss the matter. The Visitor and Minister General will pray about the request and speak to the penitent and spiritual director about it. The Visitor and Minister General shall, together, have the final say on whether or not a penitent ought to follow these inspirations and how this might be done.

ARE YOU A NUN (BROTHER, PRIEST)?

Female and male penitents are sometimes asked if they are nuns, brothers, or priests. This is because others see the visible cross or crucifix and the plain clothing and somehow think that those dressed in that way are religious. That is frequently a false assumption as many clergy and religious who wear secular dress wear bright colors and prints and often do not wear any religious symbol.

Penitents need not feel uncomfortable if they are mistaken for religious. The reason this happens is not because penitents are dressing like religious but because religious are dressing like laity. Our call is to "live the Rule of 1221." If we are faithful to that call, we will be faithful to the clothing element in the Rule and Constitutions, no matter how secular looking religious and clergy may become. If a person has a brick home and a brick Catholic Church is built next door, does that mean that the home owner ought to cover the brick with aluminum siding so that folks don't mistake the house for the parish rectory?

It's important for penitents to understand why someone may ask them if they are clergy or religious. The questioner may:

a. Have an intention which needs prayer.
b. Have a question about the Catholic Church.
c. Have a problem for which they need counsel or a listening ear.
d. Be trying to figure out how to address the individual.
e. Be looking for a religious presence in a secular world.

All of these are good reasons for wanting to speak to a religious. Rather than feel awkward about being asked if they are nuns, brothers, or priests, penitents ought to use the question as an opportunity to help someone else. How about this answer? "No, I'm a lay person who is living a Catholic Rule of Life in my own home. Might you have something you wanted to discuss with a religious or a prayer intention I could pray for?" Answering this way may minister to someone who would otherwise not have found anyone he or she felt comfortable enough with whom to talk.

The Rule and Constitutions ask us not to be conspicuous and yet, because we dress simply, people notice. Is this violating what we are trying to live? Not at all. Our way of Life asks that we not stand out because our bright and worldly colors call attention to themselves. Clergy and religious are not to call attention to themselves either, yet, if they are in religious garb, they definitely stand out. What folks are noticing about us in the CFP is not our dress but our dress combined with the crucifix or cross. If we began wearing patterns and colors and still wore the cross or crucifix, folks would notice and still ask if we were religious or priests as religious and priests wear these colors. The only way that penitents could look "just like everybody else" is to not wear the cross or crucifix at all. That would violate our CFP Constitutions.

WITNESSES TO CHRIST

God may be asking us penitents to be willing to be His witnesses in the world. Remember why folks ask if we are priests or religious. They are looking for a religious presence in a secular world. They are trying to see if God matters to anyone. They want someone to pray with them or for them or to answer their questions. Our plain garb with its cross or crucifix is a way of saying that God does matter, prayer matters, others matter, at least to us. People who are looking for answers, prayer, support, or just a listening ear, see the cross and crucifix as indicating someone who can provide those helps. Today especially, when rock stars and atheists are wearing religious symbols as jewelry, while religious are not wearing habits, we penitents have to expect to be singled out.

The original charism of the Confraternity of Penitents was "to live the Rule of 1221." We thought we were to live it for ourselves, but it is becoming increasingly clearer that we are to live it for the sake of others as well. If our simple, plain dress with the cross or crucifix says to someone that we are loving and serving the Lord in a special way, isn't that a good thing? St. Francis once told a friar that they were going out to preach. They walked up and down the hills of Assisi and returned to the friary without having said a word. The friar questioned St. Francis about the preaching mission. Francis said that they preached a good sermon by their demeanor. We need to "preach" in the same way.

The clothing part of our way of life is critical to how we live this life, and perhaps more critical to others than we know. Let us be open to preaching without words wherever we go. If someone does ask us if we are priests or religious, then we can use words to minister to them as the Holy Spirit directs.

EATING ENGAGEMENTS

Consider our days of fast and abstinence. Do penitents have to turn down luncheon dates with coworkers or friends, if they fall on days on which the Rule enjoins fast or abstinence? Not at all! Charity is the most important part of the penitential life and is written into it. Penitents certainly can go to luncheons. They can order meatless meals on abstinence days, if that's possible. If they are served meat on such days, they ought to eat it in charity. If they are served a between meal snack, they ought to enjoy it. If they go to a restaurant between meals with co-workers or friends, they can order a soft drink or fruit juice. If they go to a buffet on abstinence days, they can select the meatless items. There is absolutely no need to turn down luncheon or dinner dates or to stay back when everyone else goes for coffee!

LIVING A RULE OF LIFE

A Rule of Life is a way in which all those in the organization are to live. It is the thread, other than our faith in God, that binds us together. Living our Rule and Constitutions is a way to exercise obedience and denial of self will. If we want to change the Rule or Constitutions, or mitigate, forget, or make more stringent, parts of them, then we are not living our Rule of Life but another Rule. It takes great humility to live according to a Rule of Life. That's why many folks won't do it. May the Holy Spirit give us the wisdom, love, grace, and courage to live our Rule and Constitutions as we have them.

Christ assures us at our baptism that, if we live out our baptismal promises, we will obtain eternal life. As this Rule assists us to live out the Christian life, so it will assist us toward eternal salvation.

Madeline Pecora Nugent, CFP

THE CONFRATERNITY OF PENITENTS: A MIXED BUNCH

I have a friend who loves to attend charismatic prayer meetings because he is a great charismatic pray-er. A prayer meeting gets his highest commendation if he remarks afterwards (I paraphrase what he says), "What a mixed bunch! God can do something with that mixed bunch."

I think he could be talking about the Confraternity of Penitents. We really are a "mixed bunch."

VIVA LA DIFFERENCE!

We are looked upon as fools even by many in the Church who wonder why in the world we would want to live a Rule like ours when "Vatican II freed the Church from all those penances and fasting." Each of us could name at least one family member who condescendingly thinks we have "flipped our rocker." Speaking of rockers, some of us are old enough to spend our days in one. As of this writing (April, 2005), our oldest member is a spry ninety year old. Of course, we have some who have "barely left the cradle." The youngest member of the CFP is eighteen years old and discerning a vocation to religious life.

Within a seventy year span between our oldest and youngest member lies a mixed bunch of all ages, life styles, and income levels. One of the CFP members is now residing temporarily in a women's shelter and another one is preparing to move into a home for the able bodied elderly. A few are living in college dorms and two are doing their formation from behind prison bars. A number of our members home school their children. Some of them bake their own bread, freeze their own produce, and milk their own goats. Others work high powered jobs in major metropolitan cities. We have among us college professors, school teachers, computer technicians, veterinary clinicians, home health care professionals, hospice workers, and salesmen. Some carry the cross of mental and/or physical illness. All bear scars in one way or another, some from very deep wounds that involve parents, spouses, and/or children.

If you see us together, the differences become visually apparent. You'll immediately notice that some of us prefer a very casual look and have no idea how to use a steam iron, while others always dress as if they just picked up their garments from the cleaners. Some have the hard hitting accent of New Yorkers and others the soft slur of the South. Some are no nonsense, get to the point kind of folks and others are the sit down and chat a while types. Some have light skin and some dark, some have wrinkles and some have freckles. Some are vegetarians and some like nothing better than a good, medium rare steak. We sure are a mixed bunch.

THE TIE THAT BINDS

But if you do see us together, you'll notice one thing right away. No matter whose hair is gray or even absent, and whose is luxurious, no matter who is dressed as if they were going to work in the field and who looks like they are going to a wedding, no matter who could chat for hours and who wants to escape to a prayer chapel, we are all great buddies. It's as if we know each other even if we've never met before. Maybe it's that "off the rocker" Rule of Life we are living, or hoping to live, that binds us together. But I think it's even more than that. Those who last in the CFP are not only committed to the penitential life, but they are also committed to our motto which is love of God and love of neighbor. It's the love that makes us a family and the love that binds us together. Love of God and of one another makes a mixed bunch into a family of penitents. Love makes a Con (with) fraternity (brotherliness).

God can use a mixed bunch only if it's loving. God does not long for people who fast, who spend long hours in prayer, and who wear only certain clothing colors. God can get along very well without any penitents. The CFP Rule and Constitutions aren't for God's sake. They are for our sake. What God desires, what He craves, is love. Love is God's name. He seeks people who reflect His name back to Himself. God desires people who love Him and who love one another. The Rule of Life that we embrace must be the discipline that turns us away from self love and that transforms each of us into lovers of God and of others. Penitents are to become lovers. Love makes a mixed bunch into a confraternity, a group held together "with brotherliness."

WHY THE MIXTURE?

A mixed bunch is the best bunch to achieve God's work because it doesn't think too highly of itself. All the differences in the members keep it on course because if one person thinks he or she is something special, the others will soon give the haughty one a dose of reality. In the same way, if one member thinks he or she is no better than refuse, someone is going to remind him or her that God uses manure to grow flowers. A mixed bunch doesn't conform to any standards except uniqueness so it doesn't conform to the world's view of what makes a person successful or attractive. The only place a mixed bunch can really feel understood is in the arms of God Who called a pretty mixed bunch to serve Him right from the start. St. Paul writes:

Consider your own calling, brothers. Not many of you were wise by human standards, not many were powerful, not many were of noble birth. Rather, God chose the foolish of the world to shame the wise, and God chose the weak of the world to shame the strong, and God chose the lowly and despised of the world, those who count for nothing, to reduce to nothing those who are something, so that no human being might boast before God. It is due to him that you are in Christ Jesus, who became for us wisdom from God, as well as righteousness, sanctification, and redemption, so that, as it is written, "Whoever boasts, should boast in the Lord." (1 Corinthians: 26-31)

God can use a mixed bunch just because we are so insignificant. As long as we remember that all we have, we owe to Him and to His grace, we will keep ourselves little enough. God isn't out looking for mountain peaks. The world sees those easily. He's seeking out pebbles who know they are lying in dust. Welded together by the macadam of God's love, we in the CFP can become a little patch of highway over which others may pass to reach the kingdom. As we bond together in the mixed macadam patch of God, let us treat one another with brotherliness because we are "all in this together." Come, Lord, make us fully Yours and use us as You will. Amen!

Madeline Pecora Nugent, CFP

PENANCE AND FORGIVENESS: NEVER LOOK BACK

Section 26 of the CFP Rule and Constitutions mandates that penitents are to forgive and reconcile. While reconciliation may be difficult as the other party may resist, forgiveness requires only one—the person forgiving. This article suggests a way to forgive those who have hurt us, whether or not reconciliation is possible.

"Jesus said to him, 'Once the hand is laid to the plow, no one who looks back is fit for the kingdom of God" (Luke 9:62).

This is a good Scripture verse for us folks who come out of bad situations. We repent and are forgiven by the Lord and all our sinful thoughts and actions are wiped away. Also, on our part, it is vital for us to forgive each and every person who ever hurt us, just as we seek forgiveness from every person we have hurt. Forgiveness is a two way street and the key to healing. We choose to forgive. If that seems impossible because of our woundedness, then it's important to ask the Lord to help us to want to forgive. Asking God to help us shows a good will on our part, and the Lord can work with our good will. We mustn't allow the lack of feeling loving and forgiving to stop us from saying, "I forgive _____(name)_____ in the name of Our Lord Jesus Christ." Forgiving, just like loving, is often a choice.

PREPARING A DAY OF HEALING FORGIVENESS

A day or so before you do a forgiveness session for yourself, read the Gospel of St. John all the way through in one sitting. As you are reading, ask the Holy Spirit to guide and enlighten you. This is a good pre-preparation.

Then choose a time when you will be completely alone for about an hour or so and will not be disturbed. Again ask the Holy Spirit to guide you and help you. Then ask the Lord Jesus to cover you in His Precious Blood and protect you. Also ask the Mother of Jesus to accompany you on this journey, asking for her motherly protection.

Begin by asking the Holy Spirit to bring to your remembrance all those persons you have to forgive. Don't dredge around in your unconscious as the Holy Spirit will float these memories to the surface. Don't be surprised at what emerges. Don't panic either. Remember that you are sitting between Jesus and Mary who love you and want this more for you than you realize.

As you become aware of a memory and a person, say, "I forgive _____ in the Name of Our Lord Jesus Christ."

Sometime during this exercise, you may discover that you are very angry with God for allowing something bad to happen. You may think, "I'm so angry that I have to forgive God." But God never wrongs us. It is impossible for God, Who is Love, to act unlovingly. Come to grips with your anger and tell God that you are mad at Him. He's big enough to handle your anger! Pray, "Lord, I am angry that you allowed this to happen. But I know that you will bring good out of this for me and for others. Help me to internalize that truth. Thank you for what You will do in my life in the aftermath of this terrible thing."

You will probably also have to forgive yourself. "I forgive myself in the name of Our Lord Jesus Christ." Continue until no more names surface. Don't block any tears during this healing time. The Lord Jesus is healing you! Ask the Holy Spirit to pour the balm of His Love over your wounded heart.

When the healing session is over, rejoice and thank the Lord. Then do something active and fun for yourself and others.

DEALING WITH RECURRING MEMORIES

The world, the flesh, and the devil will throw up memories and their feelings from our unconscious. We may have to repeat our act(s) of forgiveness many times. We must not succumb to feelings of anger, resentment, bitterness, and fear. Jesus and His merciful love is with us. "He that is within you is greater than he who is in the world" (1 John 4:4).

Jesus said in the prayer He taught us, "Forgive us our trespasses as we forgive others" (Matthew 6:12). He also said in John 14:23, "If anyone loves me, he will keep my word, and my Father will love him and we will come to him and make our home with him." Is this not the best reason in the world to forgive? To keep His word results in our becoming a dwelling place of the Holy Trinity and preparing for union with Jesus.

So as we keep going down the path of life, we must not look back! Don't be like Lot's wife who got turned into a pillar of salt. Looking back can paralyze us, blind us, and prevent us from being true penitents, "the converted ones." When ugly stuff surfaces, we thank the Lord for rescuing us and ask Him to help us forgive one more time. And with

His loving, wounded arm around us (sometimes it's called a yoke), He guides us on His Way of Life to be one with Him.

Lucy St. Michael, CFP*

*Lucy St. Michael is the pen name of a life pledged member of the Confraternity of Penitents.

RECONCILIATION: AN OPEN DOOR

The motto of the Confraternity of Penitents is love of God and love of neighbor.

"You shall love the Lord your God with your whole heart, with your whole soul, and with all your mind, (and) you shall love your neighbor as yourself." (Jesus's words as recorded in Matthew 22:37-38)

It is impossible to love God if one does not love one's neighbor as well.

"Those who say, 'I love God,' and hate their brothers or sisters, are liars; for those who do not love a brother or sister whom they have seen, cannot love God whom they have not seen. The commandment we have from Him is this: those who love God must love their brothers and sisters also.' (1 John 4:20-21).

Love is so important that it brings about union with God.

"Beloved, if God has loves us so, we must have the same love for one another. No one has ever seen God. Yet if we love one another God dwells in us, and His love is brought to perfection in us." (1 John 4:11-12)

Why is this union possible only if we love?

"God is love, and he who abides in love abides in God and God in him." (1 John 4:16)

THE CORE OF THE CFP RULE

Section 26 of the CFP Rule and Constitutions are the core of the way of life for penitents. This is because the love of God and of neighbor meet in the living of this part of the Rule and Constitutions. What does section 26 say?

RULE:

26. As regards making peace among the brothers and sisters or non-members at odds, let what the ministers find proper be done; even, if it be expedient, upon consultation with the Lord Bishop.

CONSTITUTIONS:

26. In keeping with section 26 of the Rule:

26a. All are to make peace with members of the Confraternity and all others, seeking, if necessary, the consultation of the Church.

26b. The penitent must daily pray for all those who refuse to make peace with the penitent and must forgive such people all wrongs done to the penitent.

26c. The brothers and sisters are always to take the first steps toward reconciliation. Under no circumstances are penitents to hold grudges or wish ill to anyone.

THE PROOF OF LOVE

The living of section 26 of the Rule and Constitutions is a proof of love of God and of neighbor. All the other sections of the Rule and Constitutions are intended to foster love of God and of neighbor. It is obvious that a penitent who nurses resentments toward others or who refuses to forgive and reconcile does not understand the meaning of penance (conversion).

Everyone who loves has been born of God and knows God. Whoever does not love does not know God, because God is love. This is how God showed His love among us: He sent his one and only Son into the world that we might live through Him. This is love: not that we loved God, but that He loved us and sent His Son as an atoning sacrifice for our sins (1 John 4:7b-10).

The power to love and the power to forgive and reconcile come from God Who loved us first, Who forgave us, and Who, by His sacrifice, reconciled us to Himself. By God's grace alone is it possible for us to reconcile with others.

TAKE NO OFFENSE

The first step toward reconciliation is to precipitate no situation that would require reconciliation. This means not taking offense where none may be intended.

Here's a true story. A mom of two preschoolers was grocery shopping, trying to watch one child in the cart and the other exploring the store, while trying to select the necessary groceries. Several weeks later, the mom met a friend who asked, "Are you angry with me?"

Dumbfounded, the mom replied, "No. Whatever made you think that?"

The friend responded, "When I saw you in the grocery store last month, you didn't even say hello."

The mom had not even seen her friend in the grocery store! Her total attention had been on the kids, the grocery list, and the grocery shelves.

Another example involves emails. Sometimes when we don't hear back from someone to whom we sent an email, we assume that the person is angry with us or doesn't want to reply. The truth is, more likely, that the person has either been too busy to look at emails for a few days, is having computer problems, is away, or perhaps never received our email.

As penitents, we ought always look for the best in others and make excuses for them. After all, isn't this what Jesus does for us?

If we don't take offense, we will have no need to reconcile.

AN OPEN HEART

For the penitent, reconciliation means having a heart that is open to all who wish to enter and to allow them as much space as is safe. Jesus told us to be wise as serpents but guileless as doves. He meant that we are to be gentle as a dove yet as cautious as well, for doves fly at the sight of danger. We are to be wise as serpents which means that we quietly slip away from danger when we can, yet, if we cannot, we face it courageously as we defend our very spiritual lives.

Let's take a few examples.

If a penitent is at odds with a neighbor because of a boundary dispute, the penitent could safely speak to the neighbor and apologize for any wrongs done. This might mend the fences in more ways than one.

However, if a penitent was driven, as a teen, from her home by an alcoholic and abusive parent, she may find reconciliation more difficult. It may be safe to contact the parent, perhaps by phone or by letter, without listing a return address, to tell the parent that she is praying for him or her and stating the penitent's forgiveness for any wrong done.

In the one case, it is safe for the penitent to confront the one at odds and to let the other fully know the whereabouts of the penitent. In the other case, wisdom and safety may demand more caution. But in both cases reconciliation can be attempted and, hopefully, achieved to some degree. In all cases, love should be given, for the love of God.

THE FIRST STEP

Penitents are to take the first steps toward reconciliation. This reconciliation must exist within morally sound parameters. We do not ever reconcile with evil, even if it comes to us in persons who appear to be good. We are called to resist evil in all its forms, even if temptation tells us that, if we accept the evil, good will result. Such a statement is always a lie for, although God can and does bring good out of evil, He does not ever want us to do evil so that good may result. To resist evil is to bring about a greater good, the good of obedience to God's moral law. We are always to do what is right in itself.

For example, we may have upset a friend by condemning an adulterous affair which the friend insists was unavoidable and not harmful to anyone. The price which our friend demands for reconciliation is that the penitent agree that the affair was not sinful or avoidable. The penitent cannot make this concession as it involves agreeing to what is morally evil. In this case, the penitent ought to tell the friend that he or she still loves and prays for the friend and wishes to communicate with him or her. But in no way ought the penitent state that what was evil was good or necessary. The good of reconciling a damaged or broken friendship is overshadowed by the greater good of witnessing to what is morally right. In this case, the refusal to reconcile is coming from a friend who demands an immoral solution to bring about the reconciliation.

NO DEMANDS

The open door to reconciliation is not a toll gate. We demand no apologies, tokens of love, or out pouring of guilt as a price to enter that open door to our hearts or to anyone else's. We are open to all those who come sincerely, wanting to reconcile with us. And we walk through that open door to the doors of others, knocking at them first to see if they will reconcile with us.

We may go to doors that are closed and barred against us. Pleading, logic, and the witness of others have failed to crack those doors open even a little bit. The sole weapons left to us are prayer and sacrifice, so we ought to wield those weapons daily, asking God to bring about reconciliation in His time and way.

We may come to toll gates in the hearts of others who demand apologies or some other tokens from us before they will reconcile. If what is demanded is morally acceptable, then we, by all means, need to give it. But if what is asked is morally wrong, if we are asked to acknowledge wrongs we never committed or confess thoughts we never had, we cannot lie. We must always follow the laws of God Who asks the truth of us in all things. Reconciliation is to be done in truth and in love, for if it is not done in truth, it can never be done in love. Love demands truth.

THE SONG OF "SAINT FRANCIS"

The following prayer is attributed to Saint Francis of Assisi. While it was not actually written by him, it does express well his philosophy of life and the tone of the penitential life:

> (Text adapted by Sebastian Temple)
> Make me a channel of your peace.
> Where there is hatred, let me sow your love,
> where there is injury, your pardon, Lord,
> and where there's doubt, new faith in you.
> Make me a channel of your peace.
> Where there's despair in life, let me bring hope,
> where there is darkness, only light,
> and where there's sadness, ever joy.
> O Master, grant that I may never seek
> so much to be consoled as to console,
> to be understood as to understand,

> to be loved as to love with all my soul.
> Make me a channel of your peace.
> It is in pardoning that we are pardoned,
> in giving to all men that we receive,
> and in dying that we are born to eternal life.

AN INCLUSIVE LOVE

The motto of the Confraternity of Penitents is "You shall love the Lord your God with your whole heart, with your whole soul, with all your mind, (and) you shall love your neighbor as yourself." Love means a heart that is an open door to God and to all others. God's love is not selective nor should ours be. The core of the CFP Rule and Constitutions is section 26. Only when we are willing to show our love for God by our love for all others, only when we are willing to be at peace with all and to take the first steps toward that, does our Rule of Life have meaning. If we give up food, clothing, possessions, and time to follow God, but do not give up bitterness, anger, resentments, or hatred, then our other penances are meaningless. If we spend long hours in prayer but won't spend a few moments trying to make peace with another, our prayers are empty. Penance is a sham if it is not done in love.

God is a God of peace, and to love God means to embrace Him with a heart that is at peace with all. Pray for that peace. Ask God to grant the graces necessary for reconciliation and to foster in you a heart that truly desires it. If you resist reconciliation, give God your resistant spirit and ask Him to soften you in His Love. Reconciliation can only be attempted and achieved by the grace of God so let us pray for that grace. Only if one truly desires and seeks reconciliation with all can one be truly united with God Whose name is Love and Who calls us to love as He loves.

May God grant us hearts that are open doors to others so that peace and love will reign in us and between us and all.

Madeline Pecora Nugent, CFP

WORKS OF MERCY: PENITENTS' APOSTOLATE

How merciful God is!

We penitents, perhaps more than other folks, understand and love God's mercy, for we know that we have entered upon the path of penance (conversion) because God has been merciful to us. Were it not for God's mercy, we would yet be mired in our sins. We are not perfect, we know, but at least we now recognize and acknowledge our shortcomings. We at least try to steer clear of sin now instead of toying with it or even wallowing in it as we once did. We attempt to replace sin with good actions and prayers, not always succeeding but certainly sincerely trying. We thank God for having called us to this life of penance, of conversion.

Because God has been merciful to us, He calls us to be merciful to others. Because God has loved us, He calls us to love others. Love and mercy create a mystical, spiritual spiral which funnels us toward the heart of God.

The Confraternity of Penitents has a Prayer, Mission, Motto, and Action. The Action of the CFP combines the Prayer, Motto, and Mission into a goal for each penitent.

The Action of the Confraternity of Penitents is "To pray for God's specific direction in one's life so that, through humbly living our Rule of Life, each penitent may help to rebuild the house of God by bringing love of God and neighbor to his or her own corner of the world."

Prayer helps us individually to discern how God wishes to use us personally to rebuild the Church. Any successful rebuilding must have love of God and neighbor as its foundation. The love of God and of neighbor is manifest in the Spiritual and Corporal Works of Mercy. Each penitent is to engage in a specific apostolate which involves at least one of these works of mercy. Because we penitents are flung worldwide, the Confraternity does not mandate one specific apostolate, other than prayer, which each member is to embrace. Rather, we trust that God will give each of us our own apostolate involving one or more of these merciful works.

WHAT SORTS OF WORKS DO THE WORKS OF MERCY ENCOMPASS?

The **Spiritual Works of Mercy** minister to the soul. They are:

Instruct the ignorant: Teaching nursery school, day care, college, religious education; RCIA; home schooling; vocational school; adult education; vocational rehabilitation; skills instruction; teaching children in one's role as parent; subscribe someone to an instructive magazine; pass on an article or book that touched you; mentor someone and share your skills and knowledge; give surplus books and magazines to a senior center, school, library, or mail to an organization that distributes them to underprivileged nations.

Advise the doubtful: Formal and informal counseling on all levels and in all areas; letter writing; phone calls; advising children and peers; encouraging the depressed; psychological and psychiatric therapy; guidance counseling; offering sincere compliments; write letters of appreciation to government officials, business people, employees; write the wait person a compliment when you pay your restaurant bill; write love notes to family members and hide them in their dresser drawers, lunch boxes, or coat pockets; befriend a new classmate, fellow employee, or neighbor;

Correct sinners: Writing, speaking, witnessing for the faith; teaching religious education; adult education; standing up for God's righteousness; letters to the editor; calling in on talk shows; picketing. This work of mercy must be done in union with the following ones on patience, forgiveness, and comfort, because all correction must be given in charity and with sensitivity toward the feelings of the one being corrected.

Be patient with those in error or who do wrong: Parenting; charity toward employees; teaching on all levels; put money in someone else's expired parking meter; help someone find something lost; give a gift of flowers or a plant to someone who rubs you the wrong way (you might even do it secretly); listen attentively.

Forgive offenses: Not only those done to us personally but also those done to others and done by institutions, employers, governments, subordinates, clergy and religious, those in authority, and our children, spouses, and relatives; recommend someone you may see as a competitor.

Comfort the afflicted: Offering a shoulder to cry on, a listening ear, a hug, a pat on the back; sending sympathy cards; bringing meals; cleaning house, or running errands for shut ins or those suffering loss of loved ones; repairing or replacing broken treasures and toys; giving a gift of flowers; take a day trip or a movie with a person who needs some cheering up; share a funny comic strip or joke; visit those in hospitals or nursing homes who have no visitors; write a note of encouragement to someone who has received sad news; collect stuffed toys for the hospital to give to traumatized children; say "Good morning" to everyone you meet; pass on positive news; put copies of inspirational poems or sayings on the company bulletin board or water cooler; put inspirational books in public areas.

Pray for the living and the dead: Offering Masses; praying chaplets, novenas, or rosaries; praying for intentions of others; prayerful use of relics and sacramentals as tools of intercession; distribution of prayer cards; organizing prayer services, retreats, missions, days of reflection; tell someone you love them and are praying for them.

The Corporal **Works of Mercy** minister to the physical body. They are:

Feed the hungry: In one's family; soup kitchen work; donating to and working in food pantries; giving money to charities combating world hunger; collecting for the needy; giving away or selling reasonably garden produce; donating to bake sales for charitable causes; all types of kitchen work whether for free or as employment; growing food; farming; raising livestock, fish, fowl for consumption; pot luck dinners, cooking for an ill or infirm neighbor; driving someone without a car to the grocery; invite those who live alone for a meal including holiday meals; leave a muffin or cookies for your garbage collector, paper carrier, teacher, police or fire station, town hall, or mail delivery person or give them a gift of fruit, flowers, or potted plant; help folks load their groceries into their cars or hold their umbrella if it's raining; bring to work a birthday cake for a colleague; treat someone to lunch; give gift certificates for food; volunteer for "Meals on Wheels".

Give drink to the thirsty: All of those listed under Feed the hungry as well as building water pipelines and digging wells; contributing money toward alleviation of thirst; donating beverages to social gatherings; working for clean water laws; sewage treatment plant work; bring a cup of coffee or tea to a colleague; buy a box of popsicles to share on a hot day.

Clothe the naked: Donating used clothing; conducting clothing drives; making sure one's family is adequately clothed; mending; sewing; tailor work; clothing designer; raising natural fibers and animal products for clothing; working in or managing used clothing shops.

Shelter the homeless: Working in and supporting homeless shelters; renting rooms or apartments; building work; contracting; taking in boarders; managing guest houses and retreat centers; stop over shelters; safe houses for runaways and abuse victims; homes for unwed or single mothers; working with street children; half way houses; live in treatment centers; group homes; adopting; foster care; working in orphanages; housecleaning; interior design; making furniture; home furnishings and crafts; inventing; plant trees and flowers.

Visit the sick and imprisoned: Visiting by phone call, letter, email, or in person those in hospitals, institutions, prisons, shelters, half way houses; working for justice for the imprisoned, handicapped, marginalized; become a voluntary companion for an elderly person; share musical or story telling talents with the elderly; take the elderly places; offer manicures or hair dressing to nursing home residents; offer to babysit; buy disposable diapers for a new mom; push someone's wheelchair; do chores for the homebound.

Ransom the captive: Buying back those enslaved; prolife work; working for justice for oppressed; rescuing abuse victims; reporting abuse; assistance for those suffering from addictions, handicaps, social and sexual deviations; working for peace; clean up graffiti; offer to switch with a colleague when they need a day off; offer to write letters for someone who can't.

Bury the dead: Attending funerals; funeral home work; putting past offenses to rest; aid of any sort to survivors.

These are only a few of the ways in which penitents can and do engage in the spiritual and corporal works of mercy.

There are many other ways to show mercy, which don't fit neatly into the above categories but which do show love of God and of neighbor. Some of those ways are:

Return shopping carts to the store; write thank you letters; shovel someone's sidewalk or mow their law without pay; hold the door open for someone; give your place in the grocery line to someone with only a few items; pick up trash; do someone else's chores; give up your parking spot to someone else; offer to do a distasteful job; raise money for charity; leave money secretly at a needy person's house or mail it to them anonymously; share photos with those in them; donate blood; help someone in trouble; play with your children; help someone carry packages; help a mother carry a stroller up and down stairs; buy a raffle ticket for someone else (they might win); take out someone's trash.

May God inspire each penitent to perform the works of mercy to which He has called each and may every work of mercy be truly merciful and centered in love.

Mary McGarry and Madeline Pecora Nugent, CFP

PLEDGING TO LIVE A LIFE OF PENANCE: CHANNEL OF GRACE

The thoughts expressed in this article are those of Father David Engo, FBM, Spiritual Advisor to the Confraternity of Penitents

The vocation to be a penitent is a personal commitment of the heart to the service and love of God. It is a commitment made fully when one pledges for life to live the Rule and Constitutions of the Confraternity of Penitents.

The call to a life of penance comes directly from the Lord to the individual. If one hears this call and recognizes it as coming from the Holy Spirit, then he or she ought to immediately answer, "Yes, Lord. Here I am. You have called me and I am willing to follow Your call and to give my life entirely and fully to You. I run toward You, my God. Accept me into this life."

The pledge is this total surrender of one's entire self to God. The pledge is a vehicle for total union with the Lord, through a life of penance undertaken out of love for God and for neighbor. By pledging to live the Rule and Constitutions for the duration of one's life, the penitent is, in a sense, impaling himself or herself on the very cross of Christ. The penitent is saying, in effect, "Through my voluntary offering of myself to You, Lord, through a life of penance, I am ready for total union with You in every aspect of Your life, including Your passion as well as Your joys.

Because a life pledge to live a life of penance is a personal consecration of the penitent to the Lord, it is something that should never be postponed except for very valid reasons approved by the spiritual director. When a penitent pledges to live the Rule and Constitutions for life, several effects happen in the soul.

a. The penitent becomes a channel of grace for others, a mediator of God's grace, in a very real sense. This happens because the penitent has put himself or herself completely into the service of God.

b. If the penitent is part of a local gathering of penitents (a Chapter or Circle), the entire gathering, as well as each member of it, is strengthened by grace flowing through the one who has given himself or herself to the Lord through the pledge.

c. The pledge of any member gives courage to all members to continue with their formation and to move as quickly as their formation allows into making a pledge themselves.

d. Local gatherings, as well as the Confraternity itself, become increasingly stabilized with each member who pledges for life.

e. When a penitent is pledged to live a life of penance, every word and action done for the Lord sanctifies the penitent in a greater way. The penitent becomes holier because of the consecration of the pledge.

f. The pledge spiritually strengthens the person making the pledge and deepens the penitent's baptismal consecration to God.

g. The intense supernatural reality of the pledge effects the grace of total surrender and union with God. Thus the penances undertaken become much more valuable because they are fully united with God's Will and purpose.

h. The pledge is the penitent's response to Christ's call, given to the rich young man, "If you wish to be perfect, go, sell all your possessions, and come and follow Me." When the penitent "sells" himself or herself to the Lord in the total surrender of pledging to live the Rule and Constitutions for life, he or she has truly given the Lord "all your possessions." The result is that the penitent now can follow Christ completely. He or she will not be without struggle in the spiritual life, but the graces will be given to move forward with trust that God, Who now has all the penitent possesses, will make "all things work together for the good of those who have been called according to His decree" (Romans 8:28).

"Lord, I have heard Your call. I give myself totally to You. Guide me into the expression of the penitential life which You have already worked out for me from long before You created me. May I be always and in every way only Yours. Amen."

SAINT FRANCIS AND PENANCE

Penance, in its traditional definition, means conversion from human ways of doing things to God's ways. During his life, Saint Francis of Assisi passed through certain stages of conversion, common to many spiritual journeys, to a deeper intimacy with God. At any one of these steps, he could have stalled or reversed direction. Instead he continued forward, becoming a saint.

STEP ONE: LAX ATTITUDE TOWARD GOD.

The individual believes that God exists. He may pray and attend Mass, but the relationship with God is shallow. Francis Bernardone was born in Assisi, Italy, in 1182. The son of a rich cloth merchant, Francis was named by his father in honor of the nation which provided the family business with some of the finest cloth in Europe. Francis grew into a generous, kind lad who loved good times and parties. He was so free with his father's money that his friends often chose him as king of the many feasts he sponsored.

STEP TWO: DESIRE TO FOLLOW GOD IN HUMAN WAYS.

A person wants to serve God better so he begins to do what seems good, humanly speaking, yet the person has not asked what God wants done. As he matured, Francis's love of God deepened and mixed with his dreams of glory and honor. Aspiring to become a great knight, he convinced his father to buy him the finest armor. Then he set out, fighting on the side of the Pope in his war against the emperor. Captured following a bloody battle, Francis kept his spirits high while imprisoned and encouraged other prisoners to be cheerful. Finally, after his father's intervention, Francis was released. Ill, he returned home to recover.

STEP THREE: CONFUSION OVER THE PATH TO FOLLOW.

A soul begins to realize that what seemed reasonable did not bring the intended results. Questioning follows. Did I do the right thing? Am I on the right track? Francis had been sure that he was to serve God as a knight, but battle, imprisonment, and illness had dimmed his thoughts of glory. Although he had been fighting on God's side in the papal army, he had encountered, in supposedly Christian soldiers, pride, injustice, brutality, and hatred. In the delirium of his illness, Francis pondered eternal questions. What does God want of me? What am I to do with my life?

STEP FOUR: MISINTERPRETATION OF GOD'S WISHES.

The soul, not yet seasoned in discernment, may misinterpret the answer received in prayer and thus attempt to carry out a faulty agenda. Francis made a slow recovery. One night he had a dream in which he was in an enchanted castle filled with armor and presided over by a stunningly beautiful princess. "All this is you and your knights," a Voice said. Believing in dreams, Francis, with renewed joy, again clad himself in armor and set out for battle. But this time, at Spoleto, Francis's illness returned and with it a second dream and the Voice he had heard before. "Who do you think can best reward you, the Master or the servant?" When Francis answered, "The master," the Voice questioned, "Then why do you leave the Master for the servant, the rich Lord for the poor man?" "Oh, Lord," Francis breathed, "what do You wish me to do?" "Return to your own place," the Voice said, "and you will be told what to do. The dream about the armor must be interpreted in a spiritual sense."

STEP FIVE: TAKING TIME TO DISCERN.

Having realized previous errors, the soul begins to pray more fervently and to wait patiently for clear direction from the Lord. Francis shocked Assisi by his return. Was he afraid of battle? Was he crazy? The latter seemed more logical, reveling in the street and Francis stopped in a trance, struck by a vision of the princess he had seen in the castle. This time she was dressed in rags. "I have found my beloved bride," he proclaimed to his sarcastic friends, "and she is the noblest, the richest, the most beautiful bride who ever lived on this earth." He called her Lady Poverty. After this, he courted her alone, leaving his friends for the solitude of the woods, for a pilgrimage to Rome where he begged for his food, for the lepers whom he tended. All this time, Francis prayed and waited for God's promised direction. "Lord, what would YOU have me do?" Finally, in the run-down church of San Damiano, the answer came from a huge, colorful icon of the Crucified Christ. "Francis, go and repair My house, which, as you can see, is falling into ruin."

STEP SIX: ACTING ON THE DIRECTION GOD HAS SHOWN.

Revelation of God's direction may come in many ways, but, when a penitent is certain of it, he or she decisively acts. With an eager, "Yes, Lord," Francis set to work. Taking huge bolts of cloth from his father's store, he set off for a nearby town where he sold both cloth and steed and then walked back to San Damiano where he attempted to give the money to the priest. Explaining that the alms were dishonestly acquired through the sale of Pietro Bernardone's goods, the priest refused the coins. So, legend claims, Francis threw them into one of the windows of San Damiano.

STEP SEVEN: MAINTAINING DIRECTION DESPITE OPPOSITION.

Set on a path of conversion, the convert soon encounters misunderstanding from those whose spiritual position he has left behind. The soul will either move forward despite opposition or will wither under it and fall backwards. When his father learned what Francis had done, he hauled him before the bishop and demanded that Francis restore the money obtained for the goods. Since the priest had not used the money, it was easily returned. However, Francis recognized a spiritual crossroad. Disrobing in front of the assembled populace, he gave his clothes to Pietro Bernardone and cried out, "Up until today I have called Pietro Bernardone my father. For the future I shall say, 'Our Father Who art in heaven . . . .'"

STEP EIGHT: CONTINUANCE ON THE PATH OF CONVERSION.

The soul intent on serving God continues to do so joyfully despite hatred, mockery, and opposition. Alienated from his family and dressed in a workman's tunic, Francis followed the direction given him by God. He walked the streets of Assisi, begging for stones which he carried down the steep hillside to tumble-down churches in the valley below. He continued to tend lepers, even washing their wounds and eating from their bowls. His father thought him mad. His mother pitied him. Children pelted him with rocks and mud. To all he grinned, "Pax et bonum." Peace and all good.

STEP NINE: EXUBERANCE OF A NEW BEGINNING.

Opposition begins to fade as conversion persists. New friendships develop. God seems continually nearer. For two years, Francis labored alone, restoring three country churches. Meanwhile, some of the townsfolk were touched by his persistent fervor and courtesy. In 1208, Bernardo di Quintavalle and Pietro Catani, two prominent citizens of Assisi, asked to join Francis. Others followed. Silvestro. Giles. Rufino. Clare, the daughter of a respected Assisian knight who, with the women who followed her, were housed at San Damiano which Francis and others had enlarged into a cloister. Eventually Francis took his band of twelve men to Rome where the Pope authorized them to preach repentance.

STEP TEN: CONVERTING OTHERS TO THE WAY.

With the support and encouragement of like minded friends, the convert begins to evangelize. Francis and his friars minor (lesser brothers) fanned across Italy in groups of two, preaching a simple message of conversion to Christ. More friars joined Francis; more sisters joined Clare. Lay people wished to do penance so Francis laid the foundations of a lay Order called the Brothers and Sisters of Penance. Francis himself was preaching, going even to the Moslems.

STEP ELEVEN: EMBRACING SUFFERING.

Once an individual is solidly on God's path, his faith is often tested by suffering which, if borne with trust in God's wisdom, perfects belief. In Egypt Francis contracted a painful eye disease that eventually blinded him. As his health deteriorated, he was plagued with headaches and stomach pains. Unable to govern the friars, he turned the Order over to others who began to mitigate the poverty embraced by Francis and his first followers. Depression set in. In 1224, while deep in prayer, Francis was branded in his hands, feet, and side with the stigmata, the painful wounds of Christ. Unable to walk, he who forbade his friars to ride horseback had to use a donkey himself.

STEP TWELVE: FINDING JOY IN WHATEVER LIFE MAY BRING.

The penitent realizes that all that happens is in God's will and for his spiritual good. Thus, with trust and faith, the soul joyfully surrenders to all God's actions. Blind, ill Francis wrote what is perhaps his most famous piece, "The Canticle of Brother Sun." The song praises creation and the Creator and ends with an ode to death. In the early evening of October 3, 1226, death came for Francis at the Porziuncola, the little restored church which he wished to be the headquarters of his Order. Francis had asked to be laid naked on the ground "for as long as it takes to walk a mile unhurriedly," so that he could meet his Creator as he had entered the world–with nothing. As if to announce his entry into eternal life, a flock of sky larks flew over the little cell in which lay his still warm body.

People come to know and follow the Lord by many different routes, but some paths are common to many journeys. Back in the little, tumble down church of San Damiano, when Francis was trying to determine what God would have him do, he had prayed a prayer of personal surrender to God. "Lord, what would YOU have me do?" This was the prayer of Christ in the Garden. "Not My will, Lord, but Yours, be done." When we can sincerely pray that prayer, or something like it, then our own conversion venture will have begun.

Madeline Pecora Nugent, CFP

Reprinted with the kind permission of the Messenger of Saint Anthony, Padua, Italy (originally published October, 1999, in the Messenger of Saint Anthony, pages 14-16)

FACING THE FEARS OF DYING TO SELF

One of our CFP members shared the following thoughts in an email:

As I clean out my physical arena, excess clothing, jewelry, sundry possessions, I have had to face the fact that underneath all my love of Christ is a great fear. I thought it was small, because I never heard it loudly or clearly, and because I keep so busy praying and attending to family and dealing with pain that I haven't paid attention to it.

But the fear is of Death and more to the point, dying. Discovering this fear lurking under my thoughts is displacing. I feel displaced, disoriented, when I think of it. Me, of all people, afraid of death when dying is actually what I desire (in the longer run) as it brings me closer to God! Whenever I attend funerals I have trouble looking sad because I know, I KNOW, that God is merciful and wants us with Him.

It's not just that I want to live long enough to see my children grown well, or that I get to do the few activities that I would love to do (like getting to Italy!). I find that I am afraid that I will not get as close to God as I want...this is embarrassing! It sounds conceited, or presumptuous. But I look around me and at what I accomplish daily, and at how many times I miss an opportunity, and I want one more day, one more chance to pray better, to for my children or husband better—dear Lord! There is SO MUCH ROOM for improvement!

At the service this evening, Father asked about how much we love one another—if you would die on the Cross for your spouse, your children, your friends. I often think I would die for my family, but would I allow myself to be crucified? Wow.

I so want to drown, float, dance, leap with Jesus. Just mesh with Him.

But then I think that so many events, so many persons, get in the way of "my" prayer life. I met with my spiritual director and I expressed my frustration that I always see the children and other people as interfering with my relationship with God. Now I have read the Opus Dei teachings about daily work being our sanctification. I take to heart Paul's admonition to "pray without ceasing." I know that the children and my husband (indeed, each human being) are GIFTS directly from God, but I couldn't figure out how to be balanced and accepting about it all. It seems easy to compartmentalize life and not see how it all flows together.

Father said that it is NOT at all an interruption. That dealing with family and friends–interruptions–is the 2nd commandment (Christ gave us). Love your neighbor as yourself for the love of God. It is how I react to each "interruption" that then makes that relationship an "active prayer" and not the schism that I have perceived it to be.

So that seems much like what Mother Teresa of Calcutta focused upon...to serve the Christ in everyone...but I think this goes one step further for me, to not only serve the Christ in each person, but that my response is a prayer, and it can be a contemplative response, a praise response, a questioning hopeful response, even angry, righteous indignation. But just like uniting the pain to the foot of the Cross makes it intercessory prayer–prayer warfare–so does the attitude in my heart make all interactions prayer, not interruptions.

TWO DEATHS

This penitent is not far from Christ. In fact, she is much closer than she imagines herself to be. You see, recognizing that we are down right frightened about dying is admitting that we are just as scared of dying to self. Death of the body is, after all, the ultimate death of our self will, isn't it? When we physically die, we have lost total control of everything, everyone, and of ourselves.

Recognizing our fear of dying to self is the biggest step to actually doing it. When we admit our fear about giving up our own will and our own way and our own privacy, then we hear the little voice of God saying to us in our hearts, "Do you really want to die so that I can live within you?" We have to think about that, wrestle with it, admit like this penitent did that we don't really want it, and then the Holy Spirit backs off for a bit and says, "When you do really want it, let Me know."

The question will return, from time to time, "Are you willing to die for love of Me?" And we will wrestle some more and hem and haw, and the question will persist as we struggle with it. Then God will make things easier for us. He will give us something that we do not want but cannot escape, something that will break down our will for us, because we do want to die to self for Him, on an intellectual level at least. Haven't we prayed, "Lord, let me be all Yours?" So now He will show us how to become truly His alone.

We will be plunged into a new and unanticipated situation, crammed with confusion and frustration. We won't be able to turn to our own way, to the left or the right. "Follow Me," He will beckon, and we will cry, "Where, Lord? I can't even see You!"

"Just keep going," He will say. "I am with You."

"That's great," we will say, "but it would help if You gave me a little light."

"In the dark, you are to hold My Hand," He instructs. Since there is nothing else to hold, we grab for Him.

SANCTIFYING INTERRUPTIONS

Our penitent of the email sees this dying to self coming up in the dichotomy between how she wants to serve the Lord and how she actually has to serve Him in her family. Her spiritual director has given her superb advice in telling her to sanctify each moment and let the interruptions be the basis for prayer. What better model have we than Our Lord Whose public life seems to have been one constant interruption? Jesus goes to the Jordan to be baptized and begin His public ministry where John acknowledges Him to all present. As Jesus went forth into the desert for His forty days of fast, people who heard John must have stopped Him and said, "Who are You?" When He was in the desert, Jesus could not even pray in peace for satan was there with Him, to tempt Him. Then, when he returned to select His apostles and attend the wedding at Cana, His Mother interrupted Him, pointing out that the wine was in low supply. In Jesus's life, things went down hill, interruption wise, from then on. He couldn't even get away to pray or sleep in a boat or preach without someone coming up to be healed.

Scripture says an amazing thing about Jesus: "Son though he was, he learned obedience from what he suffered; and when he was made perfect, he became the source of eternal salvation for all who obey him, declared by God high priest according to the order of Melchizedek." (Hebrews 5:8-10)

If Jesus learned obedience through suffering, who are we to think we are going to learn it any other way? If we are truly going to die to self and live for God, then we are going to do it through suffering. This is because our wills are resilient and if we mow them down one day, they are going to sprout up again the next. The only way to attack self will is to dig out the root. If you have ever tried to dig out a very deeply rooted weed like burdock or dandelion or an overgrown bush, you know what hard work it is to get down to all those roots. Our self will is even more deeply rooted. So getting rid of it is a constant battle. Thank God we have God helping shovel!

BATTLING DISCOURAGEMENT

The sneaky danger in this frontal attack on our self will is discouragement. Our penitent seems to struggle with that herself. We have to remember one thing, which St. Francis de Sales pointed out most forcefully to his own penitents. We aren't going to be perfect in this life; we are going to fall, and we must not get discouraged. Satan uses discouragement to make us give up the struggle, and then we fall into greater acts of self will than ever. As long as we are getting up and attacking our self will again, we are making progress.

We eventually learn that "our time" isn't ours at all. It's God's time, as my spiritual director said to me. So we ought not be surprised when He takes it to use as He will. In the same way, our bodies aren't ours—they're His. Same with our minds, our talents, our possessions, our loved ones. The only things that really are ours, St. Francis of Assisi noted, are our sins. We can claim those! But everything else belongs to the One Who gave us life in the first place. We die to self when we can truly give it all back to Him. Over and over we will do this, like children who play the game of hot potato—tossing the hot potato back and forth between their hands until the music stops and we see who ends up with the spud. Mine, Yours, mine, Yours, mine, Yours. When we can look at all the things we are, do, and have and say, "Yours. Yours. Yours" and always and only "Yours" we will have arrived at total dying to self. For most of us, that moment won't come until our physical deaths when all we'll cart away with us, all that we will really possess, are those sins of ours. But even if we can't die to self perfectly or completely before we die once and for all, we have to keep trying.

I take heart from St. Frances of Rome. A nobleman's wife and mother of three children, she was very devout and devoted to works of charity. Alban Butler relates this of her in his Lives of the Saints:

When she was at her prayers, if summoned by Lorenzo (her husband) or asked to give orders about the house, she laid all aside to respond to the call of that duty. "It is most laudable in a married woman to be devout," she was wont to say, "but she must never forget that she is a housewife. And sometimes she must leave God at the altar to find Him in her housekeeping." Her biographers relate that once when she was reading our Lady's Office, a page was sent to fetch her. "Madonna, my master begs you to come to him," said the lad. She immediately closed the book and went. Three more times this interruption happened; but when at last she opened the book for the fifth time she found the words of the antiphon were written in gold.

So let us take heart from the trials we undergo and the falls we may take during them. We aren't made holier only through praying and attending Mass. The holiness comes in doing God's Will, moment by moment, as He unfolds it in our lives. What's happening to us is, indeed, HIS WILL, either by His permission or by His action. So however horribly things are going, God is at work to somehow bring good out of them. We may not know what that good completely consists of. But we can be certain of this: God is making us obedient through suffering. When we are perfected, we will then live for Him alone. Until that time, with God's grace to help us, we will keep digging away at the root of self will until we can answer with a resounding "yes" the question, "Do you really want to be Mine alone?"

Oh, Lord, give us the grace to answer "Yes!"

Madeline Pecora Nugent, CFP

LIKE A LITTLE LOST LAMB

Be quiet, little lost lamb
Stop your fearful trembling
The heart of the Good Shepherd
Knows there is one lamb missing
From his safe, loving fold
He will come for you soon
His perfect vision sees
The tracks your small feet made
Across the verdant pasture
He knows the sweetness
Of the poisoned spring you chose
To quench a thirsting soul
Soon his footsteps will sound
Upon the rocky soil
His tender hands will move
The thorns that hold you fast
High upon his shoulder,
He will bear you home.

—Virginia Walden Hogue (Poem 'Lost Lamb,' reprinted with permission from Maryknoll Magazine, March 2005)

So he told them this parable: "Which one of you, having a hundred sheep and losing one of them, does not leave the ninety-nine in the wilderness and go after the one that is lost until he finds it? When he has found it, he lays it on his shoulders and rejoices. And when he comes home, he calls together his friends and neighbors, saying to them, `Rejoice with me, for I have found my sheep that was lost.' Just so, I tell you, there will be more joy in heaven over one sinner who repents than over ninety-nine righteous persons who need no repentance. (Luke 15:3-7)

A GROUP FOR SINNERS

The Confraternity of Penitents is a confraternity (group that exists with the permission of a bishop) of penitents (sinners who are sorry for their past sins and who are praying for God's grace to do better). The CFP is not a bunch of holy people. It's a group of Catholics who want to be holy and who are willing to do whatever it takes to turn their lives over to God.

Repentance isn't a one shot deal. It's a continual process. We can hope that the little lost lamb, once found by the Good Shepherd, learned his or her lesson and stuck with the flock from then on out. Sticking with the flock would keep the little, senseless creature close to the Shepherd. However, knowing how dull witted sheep are, it's quite likely that the lost lamb strayed again and the Shepherd had to head out into the desert once more.

Note how gentle the Shepherd is in carting the lamb home. We don't hear of any beatings or of penning the poor creature up or hobbling it with chains to keep it from running off again. Gentle love is the antidote to racing off on one's own, even if that love has to be repeatedly given until it penetrates through a thick skull into the heart.

ANTIDOTE FOR DISCOURAGEMENT

We get discouraged if we fall back into sin. Maybe if we could admit the wisdom of St. Francis de Sales, we'd be more patient with ourselves (and with others who also fall). "If we knew well what we were, instead of being surprised at seeing ourselves fallen, we would be surprised how we could even stand." You see, we are still human and will remain so until we quit this earth. Only when we reach eternity will our humanity be transformed so that it will no longer be capable of sinning. In this life, we've got to be patient with ourselves.

All this does not mean that we are ho-hum about sin. We do the best we can, with God's grace, to keep from ever sinning again. We stay away from the occasions of sin. We avoid those situations that cause us to lose control. We squelch our urges to get back at others, to show how smart we are, or to make ourselves look better by making someone else look worse. We keep to the discipline of our lives, even when we don't feel like it. We pray even if we are tired. We forgo the food we ought not eat and are moderate in our diet and dress. We keep from splurging on things we don't need and try to use the money to help our neighbor, even if we don't have a particular concern for him, because we know it's the right thing to do. Much of the spiritual life is doing what's the right thing to do, even if we don't feel like doing it.

The little lamb got into trouble by doing what he felt like instead of what he ought to have done. And he discovered, as we all eventually do, that the green grass on the other side of the fence has got some nettles in it. Trouble is that sometimes it's embarrassing to crawl back under the barbed wire and rejoin the crew that never crossed the boundaries.

That's why the Good Shepherd comes looking for us. He makes it easier to come back because He's with us.

CARRIED ALONG HOME

When we recognize that we are being carried on the shoulders of the Shepherd, away from sin and into life, we can take heart. When the Shepherd picks us up, we might try to kick and bleat, but we can sense His grip on our struggling spirits and we know He's taking us someplace else. When we settle down and let Him have His way, we might find ourselves back in a flock of penitent souls, many of whom know exactly what it was like in the pasture we once thought was so superb. That's the value of a community like the Confraternity of Penitents. Those of us in this flock aren't going to look askance at the new lamb just carted in from the edge of the cliff or the depths of the briar patch. Chances are, some of us once frequented those spots and know all about them. How special it is to be among others who understand and who can look up to the Good Shepherd and see Him smiling down with an all-knowing, gentle grin!

If you're out there, afraid of what you've gotten into and confused that life isn't what you thought it ought to be, maybe it's time to start bleating for the Shepherd. He knows where you are, but if you call for Him, He knows you're ready to be found and will come a-running. Allow Him to pick you up and bring you into a better life. The flock He carries you to might not be the one you left, but you can be sure He's there with it. What more could you want?

Madeline Pecora Nugent, CFP

GIVING PENANCE
A GOOD NAME

A while ago, I was making phone calls, trying to nail down a retreat master for our yearly retreat. When I told Brother Isaac of the Capuchin Friars of the Renewal who we were—the Confraternity of Penitents—he remarked wryly, "Sounds like a fun group."

I laughed and told him that we are a "fun group." He chuckled knowingly because the CFR's are a penitential religious order, and he knows first hand the joys of a penitential life.

A priest once told our CFP minister (president) that he does not "like" the word "penance." After our minister spoke to him about the Confraternity of Penitents, he admitted that he "needed to do some of that Penance thing a little more often." When the minister shared with another good Catholic woman about the CFP, the woman commented, "People of Pain— that is what you Catholics like."

Let's face it. Penance has gotten a bad name in recent years. Like that good Catholic woman, people associate penance with pain, and people nowadays do whatever they can to avoid pain. Penance, to most people, means "giving up" things, and most folks don't want to give up too many. But penance is about receiving, not about giving up. It's about gain, not pain. In penance, a divine trade off takes place, a bartering with the Holy Spirit. We give God certain things and He gives us other things.

NO PAIN, NO GAIN

Several years ago our oldest son had to have a pneumothorax repaired. This is a weak place in the lung which can collapse and cause pain and difficulty breathing. James had two bouts with a collapsed lung before the surgeon decided that an operation was necessary. So one fine day, when James was perfectly healthy, he was admitted to the hospital for an operation which the surgeon described as "roughing up" the lung to cause the weak spot to toughen up and heal over. When James woke from the operation, he was in excruciating pain. When he was well, he drew a picture of the surgeon as a torturer. In the same way, penitents may have to endure some pain as they repair weaknesses in their own spiritual lives. But once they are repaired, the weaknesses no longer cause them pain or endanger the spiritual life. The catchy saying "No pain, no gain" was never more true than in the spiritual life.

SPIRITUAL EXCHANGE

SPIRITUAL EXCHANGE

Consider money. Money is of no value unless it's spent. You can't eat or wear money or build a shelter with it. Yet everyone is busily amassing money. Only misers hoard it. The rest spend their money because only by spending does one obtain what money can buy.

In the same way, holiness is not something you keep to yourself. It does not do the world much good if you stay in your home and do not reach out to others, whether through prayer or through service or, preferably, through both. Pope Francis wrote about this in his encyclical *The Joy of the Gospel*.

> 88. The Christian ideal will always be a summons to overcome suspicion, habitual mistrust, fear of losing our privacy, all the defensive attitudes which today's world imposes on us. Many try to escape from others and take refuge in the comfort of their privacy or in a small circle of close friends, renouncing the realism of the social aspect of the Gospel. For just as some people want a purely spiritual Christ, without flesh and without the cross, they also want their interpersonal relationships provided by sophisticated equipment, by screens and systems which can be turned on and off on command. Meanwhile, the Gospel tells us constantly to run the risk of a face-to-face encounter with others, with their physical presence which challenges us, with their pain and their pleas, with their joy which infects us in our close and continuous interaction. True faith in the incarnate Son of God is inseparable from self-giving, from membership in the community, from service, from reconciliation with others. The Son of God, by becoming flesh, summoned us to the revolution of tenderness.

God inspires us to offer ourselves more fully to Him through penitential practices. This offering then opens us to be able to receive more of what God wishes to give. God gives His gifts of peace, faith, love, trust, courage, and the other gifts of the Holy Spirit to those who, by their prayers and acts of charity, prepare their souls to receive these graces.

Until very recent times, Catholics understood this spiritual exchange. In modern times, the idea of having to do something spiritual to receive more of God's grace became unpalatable to some people. Some modern Catholics are like spoiled children who think that Daddy ought to give them wonderful things out of the goodness of His Heart, without their asking for these things or doing anything to deserve them or to prepare their souls to receive them. After all, if Daddy doesn't want to do that, why did He have kids?

ENTITLEMENT

This "entitlement mentality" is what has made the concept of penance odious to so many. If God isn't going to give spiritual goodies to me out of the goodness of His Heart, then I don't want them. I'm sure not going to work for them when He, by a whim of His Will, could grant them to me. What kind of a God is He to deny me something He can readily give?

The error comes in the deduction. Could God make all of us spiritual giants in an instant? The immediate answer seems to be, 'Of course. He's God. He can do anything He wants." Yes, God can do anything He wants, but He can't do something to us unless WE want it. God made our souls in His image and likeness. That means He has given us the ability to choose freely, an ability He possesses. God always chooses rightly, not because there are never evil choices before him, but because He wills to choose what is good, always. God gave us the ability to choose rightly, too, when He created our first parents. But in order for our nature to be truly like His, we had to have the freedom of choosing, which meant the freedom to choose anything. Not every choice is good.

Yes, God is able to make us saints. But He won't do it unless we will it. That allows our freedom of choice to be truly free. "Well," you might say, "I want God to make me a saint. So go ahead and do it, Lord."

Oh, but do we really mean that? Really? What is a saint? A saint is someone who lives in heaven with God and we are all, indeed, called to be saints. How does one go from earth to heaven? By doing always God's Will. One can no more expect to have done his own will all his life, and then go to heaven and do God's Will, than he can expect a wire twisted into one shape to suddenly become another shape without twisting it again.

THE PENANCE TWIST

"Let's do the TWIST!" Chubby Checker sang out in 1959 and 1960. The Twist was a dance done by an individual who twisted his whole body back and forth, up and down, to an upbeat song of the same name. You could sit and watch the Twist, but then you weren't "twisting." No one would emerge from the shadows and force you to dance the Twist. You either danced it of your own free will or you didn't. Some "twisted" in more spectacular fashion than others. Each person displayed his own idiosyncrasies. At the end of the dance, the "twisters" were generally breathless and, if they danced well, a little muscle sore. Those who "twisted" often and vigorously got a good physical workout and could actually tone up.

Penance is like the Twist. Our life experiences are the music and the beat which God provides. But we have to get into the mix and "twist." If we "twist" long enough and with enough vigor, our spiritual selves shape up.

As with any dance craze, the Twist was fun to do. A dancer could really get into the dance and make it his or her own. I used to do the Twist, and I don't ever recall seeing anyone do it with a grouchy face. You just had to grin when you were "twisting" even if you were getting plumb tuckered out. That's because the music and the dance and the company around you were exhilarating. And when you were done "twisting," you sure felt tired, but a good tired. You felt stronger, more alert, pepped up. You had a physical workout and you didn't even mind it!

Doing penance is like doing the Twist. If it's not fun, you're not doing it right. As we allow the music of our life's circumstances to echo around us, we "twist" to the beating Will of God in them. To do penance is to choose to enter the dance. To do penance in a particular way is to make the dance your own. All religious Orders which follow a Rule of Life do penance. That is, they have their members follow a specific plan for bringing their wills into conformity with God's Will.

TURNING OUR WILL BACK TO GOD'S

Every Order has a Rule and every Rule differs from every other Rule in the ways in which it requires the members to turn their wills back to God's Will. Willing to follow the Rule of the CFP is a way to turn our human wills back to God. Penance opens our souls to receive God's graces. Imagine booking a three month, all expense paid vacation in the Caribbean for the price of a banana. Our Rule's little penances cannot compare to the great graces that God wishes to give us if only we surrender our will to Him.

There is no way that a person who is properly disposed can follow a penitential Rule of Life, such as that of the CFP, without growing in sanctity to some degree. The growth is commensurate with the penitent's embracing of the Rule with abandon, obedience, and joy. But even if the Rule is embraced half heartedly, the living of that Rule is going to bring about changes in the penitent's spiritual life.

Moreover, when a penitent is properly disposed, he or she can offer their penances (those difficult life changes) to God as prayers for others. Therefore a person, who is properly disposed in prayer, fasting, and works of mercy, can offer those acts for others while he or she is simultaneously growing in greater conformity to God's Will.

THE JOY OF PENANCE

So "doing penance" is really a joy, especially if done with others. All groups doing penance ought to be joyful groups. That's because each penitent is focused on God Who is Love and on the neighbor who is God's love enfleshed, even if imperfectly. The penitent isn't focused on the hamburger he's not eating but on the God to Whom he is progressing. She's not begrudging the time spent in prayer but rather anticipating the time spent in eternity in the Presence of God. He's not complaining about clothes relinquished but rather rejoicing over the white robes of salvation awaiting those who dance in the courts of the Lamb.

The saints all recognized the joys of penance. Here are just a few of their many thoughts on the joys of a life of penance (conversion):

In the beginning there is a struggle and a lot of work for those who come near to God. But after that, there is indescribable joy. It is just like building a fire; at first it's smoky and your eyes water, but later you get the desired result. Thus we ought to light the divine fire in ourselves with tears and effort. —St. Syncletica

We should never allow even one thought of sadness to enter the soul. Have we not within us Him who is the joy of heaven! Believe me when I say that an obedient religious is a happy religious. — St. Therese Couderc

There are difficulties, sufferings, and worries. . . . But one beautiful day it will be all over, and we will find ourselves all united in heaven with the Blessed Trinity, with Mary most holy, with our dear ones and with the Sisters who have gone before us. This is our joy and our comfort. Courage! —Venerable Thecla Merlo

The heart is rich when it is content, and it is always content when its desires are fixed on God. Nothing can bring greater happiness than doing God's will for the love of God.— Blessed Br. Miguel Febres Cordero, FSC

Those whom the Holy Spirit calls to live lives of penance, by following a penitential Rule of Life, will do God's Will and thus experience His joy only if they walk on the path to which He beckons. The path of penance may twist at times. It may take sharp turns, lead into steep upgrades or down into seemingly bottomless valleys. The path of penance might wind through dry wastelands, it may bridge frightening chasms or wend through black, impenetrable forests that seem alive with frightening, invisible beasts. If the penitent follows that "light to his path," walking in the light of Him Who is Light, he will find joy in the persistent glow of that Light, feeble as it may sometimes seem. Indeed, the Light is always present in some degree for those who look for it. That Light of Christ will bring the penitent safely home to the eternal shores of peace and love where all is joy forever. Who in his right mind would not desire that?

Madeline Pecora Nugent, CFP

BUILDING BLOCKS OF THE SPIRITUAL LIFE

(This article is a composite of thoughts from several people some of whom wish to remain anonymous.)

Who is the Master Builder of your spiritual life? Yourself? Or God?

Often times on our journey into penance, we encounter what appear to be roadblocks on our spiritual journey. God may intend to use these as building blocks of our spiritual life. What are some of these and how may we allow God to use them?

Lord, I so want to be perfect. Yet I know that I am not. I want to follow You, yet feel so discouraged at times. Can You help me with my difficulties if I allow You to do so? Guide me, my Jesus, and help me to draw closer to You even now, when I do not see the way. Amen.

ABSENCE OF CONSOLATIONS:

Consolations are sweetness in prayer and tender emotions of love for God. These are often present when we begin to grow closer to God. In time, however, they usually lessen or even disappear. Do we still love God even though we no longer feel that burning, consuming love? Can we continue a spiritual journey that no longer seems as exciting or inviting as it used to?

God invites us to build our spiritual life on the God of consolations, not on the consolations of God. God wishes us to love Himself for Himself alone, not for the joys He can give us.

To build your spiritual life with this building block, persist in your spiritual life despite your feelings. Know that the Lord is building your perfection on the solid basis of your will to love Him. You will learn that you do not need His consolations nor to look for them. You need Him.

My Jesus, how I used to feel such love for You! And now I feel nothing. What is wrong with me, my Lord, in that I think that I love You only if I feel I do? Do I love my friend only when I am caught up in tears with love for him or her? Or is my love deeper and constant without those sensible feelings? My Lord, You are my true Friend, and more than Friend—You are Father, Brother, Spouse to me. Let me know that I do love You because I want to be with You always and You with me. Amen.

ARIDITY:

A desert is an arid place with no water or place of refreshment. Spiritual aridity is more than the lack of all sensible and spiritual consolations. In spiritual aridity, prayer grows wearisome, irksome, endless. Faith and trust seem dormant.

Aridity is painful. However, it is one of God's ways of detaching us from all created things, including joy in our devotion, so that we may learn to love God for His sake alone.

Aridity becomes a building block of our spiritual edifice when it teaches us humility. We realize that we cannot earn nor do we deserve God's consolations which are His freely given gifts. Aridity fosters virtue which we must embrace by acts of our will. Ask Our Lady, the saints, and your guardian angel to pray for you and with you. Ask a particular saint to prod you to maintain your spiritual exercises. In aridity, we unite with Christ in the Garden of Gethsemane and on the Cross. We persist in our spiritual life, discouraging as it may be, realizing that God is strengthening the structure through this time. God is calling us ever closer to Himself.

Oh, my Lord, help me. This desert seems devoid of any Living Water. Where are You in this dryness, my God? I no longer see You nor feel the gentle, refreshing breath of Your Love. Who will sustain me in this desert if not You, my God? It is night here in my soul. And who knows but that just over yonder, so close, so very close, is the Living Spring I seek, but the darkness keeps me from seeing It. Oh, my God, sustain me in this darkness. I put my trust in You. Amen.

FAILURE TO ENDURE:

Failure to endure is an attitude of changeableness in how we approach the spiritual life. Beginning joyfully to make changes in our lives, to root out sin, and to embrace God's Will, we slowly realize that overcoming our faults is more than simply wanting to do so. This is real work, wearying work, especially when we struggle so against our human nature that complains and protests. Weren't we contented before? Maybe we ought to simply give up and revert to how we used to be. We weren't so very bad, were we?

Failure to endure becomes a building block when we use it to build endurance. As athletes push themselves constantly to overcome weakness and build endurance, so must we in the spiritual life. Not every athlete wants to exercise endlessly, stretching muscles that complain and working out while the body shouts, "Give up! Rest!" If we want to win the spiritual race, we must "work out" when tired, move forward despite setbacks, and persist even if we want to quit.

Invite a friend or family member to go to Mass or confession with you once a month. Attend Mass at a church other than your parish. Stop for something to eat after Mass, if you have time. Make prayer time part of your morning and evening routine. Take baby steps and begin slowly but persist.

My dearest God, You are so constant in loving me and I am so inconstant in loving You. How could I make such promises of fidelity to You and now wish to abandon what I have promised? Did You ever tell me, my God, that the journey would be easy or the road short? Have You, rather, not promised the Cross and the narrow way? You Who bore Your Own Cross and Who walked the narrow way, help me to bear mine and walk with me. Let me run the race set before me and stick to the course, keeping in mind the prize that awaits me, eternal life with You. Give me perseverance, Lord. I want to be with You. Amen.

DISCOURAGEMENT/DESPAIR:

Discouragement and despair can set in when we begin to ask ourselves questions like these: Who am I fooling anyway? Look at my past sins. Look at how I was brought up. I know I am forgiven, but I am not good enough to be in any religious association. I could never live up to those ideals or be like those other people who are so holy. Why should I even try?

Discouragement and despair can become a building block when you realize that you are your own worst enemy. God came to save sinners, so you qualify! The CFP is a Confraternity of Penitents, that is, sinners who are trying to be better. If your past is sinful, great! You belong here with the rest of us. Believe in God's mercy, accept forgiveness, and move on.

Lord, here I am, a sinner. I am ashamed of my past, but You came for the likes of me. Accept me into Your Arms and forgive me. Help me to forgive myself. Amen.

OVER-EAGERNESS:

Over-eagerness is spiritually trying to do too much too quickly. It is like someone who is just learning to cook and who decides to make a gourmet meal as the first dinner or someone who is just learning woodworking and decides to build a china closet as the first project. The beginning cook does not yet know what blanching, searing, and sautéing are, nor does the beginning woodworker know how to do planing, sanding, drilling, or staining.

If our project is too grand, no matter what we are learning, we soon grow discouraged and weary. We think we can never succeed when, in fact, we could if only we moved more slowly, allowing ourselves to learn the techniques we need to achieve the goal.

Over-eagerness becomes a building block of the spiritual life when we set aside our unrealistic time frame of becoming holy and when we allow God and those who represent Him to lead us. Over-eagerness can foster obedience and patience, two virtues essential to spiritual growth. Spiritual growth is a GROWTH, and growth in every living thing takes TIME. Allowing God to grow us is a sturdy building block, in fact one of the major ones, in any spiritual edifice.

Oh, Lord, I so want to be holy! I want to serve You perfectly and totally. I know how much needs changing in my life. Why can't I do it all now, Lord? Oh, my Jesus, You know how much I need to grow. You know the pace I need to keep. You know what You want to make of me. Why am I too proud to move at Your pace, Lord, instead of fretting about being unable to move at my pace? Right now, I surrender to You all my plans and time frames, Lord. Give me peace about Your pace, Lord. I want to walk with You, not outrun You. Slow me down, Lord, so I can take the time to learn what You want to teach me. Give me patience, Lord, and total trust in You. Amen.

SCRUPLES:

Scruples are a spiritual disease which causes us to feel anxiety about having offended God for little or no reason. How can I be sure I am in the state of grace? What if God is angry with me? Does He still love me? How can I make up for what I have done?

By focusing intently on every little action or inaction of our lives, we become depressed and weary. We begin to mistrust ourselves and question God Who seems unmerciful to require a degree of perfection which we cannot seem to achieve.

Scruples become a building block of our spiritual life when we use them to purify our intentions and to meekly and obediently accept the judgment of our spiritual director or other spiritual counselor. This experience, while it may be humbling, is a growth producing one. We come to realize that God is a God of mercy and love, not a bookkeeper who is keeping minute track of every little infraction. Good Father that He is, God loves us despite our imperfections. He Who showed greatest mercy to sinners will surely be merciful to us who want to serve Him well. Overcoming scruples brings a peace about Who God is and who we are. We can love Him more, trust Him more, having been healed of this spiritual disease.

Oh, my dear, dear God. You are so perfect and I am so imperfect. Every time I look at myself, I see how I fall short of what I could be doing. I fail You at every turn, Lord. So I admit this. Now help me to go on, my Lord. Let me know that You are a Loving Father Who holds me close to His Heart and Who understands my weaknesses. Like a good papa who does not punish childish imperfections, so You do not frown at mine. You know my heart is good and my desire to follow You sincere. You love ME. Never let me doubt that. Amen.

DIFFICULTIES IN PRAYER:

Difficulties in prayer arise when the way one used to pray is no longer satisfying or useful. Am I growing lax? Do I no longer love God? Why can't I pray?

As we advance in the spiritual life, how we pray changes. In the beginning, vocal prayer is sufficient. Then meditation takes its place where the soul can gain many insights from prayerfully thinking about God, the mysteries of the Rosary, the life of Christ, the lives of the saints, and so on. As the soul advances, these forms grow wearisome and the soul cannot pray this way very well. Then prayer becomes the prayer of quiet presence to God, a loving attentiveness to Him with few or no words.

Difficulties in prayer become building blocks when we realize that God is moving us into deeper levels of union with Him. We will still pray vocal prayers and the Divine Office (if one is living according to the CFP Rule and Constitutions). We will still meditate at times or pray the Rosary. But we will allow God to lead us in our prayer so that He can make of us what He wishes. Be creative in your prayer time. Say the Rosary while taking a walk or on a treadmill. Pray the Liturgy of the Hours outdoors. Look for other ways to be creative.

My Lord, I want to spend time with You. But the time I spend seems so different than it used to. Are You calling me to spend my time with You a different way? Show me that way, my Lord. Help me to realize that I need not speak all the time to You. I need not constantly force a meditation. I need only be with You. Be with You in the silence, in my love for You and Yours for me, if that is Your wish for me. My Lord, may I be with You as You wish me to be. Amen.

DISTRACTIONS IN PRAYER:

Distractions in prayer are common. We begin to pray and find ourselves thinking about everything and everyone except about God. Why can't we keep our mind on our prayers? Is there something wrong with us spiritually?

Distractions in prayer become building blocks when we humbly realize that they are common to everyone. One good way to deal with them is to offer to God, at the beginning of prayer, all the distractions and ask Him to bless every person or situation that comes to your mind while at prayer. In that way, the distraction becomes a prayer. If you are plagued with distractions, don't go back to the beginning of your prayer and start over. Pray for the elements and people of the distraction and keep going. God knows that you are trying.

Lord, the world and all its allurements crowd me and distract my soul from You. It seems to be a constant battle. Sometimes I am so weary that I cannot even tell You how much I love You. Yet You know my innermost thoughts and desires. It seems that the only time I really pray with fervor is when I am confronted by or need in my life or someone else's. Help me to see You when I face these distractions. I pray for the people and events in them all, right now, that You will shower Your graces upon them. Help me to trust You and leave all in Your Hands, including my ability to pray. Amen.

COMPARISON WITH OTHERS:

Comparison with others occurs when we look at others and see that we fall short of where they are on the spiritual journey. We feel they are advancing more quickly than we are, or that they are not experiencing the difficulties we have, and we feel insufficient next to them. We are embarrassed by our slow pace or our spiritual difficulties and become tempted to abandon the spiritual walk because we don't see ourselves being as "good" as others.

Comparison with others can become a building block when it births in us a realism about spiritual growth. Just as every variety of plant grows at its own pace, and matures its fruit in its own genetic time table, so does God grow us according to the timetable for the spiritual fruition of our own souls. A tomato is not a carrot nor does it grow the same way. When we realize that God knows best, for He has created us to be who we are, we cease comparing ourselves with others and peacefully and trustingly allow the Master Builder to build us into the structure He has designed.

Dearest Jesus, I look at the saints in Your Kingdom and those around me in my life, and I think that I am so far from them that I shall never attain sanctity. But where I am now does not matter, does it, Lord, if I am where You want me to be? What matters is that I move closer to You in the ways and at the pace You set. For You want me to be with You eternally, and that is what I want, too, Lord. Give me patience with my spiritual progress, Lord. Grow me as You see fit. I know You will achieve Your Will in my life if only I allow You to do so. So may I be perfectly content with Your work in me. May I know that, if I allow You a free hand, You WILL bring me to Eternal Joy with You. Amen.

BUSYNESS:

Busyness is common to us all. Often after we begin to grow in the spiritual life, our lives suddenly become super busy. There is a saying, "If the devil can't make you sin, he'll make you busy." Workloads increase, the computer crashes, someone gets very ill, we are expecting a new baby, we must move, we need to get another job, we decide to go back to school, the kids take up sports and we must drive them, and so on. Things like these take up super amounts of time. Suddenly we feel that we are under so much pressure that we just can't pursue the spiritual life as we would like. And so we are tempted to quit.

Busyness can become a building block in our spiritual edifice when we use it as a means of surrender to God's Will and to trust Him for our growth and not ourselves. If we are busy because of circumstances beyond our control, we need to realize that these situations are part of God's plan for us. Ask Him how He wants you to follow Him now. Busyness makes us realize that God is flexible. What worked last week in our walk with Him may not work this week, but that is OK as long as we are still walking with the Lord.

Help, Lord! How am I ever going to cope with all that is going on in my life? Here I envisioned myself spending quality time with You, and I don't even have time to eat in peace. My Lord, what is happening here? Give me the grace to calm down, to take a deep breath, and to feel You here with me, right now. If I can't meet my expectations, then help me to lower my expectations. If folks need me, let me respond to them in love as You did. I want to follow You my way, and You are having me follow You in Your Way. So be it, my Lord. I surrender to the duties and obligations that I am now facing. Show me how to love and serve You better through them. Amen.

There really are no excuses if you want to unite yourself more closely with the Lord. Every spiritual roadblock can become a building block. May God show you how!

DIRECTORY

The Directory of the Confraternity of Penitents is a detailed description of procedures and protocol which supplements the Rule and Constitutions. Because the Confraternity is growing and evolving, the Directory will necessarily change to meet the needs of the Membership. Therefore, with the exception of the areas listed in the Minister General section of the Constitutions, the Minister General, with the advice of some or all of the CFP Officers and Advisors, and the approval of the Visitor, may make changes to the Directory at any time, as deemed necessary.

We ask God's blessings upon our efforts and seek His grace in surrendering to His guidance, for the Confraternity belongs to Him.

May 2010

"Blessed are those who cherish the name of Mary. Her favor will sustain them in the midst of trials, and they will bring forth fruits of salvation." *St. Anthony of Padua*

<u>Prayer to Our Sorrowful Mother
for the Church and the Pontiff</u>

Most Holy Virgin and Mother, your soul was pierced by a sword of sorrow in the passion of your divine Son, and in His glorious resurrection, you were filled with unending joy in His triumph! Obtain for us who call upon you, to be such partakers in the adversities of holy Church and in the sorrows of the Sovereign Pontiff as to be found worthy to rejoice with them in the consolations for which we pray, in the charity and peace of the same Christ our Lord. Amen.

DIRECTORY OF THE CONFRATERNITY OF PENITENTS

PURPOSE

FAMILY IN THE CHURCH

Penitents should never entertain spiritual pride. They must remember that the Rule is no more than a means of following Christ through a specific method of personal conversion. All the faithful are called to the goal and end of holiness but may be called to follow the Master by other means or other Rules.

Confraternity Members and Associates are living a religious Rule of Life but as lay people. Because they are laity, CFP Members and Associates refrain from wearing clothing that could give the impression of a religious habit. This is done by following the clothing guidelines in the CFP Rule.

The CFP Rule of Life is published in the CFP Handbook and on the web site of the Confraternity.

CANONICAL STATUS

Bishop Kevin Rhoades' letter of 3 January 2014 followed Bishop Thomas Tobin's letter of 11 February 2009, both letters confirming the canonical status of the Confraternity of Penitents as a Private Association of the Faithful. Copies of these letters are found in Appendix U.

PUBLICITY

Publicity spreads the message of penance to others. The primary purpose of publicity is to encourage others to conversion (penance), whether or not they ever live the CFP Rule. Letterhead, web pages, and other Confraternity documents and publications may use the Vision, Prayer, Motto, Action, and/or Mission of the CFP as part of their message and may display the San Damiano Crucifix, the crucifix of conversion. The Charism of the CFP is publicized via the web site penitents.org and via the print media to include a monthly newsletter and occasional magazine and newspaper articles. Members and Associates without internet access, as well as CFP Spiritual Assistants and Spiritual Advisors, receive the newsletter free via postal mail. Any others wishing the printed newsletter pay for a yearly subscription, records of which are kept by the CFP Treasurer.

The CFP may be promoted locally by CFP Members and Associates through Days of Recollection or other events, with the permission of the Regional Minister, Minister General, the appropriate local clergy and, if necessary, their diocesan Bishop. Local events will be posted on the CFP website through the CFP Office.

The Diocese of Fort Wayne - South Bend must approve in advance any widespread publicity regarding the CFP. Such publicity shall be conducted through the CFP Office with the direction of the Visitor and the Minister General.

SPIRITUAL DIRECTOR

A Spiritual Director is indispensable in assisting anyone who wishes to advance in the spiritual life. Spiritual Directors provide guidance, feedback, and support in developing union with God. All CFP Members and Associates are to have a Spiritual Director by the middle of their first year Novice formation and to continue to have a Spiritual Director as long as they live the CFP way of life. No one is allowed to pledge to live the CFP Rule without the permission of a Spiritual Director. Members and Associates are responsible for obtaining their own Spiritual Directors. The CFP Office can offer guidance. Without a Member's consent, no one is to question a Spiritual Director regarding a directee. Spiritual Directors are not obligated to share information on their directees.

CFP leaders or the Minister General can answer any questions that a Spiritual Director may have regarding spiritual direction of penitents or regarding the Confraternity or its way of life. If a leader is unsure of the answer, he or she should apply to higher levels of leadership to obtain the information. Letters from the Diocese of Fort Wayne - South Bend, attesting to Diocesan permissions in regard to the Confraternity of Penitents, are available for Spiritual Directors who request them.

Spiritual Directors are to be Roman Catholic priests, deacons, or religious who are totally in agreement with all the teachings of the Roman Catholic Church and also totally in favor of the CFP Rule of Life and of the penitent's desire to live it. The Visitor must approve any lay Catholic who will serve as Spiritual Director for a CFP Member or Associate. Spiritual Directors ought to meet privately and in person with the penitent, if at all possible. If not possible, spiritual direction may be given via phone, postal mail, or email. In the absence of other options, a person's confessor can serve as a Spiritual Director provided that he agrees to offer brief spiritual direction in the confessional. So as not to cause inconvenience to others by taking up so much of the priest's time, penitents who will be receiving spiritual direction during confession ought to consider confessing weekly. Penitents who lose a Spiritual Director should seek a replacement as soon as possible. Penitents cannot continue as Members and Associates of the Confraternity of Penitents unless they have a Spiritual Director or are actively seeking one.

LEGALITIES

TAX EXEMPT STATUS

The Confraternity is registered, at its Indiana Office address, as a non profit, tax exempt entity with the State of Indiana, USA, and as a 501c3 organization with the United States Internal Revenue Service. Tax free status means that the Confraternity of Penitents, or any of its Chapters and Circles, does not pay taxes on items or services for Confraternity use. In addition, all contributions to the Confraternity of Penitents, over and above the actual cost of goods received, are tax deductible. The CFP Office files the paperwork necessary to retain the tax exempt status.

The Confraternity of Penitents also carries a group exemption so that all CFP Chapters and Circles, that are registered with the Internal Revenue Service under the parent organization of the Confraternity of Penitents, also benefit from the tax free status. The CFP Office registers new Chapters and Circles with the IRS, and it also updates information yearly on existing ones.

CFP OFFICERS

In order to maintain its tax free status under the state of Indiana, the CFP must have four elected or appointed Officers who fill the roles of President, Vice President, Secretary, and Treasurer. The President cannot simultaneously hold the office of Secretary. The CFP Minister General shall be listed as the President; the Ministerial Assistant as the Vice President; the CFP Messenger as the Secretary; the CFP Treasurer as the Treasurer.

REQUIRED COUNCIL MEMBERS

The State of Indiana also requires a minimum of three elected or appointed directors to serve on a Council of directors. The CFP Articles of Incorporation state that the Council of directors shall consist of a minimum of seven directors and a maximum of

416

eleven directors. The four CFP Officers (Minister General, Ministerial Assistant, CFP Messenger, CFP Treasurer) will automatically serve on the Council of directors. The Minister General shall appoint the additional directors (three to seven in number) from the CFP Membership, Associates, Lay and/or Spiritual Advisors, to act as consultants to the Minister General. The Visitor shall approve these appointments.

At least one yearly Council meeting must be held and a quorum (50% plus one) of directors present to conduct business. For convenience, the annual meeting is held in conjunction with the annual CFP Life Pledged Chapter or CFP retreat. Annual reports of CFP activities, Regions, and finances, as well as minutes from the previous Council meeting, are mailed to CFP Council members by two weeks before the scheduled meeting to be reviewed at the Council meeting. The Visitor, or another Roman Catholic priest, deacon, or religious, shall be present at all Council meetings. The Directory is reviewed at least once yearly at the Council meeting although anyone may address the Directory at any other time.

CFP OFFICE

The Confraternity of Penitents' Office is located at 1702 Lumbard Street, Fort Wayne, Indiana 46803 USA. The Minister General oversees the office work and also may appoint or hire an office manager and/or assistants whose decisions will be subject to the Minister General for approval.

The CFP Office retains paper and electronic files on each Member, Associate, and Affiliate and on Confraternity business.

Each Member's and Associate's file consists of formation applications, baptismal certificate, letters from Formators attesting to successful completion of formation, documents of pledging, date of death or withdrawal from the Confraternity, and other important information. If someone withdraws from the CFP, requests a leave of absence, or drops from formation, the Office will keep their records for a minimum of five years, although files may be kept longer. The file on Affiliates consists of name, address, Affiliate application, and pertinent contact information.

The Confraternity Office shall also retain original copies of government and tax documents, letters to and from Diocesan officials, and paperwork which details the history and activities of the CFP such as newsletters, retreat reports, Council meeting minutes, and so on. All important paperwork regarding the Confraternity is to be forwarded to the CFP Office.

Electronic files of all pre-inquirers, Inquirers, Associates, and Members include their name, address, phone number, email, year of formation or of pledging, Chapter/Circle affiliation, documentation of Baptismal Certificate, birth date, Formator, Regional Minister, and so on. Changes, deletions, and additions to this list should be made to the CFP Office as they occur.

As needed or requested, the CFP Office makes information filed at the Office available to Regional Ministers, Visitor, diocesan officials and/or the Bishop. The Minister General, with the consent of the Visitor, must approve requests from any other persons for this information. In addition, permission must be granted by the person(s) whose information will be shared.

CFP photos and photo albums are kept at the CFP Office. Photos may be used in a public manner with the approval of the persons photographed.

The CFP Office postal mails or emails information on the CFP to those requesting it, processes requests for CFP leadership to conduct a retreat or day of recollection, and handles any business involving the international nature of the Confraternity. The Office writes, edits, and publishes the CFP Handbook which contains all formation lessons, the CFP Rule and Constitutions, and much other information. It is also responsible for updating and publishing this Directory.

The CFP Office maintains three CFP email addresses, copenitents@yahoo.com, cfpenitents@gmail.com, and bspenance@hotmail.com, and responds to contacts through them and through postal mail or phone. It maintains various email lists to include a public email list which can be subscribed to via the web site, a list for CFP Members, Inquirers and Associates only, an Affiliate list, and a list for those celebrating Eucharistic Adoration for CFP intentions, supporters, officials, and participants. Urgent prayer requests and general information are sent to the public list. Specific information regarding Membership goes to the Membership list. Inspirational thoughts on the Eucharist are sent to the Adorer List. Any specific mailings to Affiliates go to the Affiliate list.

It is the responsibility of the CFP Office to insure that the CFP web site www.penitents.org is maintained.

GIFT SHOP

The CFP Holy Angels Gift Shop may be located at the CFP Office or another location. The CFP Holy Angels Gift Shop is an on line gift shop carrying items, offered for a suggested donation, that promote penance and that instruct in the Catholic Faith. The Gift Shop manager and accountant, both of whom are appointed and/or hired by the Minister General with the advice of the Officers, maintains and manages the Gift Shop. With the approval of the Minister General, the manager locates items to offer and sets prices and postage expenses. Before production and sale, any items alleging to be products of the CFP and/or carrying the CFP name must be approved by the Minister General and Visitor with the advice of the CFP Officers.

Gift Shop profits above operating expenses revert to the Confraternity Treasury. Both the manager and the accountant present a yearly report to the CFP Officers at the yearly Council meeting. The CFP Office maintains the Gift Shop web pages.

BUSINESS

Business is on going in the CFP, with leaders acting and consulting via postal mail, phone, and electronic means. English is the primary language for all CFP documents and correspondence. The Minister General and Visitor approve translations into other languages.

The CFP is a family in the Church, and any Member may speak to any other at any time and about any topic. However, both Members and Associates must agree to the exchange of personal information (phone numbers, emails, addresses, and so on) before contact information is shared.

Anyone may make suggestions, which are brought to the attention of the appropriate CFP leadership for consideration.

CFP leaders determine their own work hours and receive no monetary compensation for their work. They maintain regular communication with other leaders, Members, Affiliates, and Associates. They keep confidential any "confessions" and personal information. CFP leaders encourage penitents, walk with them on the spiritual journey, and pray for all doing penance worldwide. .

MONIES

The CFP Treasurer handles all monies directly connected with the parent organization. The Treasurer makes a monthly report of income and expenses to the Membership and a yearly report at the annual Council meeting. Regular expenses may include phone bills, internet access, postage, printing, web site registration, filing fees, retreat master expenses and stipend, and so on. Before being incurred, any at large expenses in these categories (20% or more of the total CFP Treasury) must be approved by the Minister General with the consent of the Officers.

Unless a Region has its own Treasurer and bank account, Regional Ministers may request from the CFP Officers that expenses to be incurred regarding their Region be reimbursed by the CFP Treasurer. An estimate of the money to be reimbursed should accompany this request. If the Officers approve the reimbursement, the Regional Minister shall submit to the CFP Treasurer proof of the expenses so that reimbursement can be made. This same procedure is to be followed by any other person who requests reimbursement of expenses from the CFP Treasury.

The CFP Treasurer will maintain an Alms Fund. Those requesting alms will write a letter of application to their Regional Minister and include three references, one of which must be from their parish priest on parish letterhead, attesting to the need. If deemed worthy of consideration, the Regional Minister shall discuss the request with the Minister General, Treasurer, and other CFP Officers and a decision reached.

With the approval of the Council, the CFP Treasurer may have an assistant or assistants who will be in charge of certain specific accounts. The Treasurer, or an assistant

Treasurer directly responsible to the Treasurer, shall file the necessary yearly tax report with the United States Internal Revenue Service.

STRUCTURE[45]

The detailed structure of the Confraternity includes various Officers and advisors as well as Members and others, who, by the grace of the Holy Spirit, comprise the structure of the CFP within the Church. This structure is as follows:

Visitor[46] *(Priest appointed or approved by Bishop of the Diocese of Fort Wayne - South Bend, Indiana USA. No term of office)*

|

Minister General *(The Founder,*[47] *whom the Holy Spirit used to bring about the Confraternity, will occupy this position for life or until unable to serve. Thereafter, the Minister General will be elected by Life-Pledged Members from their number. Elected term of office: 6 consecutive one year terms. Chair of CFP Council of Directors)*

|

CFP Officers: CFP Ministerial Assistant, CFP Treasurer, CFP Messenger *(Life Pledged Members elected by Life Pledged Members unless there is an insufficient number of capable Life Pledged Members willing to serve. Act as consultants to the Minister General. Term of office: 1 year. Members of CFP Council of Directors)*

|

Three to Seven Additional Council Members *(CFP Members and/or others appointed by Minister General. Act as consultants to Minister General. Term of office: 1 year).*

|

Lay and Spiritual Advisors *(Appointed by Visitor, and/or Minister General to act as consultants to the Confraternity. No term of office.)*

Regional Spiritual Advisors *(Roman Catholic priests, deacons, or religious chosen by*

---

45   The Confraternity of Penitents acknowledges that God, through the Pope and the Magisterium, is the ultimate Authority regarding the Confraternity of Penitents.

46   Subject to the Bishop of the Diocese of Fort Wayne - South Bend, the Visitor has ultimate authority over the internal operation of the Confraternity of Penitents.

47   Acknowledging the Divine Foundation of the Confraternity of Penitents, the Confraternity likewise recognizes Madeline Pecora Nugent as the person who corresponded with the call of the Holy Spirit to found the CFP. It was she who, in July of 1994, received an interior call, "I want you to live the Rule of 1221." In the fall of the same year, she received a second interior call to "Pray for more people to live the Rule of 1221" and, later that same year, to "Pray that more people would live the Rule of 1221 and enter this fraternity. And pray that more people would live the Rule of 1221 nationwide and worldwide." Madeline, in consultation with her spiritual director and others, acted on that call by laying down the organizational foundation for what first was called the Brothers and Sisters of Penance and which has been refounded as the Confraternity of Penitents.

Regional Ministers to act as consultants in Church matters. No term of office)

|

Regional Ministers *(Appointed by Minister General: Term of office: 1 year)*

|

Assistant Regional Ministers, Regional Treasurers, Regional Messengers
(Appointed by Regional Minister as needed: Term of office: 1 year),

|

Chapter and Circle Spiritual Assistants *(Roman Catholic priests, deacons, religious. No term of office)*

|

Chapter and Circle Officers: Minister, Assistant Minister, Messenger, Treasurer
(Elected within Chapter and Circle: Term of office: 1 year)

|

Formators *(Appointed by Minister General, Regional Minister, and/or Chapter/Circle Minister: Work with Members and Associates in formation. Maximum number of Members and Associates per Formator: five. Term: Until Member pledges.)*

|

Members *(Minimum of 4 years in formation, then pledge for life or a year. May vow for life with permission of Spiritual Director.)*

|

Associates *(Do formation but cannot pledge, vote, hold office, or become Formators)*

|

Affiliates *(Clergy, Religious, Laity who pray for and support the CFP)*

RIGHTS, DUTIES, OBLIGATIONS

CHAPTERS AND CIRCLES

Chapters and Circles are to choose a patronal title for their group, considering especially either a title for any person of the Blessed Trinity, a title of the Blessed Mother, or the name of a saint or beati of the Roman Catholic Church. Every Chapter and Circle shall have a different name which must be approved by the Regional Minister, Minister General, and Visitor. If they wish, Chapters and Circles are permitted to make their own banner which ought to include the CFP symbol of the San Damiano Crucifix as well as the name of their local group and image of their patron, if desired. Banners must be approved by the Minister General, Regional Minister, and Visitor and may be used publicly.

Once the Chapter or Circle is established with Officers, title, and Spiritual Assistant, its Chapter or Circle Minister, or another Member designated by the Minister, must complete the Chapter and Circle Application and mail it to the CFP Office. Established Chapters and Circles also inform their diocesan Bishops of their existence. A sample letter of introduction to a Bishop is found in Appendix K of this Directory. The Regional Minister can assist in composing this letter. Chapters and Circles should keep their diocesan Bishop informed at least yearly regarding local meetings and activities, and they are to follow his directives.

Chapter and Circle Members and Associates gather at least monthly in either a Member's home, a parish meeting room, or any other suitable location at a time agreeable to the Membership. Gatherings in parishes require the permission of the parish priest. Those who do not or cannot attend Chapter or Circle meetings regularly are not considered part of said Chapter or Circle unless their absence is necessitated by illness or infirmity (for example, Confraternity Members and Associates who used to attend meetings but have become shut-ins.)

Unless otherwise arranged, the Minister conducts the monthly meeting which should be joyful and positive and begin and end with the Meeting Prayers which are in the Prayers section of this Handbook. A meeting may also include the Mass, part of the

Divine Office, the Rosary, or other prayers. The gathering includes a brief business meeting, covering the Messenger's minutes, the Treasurer's report, and any other items of interest. There should also be a teaching given by the Spiritual Assistant. Formation may cover elements of the Roman Catholic Faith, the Confraternity, and the Rule and involve faith sharing by all present. Members and Associates also review formation lessons for the month and share their responses to the questions. Assigned Formators within the group keep a ledger of lessons successfully completed and inform their Minister and their Regional Minister at the end of the formation year (prior to Ash Wednesday). The gathering should also include a time of fellowship, possibly with a meal or refreshments.

At the beginning of each formation year (that is, Ash Wednesday), each Chapter or Circle should send to the CFP Office a report containing the following information: Chapter or Circle name, location, contact information, Spiritual Assistant, Officers, and Membership by name and year of formation.

Such local gatherings strengthen the penitents in faith and in living the Rule, and they foster the loving community called for by the CFP Rule. The Regional Minister assists in the formation and growth of Chapters and Circles as detailed in the Regional Minister section of this Directory.

Once a Chapter is established, it retains its Chapter designation even if the Membership falls below five. Should the Membership of the Chapter or Circle be reduced to one, the group shall be designated as "inactive" until at least one additional Member joins.

VISITOR

The CFP Visitor, Spiritual Advisors, and Diocesan officials address questions of Church doctrines, regulations, and Canon Law.

The Visitor must be easily accessible and is on all Internet CFP mailing lists unless otherwise requested. He is informed of all important CFP decisions and affairs, and he offers input into them. The Visitor also advises the Minister General on all matters involving the Faith and the Church and on important spiritual, organizational, and Member matters which involve the Confraternity. As necessary, the Visitor takes disciplinary and/or corrective action if any Confraternity matter or individual deviates from official Church teaching or from what is contained in the CFP Rule and Constitutions.[48] The Visitor exercises final approval over all matters involving the Confraternity of Penitents.

Because the Visitor is a busy person, only those CFP matters which definitely need his attention are presented to him. Therefore, anyone who wishes to consult the Visitor directly is to present the request first to either their Regional Minister or to the Minister General who will determine if only the Visitor can be consulted about the matter or if another CFP Spiritual Advisor or leader could help.

---

48   Details on the Visitor's disciplinary authority are in the Difficult Members and Associates Section of this Directory.

The Visitor and Minister General work closely together. The Visitor has the final say regarding the text of printed matter not involving the Rule or Constitutions of the CFP. He consults the Minister General for input prior to making any decisions which involve the Confraternity as a whole or any Member in particular.

MINISTER GENERAL

With the permission of the Diocese of Fort Wayne – South Bend, the Founder of the Confraternity of Penitents will be confirmed in the position of Minister General annually for the remainder of her life or until unable to serve.

When the Founder can no longer serve, her successor as the Minister General will be elected by Life-Pledged Members from their number. The Minister General's term of office shall be confirmed annually for six consecutive years. The Visitor must approve the choice of the Minister General and the Bishop must be informed.

At least once yearly, the Minister General prepares a report for the Bishop's office that summarizes the CFP activities and Membership for the year. This may be also sent to other appropriate Church officials.

Unless the Minister General makes other arrangements, he or she approves all appointments to any CFP office or committee before they take effect.

All emergencies in the CFP are immediately brought to the attention of the Minister General who determines, through prayer and in consultation with the CFP Officers and the Visitor, the proper course of action.

The Minister General determines the number of Regions and their geographical boundaries.

MINISTERIAL ASSISTANT

The CFP Ministerial Assistant is the Minister General's primary assistant and completes the duties assigned by the Minister General. These include:
Appointing the Nominating Committee for all international elections
Serving on the CFP Retreat and Life-Pledged Chapter Committees along with those who have volunteered to be on these committees
Appointing additional Retreat Committee members as needed
Assigning Mentors, from CFP Life-Pledged Members, for those about to be pledged who have not selected a particular life pledged member as mentor.

CFP MESSENGER

The CFP Messenger records the minutes of the annual Council meeting and sends them, through the CFP Office, to all life pledged members. Annual reports of CFP activities, regions, and finances as well as minutes from the previous Council meeting are mailed to CFP Council members by two weeks before the scheduled meeting to be reviewed at the Council meeting. The CFP Messenger will take minutes/notes of all discussions at the Annual Pledged Chapter and will distribute them through the CFP Office, along with any handouts provided to members in attendance, to all Life Pledged members unable to attend the Chapter.

CFP TREASURER

The CFP Treasurer oversees the CFP bank account, Alms Fund, and Retreat Fund, and any other bank accounts for the CFP, pays all CFP bills, and deposits all CFP funds.[49] With the permission of the Minister General, there may be more than one Treasurer.

LAY AND SPIRITUAL ADVISORS

Lay and Spiritual Advisors offer guidance to the Minister General in decision making regarding the Confraternity. Regional Ministers may appoint Spiritual Advisors as consultants within their Regions. Ultimate approval of all Lay and Spiritual Advisors rests with the Visitor.

REGIONAL MINISTERS AND OTHER REGIONAL OFFICERS AND ADVISORS

Regional Ministers keep accurate Membership lists and inform the CFP Office of any changes in Membership data. This should be checked periodically. A sample letter to Regional Members and Associates, for whom the Regional Minister does not have updated information, is in Appendix L of this Directory.

Either the Minister General, the Regional Minister, or the Chapter or Circle Minister, or any two or three in consultation with each other, appoints Formators for specific Members and Associates. The Minister General approves all such appointments and retains contact with all Regional Ministers either personally or through a delegate.

Regional Ministers oversee all Formators in their Regions, either directly, through an Assistant Regional Minister, or through Chapter or Circle Ministers. They are in touch regularly with all penitents in their Regions. Regional Ministers may themselves be Formators for up to five Members or Associates either within or outside their Region. Unless they are removed from the role of Formator or request discontinuance of that role, they continue as Formators after their year long appointment as Regional Minister ends.

Regional Ministers insure that formation applications are received by the CFP Office and that Membership information in their Region is kept up to date. They may do this by themselves collecting all formation and pledging applications and supplementary materials from penitents in their Regions, and submitting them to the CFP Office. Or

---

49   The CFP Treasurer's duties are detailed under the Legalities Section (Monies Subsection) of this
       Directory

they assign this task to an assistant or may have those in formation submit such applications to the CFP Office directly.

At their discretion and with the Minister General's approval, Regional Ministers may appoint an Assistant Regional Minister, Regional Treasurer, and Regional Messenger as well as a Regional Spiritual Advisor who must be totally in conformity with the teachings of the Roman Catholic Church and completely supportive of the Rule, Constitutions and Structure of the CFP, as a consultant in Church matters.

At least once yearly at the Life-Pledged Chapter, the CFP Office updates Regional Ministers on all pre-inquirers, Inquirers, Members in formation, Associates, Affiliates, and Pledged and/or Vowed Members in their Regions, according to the official CFP address list. Regional Ministers maintain a Regional address list with note of Formator and year of formation for each penitent. Any discrepancies between this list and that supplied by the CFP Office are reported to the CFP Office which ascertains the correct information.

Regional Ministers encourage and assist with the development, continuance, and growth of Chapters and Circles within their Region. They foster the emergence of new groups by putting Members and Associates, who live in close proximity, in touch with one another, as long as each party agrees. Regional Ministers periodically contact emerging and existing Chapters and Circles, through their Ministers or other contacts, to ascertain the status of their Membership and the activities of the local group. Regional Ministers are alert to the location of new Inquirers and pre-inquirers and, if they are near any existing Chapter or Circle, put the local group's Minister in touch with these inquiring people. Once these Inquirers are attending local gatherings, the Regional Minister shifts primary contact with them to their Chapter or Circle Minister. The Regional Minister keeps the Minister General informed of Chapter and Circle developments as they occur.

In regard to any regional activities, Regions are to be self supporting financially. With the permission of the Minister General and their Regional Officers, they may initiate fund raisers, collect donations, and disburse funds. They may not, however, require Membership dues. All Regional Treasurers must present an annual report of income and expenses to the CFP Office.

With the permission of the Minister General and Council of directors, Regional Officers may also plan and conduct regional Council of directors meetings and gatherings of CFP Members.

CHAPTER OR CIRCLE SPIRITUAL ASSISTANT

The Spiritual Assistant, after consultation with the Chapter or Circle Minister and other Officers, has final authority in the Chapter or Circle regarding Members and Associates and their observance of the CFP Rule, provided that the Rule, Constitutions, and Church teachings are not modified or disregarded.

The Spiritual Assistant shall meet with the Chapter or Circle monthly, except for occasional, unavoidable absence, and will provide teaching to the Chapter and Circle attendees regarding the Rule and the Catholic Faith. He or she will be available to Members and Associates for consultation and advice and may grant dispensations to the Rule in singular instances.[50] Additional duties are detailed in the Special Situations Section of this Directory.

REGIONAL, CHAPTER, AND CIRCLE OFFICERS: GENERAL INFORMATION

Regional, Chapter, and Circle Officers assure that, within their jurisdiction, CFP business is being conducted efficiently and penitents are being properly formed in the CFP way of life. Assistant Ministers, Messengers, and Treasurers are subject to their appropriate Minister (Chapter/Circle or Regional). Chapter and Circle Ministers are subject to their Regional Ministers. Regional Ministers are subject to the Minister General, following the Order of Governance delineated in the Constitutions.

In Chapters and Circles, the founding members, in consultation with the Regional Minister and with the approval of the Minister General, determine an initial slate of Officers, consisting of, at minimum, a Minister and Messenger. Once the Circle or Chapter grows to a size warranting it, an Assistant Minister, Treasurer, and other Officers, may be added.

REGIONAL, CHAPTER, AND CIRCLE MINISTER AND ASSISTANT MINISTER

Ministers are penitents' primary contacts with the Confraternity. They should be true examples of humility, faith, honesty, and love to the Membership and should embrace the observance of the CFP Rule with joy. They should have good skills in dealing with others, be able to identify with others, and be capable of seeing things from other viewpoints while also remaining faithful to the Rule, Constitutions, and the Church. Duties specific to the Regional Minister are listed earlier in this Directory. The duties listed in this section are common to Chapter, Circle, and Regional Ministers but within their own jurisdictions–Chapter and Circle Ministers exercise jurisdiction over Chapter and Circle Members and Associates and Regional Ministers over isolated Members and Associates. All decisions of the Ministers are subject to the Minister General's approval.

Within its jurisdiction, the Minister is responsible for the governance of the group, for organizing, publicizing, and conducting business meetings, and for setting up guidelines, within the parameters of the CFP Rule and Constitutions. The Minister advises on distribution of funds to the brothers and sisters as needed, in consultation with other

---

50   The CFP Visitor alone can grant any major dispensations.

Officers. He or she visits ill penitents weekly (in person, via phone, email, or postal mail) and reminds them of penance. The Minister may make minor dispensations to the Rule on occasion (major dispensations require the Visitor's approval.).

Ministers, or someone designated by them, are to inform the CFP Office of all changes regarding Membership data (address, phone number, email, marital status, formation level, etc.) within their jurisdictions. In addition, Chapter and Circle Ministers and Regional Ministers ought to make one another aware of any changes regarding Members and Associates over which they both exercise jurisdiction. .

While Members and Associates may ask questions of anyone in the Confraternity, who ought then try to find the correct answer, their primary contact will be their Chapter or Circle Minister if the individual is part of a local group; if not, then the Regional Minister. Questions should be answered only if the Minister is certain of the answer. If unsure, the Minister should consult, depending on the issue, the Catechism of the Catholic Church, the CFP Officers, Minister General, a Spiritual Advisor of the CFP, Spiritual Assistant of the Chapter or Circle, or the Visitor. If the situation involves counseling, the Minister should consult the Minister General before speaking to the individual

Ministers may create mailing lists for penitents in their Regions. They should, however, refrain from forwarding any unnecessary material that is not directly connected with the formation and spiritual growth of penitents, such as "cute" emails, motivational messages, good links, and political information. They also must not forward theological pieces that are not approved Church documents, Church approved prayers, or writings of the saints. Before being mailed, any such items should be first checked with a Spiritual Assistant, Spiritual Advisor, or the Visitor for theological accuracy.

The CFP Office will alert the Ministers to new pre-inquirers within their jurisdictions. The Ministers contact pre-inquirers and offer to be of assistance to them. They encourage pre-inquirers to submit an Inquirer Application. The Minister shall inform the CFP Office should a pre-inquirer express a desire not to pursue further inquiry.

Beginning with Inquirers, the Minister is primarily responsible to see that formation is being done appropriately for CFP Members and Associates within their jurisdiction. The CFP Office either postal mails or emails copies of Inquirer applications to the Minister. If the Minister receives an Inquirer application directly from a prospective Inquirer, the Minister shall mail a copy of the Inquirer application to the CFP Office.

Within a few days of receiving the Inquirer Application, the Minister, either directly or through a designee, contacts Inquirers, informing the CFP Office when the Inquirer has responded to the contact. Within two weeks of receiving the Inquirer Application, the Minister interviews new Inquirers prior to admittance to the Inquiry stage (See Appendix F for interview questions) and explains the obligations of Membership to them, making sure that they understand the obligations of the Rule and Constitutions. The Minister encourages Inquirers to pray about their discernment of a call to live the Rule and Constitutions. He or she invites them to complete the Inquirer Reflections and, as is applicable, to share on the on-line Members' Forum, to participate in the monthly on line chat gathering, and to attend local CFP gatherings. The Minister submits a summary of the Inquirer Interview to the CFP Office, to be placed in the Inquirer's file. If the Minister is unsuccessful at establishing contact with the new Inquirer within two weeks of reception of the Inquirer Application, the CFP Office will attempt to initiate contact and conduct the Inquirer Interview.

The Minister instructs Inquirers on how to apply to enter formation and obtains applications for them if necessary. The Minister maintains contact with all Inquirers within their jurisdiction until they enter the Postulancy at which time the penitent's Formator assumes primary contact.

Ministers insure that applications to formation and pledging are completed at the proper time and submitted to the CFP Office for filing. They check to be sure that formation is being done properly and that Members and Associates are comfortable with their Formators. With the permission of the Minister General, they may organize and publicize Days of Recollection, mini-retreats, and other religious gatherings for penitents and the general public, to assist in formation and promote penance (conversion). Ministers consult discreet brothers and sisters regarding whether or not to pledge those who have completed formation and may, if they desire, interview the candidate about to pledge. They are responsible for keeping peace within their jurisdiction. This is discussed in detail in the "Difficult Members and Associates" section of this Directory.

The Minister has authority over leaders within his or her jurisdiction. Ministers may appoint leaders to various positions. If the Minister is going to be away for a time, he or she informs penitents within his or her jurisdiction and designates a temporary replacement. Upon his or her return, the Minister informs the penitents and resumes work. Ministers who experience a computer crash or similar problem shall inform those whom they can, as well as the CFP Office and the Minister General, one of whom will notify others who need to know.

The Assistant Minister assists the Minister as requested in the completion of the Minister's duties. In Chapters and Circles, the Assistant Minister conducts a meeting of the local gathering if the Minister is absent and assumes the office of Minister if the Minister can not complete the term. When their term of office is completed, with the counsel of brothers and sisters, Ministers are to elect two other Ministers, Treasurer, and Messenger to serve the Membership. Election of new Officers by the existing Ministers applies primarily to Regions as local gatherings elect their own Officers from their Membership.

Additional duties of Ministers are listed in the Special Situations section of the Directory.

REGIONAL, CHAPTER, AND CIRCLE TREASURER

The Treasurer is in charge of the finances of the group and so must be honest and capable regarding money as well as held in respect by the local group. The Treasurer collects and deposits monies, distributes funds, gives a stipend as deemed appropriate to the Spiritual Assistant and to the church or other location where a CFP meeting is held, pays expenses, maintains financial records, and reports monthly and annually to the local group. The Treasurer should make a yearly report on income and expenses to their Regional Minister and to the CFP Office.

The local group is self supporting financially and must meet all the expenses incurred therein. It is not to incur debts, and, should it inadvertently do so, these must immediately be paid. All Officers must agree upon the use of the group's funds including the reimbursement of expenses incurred by any CFP leader whose visit is requested or necessary. The group may choose to establish a fund for needy Members and Associates. Disbursement of Alms shall be determined by the Officers in consultation with the Spiritual Assistant.

Upon dissolution of the Chapter or Circle, any remaining funds in all accounts, following payment of bills, are deposited in the CFP General Treasury. If the Chapter or Circle is in debt, the group's Minister, Treasurer, and Spiritual Assistant shall consult the CFP Visitor and the Minister General. Together they shall formulate a plan to pay the debt.

REGIONAL, CHAPTER, AND CIRCLE MESSENGER

Since the Messenger keeps records of the group and handles correspondence as deemed appropriate by the Minister, he or she ought to be capable of organizing and communicating data well. The Messenger should be concerned with accuracy and be a respected Member of the local group. The Messenger publishes to the other brothers and sisters the names of those who have died, records and publishes what is said and done in the meetings, and keeps attendance and Membership records. Minutes are reviewed and approved or amended at the following month's meeting and are retained within the local group. If the group is dissolved, all records should be sent to the Confraternity Office.

FORMATOR

Formators are critical to the Confraternity of Penitents because they assist the Members and Associates in understanding the Rule and the Catholic Faith and in applying the Constitutions of the Rule to their own lives. They are to be honest, faithful, and trustworthy Members of the CFP with skill at working with others and who are capable of responsible leadership. They must also be dedicated to living the CFP Rule and must be in total agreement with the Catholic Church's teachings. They are appointed by the Minister General, or, with his or her permission, by the Regional Minister or Chapter/Circle Minister. The Minister General must approve all Formators. They must have already completed the year of formation of those whose lessons they review.

As a general rule, Formators will be assigned no more than five Formattees at one time. They are to respond to those lessons in a timely manner with helpful comments and instruction. They shall keep accurate ledgers of lessons completed successfully.[51] They need not keep copies of the lessons but ought to inform the individuals to keep copies themselves. Formators determine who qualifies, by successful completion of lessons, and with the permission of their Spiritual Director, to advance to the next year of formation or to pledge, thereby generally working with Members and Associates until they either complete formation and pledge for life or else leave formation in the CFP. Formators are to periodically update their Chapter/Circle Minister and Regional Minister on the status of those whose lessons they review and must do so at least annually.

MEMBER

Members are expected to pray for the Confraternity, to follow all the teachings of the Roman Catholic Church, and to be at peace with all. Members monetarily contribute to the Confraternity as they are able, by submitting donations to either the International Office, their Regional Treasurer, or their Chapter or Circle.

Each Member is to participate in an apostolate from either the Spiritual or Corporal works of mercy. They may also assist the Confraternity in one of the organization's apostolates such as:

* Collecting and distributing used breviaries
* Prolife prayer and support of women in pregnancy crisis
* Promoting the Oratory of Divine Love weekly Catechism and Scripture study
* Distributing printed, computer generated "Blessings" for framing
* Encouraging the Young Knights and Maids of Errantry
* Eucharistic adoration for CFP Members and Associates, intentions, and the Church

Members continue formation according to the program of the CFP outlined in the Formation Section of the Directory. They are not responsible for living any parts of the Rule beyond those required of them at their current stage of formation. Members who wish to live more of the Rule at any given stage should discuss their desire with their Formator and Spiritual Director and a prudent decision reached.

If they wish, Members may place the initials CFP after their names as long as they are Members of the Confraternity of Penitents.

Clergy, religious, and laity in Third Orders or other Catholic Associations, who wish to complete formation, will do so in the usual manner and time frame and may become Members of the CFP if their organization allows. CFP Members in Third Orders or forms of Consecrated Life must continue to fulfill all the obligations and commitments required by the other groups unless dispensed from doing so.

---

51   Should a Formator resign, the ledger is transferred to his or her successor.

All groups to which a CFP Member belongs must be entirely faithful to the Roman Catholic Church and its teachings. If a Roman Catholic applicant or CFP Member belongs to a group which opposes any of the Church's teachings or authority, the Visitor will make a determination on the suitability of such a candidate for the Confraternity.

Penitents may discuss the Rule with others but ought not to attempt to persuade other groups or other groups' Spiritual Assistants to adopt the CFP Rule.

Penitents who wish to transfer from any other Lay Association or Third Order to the Confraternity of Penitents will first complete the usual three months of Inquiry. During this time, they will be asked to submit their current Rule and Constitutions as well as copies of their completed formation lessons (if any) plus their answers to them. Their level of formation following Inquiry will depend upon the similarity of their current Rule, Constitutions, and formation plan to that of the Confraternity of Penitents. Depending on the similarity, they may be able to transfer at their current level of formation. However, all transfers will be asked to complete all CFP formation lessons, beginning with the Postulancy, in areas that differ from those already completed in their current organization. If they wish, they may complete these concurrently with their ongoing CFP formation lessons. Those already professed in another organization whose Rule and Constitutions are very similar to those of the Confraternity will be interviewed to determine if they could be accepted as temporarily pledged in the CFP until they have completed all the necessary CFP formation in order to pledge for life in the Confraternity. Temporarily pledged members will not be eligible for any leadership roles in the CFP nor will they have voting privileges during the time of temporary profession.

ASSOCIATE

With the permission of the CFP leadership sponsoring the event, Associates may attend CFP functions or meetings. They are expected to conduct themselves in a neutral or supportive manner relative to the Roman Catholic Faith and must abide with the totally Catholic nature of their formation. They are subject to the same disciplinary procedures as applied to Members, as listed in the CFP Rule and Constitutions and the Directory. Associates cannot pledge, hold office, vote, or become Formators.

Associates are either non-Catholics or Roman Catholics who have one or more of the following impediments:

* They do not have spousal permission.
* They are Members of Third Orders which will not allow Membership in the CFP.[52]

---

52   As of March 2010, the CFP was aware of the following Third Orders which disallow dual Membership: Secular Franciscan Order, Third Order of Mount Carmel, Third Order Dominicans, Benedictine Oblates, Tau Maria. Associates in Third Orders or forms of Consecrated Life must continue to fulfill all the obligations and commitments required by their Orders unless dispensed from doing so.

* They had previously dropped from formation in the CFP but have reentered formation.[53]
* They have rescinded a pledge to the CFP Rule but have asked to be readmitted (these will be known as Associates who have completed formation).[54]
* They have other special circumstances such as certain types of mental illness which makes Membership in the CFP impossible or difficult.
* They do not wish full membership status.

Within their own areas of jurisdiction as defined earlier in the Directory, the Regional Minister for isolated applicants or the Chapter/Circle Minister for local ones, in consultation with the Minister General, shall determine which applicants shall be accepted as Associates and shall name their entry level of formation.

After remaining for a period of time as an Associate, Associates who feel that they could be accepted as Members may apply for Membership in the Confraternity of Penitents. In Chapters or Circles, Associates submit to their Chapter Minister a letter of request for Membership, stating the reasons for the request, as well as a letter from the Associate's Spiritual Director agreeing to the request. Associates not in Chapters and Circles submit the letters of request to their Regional Minister. The letters of request are reviewed by those receiving them and in consultation with the Minister General. When a decision on re-admittance is reached, the Minister informs the Associate as well as the CFP Office. If admitted into Membership, the new Member continues formation at his or her current lesson.

Associates who have completed formation as Associates and who become able to meet the requirements for Membership are interviewed by their Minister and by the Minister General. The Minister and Minister General consult together to determine if the Associate's request for Membership ought to be granted. If so, the Associate shall follow the procedure for Pledging which is detailed in the Formation Section of the Directory. Associates who have been away from formation for a year or more should first complete, with a life pledged member, a review of the Rule and Constitutions as well as an evaluation of how they are living the way of life of the CFP. After making the necessary life style adjustments to adhere to living the Rule and Constitutions, the Associate may proceed to the three lessons prior to pledging.

Year pledged members who do not renew their pledge and life pledged (including privately vowed) members who rescind their pledge (and vow if applicable) automatically become Associates who have completed formation. This status stands in perpetuity;

---

53 The applicant's Minister (Chapter/Circle if in local group; Regional Minister otherwise) should ascertain from the applicant the reasons why he or she had left the Association previously to determine how best to avoid a similar situation.

54 See the Special Situations section of this Directory.

nothing can negate the fact that this individual has completed formation in the Confraternity of Penitents and, by that very fact, is associated with the CFP.

AFFILIATE

The following obligations must be fulfilled for Affiliate status:

* Completion of the Application for Affiliation, found in the CFP Handbook and on the web site.
* Promotion of penance (conversion) in ways suitable to the Affiliate's vocation.
* Offering attendance at one Mass per year for deceased penitents.
* Fully living section 26 of the Rule and Constitutions which enjoins peace with all.
* Being consecrated to Our Lady and praying a daily Marian Consecration prayer of their choice.
* Praying daily the Affiliates' Prayer, found in the Prayer section of this Handbook.

Priests, Deacons, and Religious Affiliates are also asked to consider becoming Spiritual Assistants for CFP Chapters or Circles and/or Spiritual Directors for CFP Members and Associates as their time, wishes, and obligations permit. Priest Affiliates are asked to celebrate one Mass yearly for all deceased penitents.

With the permission of the CFP leadership sponsoring the event, Affiliates may attend CFP functions and meetings. CFP leaders retain contact with Affiliates as they wish. The Confraternity of Penitents is most grateful for its Affiliates and prays daily for them.

HERMITS

The Confraternity of Penitents welcomes Diocesan Hermits, who are living a Rule of Life similar to ours, into alliance with the Confraternity. They must submit their Diocesan approved Rule of Life to the Minister General of the CFP who will present it to the Visitor and the Confraternity Council for consideration. If the hermit's Rule is deemed to coincide with the Rule of the Confraternity of Penitents in all major areas, the hermit will be invited to become an ally to the Confraternity. Once accepted, the hermit may then attend Confraternity retreats and days of recollection as well as Chapter and Circle meetings and other Confraternity functions. The hermit will be eligible to be a spiritual director to Confraternity members and a spiritual adviser to Confraternity Chapters and Circles.

PRISONERS AND FORMER PRISONERS

Prisoners applying for formation in the Confraternity of Penitents may become part of the CFP's Alessandro Ministry, named after Alessandro Serenelli, the convicted and later repentant murderer of Saint Maria Goretti. Prisoners must complete all Inquirer Reflections and Inquirer Intake Questions prior to postulancy. They must also reveal the nature of the crimes <u>for which they have been</u> incarcerated and have made restitution for them, or are trying to make restitution as much as is possible and prudent, before continuing with formation.

Prisoners must be made aware in writing that all information shared with the Confraternity is not under the seal of confession and that members of the Confraternity are bound by and will follow all mandatory reporting laws.

Because of the unique prison environment which often makes living the Rule easier inside of prison than outside, incarcerated persons shall be permitted to participate in formation in the Confraternity of Penitents in the same manner as other penitents but without being formally admitted into the Confraternity as members. Should they complete their four years of formation while still in prison, they may continue with ongoing formation as do other penitents, again without being formally admitted as members of the CFP. Upon release from prison, former prisoners will be eligible to become Associates of the Confraternity of Penitents. They will continue as Associates for a minimum of two years, without any infractions of the law, continuing their formation, and living the Rule as their formation requires, before being eligible to apply for membership and pledging.

Should a former prisoner wish to continue with the discipline of life of the Confraternity of Penitents and apply for formal membership, he or she should meet with the Minister General and Visitor to discuss what this process would entail. Requirements <u>may</u> include but are not limited to assurances of worthiness of life through a minimum two year waiting period, psychological evaluation, regular background checks, etc.

Should a prisoner, who is serving a life term without parole and who has completed formation successfully, request evaluation of status within the Confraternity, the Minister General and Visitor shall conduct the evaluation and make a recommendation to the Bishop who will decide if the person can be admitted as a CFP member, can pledge, and/or can vow to live the CFP Rule and Constitutions for life while incarcerated. However, due to limitations of prison life, a prisoner will be unable to hold office or be a formator.

ELECTIONS

Apart from appointments to certain offices, elections are the Confraternity's primary way of selecting its leaders. Leaders of the CFP are responsible for its governance and for working with the Membership. All leaders should be people of prayer who are committed to the CFP way of life and Charism. They are to be models to others on how to live the Rule with love and joy.

Although there are no consecutive term limits to elected or appointed offices, it is prudent to elect or appoint new Officers yearly, to avoid exhaustion and to give other Members the opportunity to serve. Clergy and Religious, who serve the CFP as Visitor, Spiritual Advisors, and Spiritual Assistants, have no terms of office.

Vacancies among leaders are discussed in the Special Situations section of the Directory.

ELECTIONS: GENERAL INFORMATION

In small Chapters or Circles, elections may take place with nominations from the floor. In larger groups and in the Confraternity as a whole, the following procedures take place.

In advance of the elections, a Nominating Committee is formed of at least three Members, Associates, or others ineligible to vote or to hold office. The Nominating Committee elects one of its number as Chairperson.

The Nominating Committee sees that the elections are properly held, by identifying suitable candidates for each office and by distributing and collecting ballots and tabulating results.

Each Member eligible to vote receives, by postal mail, one ballot, which lists the candidates nominated for each office, one envelope marked "Ballot," and one larger, stamped envelope addressed to the Chairperson of the Nominating Committee. This envelope shall have the name of the voter written in the upper left-hand corner. The Member indicates on the ballot his or her choice of Officers. The ballot is then sealed in the "Ballot" envelope and that envelope sealed within the stamped and addressed envelope and mailed. Upon the arrival of each ballot, the Chairperson of the Nominating Committee records who has submitted the ballot and then removes the sealed Ballot Envelope from the mailing envelope. All of the sealed ballots are retained until the Chairperson of the Nominating Committee opens the ballots in the presence of two witnesses, one of whom must be a priest, deacon, or religious of the Roman Catholic Church. The ballots are counted twice to verify the results and the new Officers duly recorded. The priest, deacon, or religious then destroys the ballots. The nominee who receives the majority of the votes assumes office. Should there be a tie, the Chairperson of the Nominating Committee immediately conducts a re-election. The vote is kept confidential except for the results, which the Chairperson makes known immediately to the appropriate Minister and to those voting. The Minister (if in a local group) or CFP Office (for total Confraternity) shall promptly make the results known to the remainder of the Membership.

The incumbent contacts the new Officer to insure a smooth transition.

YEARLY CONFIRMATION OF FOUNDER AS MINISTER GENERAL

The CFP Rule calls for yearly election or appointment of Officers. In order to fulfill this requirement while maintaining the CFP Structure, which has been advised and accepted by the Diocese of Fort Wayne – South Bend, the Founder is yearly confirmed as Minister General. While the Founder is serving as Minister General, a notice, requesting confirmation of the Founder as the Minister General, is submitted to all Life-Pledged Members along with the Letter of Nominations. A sample letter is in Appendix A of this Directory.

ELECTION OF MINISTER GENERAL

Only Life-Pledged Members are eligible to be elected to the office of Minister General. When a vacancy of the office of Minister General is anticipated or unexpectedly occurs, the Ministerial Assistant convenes the CFP Officers who appoint a Nominating Committee of three Year-Pledged Members, Associates who have completed formation, and/or third year Novices. The Nominating Committee identifies three Life-Pledged Members who are qualified to fill the office of Minister General and who agree to accept the role and serve for six years if so elected. All Life-Pledged Members then receive a letter soliciting their vote in this election. A sample letter is in Appendix B of this Directory. Upon the Visitor's approval of the new Minister General and upon notification of the Bishop's office, the Minister General shall assume office. The CFP Office shall make the choice of Minister General known to the CFP Membership.

The elected Minister General shall serve a six year term beginning January 1 following the election. Should the office of Minister General become vacant between terms, the newly elected Minister General shall serve the remainder of the year plus five consecutive years. At no time shall an elected Minister General's term exceed six full years.

YEARLY CONFIRMATION OF ELECTED MINISTER GENERAL

To satisfy the CFP Rule as well as the requirements of the State of Indiana's Corporations Act, the elected Minister General must be approved yearly throughout the six year term. Therefore, each year, when the Letter of Nominations is submitted to the Life Pledged Members prior to the elections, all Life-Pledged Members receive an additional letter asking that they confirm the elected Minister General for the coming year. A sample letter is in Appendix C of this Directory.

MINISTER GENERAL'S OATH OF OFFICE

Before the Minister General may assume office, the CFP Visitor, or a Roman Catholic Priest appointed by him, shall receive the Minister General's Oath of Office. In the presence of the Visitor or his representative, and two additional witnesses, the Minister General shall read and sign the Oath, which shall then be filed at the CFP Office. The text of the Oath is as follows:

Humbly asking God's grace, I, (NAME), having been duly elected as Minister General of the Confraternity of Penitents for the next six years, do solemnly promise before God and before you, Father, in the presence of these witnesses, that I will, for the duration of my term of office, uphold the Rule, Constitutions, and Directory of the Confraternity of Penitents. I promise to live in peace and harmony with all in the Confraternity and outside of it, to exercise my duties with love, and to consult other Confraternity leaders and advisors in making the decisions that will be brought before me. I promise to spread the message of penance worldwide and to insure that those seeking to live a life of penance are assisted on their journey. I promise to remain faithful to all the teachings of the Roman Catholic Church, to the Magisterium and Pope. I promise to be obedient to you, Father Visitor, and to our Bishop, and to treat all, including the least, with the charity of Christ. I promise to be, to the best of my ability, a person of prayer, to consult the Holy Spirit in all decisions, and to follow His lead. I also promise to pray daily for all involved in any way with the Confraternity of Penitents, for its intentions, and for all doing penance worldwide. I ask your prayers, Father, and those of all my brothers and sisters in the Confraternity, in this regard.

_____ (SIGNATURE OF MINISTER GENERAL)
_____ (DATE SIGNED)
_____ (VISITOR OR REPRESENTATIVE)
_____ (SIGNATURE OF FIRST WITNESS)
_____ (SIGNATURE OF SECOND WITNESS)

ELECTION OF CFP OFFICERS

CFP Officers are vital to the efficient operation of the Confraternity of Penitents. They should be capable, prayerful, joyful individuals, Life Pledged Members of the CFP, who possess a true loyalty to the Roman Catholic Church and a deep understanding of the CFP way of life. By August 1 of each year, the Ministerial Assistant, in consultation with the Minister General and the other CFP Officers, appoints a Nominating Committee of three either non-pledged or year pledged Members of the CFP and/or three Associates who have completed formation. The Nominating Committee is responsible for all matters concerning the elections. By September 15, the Nominating Committee proposes a slate of CFP Officers, selected with their permission from the Life Pledged Members and approved by the Minister General. On that date, the proposed slate is made known to all Life Pledged Members via postal mail. A sample Letter of Nominations is in Appendix D of the Directory. All Life Pledged Members have a chance to nominate, vote, and be elected. The office of Minister General must be held by a Life-Pledged Member.

On October 12, the full slate of candidates, who have agreed to serve if elected, is sent by ballot to all eligible voters. A sample ballot letter is in Appendix E. Ballots are returned to the Chairperson of the Nominating Committee. Once the results of the election are ascertained, the Chairperson immediately shares the outcome of the election with the Minister General, those elected and those voting. By the end of December, the CFP Office informs the general Membership of the new Officers.

CHAPTER AND CIRCLE ELECTIONS

All CFP Chapters and Circles have Officers who assist in running the local gatherings and who serve their Membership. When a Chapter or Circle is first formed, those fulfilling the offices of Minister and Messenger are appointed by the Regional Minister in consultation with the Minister General. Later, an Assistant Minister and Treasurer may be elected by Members of the local group, from among their number. Until a Chapter or Circle has a sufficient number of qualified Life Pledged Members eligible to vote and hold office, Members in formation as well as Pledged Members elect Officers from among their own number. In this case, the Nominating Committee, if the group is large enough to warrant one, consists of those ineligible to vote such as Inquirers, Affiliates, and/or Associates of the Confraternity. When there is a sufficient number of qualified Life Pledged Members, then Life Pledged Members only are eligible to nominate, to vote, and to be elected. In an election consisting of only Life Pledged Members, the Nominating Committee should consist of Members who are in formation and/or Associates who have completed formation.

If the pool of candidates is large, a slate of those running for each office, comprised of Nominating Committee selections and nominations from the voting Membership at large, shall be made available to all voting Members at least one week prior to the actual election. In smaller Chapters and Circles, nominations may be taken from the floor at the time of the elections. All those nominated must agree in advance to serve if elected.

Elections are conducted by a secret ballot at a local gathering at which a majority of those Members eligible to vote are present. Absent voters may designate proxy voters or may return their ballots, sealed in an envelope, prior to the election. The Minister is elected first. Then, when that office is filled, the Assistant Minister is elected, then the Treasurer, and lastly the Messenger. Officers begin to serve in January following the election.

FORMATION

This Section discusses normal formation procedures for those entering and advancing in formation. Situations not covered here are in the Special Situations section of the Directory.

LESSONS

The date of entering into formation is either Ash Wednesday or August 1 for Postulants and Ash Wednesday for all others. In Chapters and Circles, the Chapter or Circle Minister determines if someone may enter formation within one month after these dates. For isolated Members and Associates in Regions, the Regional Minister makes that decision.

All formation lessons are in the CFP Handbook and on the CFP web site. They can be mailed to Members and Associates who request them and who cannot afford a Handbook. Regional Ministers may grant free Handbooks to those Regional Members and Associates who are at the Novice 2 level or above and who cannot afford them. All other requests for free handbooks must be discussed with the CFP Treasurer and Minister General and a decision made.

Unless granted a dispensation by the Visitor, Members and Associates answer the questions briefly in written or typed format and submit their written answers to their assigned CFP Formator. Answers may be submitted on the CFP Members' Forum, via email or postal mail, or in person. The Formator discusses the answers with the Member and offers helpful feedback. If either the Formator or the Member has concerns about the other, the person should consult his or her Chapter or Circle Minister or, for isolated penitents, the Regional Minister. If necessary, the Minister General may also be consulted.

FORMATION APPLICATIONS

Applications can be found in the CFP Handbook and on the web site. Inquirer, Postulant, and Novice 1 applications may be submitted via email and do not require the signature of a Spiritual Director. Novice 2, Novice 3, and Pledged applications are to be submitted in writing and signed by the penitent and his or her Spiritual Director. The Minister shall promptly inform the applicant of his or her acceptance into the stage of formation or shall explain the reasons for denial. All Members and Associates in formation are to submit an application yearly, generally prior to Ash Wednesday, until a Member pledges for life or until an Associate completes formation.

Following Ash Wednesday, the CFP Office either postal mails or emails a letter of welcome to all those who have been accepted into the current formation year. A sample letter is in Appendix H.

INDUCTION INTO FORMATION

The Ceremony of Induction formally welcomes the Member into each formation year while also offering prayers and asking a blessing upon the Member's commitment. While encouraged, the Ceremony of Induction is not mandatory. The rites for Induction Ceremonies are in the Ceremonies section of the CFP Handbook and may be adapted as circumstances require. Induction Ceremonies may take place within Chapters and Circles, and they are generally celebrated during one of the Masses at the annual CFP Retreat. While Induction generally takes place in the presence of the one presiding, Members and Associates in unusual situations may be inducted on the phone or in an on-line chat room.

INQUIRY

All Inquirers must complete an Application of Inquiry which will be retained at the CFP Office with a copy sent to their appropriate Minister (Chapter or Circle if near a local group, Regional otherwise).

After receipt of the Application but before acceptance as an Inquirer, the appropriate Minister shall conduct an interview, in person or via phone, with the prospective Inquirer. The interview shall consist of questions which discern as much as possible about the candidate's background, history, and motivation for embracing a life of penance within the CFP. The Minister records answers to these questions for the Inquirer's file, forwarding a copy to the CFP Office as well. A list of questions is in Appendix F. The Minister shall determine whether an applicant shall be accepted and whether his or her status be that of Member or Associate.

If they wish, Inquirers may share on Inquirer Reflections found in the Handbook and on the web site. These help the Inquirer further to discern a call to a life of penance. After a minimum three month period of Inquiry, the appropriate Minister (Chapter/Circle if in a local group, Regional otherwise) should invite the Inquirer to complete the Postulant application for entry into formation at the beginning of the upcoming formation year.

At the beginning of a new formation year, (Ash Wednesday or August 1 for Postulancy), the CFP Office, through the Regional and Chapter/Circle Ministers, checks on the status of all Inquirers. If they wish to enter formation, they shall complete the Postulant Application and return a copy to their Regional Minister and Chapter or Circle Minister (if applicable) as well as to the CFP Office. If they wish to continue their period of Inquiry, they submit an Inquirer application for the current year.

POSTULANT

The Postulancy is the only stage of formation which may be completed in less than twelve months' time. The Postulancy may last twelve months beginning on Ash Wednesday or no less than six months, beginning on August 1, provided that all twelve Postulant lessons are completed by the following Ash Wednesday.

In assisting Inquirers to determine if they are capable of completing the Postulancy between August 1 and the following Ash Wednesday, the Minister may ask the following or similar questions:

* Do you want to enter formation now? Why?
* Are you a disciplined, hard working person who has the time to complete the lessons in less than twelve months?
* Will you consistently implement the activities suggested in the Postulancy (they are on the Getting Started page of the web site) so that you will be doing them daily?
* Will you keep in touch with your Formator regularly if you have difficulties?
* Can you read material, digest it, and answer questions briefly and to the point?

If the answers to the above questions are all yes, then the Inquirer could probably enter the Postulancy on August 1 and complete the formation by Ash Wednesday.

Upon receipt of a Postulant Application, the immediate Minister shall determine if the Inquirer may proceed into the Postulancy at the time requested. Any irregular living situation must be rectified in keeping with Church and moral guidelines before entrance into postulancy.

NOVICE

Each of the three Novice years must be a minimum of twelve months in length. Lessons are in the CFP Handbook and on the web site.

PLEDGE

Those wishing to pledge must have successfully completed the Postulancy and three years of Novitiate as well as three lessons prior to pledging. These three lessons must be completed each year until the Member makes a Life Pledge or until the Member elects to become an Associate who has completed formation. These three lessons, found in the CFP Handbook and on the web site, discuss the seriousness of the commitment and must be reviewed with a Mentor. The Member may select a Mentor, to be approved by the CFP Ministerial Assistant, or the Ministerial Assistant may assign one. The Mentor must be a Life-Pledged Member of the Confraternity other than the penitent's Formator.

The Member must have submitted to the CFP Office the following documents (see Appendix R) to be held on file:

* An updated Baptismal Certificate. The Baptismal Certificate is requested when a member enters First Year Novice formation, if it had not been submitted earlier, so that so that it is on hand when needed. If it is impossible to obtain an updated Baptismal Certificate, a copy of the original Baptismal Certificate is acceptable, but it should be accompanied by copy of the penitent's Marriage Certificate (if applicable) and a letter on parish letterhead from the Member's parish priest. The letter should indicate that the penitent is in good standing in the parish. If it is impossible to obtain any copy of any Baptismal Certificate, or of any one of the other documents mentioned herein, the Diocese of Fort Wayne – South Bend is to be consulted and their directives followed.

* For converts, a copy of a document indicating that they have entered into full communion with the Church, including the date of entry. This may be a special RCIA certificate, a "Profession of Faith" certificate, or any document which indicates that the Member is a Catholic such as a letter from their parish priest.

* The Pledged Application found in the CFP Handbook and on the web site, completed, signed, and dated by the penitent and his or her Spiritual Director. The Spiritual Director may also write a letter of recommendation for pledging.

* A signed and dated letter from the penitent's Formator, stating that the penitent has successfully completed all four years of formation and that, in the Formator's opinion, the penitent is ready to pledge.

* A letter from the Mentor assigned to the penitent. In the letter, the Mentor must state that the penitent has successfully completed the three lessons prior to pledging, that he or she has interviewed the penitent and insured that he or she clearly understands the seriousness of the obligations and commitments of a Pledged Member. The Mentor must also state that he or she believes that the penitent is prepared to undertake the commitment.

* A letter from the Member about to be pledged, stating that he or she has made a day of recollection or a retreat prior to pledging (either informally at home or as a formal, Church sponsored event) and including the date, location, and summary of their thoughts about the event in relation to their Pledging.

* If applicable, a signed and dated letter from the appropriate superior of any other Association to which the penitent has pledged (professed) to live a Rule of Life,

stating that the penitent has the permission of the Association to pledge to live the CFP Rule.[55]

The Ceremony for Pledging is in the CFP Handbook. This may be used during any Mass or as a private ceremony. Pledging should be recorded in a formal document containing the Formula of Pledging handwritten in advance by the penitent, following the model in the Pledging Ceremony. This formula may be expanded as the penitent desires as long as the integrity of the original is kept. The final form of the Pledge, if differing from that in the Handbook, must be approved by the penitent's Spiritual Director and the Minister General. The Pledge cannot be made on line or over the telephone. It shall be read orally by the Member, be received by a Roman Catholic priest, deacon, or religious, and be witnessed by at least two other persons. The document must be signed and dated by the penitent, the one receiving the pledge, and at least one of the witnesses and then forwarded to the CFP Office where it is kept in the penitent's file.

At the time of the Pledging, the Confraternity presents all penitents with a small San Damiano crucifix and a Certificate of Pledging which are theirs to keep. Like the Pledging document, the Certificate is to be signed and dated by the penitent, the priest or deacon, and at least one witness.

Samples of Pledging Certificates are in Appendices N and O of this Directory.

Those who Pledge for Life also receive a cord with four knots (one each for poverty and chastity according to one's state in life, humility, and consecration to Our Lady), and a Brown Scapular designed by Charles Untz which reads "Mary" and "My Lady" with a crown of twelve stars. The cord and Scapular, if chosen to be worn, are to be concealed by one's clothing. Those not enrolled previously in the Brown Scapular are to be enrolled at the time of pledging. Life pledged members shall be known as brother (Baptismal Name) or sister (Baptismal Name) within the Confraternity. The title "brother" and "sister" shall be written in lower case to indicate the lay status of the penitent and the minority of the penitent before God.

Monthly formation will continue for Members and Associates after they complete formation. For this, with the permission of their Spiritual Directors, they shall select writings or lives of the saints or official documents of the Church. The Minister General may supply some reflections on selected texts.

VOW

The vow(s) may be taken at the time of pledging or in the future. As long as the CFP is a Private Association of the Faithful, vows cannot be taken during a public Mass but

---

55   Under Canon Law, an individual may profess (pledge) to observe the Rules of more than one Association provided that they both agree. The Confraternity permits those professed to the CFP Rule to also observe the Rules of other Associations approved by the Roman Catholic Church.

must be received privately by the Spiritual Director or any other priest, deacon, or religious of the Roman Catholic Church. The vow must be made in the presence of at least one other witness. The Spiritual Director will direct the penitent and see that the vow is kept. Vows are written out by the penitent and then signed and dated by the penitent, priest, deacon or religious, and the witness as well as the Spiritual Director if he or she is not the one receiving the vow. A copy of the document is to be forwarded to the CFP Office to be kept in the Member's file. Vowed Members also receive a Certificate of Vowing, a sample of which is in Appendix P of this Directory.

If desired and with the approval of their Spiritual Directors, penitents who take vows may assume a Confraternity name after a saint, to be used within the confines of the Confraternity only. In correspondence between Members and Associates, or in documents that only Members and Associates have access to, the secular name followed by the Confraternity name may be used. In oral conversation among CFP Members and Associates, they may use whichever name they prefer. Confraternity names are not to be used in any documents that are accessible to the general public nor will they be used on official Confraternity documents.

Those who take private vows have permission to celebrate the feast day(s) of the saint(s) of their vowed name as a Solemnity, following the guidelines of sections 6 and 9 of the CFP Rules and Constitutions. Those whose saint has several feast days are to choose one day on which to celebrate their private Solemnity in honor of their saint.

ONGOING FORMATION

Ongoing formation is critical for all penitents as it insures a deepening of knowledge of the Catholic Faith and the penitential life while fostering a stronger commitment to be totally surrendered to the Will of God and to act in union with Him. The Minister General, through the CFP Office, sees that ongoing formation is supplemented by the following:

* Days of Recollection which are days set aside for spiritual matters. The CFP will sponsor at least one yearly Day of Recollection. Chapters and Circles are encouraged to organize a minimum of one yearly Day of Recollection. Suggestions on how to organize a Day of Recollection are in Appendix Q of this Directory. Each CFP Member ought to make a yearly Day of Recollection, preferably at the beginning of each formation year. This may be done privately in one's home if a public Day of Recollection is not available.

* A Yearly Retreat/Reunion/Conference: The Retreat is conducted by a Member of the Roman Catholic clergy or a Roman Catholic Religious. The Conference, in conjunction with the Retreat, is conducted by CFP Members via a committee appointed by the

Ministerial Assistant. CFP Members and Associates are encouraged to make a yearly retreat.

* The Members' Chat Room, accessible only to CFP Members, Inquirers, and Associates, provides ongoing formation and opportunities for sharing on the CFP way of life. An On Line Chat Gathering is held monthly for all Members, Inquirers, and Associates. A Member of the Confraternity or a guest will conduct the 90 minute gathering which will include prayer, teaching, and formation in the Rule of Life. Class Chats may also be held in the chat room as Members desire. The chat room may be used at other times if approved in advance by the Minister General.

The following are On-Going Formation experiences for Pledged Members:

* Monthly Hermitage Day: Pledged Members are to set aside one day per month for a private hermitage experience. This would involve a minimum of six hours of private prayer, reflection, meditation, and spiritual reading in solitude. Penitents are encouraged to attend Mass on a hermitage day. However, Mass attendance, since it is not done in solitude, should be in addition to the six hours of solitude hermitage experience. The hermitage day may be done anywhere a penitent can be alone, whether that be at home, in a quiet outdoor setting, or in a church, for example. To foster the experience of solitude, the penitent should refrain from using a phone, computer, or other technological communication device during the hermitage hours so that the time spent is between the penitent and God.

* Yearly Life Pledged Chapter and Spiritual Leadership Training for Life Pledged Members only or those preparing to pledge for life. Every Life-Pledged Member should attend a Life Pledged Chapter and Spiritual Leadership Training Course at least once every five years. If possible, Members should attend a Spiritual Leadership Training Session before being assigned leadership in the Confraternity of Penitents.

SPECIAL SITUATIONS

While the previous sections of this Directory deal with normal protocol and procedures, problems and special situations sometimes arise. These include, but are not limited to, formation irregularities, discontinuance with the Confraternity, and other difficulties with Members and Associates.

FORMATION IRREGULARITIES

WAIVER OF THREE MONTH INQUIRY PERIOD

If the Minister deems appropriate and the Minister General agrees, the three month Inquiry period may be waived or shortened, although this should be a rare exception.

EXTENSION OF THREE MONTH INQUIRY PERIOD

The period of Inquiry may be extended upon the Inquirer's request by their informing their appropriate Minister or the CFP Office. If this extension goes beyond Ash Wednesday of any given year, they are to complete the inquirer application again, mark it "continuing inquiry," and submit it to the CFP Office by Ash Wednesday.

LEAVE OF ABSENCE FROM FORMATION

Members and Associates desiring a leave of absence from formation request such leaves in writing from their Formator who will grant the leave of absence if the Minister General approves. The Formator shall then notify the CFP Office, the Regional Minister, and, if applicable, the Chapter or Circle Minister. The CFP Office shall note in the penitent's file the level and lesson of formation at which the leave was granted.

RETURNING TO FORMATION FOLLOWING LEAVE OF ABSENCE

Upon applying to resume formation following a leave of absence, the penitent's Minister (Chapter/Circle if in a local group; Regional, otherwise), in consultation with the Minister General, shall determine the entry stage of formation and so informs the CFP Office. Depending on the length of the leave, the Member or Associate may be asked to repeat formation lessons previously completed. The appropriate application should be completed and submitted to the CFP Office.

PROLONGED FORMATION

Members and Associates desiring to prolong their formation must discuss this option with their Formator, appropriate Minister, and the Minister General, all of whom must concur with this change. Prolonged formation generally involves completing only part of the lesson each month or at some other interval so that all the lessons are eventually completed by the commencement of a future formation year when entry into the next level of formation may take place. The Formator has the responsibility for keeping track of the completion of the lessons. A formation application must be completed yearly and submitted to the CFP Office.

CONTINUING FORMATION

Members who do not complete a year of formation by Ash Wednesday are allowed to continue that year of formation, with the approval of their Formator, Regional Minister, and the Minister General. By Ash Wednesday, they must complete the appropriate application for the year and return a copy of it to the CFP Office, to their Formator, and to their Regional Minister.

POSTPONED FORMATION

For good reason, a Member's application for formation or pledging may be temporarily denied. This postponement must be made with the consensus of the Minister General and the Visitor. The applicant, if an Inquirer whose Postulancy is to be postponed, or Member whose formation or pledging is to be postponed, will remain at his or her current level of inquiry or formation without penalty until the appropriate Minister (Chapter or Circle, if in a local group, Regional otherwise), in consultation with the Minister General, determine that advancement into formation is wise. At that time, the individual shall complete a new formation or pledging application.

The Visitor must approve any postponement that exceeds twelve months duration.

INCOMPLETE FORMATION

Generally Members and Associates will complete their formation lessons within a year's time and move on to the next year of formation. All lessons in a given year of formation must be successfully completed by Ash Wednesday in order for a penitent to proceed in formation. Those with incomplete lessons may choose to continue their formation year, without penalty. That is, they do not have to begin with lesson 1 but can continue completing the lessons until they finish them. Penitents continuing a formation year past Ash Wednesday should complete the appropriate application for their current year, stating that they are continuing.

INACTIVE FORMATION

Frequently those inquiring or in formation do not maintain contact with the Confraternity. About one month prior to Ash Wednesday of each year, Regional Ministers and Formators shall attempt to contact Inquirers and those in formation who have not been in contact with anyone in the CFP, to the best of their knowledge, for the past six months or more. If the Regional Minister or Formator cannot make contact or elicit a response, the CFP Office will postal mail a letter to these individuals. The letter shall ask their intentions and inform them that, if they do not confirm their status by the date specified in the letter, they shall automatically become friends of the CFP. A sample letter to inactive Inquirers is in Appendix G of the Directory. A sample letter to inactive Members and Associates is in Appendix I. The CFP Office will make the appropriate changes in status after the date specified and will so inform the Regional Minister and Chapter or Circle Minister, if applicable.

SIMULTANEOUS FORMATION

At the discretion of their Formator, a penitent may be permitted to move to the next level of formation while simultaneously completing the previous one. Such an exception must be approved by the appropriate Minister (Chapter or Circle if in a local group, Regional, otherwise), the penitent's Spiritual Director, and the Minister General.

REPEAT FORMATION

With the permission of their Formator, Members and Associates may decide to repeat a year of formation. Since the Member is beginning the year of formation again, the Member completes a new formation application. The Member should note on the application that this is a request to repeat the formation year.

PLEDGING PRIOR TO COMPLETION OF FORMATION

Only the CFP Visitor, in agreement with the Minister General, may grant a Member's request to pledge before formation is completed. This may be done only if the Member is in imminent danger of death or incapacity which must be proven via at least two signed, postal mail letters from two different physicians or other medical experts. If a Member's imminent death or incapacity is proven, the Visitor, in agreement with the Minister General, may allow the Member to pledge to live the Rule, for life or for a year, with the stipulation that the Member, if a measure of health returns, will continue with formation in the normal manner and time frame. With permission of their Spiritual Director, such Members may also privately vow to live the Rule for life. Members so pledged or, pledged and vowed, cannot hold office or participate in elections until their formation is complete.

DISCONTINUANCE WITH THE CONFRATERNITY

The Confraternity recognizes that many who begin with the CFP discontinue their association as the Lord calls them elsewhere. The CFP wishes well to these individuals and will continue to hold them in prayer. The appropriate Minister (Chapter or Circle if in a local group; Regional otherwise) of the person who is withdrawing may question the person as to the reasons for their leaving, to see if the CFP has failed them in any way. Those who discontinue will be retained on the CFP public email lists and postal mail newsletter list (if they wish to pay for a newsletter subscription) as friends of the Confraternity unless they request otherwise. A sample letter to a discontinuing Member or Associate is in Appendix M of the Directory.

DENIAL OF INQUIRY

Inquirers are presumed to be accepted upon receipt of their Inquirer Application. However, occasionally a Minister may have doubts about the suitability of the person to be accepted. If so, the Minister ought to conduct at least two interviews with the individual. In order to make a final decision, the individual's pastor may be consulted, if the applicant agrees. If the Minister feels that the individual's application to the Inquirer Stage should be denied, the Minister General and Visitor must concur with the decision. The Inquirer shall be gently told, via postal mail letter from the CFP Office, that the Confraternity believes that he or she has a vocation to another form of life, wishes the person well, and promises them the prayers of the Confraternity.

DENIAL OF CONTINUANCE WITH THE CONFRATERNITY

Generally Inquirers proceed into the Postulancy and thereupon into each level of formation to pledging unless they themselves wish to withdraw. However, CFP leaders may occasionally believe that it would be best for an individual and/or for the CFP that the person withdraw from the Confraternity. Such decisions are based on serious concerns about a person's suitability in relation to the CFP.

Concerns should be brought before the appropriate Minister (Chapter or Circle if in a local group; Regional otherwise), Minister General, and Visitor for evaluation. The procedures provided in the Rule and Constitutions are applied in determining whether an individual shall be denied continuance with the Confraternity. Should this seem probable, the following procedures shall be followed unless the matter involves heresy, scandal, or serious, unresolved infractions of Section 26 of the CFP Rule and Constitutions. In these three cases, the Bishop is to be consulted and his decision followed.

* For Members or Associates in formation, the CFP Office shall inform the individual that the CFP believes that their continuance with the Confraternity is not prudent. Reasons for this shall be given. The individual will be asked if he or she would like to appeal this decision. If so, the individual shall appear before the Visitor, Minister General, and at least one other CFP leader to discuss the concerns after which the Visitor, in consultation with the other leaders who are present, shall make a final decision.

* For Pledged Members of the Confraternity, the CFP Office shall postal mail a letter of concern stating the reasons for terminating their continuance with the Confraternity. The Member, and any witnesses in his or her behalf, shall be invited to a meeting with the Visitor, Minister General, and at least one other CFP leader to evaluate the concerns. The Visitor, in consultation with the CFP leaders, shall make a final decision.

If denied continuance with the Confraternity, an individual may appeal to the Bishop for re-admittance.

Those denied entry to or continuance with the CFP shall have their addresses retained on a list kept on file at the CFP Office, with the date of discontinuance noted. These individuals may continue to receive emails through the CFP public email list, if they so wish and their Minister approves. They may reapply for reentry at a later date. If accepted, their status initially shall be that of Associate.

RELEASE FROM PLEDGE OR VOW

A Pledge and a vow are serious commitments to God to live the CFP Rule. Certainly they should not be taken in an indifferent spirit, nor should they be rescinded without great cause. Those requesting release from a Pledge or commutation of a vow ought to contact their appropriate Minister (Chapter or Circle if in a local group, Regional otherwise) with their request. The Minister General ought to also be informed. The Member should be prepared to explain the reasons to the Minister and to undergo an interview with a priest, deacon, or religious regarding the request. If the Member is part of a Chapter or Circle, the Spiritual Assistant, with prior approval of the Visitor, shall conduct this interview and release the Member from the Pledge if he or she deems it appropriate. If this is an isolated Member, the Regional Spiritual Assistant, if there is one, with prior approval of the Visitor, or the Visitor himself, will conduct the interview and, if deemed appropriate, grant the release. These same individuals may interview a vowed Member regarding release from a vow. For a greater or equal good, a vow can be commuted by the Spiritual Director (provided this is a Catholic Priest), Confessor, Parish Priest, the CFP Visitor, or the Bishop.[56] Those released from a pledge (and possibly vow) automatically become Associates who have completed formation, a status which will remain in perpetuity unless Membership is granted at a later date.

---

56   Only those specified by Canon 1196 can completely release a person from the private vow. "In addition to the Roman Pontiff, the following can dispense from private vows for a just cause provided that a dispensation does not injure a right acquired by others. 1/the local ordinary and the pastor with regard to all their subjects and even travelers, 2/the superior of a religious institute or society of apostolic life if it is clerical and of pontifical right with regard to members, novices, and persons who live day and night in a house of the institute or society, 3/those to whom the Apostolic See or the local ordinary has delegated the power of dispensing."

VACANCIES AMONG LEADERS

UNEXPECTED VACANCIES

Unexpected vacancies occur when a Member of the CFP leadership, Visitor, Spiritual Assistant, or Spiritual Advisor dies or becomes suddenly incapacitated or unable to serve before the end of their term of office.

LEAVES OF ABSENCE/RESIGNATION OF LEADERS

Leaves of absence occur when a leader foresees difficulties and requests either a temporary release (leave of absence) or permanent release (resignation) from duty.

Those desiring a leave of absence or resigning from office must first speak to their appropriate Minister. No one desiring to leave their office shall be forced or persuaded to remain in it, but discussion of any problem should take place in advance of any formal departure in order to allow the CFP to find a suitable replacement.

Letters requesting a leave of absence or to resign from office must be submitted in writing to the appropriate Minister. To ensure a smooth transition between leaders, a minimum of three weeks notice must be given before a leave of absence or resignation takes effect.

A letter requesting a leave of absence must state the duration of the absence requested after which the leader shall resume duties if his or her term of office would not be over. Such a leave shall not exceed six months. If, after the elapsed time, a leader is unable or unwilling to resume their duties, the leader must submit their resignation in writing to the appropriate Minister.

The Chapter or Circle Minister grants leaves of absence and accepts resignations for leaders and Spiritual Assistants within the Chapter or Circle.

Regional Ministers grant leaves of absence and accept resignations for Regional Officers, Regional Spiritual Advisors, Chapter and Circle Ministers, and Formators in the Region.

The Minister General grants leaves of absence and accepts resignations for Regional Ministers and CFP Officers.

The Visitor grants leaves of absence and accepts resignations of the Minister General.

The Bishop grants leaves of absence and accepts resignations of the Visitor.

INEFFECTIVE LEADERS

All leaders are expected to serve well and efficiently in the capacity to which they were elected or appointed. However, humanly speaking, this is not always possible. If anyone feels that a leader is ineffective in his or her role, the concerned party should write a letter of concern to the immediate superior of the leader according to the CFP Structure Chart, detailing the problem.

The appropriate Minister (Chapter or Circle if the leader is a local leader, Regional if a Regional leader, Minister General if an international leader) shall contact the leader and attempt to rectify the situation. If this is not successful, and the leader continues to perform poorly or incorrectly, the immediate Minister of the leader in question shall consult the Minister General. Together they will determine if a leader cannot serve as required. If so, the Minister shall remove the ineffective leader from office while exercising charity toward him or her.

Should the leader be involved in a serious matter, the guidelines under "Difficult Members and Associates" shall apply.

FILLING OF VACANT OFFICES

Vacant offices are filled as follows:

With regards to Church authorities within the Confraternity:

* The Minister General shall appeal to the Bishop of the Diocese of Fort Wayne – South Bend, Indiana, for a replacement of the Visitor.
* The Minister General shall appeal to the Visitor for replacement of any Spiritual Advisors.
* The Regional Minister shall find a replacement for the Regional Spiritual Advisor.
* The Chapter or Circle Minister shall find a replacement for the Chapter or Circle Spiritual Assistant.

The Minister General and, where applicable, the Visitor shall approve the selections.

If the office of Minister General becomes vacant, the Ministerial Assistant shall immediately convene the CFP Officers and Life Pledged Members and an election held at once according to the Procedures found under the Election of Minister General section of the Directory.

If a vacancy occurs among the CFP Officers or Council of directors, the Minister General, in consultation with the remaining CFP Officers and Council members, shall appoint a replacement.

If the office of a Regional Minister becomes vacant, the Minister General, in consultation with CFP Officers and others, shall appoint a replacement. Regional Ministers shall appoint replacements for other Regional Officers.

If the office of a Chapter or Circle Minister becomes vacant, the group's Assistant Minister shall assume the office of Minister. For other vacancies within a Chapter or Circle, the Minister will appoint replacements.

If a vacancy occurs among Formators in Chapters or Circles, the Chapter or Circle Minister, in consultation with the other Officers, shall appoint a replacement. If a vacancy occurs among Formators on the Regional or international level, the Minister General shall, in consultation with Regional Ministers and CFP Officers and other Council members, appoint a replacement.

Leaders appointed to vacated offices shall complete the term of office by serving until December 31 of the year in which they were appointed.

RETURNING TO
THE CONFRATERNITY

RETURNING TO FORMATION

Applicants who have previously dropped from formation in the Association and who are readmitted to formation will reenter as Associate Postulants if two years or more has elapsed since their withdrawal. If the time of withdrawal has been less than two years, their Regional Minister, in consultation with the Minister General and with the applicant, shall determine their entry level of formation.

RETURNING AFTER WITHDRAWAL, WITH FORMATION COMPLETE

Occasionally Pledged Members of the Confraternity formally withdraw from the Association. Even if they continue to live the CFP Rule of Life on their own, they are incapable of living it fully as the Rule retains a strong community aspect. Therefore, the Confraternity considers those who have withdrawn from the CFP as also having rescinded their pledge. They would then automatically become Associates who have completed formation. Should an individual wish to return to active participation in the Confraternity, he or she shall write a letter to the CFP Office, stating the request. This must be accompanied by written approval of his or her Spiritual Director. If the request is granted, the individual shall be accepted as an active CFP Associate who has completed formation.

If, after a period of time as an Associate, the individual wishes to apply for Membership, he or she must write a letter of request to the CFP Office. This is to be accompanied by a letter from his or her Spiritual Director, agreeing to the request. The applicant shall be interviewed by the appropriate Minister (Chapter/Circle if in a local group; Regional, otherwise) and by the Minister General. The interview shall explore the reasons for their previous withdrawal from Membership in the Confraternity, the motivation for their request for re-admittance, and the extent to which they are currently living the CFP Rule of Life. The Minister and Minister General, in consultation with the Visitor, shall determine if granting the applicant's request is prudent. If so, they shall then determine what is required of the Associate prior to re-pledging, even up to repeating the full period of formation at the normal pace.

Before re-pledging, the individual must complete the three lessons prior to Pledging, must have an interview with a designated CFP Mentor, and must have the necessary documents on file with the CFP Office as listed in the Pledging section of the Directory.

Those who had previously withdrawn from the Confraternity but who are readmitted as Members enjoy all the privileges of Membership and, upon re-pledging, the full privileges of Pledged Members.

OTHER DIFFICULTIES

TROUBLE WITH AUTHORITIES

If trouble is made for penitents within their civil region, the Ministers shall do what is expedient on the advice of the Bishop. If trouble is made for those in a Chapter or Circle, they shall follow the advice of their Spiritual Assistant.

CONFLICT OF INTEREST

A conflict of interest involves any activity which is in violation of the Rule, Constitutions, and/or Directory of the Confraternity of Penitents. The Minister General, with the advice of the CFP Officers, shall determine if any Member is engaged in a conflict of interest. The Visitor with the advice of the Minister General, may dismiss from the CFP anyone whose conflict of interest persists despite correction.

DIFFICULT MEMBERS AND ASSOCIATES

The Confraternity of Penitents acknowledges that difficulties with Members and Associates occasionally arise. Difficult Members and Associates are those who cause or extend discord, harass others, promote teachings contrary to the Doctrine of the Church, the Faith and the Confraternity, and/or give scandal. No matter on what level these occur, the Minister General and Visitor are to be appraised of the difficulty and must approve any course of action before it is taken.

In Chapters and Circles, difficult Members and Associates are dealt with by their Minister and Spiritual Assistant according to the provisions of the Rule contained in Rules and Constitutions 32, 34, 35, 36, and 39. If this is not successful, the problem is referred to their Regional Minister and Regional Spiritual Advisor, and, if necessary, to the Minister General and the Visitor. If resolution is not achieved, the Bishop shall be consulted and his decision followed.

Following the CFP Rule, the Minister's responsibilities in dealing with difficult Members and Associates are as follows:

* Ministers are responsible for keeping peace within their jurisdictions.
* They are to make peace among those in their jurisdiction who are at odds, consulting the Bishop if necessary.
* The Minister reports public faults of Members and Associates to the Spiritual Assistant or Visitor for punishment or correction.
* The Minister also discusses incorrigible Members and Associates with discreet brothers and sisters, denounces them to the Spiritual Assistant or Visitor if warranted, and, if necessary, expels such Members and Associates from any CFP gathering. If they are to be ejected from Membership in or Association with the Confraternity, the guidelines listed earlier in this section of the Directory are to be followed.
* The Minister makes any public offences known to the proper civil or Church authorities.
* The Minister reports any scandal involving a Member to the Spiritual Assistant, and/or Visitor.
* The Minister corrects faults of those who have erred and sees that the disciplinary action(s) or satisfaction recommended by the Visitor or Spiritual Assistant is executed. Otherwise, the penitent is to be deemed contumacious.
* The Minister addresses harassment issues with the Visitor or Spiritual Assistant and presents appeals on dismissal from Members and Associates to the other Officers, the Spiritual Assistant, and the Visitor.

Should any Member or Associate be accused of a serious infraction of the moral or civil law, the Minister shall investigate the accusation and determine whether it might be might be accurate. If so, he or she contacts the next immediate superior, the Minister General, and the appropriate religious authority in the Confraternity (Spiritual Assistant, Regional Spiritual Advisor, or Visitor) regarding the matter. If the accusation involves a leader, that leader's duties in the CFP are temporarily suspended while the investigation proceeds.

If a matter in question is being addressed by civil authority or the authority of the Church, investigation by the CFP leadership will be postponed indefinitely. Any CFP leader under such investigation is automatically removed from office. Once the matter is legally resolved, the appropriate Minister, Minister General, appropriate religious authority in the CFP, and Visitor will consult together to determine the Confraternity's response.

If no legal action is being taken, the CFP Office will arrange a meeting between the accused party, the appropriate Minister, the Minister General, the appropriate CFP religious authority, and the accuser as well as any witnesses for either side. All sides shall be able to present their testimony which shall be recorded by electronic media or secretary. A decision shall made in the presence of at least one witness for each side of the matter. The religious authority, or person designated by the religious authority, shall immediately make the proceedings and the recommended decision known to the Visitor who shall present the information to the Bishop. If a decision cannot be reached, the Visitor shall resolve the matter and make a recommendation to the Bishop. In all cases, the final decision regarding the accusation shall rest with the Bishop or the Visitor at the discretion of the Bishop.

DIFFICULTIES WITH THE MINISTER GENERAL

If the Visitor wishes to expel the Minister General, his decision must be approved by the Bishop before taking effect.

DIFFICULTIES WITH CFP RELIGIOUS AUTHORITIES

If the Minister, in consultation with the officers in his or her jurisdiction, deems it necessary to request the resignation of their Spiritual Assistant or their Regional Spiritual Advisor, the Minister shall consult the Visitor and Minister General for approval before taking action.

Should the Minister General and Visitor be unable to come to an agreement about a decision involving the Confraternity, the matter is taken to the Spiritual Advisors for input and then, if needed, to the Bishop for resolution.

Should anyone feel that the Visitor is creating difficulties for the Confraternity, the Minister General shall be informed. If working with the Visitor to resolve the problem is unsuccessful, the Minister General shall seek the guidance of the Spiritual Advisors. Depending on their recommendations, the Minister General may take the matter to the Bishop who alone has the authority to discipline or remove a Visitor from service to the CFP.

DIRECTORY APPENDICES

"So pleasing to God was Mary's humility that He was constrained by His goodness to entrust to her the Word, His only Son. And it was that dearest Mary who gave Him to us." *St. Catherine of Siena*

The Way to God

If my days were untroubled and my heart always light, would I seek that fair land where there is no night? . . . If I never grew weary with the weight of my load, would I search for God's Peace at the end of the road? . . If I never knew sickness and never felt pain, would I search for a hand to help and sustain?

If I walked not with sorrow and lived without loss, would my soul seek sweet solace at the foot of the cross?. . .If all I desired was mine day by day, would I kneel before God and earnestly pray?. . If God sent no "Winter" to freeze me with fear, would I yearn for the warmth of "Spring" every year?

I ask myself this and the answer is plain; if my life were all pleasure and I never knew pain. . . I'd seek God less often and need Him much less, for God's sought more often in times of distress . . . And no one knows God or sees Him as plain as those who have met Him on the "Pathway of Pain."

APPENDIX A: SAMPLE OF YEARLY LETTER REQUESTING CONFIRMATION OF THE FOUNDER AS MINISTER GENERAL

The following letter is a sample of one to be sent to all Pledged Members at the time of the yearly CFP elections.

NOMINATING COMMITTEE CHAIRPERSON'S NAME, ADDRESS, EMAIL, PHONE, DATE

Dear Life-Pledged Members of the Confraternity of Penitents,

Blessings and all good.

The office of Minister General is the primary governing office of the Confraternity of Penitents. With the permission of the Diocese of Fort Wayne – South Bend, Indiana, USA, Madeline Pecora Nugent, as "Founder" of the Confraternity of Penitents, has been appointed to serve in this office for the remainder of her life or until she is no longer able to serve. At this time of CFP elections, to satisfy the provisions of our Rule and of the State of Indiana Non Profit Corporations Act, you are asked to pray and discern your agreement with this confirmation for the upcoming year. If so, please complete this form:

I, _____(PRINT NAME), as a Life-Pledged Member of the Confraternity of Penitents, support the confirmation of Madeline Pecora Nugent as Minister General for the year _____(UPCOMING YEAR)..

*Signed:*_____*(SIGNATURE)*

Date: _____

Address: _____

By November 1 of this year, please mail this confirmation form to
_____ *(CHAIRPERSON OF NOMINATING COMMITTEE),*
_____*(ADDRESS OF CHAIRPER-*
SON OF NOMINATING COMMITTEE)

APPENDIX B: SAMPLE BALLOT LETTER FOR ELECTING A MINISTER GENERAL

The letter is a sample of one to be sent to all Life Pledged Members at the time of election of a Minister General.

Dear Life-Pledged Members of the Confraternity of Penitents,

Blessings and all good.

The office of Minister General is (or soon will be) vacant. This is the primary governing office for the Confraternity of Penitents. The Minister General must be committed to promoting the Charism of the Confraternity, to upholding every part of the Rule, Constitutions, and Directory, to seeing that formation is conducted properly, and to promoting the message of the Confraternity worldwide. All Life-Pledged Members, by virtue of their life pledge, are eligible to hold the office of Minister General and participate in the elections.

To fill this position, a Nominating Committee has identified the following three suitable candidates, all of whom are Life-Pledged Members of the Confraternity of Penitents and who have agreed to accept the office for six consecutive years (confirmed annually), should they be elected. Their names, contact information, and qualifications are as follows:

NAME OF FIRST CANDIDATE, ADDRESS, CONTACT INFORMATION, QUALIFICATIONS

NAME OF SECOND CANDIDATE, ADDRESS, CONTACT INFORMATION, QUALIFICATIONS

NAME OF THIRD CANDIDATE, ADDRESS, CONTACT INFORMATION, QUALIFICATIONS

Before making your selection, we encourage you to contact these individuals. After prayer and discernment, please complete the attached ballot with your vote for Minister General. You may write in the name of any other Life-Pledged Member if you so choose.

As soon as possible, please contact the Chairperson of the Nominating Committee if you wish to vote by another means.

I vote for _____ (NAME) for Minister General.

Place this ballot into the blank envelope marked "Ballot" and seal. Place the sealed "Ballot Envelope" into the enclosed stamped envelope and mail to the Chairperson of the Nominating Committee whose address appears on the envelope.

Ballots must be received by _____(DATE) to be counted.

The candidate receiving the majority of the votes shall assume the office of Minister General. Should there be a tie, a new election will be held between the tied candidates.

As soon as the results are ascertained, the Nominating Committee Chairperson shall make the elected Minister General known to all Life-Pledged Members, to the Visitor, and to the Bishop of the Diocese of Fort Wayne – South Bend. The elected Minister General must be approved by the Visitor and accepted by the Bishop before assuming office.

APPENDIX C: SAMPLE LETTER REQUESTING ANNUAL CONFIRMATION OF ELECTED MINISTER GENERAL

The following is a sample letter, requesting annual confirmation by Life-Pledged Members of an elected Minister General who is currently completing the six year term of office.

Dear Life-Pledged Members of the Confraternity of Penitents,

Blessings and all good.

At this time of CFP elections, you are asked to support the confirmation of _____ (NAME) as Minister General for the upcoming year. Having been elected to the office of Minister General in _____ (YEAR), _____(NAME) has _____(NUMBER) years of his or her six year term remaining. Each year, a majority of Life-Pledged Members must reconfirm this election. Please complete the following form and return it to the Ministerial Assistant.

If you wish to make the confirmation known by another means, please contact the Ministerial Assistant as soon as possible.

I approve/disapprove (PLEASE CIRCLE ONE) of the confirmation of _____ (NAME) as Minister General for the year _____ (DATE).

Your Name:_____

*Your Signature:*_____

*Date:*_____

Please return this form to _____ *(NAME), the Ministerial Assistant of the*
CFP at _____ *(ADDRESS)*

Forms must be received by November 1 to be counted.

If a majority of Life-Pledged Members disapprove of the confirmation of Minister General, you
will be contacted regarding the election of a replacement.

APPENDIX D: SAMPLE LETTER OF NOMINATIONS FOR CFP OFFICERS

The following is a sample letter of Nominations for CFP Officers, soliciting nominations from Life Pledged Members for the yearly election.

NOMINATING COMMITTEE CHAIRPERSON'S ADDRESS, EMAIL, PHONE, DATE

Dear Life Pledged Members of the Confraternity of Penitents,

Peace to you and God's blessings!

As you know, Confraternity Officers are elected yearly with new terms beginning January 1. Now it is time to begin the election process for the coming year. Only Life Pledged Members are eligible to be nominated, vote, or be elected as Officers of the Confraternity of Penitents. All Life Pledged Members are asked to consider themselves open to election as stated in section 28 of our Rule and Constitutions.

As the Nominating Committee, we propose a slate of CFP Officers, all of whom have agreed to serve if elected. They are:

CFP Ministerial Assistant: Name, Address, Contact Information, Qualifications

CFP Messenger: Name, Address, Contact Information, Qualifications

CFP Treasurer: Name, Address, Contact Information, Qualifications

You, as a Life Pledged Member of the CFP, have the opportunity to put forward any other Life Pledged Member for any of the above offices. All nominees must be in good standing in the Church and in the Confraternity and must agree to serve if elected. A Member may hold only one elected office during any given term.

CFP Officers will serve as advisors to the Minister General. The CFP Ministerial Assistant will be the Minister General's primary assistant in fulfilling his or her duties and will be in charge of planning the annual CFP Retreat/Reunion/Conference and the Life Pledged Chapter. The CFP Treasurer will handle all funds for the Confraternity. The CFP Messenger will record and publish the minutes at the yearly CFP Council meeting which all CFP Officers and other Council members must attend, if possible. CFP Officers will perform their duties, as much as possible, from their own homes.

Terms of office will be one year.

Additional Life Pledged Members eligible to be nominated at this time are:

NAMES AND ADDRESSES OF ALL LIFE PLEDGED MEMBERS NOT ON SLATE AND ELIGIBLE FOR ELECTION AS DETERMINED BY THE NOMINATING COMMITTEE

NOMINATION FORM

I nominate the following individual(s) for office. Please list the name(s) and office(s) below:

SIGNED:

All nominations must be received by the Chairperson of the Nominating Committee, NAME, ADDRESS, EMAIL, PHONE, by October 10 to be placed on the ballot. Nominations received after that date will not be included.

Thank you and God bless you.

NAMES OF NOMINATING COMMITTEE WITH CHAIRPERSON FIRST

APPENDIX E: SAMPLE BALLOT LETTER FOR ELECTING CFP OFFICERS

The following is a sample ballot letter for the yearly election of CFP Officers.

NAME, ADDRESS, EMAIL OF NOMINATING COMMITTEE CHAIRPESON
Dear Life Pledged Member of the Confraternity of Penitents,
Blessings and every good.
As you know, we are in the process of conducting elections for the Confraternity of Penitents. The following slates have been put forward:
The slate proposed by the Nominating Committee is as follows:
CFP Ministerial Assistant: Name, Address, Contact Information, Qualifications

CFP Messenger: NAME, ADDRESS, CONTACT INFORMATION, QUALIFICATIONS

CFP Treasurer: NAME, ADDRESS, CONTACT INFORMATION, QUALIFICATIONS

Life Pledged Members of the Confraternity have nominated the following slate:

CFP Ministerial Assistant: NAME(S), ADDRESS(ES), CONTACT INFORMATION, QUALIFICATIONS

CFP Messenger: Name(s), Address(es), Contact Information, Qualifications

CFP Treasurer: NAME(S), ADDRESS(ES), CONTACT INFORMATION, QUALIFICATIONS

Each Life Pledged Member has one vote per office. Candidates who receive the majority of votes shall hold the office. In the event of a tie for an office, a reelection will be held immediately and will proceed through the same procedures as the original election.

The Nominating Committee will keep the vote confidential except for the results of the election which will be submitted only to the Minister General who shall immediately make the results known to the full Membership.

If any Life Pledged Member feels that an election was conducted improperly, he or she may appeal to the Minister General for a new election.

Please pray about and then submit your vote for our CFP Officers. May the Holy Spirit guide the election of our CFP Officers for the coming year.

Sincerely,

NAMES OF NOMINATING COMMITTEE MEMBERS WITH CHAIRPERSON NAMED FIRST
Ballot

Please write in your choice for the following offices:

Ministerial Assistant _____

CFP Treasurer _____

CFP Messenger _____

Please place this ballot in the envelope marked "Ballot" and seal the envelope. Place the sealed "Ballot Envelope" in the enclosed stamped envelope and mail it to the Chairperson of the Nominating Committee whose address appears on the envelope.

Ballots must be received by November 1 in order to be counted.

APPENDIX F: SAMPLE QUESTIONS FOR MINISTER'S INTERVIEW OF INQUIRERS

The appropriate Minister (Chapter or Circle for local groups; Regional otherwise) interviews Inquirer applicants to determine their suitability for entering the Inquiry stage of the Confraternity of Penitents. Some sample questions to ask are:

What attracted you to the Confraternity of Penitents?

How did you find out about us?

Why do you feel God is calling you to inquire with us at this time?

What do you hope to gain if you were to join the CFP?

Have you inquired with other lay associations or Orders? Which ones? What were your thoughts about them?

What are you looking for in a community of lay Catholics?

How does your family feel about your inquiring? Is your family supportive? Does your family understand your interest?

What was your family like when you were growing up?

What is your family like now?

Are you married? If so, is your marriage considered valid by the Catholic Church?

If you are single, do you live alone or with someone else? What is your relationship to that person (those persons)?

How does your past life compare to where you are now?

When were you first attracted to God?

Did you have a conversion?

Why do you want to become a penitent? What are your goals in the spiritual life?

Do you spend time in prayer? What is your prayer life like?

How often do you attend Mass?

How often to you frequent the Sacraments?
What are your views on obedience to authority?
Do you agree with all that the Roman Catholic Church teaches?
Do you have a Spiritual Director?
What is your health like? Do you have any medical problems? Are you on any medications?

APPENDIX G: SAMPLE LETTER TO INACTIVE INQUIRERS

Inquirers who have not made contact with the Confraternity for six months or more are sent a letter, by email if applicable or, if no response to the email letter, by postal mail. Similar to the letter below, the correspondence is to ascertain whether the inquirers continue to be interested in the CFP. If the letter does not elicit a response, the status of the Inquirer automatically changes to that of friend of the Confraternity.

Dear (NAME OF INQUIRER),

Peace to you in the Names of Our Lord and His Mother!

Some time ago you expressed interest in the Confraternity of Penitents. We were most happy then to hear of your interest, and we hope that you are still interested. However, we have not heard from you in some time.

If you are still discerning whether or not to enter formation, please let us know that you wish to remain an Inquirer.

If we do not hear from you within the next month, we will assume you are no longer interested in entering formation. We will, therefore, change your status to that of friend of the Confraternity. Thereafter, if ever you are interested in reentering the Inquiry stage, please contact us.

Whatever you decide, thank you again for your interest in the Confraternity of Penitents. May God bless you in your journey in His Love.

Please pray for us as we pray daily for you.

Sincerely yours in Christ!

The Confraternity of Penitents

APPENDIX H: SAMPLE WELCOME LETTER TO CURRENT FORMATION YEAR

At the beginning of each formation year (Ash Wednesday), the CFP Office postal mails or emails each Member who is advancing into formation this or a similar letter.

Dear _____,

Blessings to you!

We have received and accepted your formation application. We praise the Lord that you wish to begin, continue, repeat, or advance in your formation as a penitent. We look forward to mutual sharing with you about our Rule and Constitutions, our Faith, and our Lord.

Formation begins with Postulancy and continues through the three years of the Novitiate. While the Postulancy may be completed in less than twelve months, each Novice year must last a minimum of twelve months in length, although the year of formation may be extended upon request.

Your Formator will be in contact with you regarding how to submit your lessons. Please be sure to read the entire lesson in either the CFP Handbook or on line before completing your lesson and returning answers to your Formator.

Please do not hesitate to contact us with any questions or concerns.

Grateful to Our Lord, we will hold you in our prayers during this formation year and ask you for your prayers.

In the Love of Christ,
The Confraternity of Penitents

APPENDIX I: SAMPLE LETTER TO INACTIVE PENITENTS IN FORMATION

Penitents who have not completed any formation lessons for six months or more, and who have not been in touch with their Formators regarding their formation, are postal mailed the following letter, or one similar to it, to ascertain their continued interest in the Confraternity.

Dear _____ (NAME),

Peace to you in the Names of Our Lord and His Mother!

Some time ago you entered the (year of formation) in the Confraternity of Penitents. We were most happy then to hear of your interest and hope you are still interested in the Confraternity. However, we haven't received any lessons from you in six months, and we were wondering if you are still interested in pursuing formation in the Confraternity.

Please let us know if you are having difficulties of some sort. If it is too difficult to catch up now, we suggest that you suspend your formation until Lent and then begin again. You need not repeat any lessons you have already completed. If we do not hear from you sometime in the next month we will change your status to that of friend. Thereafter, if ever you are interested in resuming formation, please contact us.

Thank you again for your interest in the Confraternity of Penitents. May God bless you in your journey in the Love of God.

Please pray for us as we pray daily for you. Sincerely yours in Christ!

The Confraternity of Penitents

APPENDIX J: SAMPLE LETTER TO A BISHOP INTRODUCING A CFP CHAPTER OR CIRCLE

Once established, Chapters and Circles ought to introduce themselves to the bishop of the diocese in which they are meeting. Here is a sample letter to a bishop, introducing a Chapter or Circle. The letter should be mailed on CFP letterhead, and a CFP information handout, CFP monthly newsletter, and CFP prayer card should be mailed with this letter. Letterhead and other items are available from the Confraternity office.

The Regional Minister can assist in refining and adapting this letter:

NAME OF CHAPTER OR CIRCLE
NAME OF CHAPTER OR CIRCLE CONTACT (GENERALLY THE MINISTER)
ADDRESS OF CHAPTER OR CIRCLE
PHONE NUMBER
EMAIL
DATE

BISHOP'S NAME
BISHOP'S ADDRESS

Dear Bishop _____:

May the Lord grant you His peace!

This letter is to inform you about the existence of _____ (NAME OF CHAPTER OR CIRCLE) of the Confraternity of Penitents within this diocese and to humbly request your support and prayers.

The Confraternity of Penitents is a private Catholic association of the faithful whose members are following a primitive Rule for penitents, which was created especially for the laity under the leadership of Cardinal Hugolino de Conti de Segni in 1221. Members follow this Rule according to its Constitutions which have been accepted by Bishop Kevin Rhoades of the Diocese of Fort Wayne - South Bend, Indiana USA (initial acceptance on 30 January 1998 by Bishop Thomas Mulvee of the Diocese of Providence, Rhode Island, USA, where the Confraternity of Penitents was established.) A copy of Bishop Rhoades' letter of 3 January 2014 is enclosed.

Worldwide there are presently _____(NUMBER AVAILABLE FROM THE CFP OFFICE) pledged members of the CFP and approximately _____ (NUMBER AVAILABLE FROM CFP OFFICE) in formation. Within this diocese, _____(NAME OF LOCAL CHAPTER OR CIRCLE) of the Confraternity of Penitents, has_____(NUMBER) inquirer(s), _____(NUMBER) member(s) in formation, and _____(NUMBER) pledged member(s). We are most grateful to have as our Spiritual Assistant _____(NAME) who is _____ _____(BRIEF IDENTIFYING INFORMATION ABOUT THE SPIRITUAL ASSISTANT SUCH AS WHAT CHURCH OR ORDER HE OR SHE BELONGS TO, HIS OR HER MINISTRY, ADDRESS, AND SO ON.)

Much information on the Confraternity, including our Rule and Constitutions, is on the Internet at www.penitents.org Upon your request, I would be glad to provide you with a copy of the Confraternity Handbook which contains the Rule, Constitutions, Structure, and formation lessons for the Postulant and Novice years as well as much other information. In the meantime, I have enclosed our current newsletter and will see that you receive the newsletter monthly.

If you would wish to meet with me regarding _____(NAME OF LOCAL CHAPTER OR CIRCLE), I will be happy to do so at your convenience.

I look forward to hearing from you.

Sincerely Yours in Christ,

YOUR SIGNATURE
YOUR TYPED NAME
YOUR OFFICE IN YOUR LOCAL CHAPTER OR CIRCLE

Enclosures:
Letter from Bishop Kevin Rhoades
CFP Informational Handout
CFP Prayer Card
CFP monthly newsletter

"You shall love the Lord your God with your whole heart, with your whole soul, and with all your mind, (and) you shall love your neighbor as yourself." (Matthew 22:37-38)

APPENDIX K: SAMPLE REGIONAL MINISTER'S LETTER TO REGION

The following is a sample letter which Regional Ministers may send to the Regional Members and Associates whom they have not heard from in some time.

NAME OF REGIONAL MINISTER
ADDRESS
EMAIL
PHONE

DEAR _____,

We send greetings from the Confraternity of Penitents through our Lord, Jesus Christ and pray for His richest blessings upon you.

If you are receiving this message, it is because we have you listed as in formation with the CFP or as a Formator in the Region of _____ *If this is not the case, please reply and let us know how to update our records. If you have discontinued your association with the Confraternity, it would be most helpful and very much appreciated if you would let us know whether this is due to any inadequacy or failure on our part or that of the Confraternity or whether discernment with God has simply led you in another direction.*

We are writing at this time to see how you are doing in formation and to inquire if there are any questions or concerns with which we might be of assistance. We hope and pray that all is well with you and that you are progressing "in wisdom and age and favor before God and man" as Jesus did under the tutelage of Mary and Joseph. (See Luke 2:52)

In your reply, if you would be so kind as to indicate your year of formation and the lesson on which you are working for this month, we will be able to determine that all our records are current. We thank you for this kindness.

Please do not hesitate to ask for our assistance if we might be helpful to you. If all is well, we would be grateful to hear that, too. Please be assured of our daily prayers and those of the entire Confraternity.

Your servant in Christ,

_____

CFP Regional Minister for _____

APPENDIX L: SAMPLE LETTER TO SOMEONE LEAVING THE CONFRATERNITY

It frequently happens that inquirers, Members, or Associates discern that the God is calling them to another way of life and so they discontinue formation or inquiry with the Confraternity. Most of these people remain friends of the Confraternity and some may become Affiliates. This is a sample letter to someone who is leaving, written by the CFP leader who had jurisdiction over the penitent either as Minister or Formator.

Dear_____,

I am so sad that you are withdrawing from formation! But the CFP is often a time of discernment, and following the Boss is all that matters. Perhaps there will be a time when He will draw you back into our Confraternity.

You probably know by now that once you come into the CFP you are always one of us: in our hearts, in our prayers and on our mailing list as a "friend." Perhaps you would consider becoming a CFP Affiliate (information enclosed) and thus retaining contact with the CFP in this manner.

Godspeed to you and may the Lord shower you with every blessing and grace as you continue to walk beside him.

Please feel free to write at any time; stay in touch. I have come to think of you as a beautiful friend.

God bless,

YOUR NAME
YOUR TITLE IN THE CFP

APPENDIX M: CERTIFICATES

The following pages contain certificates for Affiliation, Year Pledge, Life Pledge and Vow. Certificates should be copied and used as needed.

CERTIFICATE OF AFFILIATION WITH THE CONFRATERNITY OF PENITENTS

This is to certify that on

_____

_____

was welcomed by the Confraternity of Penitents as an Affiliate.

While not a Member of the Confraternity, an Affiliate is a respected prayer partner and, by virtue of this Affiliation, is to pray daily, and to offer one Mass yearly, for the Confraternity and all its members. The Affiliate is also to be consecrated to the Blessed Mother, to promote penance (conversion), and to maintain peace with all. The status of Affiliate of the Confraternity of Penitents remains in effect as long as these stipulations are met. May God grant you the grace to keep your the requirements of your Affiliation. The Confraternity of Penitents promises you our daily prayers.

Confraternity of Penitents, 1702 Lumbard Street, Fort Wayne IN 46803 USA www.penitents.org

YEAR PLEDGE
IN THE
CONFRATERNITY OF PENITENTS

On the _____ day of _____

in the year of Our Lord

_____

By the grace of God and under the motion of the Holy Spirit, having successfully completed four years of formation in the lifestyle and having discerned the Will of God, and with the approval of a spiritual director,

_____

Pledged to live for one year the Rule of Life of the Confraternity of Penitents.

Pledged to:

_____

Witnessed by:

_____

Signed:

_____ *(Pledged Penitent)*

_____ *(Priest or Deacon)*

_____ *(Other Witness)*

_____ *(Confraternity Visitor)*

"You shall love the Lord your God with your whole heart, with your whole soul, and with all your mind, (and) you shall love your neighbor as yourself." (Matthew 22:37-38)

LIFE PLEDGE
IN THE
CONFRATERNITY OF PENITENTS

On the _____ day of _____

in the year of Our Lord

_____

By the grace of God and under the motion of the Holy Spirit, having successfully completed four years of formation in the lifestyle and having discerned the Will of God, and with the approval of a spiritual director,

_____

Pledged to live for life the Rule of Life of the Confraternity of Penitents.

Pledged to:

_____

Witnessed by:

_____

Signed:

_____ *(Pledged Penitent)*

_____ *(Priest or Deacon)*

_____ *(Other Witness)*

_____ *(Confraternity Visitor)*

"You shall love the Lord your God with your whole heart, with your whole soul, and with all your mind, (and) you shall love your neighbor as yourself." (Matthew 22:37-38)

VOWED LIFE
IN THE
CONFRATERNITY OF PENITENTS

On the _____ day of _____

in the year of Our Lord

_____

By the grace of God and under the motion of the Holy Spirit, having successfully completed four years of formation in the lifestyle and having discerned the Will of God, and with the approval of a spiritual director,

_____

_____

Vowed to live for life the Rule of Life of the Confraternity of Penitents.

Vowed to:

_____

Witnessed by:

_____

Signed:

_____ *(Pledged Penitent)*

_____ *(Priest or Deacon)*

_____ *(Other Witness)*

_____ *(Confraternity Visitor)*

"You shall love the Lord your God with your whole heart, with your whole soul, and with all your mind, (and) you shall love your neighbor as yourself." (Matthew 22:37-38)

APPENDIX N: SAMPLE FORMAT FOR A CONFRATERNITY OF PENITENTS DAY OF RECOLLECTION

Goals of a CFP Day of Recollection:

1. It affords penitents a day to quietly reflect together on their spiritual journey toward a life of deeper penance (conversion).
2. It evangelizes the general Catholic population.
3. It informs others about the existence of the Confraternity of Penitents.

Tips for a Successful Day of Recollection

1. Choose a location with ample, free parking. A parish meeting hall is ideal.
2. Select a vibrant priest, deacon, or religious to conduct the day (a priest can have Mass and Confessions).
3. Center the Day of Recollection around a season. Lent is especially effective.
4. Provide beverages. Have attendees bring a bag lunch. Have some extra food for those who forgot.
5. Near the beverages, place a basket with a few dollars in it, for a free will offering. Give the offering to the priest or religious and to the meeting location.
6. Begin and end on time.
7. Two to three weeks in advance, send bulletin announcements to all Catholic parishes within reasonable driving distance. Also send brief write ups to local and diocesan papers. Posters and flyers are helpful.
8. Ask folks to maintain a quiet, reflective atmosphere and encourage silence by playing soft, instrumental hymns during the quiet time.
9. If you pray Daytime Prayers, hand out copies of the psalms for attendees to follow.

10. Post the schedule on a large poster, blackboard, or white board.
11. Have name tags.
12. At the beginning, welcome all, point out restrooms, offering basket, beverages. Go over silent nature of the day, tell where confessions will be held, and so on.
13. Have free handouts on the CFP and a sample CFP Handbook. Point out location in a welcome talk.

Sample Schedule

9 a.m. Registration

9:30 a.m. Welcome, Mid morning Prayer, followed by Mass and homily, then quiet time and confessions

11:00 a.m. First Conference

Noon: Angelus, Midday prayer followed by bag lunch

12:45 p.m. Second Conference

1:30 p.m. Third Conference

2:15 p.m. Holy Hour with Exposition, Rosary, Chaplet of Divine Mercy, Midafternoon Prayer. Confessions heard at this time.

3:30 p.m. Benediction

Format for Bulletin Announcement

Keep the bulletin announcement short. Give the full location, beginning and ending times, date, presenter, content, contact. State that the day is sponsored by the CFP.

This announcement can also be sent to local newspapers and radio stations.

Enclose a note with the announcement, asking that it be placed in the parish bulletin, preferably for the two weekends in advance of the Day of Recollection. It is especially helpful if you can hand deliver the note to the parish.

A _____*(Lenten, Advent, other occasion)* Day of Recollection will be held at _____ *(name of parish and exact location. Be sure to give the street name and number as well as the town or city)* on _____ *(give the full date and day of week, month, day, and year)* from _____ *(beginning time)* to _____ *(ending time)*. The presenter will be _____ *(name of priest, deacon, male or female religious who will be giving the talks. Give some identifying information about this person such as their religious Order, parish, expertise, and so on)* The day will feature *(list all from this list that will be part of the Day of Recollection: Mass, Holy Hour, Confessions, Conferences, Rosary, Divine Mercy Chaplet, Adoration, Benediction, Faith Sharing). Tell how lunch will be served. Will you have everyone bring a bag lunch and you provide beverages? Will lunch be available for a fee? Pot* *luck lunch? Catered lunch? If you have a fee for the lunch or will be taking up a free will offering, state it here. Also state if any religious items will be available for donation or purchase).* All welcome. Sponsored by the Confraternity of Penitents *(if a Chapter or Circle is the sponsor, give its name also)* For more information, call _____ *(contact's name)* at _____ *(contact's phone number)* or email _____ *(contact's email)*

APPENDIX O: DOCUMENTS NEEDED FOR PLEDGING

_____ (NAME OF PENITENT)

Prior to Pledging, the Member must have submitted to the CFP Office the following documents to be held on file[57]:

_____* An updated Baptismal Certificate. If it is impossible to obtain an updated Baptismal Certificate, a copy of the original Baptismal Certificate is acceptable, but it should be accompanied by copy of the penitent's Marriage Certificate (if applicable) and a letter on parish letterhead from the Member's parish priest. The letter should indicate that the penitent is in good standing in the parish. If it is impossible to obtain any copy of any Baptismal Certificate, or of any one of the other documents mentioned herein, the Diocese of Fort Wayne – South Bend is to be consulted and their directives followed.

_____* For converts, a copy of a document indicating that they have entered into full communion with the Church, including the date of entry. This may be a special RCIA certificate, a "Profession of Faith" certificate, or any document which indicates that the Member is a Catholic such as a letter from their parish priest.

_____* The Pledged Application found in the CFP Handbook and on the web site, completed, signed, and dated by the penitent and his or her Spiritual Director. The Spiritual Director may also write a letter of recommendation for pledging.

_____*A signed and dated letter from the penitent's Formator, stating that the penitent has successfully completed all four years of formation and that the penitent is prepared to pledge.

---

57   (CODE: X means the CFP Office has this document on file. A blank space means this document is needed. A NN means the document is not needed).

_____*A letter from the Mentor assigned to the penitent. In the letter, the Mentor must state that the penitent has completed the three lessons prior to pledging and that the mentor has interviewed the penitent and insured that he or she clearly understands the seriousness of the obligations and commitments of a Pledged Member. The Mentor must also state that he or she believes that the penitent is prepared to undertake the commitment.

_____* A letter from the Member about to be pledged, stating that he or she has made a day of recollection or a retreat prior to pledging (either informally at home or as a formal, Church sponsored event) and including the date, location, and summary of their thoughts about the event in relation to their Pledging.

_____* If applicable, a signed and dated letter from the appropriate superior of any other Association to which the penitent has pledged (professed) to live a Rule of Life, stating that the penitent has the permission of the Association to pledge to live the CFP Rule.[58]

PLEDGING PRIOR TO COMPLETION OF FORMATION

_____* If, due to impending, life-threatening illness, debilitation, or accident, it appears prudent that a member pledge prior to completion of formation, two notes from two different doctors are required, stating that the penitent's life is in grave danger.

_____* Note signed by Visitor and Minister General, stating their agreement that the penitent may pledge prior to completion of formation.

---

58   Under Canon Law, an individual may profess (pledge) to observe the Rules of more than one Association provided that they both agree. The Confraternity permits those professed to the CFP Rule to also observe the Rules of other Associations approved by the Roman Catholic Church.

APPENDIX P: SAMPLE PHYSICIAN'S NOTE FOR PENITENT WHO MUST PLEDGE BEFORE COMPLETION OF FORMATION

In my professional judgment as physician for _____(name of penitent), I believe that _____'s (name of penitent) physical condition is grave and that any unfinished business which he or she wishes to undertake should be prudently completed as soon as possible.

Sincerely,

(signed)

(Please print name)_____

Address _____

_____

Date_____

Professional seal or please enclose stationary of medical office which shows the physician's name.

APPENDIX Q: SUMMARY OF REGIONAL MINISTER DUTIES

Summarized from Directory of Governance

Regional Ministers serve one year terms from January through December.

The Regional Minister is one of the most important servant leaders in the Confraternity of Penitents because the Regional Minister is the primary contact for all new isolated inquirers to the CFP. Thus, the Regional Minister is the personal face of the Confraternity to the new inquirer. For this reason, even when the Regional Minister's term ends, former Regional Ministers are encouraged to continue correspondence on a friendship level with Members and Associates of their former regions.

Regional Ministers assume jurisdiction over their regions.

Chapter and Circle Ministers assume jurisdiction over their local groups. Therefore the Chapter or Circle Minister is to assume in their local group all duties listed below that apply to a local group.

In cases in which the Minister General is to be consulted for approval, the Chapter or Circle Minister must also consult the Regional Minister.

REGARDING PRE-INQUIRERS AND INQUIRERS, THE REGIONAL MINISTER:

- Answers questions of pre-inquirers and invites them to submit inquirer application.
- Informs CFP Office if pre-inquirer withdraws from pursuit of a CFP vocation.
- Contacts new Inquirers by either phone, email, or postal mail within a few days of receiving notice of new Inquirer.
- Requests a response from the Inquirer regarding arranging the Inquirer Interview.

- Tells CFP Office when Inquirer has responded to Minister's contact.
- Conducts the Inquirer Interview within 2 weeks of the date of the Inquirer Application (if the CFP Office does not hear that mutual contact has been achieved with the new inquirer during these initial two weeks, the CFP Office will attempt to initiate contact with the intention of conducting the Interview)
- Determines if new inquirer shall be Member or Associate
- Upon the completion of the Inquirer Interview, accepts the new inquirer into inquiry (unless there are "red flags")
- Alerts the CFP Minister General if there seem to be "red flags" about the inquirer
- With approval of Minister General and Visitor, may deny entry into inquiry
- Sends copy of inquirer interview to CFP Office
- Invites inquirer to be in touch with questions or concerns
- Responds to the Inquirer Reflections with the new inquirer
- Invites inquirer to enter postulancy once a minimum of three months of inquiry has been met
- May waive the 3 month inquiry period, with approval of Minister General
- Checks with all inquirers eligible for formation prior to each formation entry date, to ascertain continued interest
- Approves those desiring to enter postulancy
- Grants extension of inquiry period
- Contacts inactive inquirers to ascertain continued interest and informs Minister General of results

REGARDING MEMBERS AND ASSOCIATES IN FORMATION, THE REGIONAL MINISTER:

- Advises Minister General on assigning Formators in or from region
- May appoint Formators with approval of Minister General
- Oversee Formators in region to make sure that formation is being done successfully
- If desired, may collect formation applications and submit to CFP Office
- Keeps list of those in formation and their Formators
- Checks with Members and Associates approximately every two months to see if they have any questions or concerns and to ascertain how formation is going.
- Approves those moving into next year of formation
- Welcomes Members into next year of formation
- May approve entry level into postulancy up to one month after normal entry date (Ash Wednesday or August 1)
- May grant free CFP handbook to Novice 2 and above who cannot afford the cost

- Along with Formator and Minister General, approves prolonged, postponed, simultaneous, and continued formation as well as reentry into formation
- In consultation with Minister General, determines entry level of formation for Members who have dropped from formation or taken a leave of absence
- If Formator is unsuccessful at contacting an inactive Formatee, Regional Minister attempts to contact Members and Associates who have not submitted lessons in six months or more. Informs CFP Office of the results.
- With Minister General and Visitor, determines if those who had pledged and dropped but who apply for re-admittance are to be approved

REGARDING PLEDGED MEMBERS AND ASSOCIATES WHO HAVE COMPLETED FORMATION, THE REGIONAL MINISTER:

- Retains contact periodically on a friendship basis
- Alerts the CFP Office if any pledged Member or Associate is in need in any way

IN THE AREA OF KEEPING PEACE, THE REGIONAL MINISTER:

- Alerts Minister General to any difficulties in the region
- Consults bishop in region, if necessary, if regional Member or Associate is incorrigible
- Takes disciplinary action against incorrigible Members or Associates not able to be dealt with in Chapter or Circle
- Keeps peace in region
- Reports public faults of Members and Associates to Visitor and makes them known to civil or Church authorities.
- Reports scandal involving a Member or Associate to the Visitor
- Corrects faults of those who have erred and sees that the disciplinary action(s) or satisfaction recommended by the Visitor is executed.
- Addresses harassment issues with Visitor
- Presents appeals on dismissal from Members and Associates to the other Officers and the Visitor
- Investigates serious infractions of the moral or civil law involving Members or Associates and contacts Minister General and Visitor if accusation seems accurate and, with them, determines Confraternity's response
- Consults with Visitor and Minister General if Regional Spiritual Assistant or Regional Officer needs to be dismissed or reprimanded

IN REGARD TO CHAPTERS AND CIRCLES, THE REGIONAL MINISTER:

- Approves names and banners (if any) of new Chapters and Circles to be confirmed by Minister General and Visitor
- Maintains regular contact with Chapter and Circle Ministers
- May assist Chapter Minister in composing letter to bishop about Chapter existence
- Assists in growth of Chapters and Circles by putting Members in close proximity in touch with each other, with their permission
- In new Chapters and Circles, assists in appointing initial officers
- Keeps Minister General informed of Chapter and Circle developments

IN GENERAL, THE REGIONAL MINISTER:

- Maintains regular contact with isolated regional Members and Associates
- Retains address list for those in region
- Informs CFP Office of change to membership data
- Consults Minister General if unable to answer questions about CFP
- May appoint Regional Spiritual Advisor with approval of Visitor
- Consults Visitor or Regional Spiritual Assistant if unable to answer questions on spiritual matters
- May appoint Regional Officers (1 year terms) with approval of Minister General
- Receives requests for alms from regional Members or Associates (requests must be accompanied by 3 letters of referral, one from parish priest). Discusses those worthy of consideration with Minister General, Treasurer, CFP Officers and decision reached
- Determines if Visitor ought to be consulted if Member or Associate has a question
- May initiate fundraisers for region, with Minister General's approval and approval of Regional Officers
- May conduct Regional Council of Directors meetings and gatherings of regional Members and Associates, with Minister General and Council's approval
- Keeps in touch weekly with ill Members and Associates in region
- May make minor dispensations to Rule for region with approval of Minister General and Visitor
- Informs CFP office if absent from region for a lengthy time
- Accepts letters requesting Membership from Associates, approves or disapproves, and shares decision with Minister General who must confirm
- May contact those leaving CFP to determine reasons for departure
- Along with Minister General and Visitor, determines if Members should be disallowed continuance with the Confraternity

- With Minister General and Visitor, grants leaves of absence and resignations from Regional leadership
- Sees that Regional Officers adequately perform their duties. Contacts Minister General if problems.
- Appoints replacement for vacant Regional Offices
- Consults Directory of the CFP for details of duties and for sample letters to Members and Associates on duties discussed above

REGARDING AFFILIATES

- All Regional Minister directives regarding contact with and keeping peace and disciplinary actions regarding Members and Associates apply also to Affiliates.

OBLIGATIONS OF THE CONFRATERNITY TOWARD REGIONAL MINISTERS

- To pay for any expenses incurred in fulfilling Regional Minister duties. These include postage, printing, and phone expenses.
- To support, pray for, and advise Regional Ministers in their duties
- To replace Regional Ministers yearly
- To follow up on Inquirers, Members, and Associates who are not hearing from the Regional Minister in a timely manner and to rectify the problem.

APPENDIX R: BISHOPS' LETTERS CONFIRMING CANONICAL STATUS OF THE CONFRATERNITY OF PENITENTS

Bishop Kevin Rhoades' Letter to the Confraternity of Penitents, January 2014

DIOCESE OF FORT WAYNE - SOUTH BEND

915 South Clinton Street • Post Office Box 390
Fort Wayne, Indiana 46801

January 3, 2014

Madeline Pecora Nugent, Minister General
Confraternity of Penitents
1702 Lumbard Street
Fort Wayne, IN 46803-2626

Dear Madeline,

I am happy to grant my recognition and approval of the Confraternity of Penitents, a private association of the Christian faithful according to the norms of the Code of Canon Law.

It is a blessing to have the Confraternity of Penitents now headquartered in the Diocese of Fort Wayne-South Bend. I am grateful for your witness to the Holy Gospel according to the teaching, example, and spirit of Saint Francis of Assisi. I pray that the Lord will bestow many blessings upon you and the members of the Confraternity and, indeed, through you upon many others.

I am happy to appoint Father Jacob Meyer to serve as your spiritual advisor and as my "Visitor" to the Confraternity. I believe Father Jacob's zeal for the Gospel and his priestly guidance will be beneficial to you.

May God bless you! May the Blessed Virgin Mary, Saint Francis, and Saint Clare intercede for you always!

Sincerely yours in Christ,

Kevin C. Rhoades

Most Reverend Kevin C. Rhoades
Bishop of Fort Wayne-South Bend

KCR / dl

Telephone: 260-422-4611 • Fax: 260-969-9145 • www.diocesefwsb.org

Bishop Thomas Tobin's Letter to the Confraternity of Penitents, February 2010

Office of the Bishop
Diocese of Providence
One Cathedral Square
Providence, RI 02903
Phone: (401) 278-4546

February 11, 2009

Madeline Pecora Nugent, Minister General
Confraternity of Penitents
520 Oliphant Lane
Middletown, RI 02842-4600

Dear Ms. Pecora Nugent:

In response to your request, I wish to affirm my support of the Confraternity of Penitents (CFP), specifically its members' commendable efforts to live according to the First Rule of the Third Order of Saint Francis of 1221, as outlined in the CFP's own Constitutions.

It is my understanding that the Confraternity was founded in 1995 as the "Brothers and Sisters of Penance", and that after subsequent discernment, was refounded and renamed in 2003. In the same year, Bishop Mulvee granted permission for the Rule to be lived out in the Diocese by the CFP's members. I have subsequently confirmed the Confraternity's canonical status as a "private association of the faithful."

To aid the Confraternity's sense of purpose, I would ask that you refer to the relevant sections of the *Code of Canon Law*, particularly those which define "Associations of the Christian Faithful" (cc. 298-299; 304-309) and "Private Associations of the Christian Faithful" (cc. 321-326).

I encourage your continued contacts with Father Michael Sisco, the Confraternity's "Visitor" and spiritual advisor. His counsel will be helpful as you continue to discern the Lord's will, and as you pray for steady growth.

Grateful for the Confraternity's good example, and extending to you my special blessing, I remain,

Sincerely yours,

+Te S. Te

Thomas J. Tobin
Bishop of Providence

THE WILL OF GOD

The will of God will never take you,
Where the grace of God cannot keep you.
Where the arms of God cannot support you,
Where the riches of God cannot supply your needs,
Where the power of God cannot endow you.

The will of God will never take you,
Where the spirit of God cannot work through you,
Where the wisdom of God cannot teach you,
Where the army of God cannot protect you,
Where the hands of God cannot mold you.

The will of God will never take you,
Where the love of God cannot enfold you,
Where the mercies of God cannot sustain you,
Where the peace of God cannot calm your fears,
Where the authority of God cannot overrule for you.

The will of God will never take you,
Where the comfort of God cannot dry your tears,
Where the Word of God cannot feed you,
Where the miracles of God cannot be done for you,
Where the omnipresence of God cannot find you.

Made in the USA
Middletown, DE
07 January 2023

20848913R00292